Argument and Persuasion

Also by Nancy Cavender
(co-authored by Len Weiss)

Thinking in Sentences
Thinking/Writing

Also by Howard Kahane

Logic and Philosophy
Logic and Contemporary Rhetoric
Thinking About Basic Beliefs

Argument and Persuasion
Text and Readings for Writers

Nancy Cavender
COLLEGE OF MARIN
Department of English

Howard Kahane
UNIVERSITY OF MARYLAND
BALTIMORE COUNTY
Department of Philosophy

WADSWORTH PUBLISHING COMPANY
Belmont, California
A Division of Wadsworth, Inc.

ENGLISH EDITOR:	Angela Gantner
PRODUCTION EDITOR:	Robin Lockwood, Bookman Productions
PRINT BUYER:	Randy Hurst
DESIGNER:	Hal Lockwood
COPY EDITOR:	Betty Berenson
COMPOSITOR:	Weimer Typesetting Company
COVER:	Juan Vargas

Printed in the United States of America

2 3 4 5 6 7 8 9 10—93 92 91 90

Library of Congress Cataloging in Publication Data

Cavender, Nancy.
  Argument and persuasion.

  Includes index.
  1. Rhetoric.   2. Persuasion (Rhetoric)   3. Authorship.
4. Debates and debating.   I. Kahane, Howard, 1928–
II. Title.
PN187.C35   1989   808'.042   88-27666
ISBN 0–534–098703

Contents

◁ CHAPTER THREE ▷

Methods of Developing Arguments
35

◁ CHAPTER FOUR ▷
Essay Analysis: Evaluating Argumentative Essays
49

◁ CHAPTER FIVE ▷
Cogent and Fallacious Arguments
65

◁ CHAPTER SIX ▷

Responding to Political Rhetoric
87

READINGS
103

The Quality of Modern Life   291

Political Rhetoric   321

Additional Readings   345

Preface

This text deals with the writing and evaluation (analysis) of argumentative essays. It is a "how to" book, not a technical treatise, and theoretical considerations are kept to a minimum.

The text is divided into two parts. The first introduces students to the basic concepts and tasks relevant to the evaluation and construction of argumentative essays. The second contains argumentative essays, arranged according to subject matter provided as models and information sources for students to use when writing their own essays. The works chosen range from essays by Machiavelli and Gore Vidal to popular magazine articles and product advertisements. (A few essays that belong to other, related genres are also included, for example, Swift's *A Modest Proposal*, to illustrate how other devices can be used effectively in the service of rational persuasion.)

The point of discussing the evaluation as well as the writing of argumentative essays in the same text is that evaluation is an integral part of the writing process. In fact, evaluation enters into the writing process twice, first when reading what others have written on the chosen topic and second when involved in one's own writing effort.

While we have not neglected the usual material on argument validity and other logical considerations, we have stressed the other aspects of good essay writing: formulating good reasons in support of a well-focused thesis, developing convincing supporting evidence, and raising and replying to counterarguments. Much greater emphasis is placed on the twin notions of *world views* and *background beliefs* and on writing for an *audience* than on theoretical questions concerning deduction and induction. Technical terms are introduced only when genuinely necessary. Nevertheless, our explanations of argument cogency, deductive and inductive validity, and fallaciousness are more comprehensive and more *accurate* than in most other texts, as we explain in Chapter 5.

We owe a larger than usual debt to the publisher's readers, Craig W. Cutbirth, Illinois State University; Donald Fucci, Ramapo College of New Jersey; Susan Harland, University of Pittsburgh; Deborah Kinerk, University of Washington; Donald Lazere, California Polytechnic State University, San Luis

Obispo; Edward McCarthy, Harrisburg Area Community College; Denise E. Murray, San Jose State University; Sandra J. Oster, Portland State University; Roger Seamon, University of British Columbia; and Victor J. Vitanza, University of Texas at Arlington.

NANCY CAVENDER
HOWARD KAHANE
Dorney, England
July 1988

Argument

Learning how to write cogent and persuasive argumentative essays takes a good deal of practice guided by an understanding of the nature of rational argument. Although arguments may extend to book length, and indeed often do, let's start by considering the basic structure of very simple arguments before moving on to more complicated cases and to complete argumentative essays.

Laying Bare an Argument's Structure

The **reasons** a person gives in support of a claim, together with that claim, form an **argument**. Logicians call reasons **premises**, and claims **conclusions**, or **theses**. Here is a simple example of an argument:

> Since it's always wrong to kill a human being (*premise*), and having an abortion kills a human being (*premise*), it follows that abortion is wrong (*conclusion*).

The word *since* indicates that a premise follows; the expression *it follows that* signals the conclusion. Some other common indicator expressions that signal premises are *because, for,* and *in view of.* Words such as *hence, so,* and *therefore* usually indicate conclusions.

The first task in figuring out the structure of an argument is to identify its conclusion. Finding supporting reasons or premises is the second task. Reasons may be either *explicitly* stated or, when context and subject matter make it expedient, *implied.* For example, in this little argument, at least one reason is implied:

> "She's charming and sexy and has tons of money (premise), so he'll ask her to marry him (*conclusion*)."

(The implied premise is that he'd want to marry almost any charming, sexy, rich woman he could talk into it.)

Finding the conclusion and recognizing the reasons offered in support of the conclusion, and any reasons in support of the reasons, constitute the investigative part of argument analysis, in which we try to find out what an argument says.

1

EXERCISE 1-1

For each of the following arguments, identify the conclusion and the reasons given in support of the conclusion.

EXAMPLE

Argument (from *The Economist*, 7 April 1984)

> It is difficult to gauge the pain felt by animals because pain is subjective and animals cannot talk.

Argument Structure:

> *Conclusion:* It is difficult to gauge the pain felt by animals.
>
> *Reason:* Pain is subjective.
>
> *Reason:* Animals cannot talk (cannot tell us about their pains).

EXAMPLE

Argument (from Goethe):

> Death cannot be evil, being universal.

Argument Structure:

> *Conclusion:* Death cannot be evil.
>
> *Premise:* Death is universal.
>
> *Implied Premise:* Whatever is universal cannot be evil.

1. Since there are no mental diseases, there can be no treatments for them.

   —Thomas Szasz

2. Forbear to judge, for we are sinners all.

   —Shakespeare

3. He that loveth not, knoweth not God; for God is love.

   —New Testament

4. There's no country as great as the smallest city in America. I mean, you can't watch television. The water won't even run right. The toilets won't flush. The roads, the cars . . . there's nothing as great as America.

   —Muhammed Ali (Cassius Clay)

5. If marriages were *really* falling apart, divorced persons wouldn't be as eager as they are to find another partner as speedily as possible.

   —*Chicago Daily News*

6. The earth has a spherical shape. For the night sky looks different in the northern and the southern parts of the earth, and that would be the case if the earth were spherical in shape.

   —Aristotle

7. It is worth noting that over the past fifteen years—a period during which U.S. women began using the pill regularly—life expectancy among U.S. women has *increased* significantly. That fact alone should make it obvious that the pill is not a *major* health hazard.

—Michael H. Hart

8. Good sense is of all things in the world the most equally distributed, for everybody thinks himself so abundantly provided with it, that even those most difficult to please in all other matters do not commonly desire more of it than they already possess.

—Descartes

Evaluating Arguments

The point of figuring out the structure of an argument is to determine whether or not the argument is *cogent* and thus should persuade us to accept its conclusion. This is true not only with respect to the arguments that we ourselves construct but also those we encounter in the investigative—prewriting—stage when we are still zeroing in on our topic. (The prewriting stage will be discussed later.)

To be completely **cogent,** an argument has to satisfy three conditions (discussed below). Arguments that fail to satisfy all three of these criteria are said to be **fallacious.**

BELIEVABLE PREMISES

The first criterion of cogent reasoning requires that we bring to bear whatever we already know or believe—our relevant **background beliefs**—to determine whether we should accept the premises of the argument being assessed.

Take the first premise of the abortion argument discussed a few pages back, namely, that killing a human being is always wrong. Since most of us are not pacifists, when we bring our background beliefs to bear on this premise, we should find it *questionable* and thus not acceptable without further reasons or evidence. (Good writers generally provide additional support or reasons for premises that readers might find questionable. But in the case of this simple argument, no additional support is provided.)

Now, by way of contrast, consider the premises of the following argument:

The Chicago Bears didn't play in the 1988 Superbowl.
Walter Payton played for the Chicago Bears during that season.
So Payton didn't get to play in the 1988 Superbowl.

Professional football fans will instantly see that these premises are in accord with their background knowledge and thus are acceptable.

VALID REASONING

The second criterion of cogent argument is that the premises of an argument must genuinely support its conclusion, or as logicians would say, the argument must be **valid**. There are at least two fundamentally different ways in which premises may support conclusions. The first way yields *deductively valid* arguments, the second *inductively valid* arguments.

The fundamental property of a **deductively valid argument** is this: if all of its premises are true, then its conclusion *must* be true also, because what is asserted by the conclusion of a deductively valid argument has already been stated by its premises, although usually not in so many words.

Here is a simple example:

Everything made of copper conducts electricity (*premise*).
This wire is made of copper (*premise*).
So this wire will conduct electricity (*conclusion*).

When taken alone neither of the two premises makes the claim that the wire will conduct electricity. But when taken together they do make that claim, not explicitly, but implicitly. We cannot imagine what it would be like for both premises to be true and yet the conclusion turn out to be false. Indeed, it would be contradictory to assert both of these premises and then deny the conclusion.

It is important to note that the deductive validity of an argument has nothing to do with whether its premises are true. Validity concerns the nature of the *connection* between premises and conclusion, not the truth or believability of the premises. Determining that an argument is deductively valid tells us that *if* its premises happen to be true, then its conclusion must be true also—it does not tell us *whether* its premises are true. Here, for instance, is a deductively valid argument that contains an obviously false premise: "If more people read Agatha Christie's novels than read Shakespeare's plays, then her novels must be better than Shakespeare's plays (*false premise*). Her novels are read by more people than are Shakespeare's plays (*premise*). So her novels must be better than his plays (*conclusion that happens to be false*)." The argument is deductively valid because the claim made by its conclusion has already been asserted by its premises, even though in this case only implicitly.

The fact that a deductively valid argument cannot move from true premises to a false conclusion constitutes the chief characteristic and primary virtue of deductive reasoning. But deduction is limited. It cannot yield a conclusion that is not implicit in the premises from which it was derived. *Induction* is needed to perform this task.

Inductively valid arguments, unlike deductively valid ones, have conclusions that go beyond what is contained in their premises. The idea behind valid induction is that of *learning from experience*. We observe many patterns, resemblances, and other kinds of regularities in our experiences, some quite simple (sugar sweetens coffee), some very complicated (objects move according to

Newton's laws). Valid inductions project regularities noticed in our experiences so far onto specified other experiences or possible experiences.

The great virtue of inductive reasoning is that it provides us with a way of reasoning to genuinely new beliefs, and not just to psychologically new ones that were implicit in what we already knew, as in the case of valid deductions. However, this benefit is purchased at the cost of an increase in the possibility of error. The truth of the premises of a deductively valid argument guarantees the truth of its conclusion, but a perfectly good induction may contain all true premises and yet have a false conclusion. Even the best "inductive leap" may lead us astray because the pattern noticed in our experiences so far may not turn out to be nature's overall pattern. An example is the inductive conclusion scientists once drew that asbestos never conducts electricity, based in part on their observation that it had never done so in their experience. When they started cooling things down close to absolute zero, however, it turned out that asbestos, indeed every substance, does conduct electricity. (Deductive and inductive validity are discussed in more detail in Chapter 5.)

INCLUSION OF RELEVANT INFORMATION

The third criterion of cogent reasoning and argument requires that we not suppress relevant information.* In particular, it tells us to resist the temptation to neglect evidence contrary to what we want to believe.

Consider a rather simple inductive argument, say this one that started going the rounds in 1980 (earlier versions circulated as far back as 1920):

> Every U.S. president elected at twenty-year intervals has died in office, starting with William Henry Harrison in 1840, and continuing with Lincoln in 1860, Garfield in 1880, McKinley in 1900, Harding in 1920, Franklin Roosevelt in 1940, and Kennedy in 1960. So the odds are not good for Ronald Reagan. (Only one other U.S. president, Zachary Taylor, elected in 1848, has ever died in office.)

This argument has the form of a simple analogy:

> So far, every president elected at twenty-year intervals has died in office (*premise*). Ronald Reagan was elected after that kind of interval (*implied premise* not actually stated since everyone can be expected to know that Reagan was elected in 1980). Therefore, Ronald Reagan will probably die in office (*conclusion*).

In evaluating this argument, note first that it presents a good, or valid, analogy. The premises do indeed provide evidence supporting the conclusion, even if not overwhelming evidence. The fact that all those presidents died in a

---

*This is an extremely stringent requirement that in everyday life is beyond the ability of most of us most of the time. The point is to come as close as we can to satisfying it, bearing in mind the seriousness of the issue and the cost in time and effort of obtaining or recalling relevant information. (One of the marks of genius is the ability to recognize that information is relevant when the rest of us aren't likely to notice.)

way that fits this odd pattern is a modestly good reason for believing in the existence of a presidential twenty-year jinx. Second, note that the argument's premises are warranted—in fact we can be virtually certain of their truth. All of those presidents did die as described and Reagan was elected in 1980. What ruins the argument, fortunately, is that it suppresses well-known *higher level* counterevidence, in particular about what sorts of things cause deaths—mere passage of twenty years not being one of them. So the argument is not cogent, even though it has true premises connected correctly to its conclusion. We discover that it is not cogent by bringing to bear well-known and relevant background evidence.

Although logicians have concentrated their efforts primarily on the nature of deductive and inductive validity, in everyday life argument evaluation often, perhaps even usually, centers on the other two criteria of argument cogency. Arguments in which appeals to an authoritative source constitute the principal support for a conclusion are a case in point.

Consider the following simple example:

> According to the Union of Concerned Scientists, we won't be able to build the proposed "Star Wars" defense system against nuclear weapons for many years to come (*premise*). Therefore, the system won't be built for many years to come (*conclusion*).

Although not valid as it stands, this argument can be made valid simply by adding a premise to the effect that the authorities appealed to know what they are talking about and will tell us the truth. Adding such a premise merely makes explicit a claim that was implicit in the original argument, indeed a claim that is implicit in all arguments that appeal to an authority. So the structure of this argument, as of all arguments that appeal to an authority, is this:

1. Authority A says that so and so is the case.

2. Authority A knows the truth of the matter and will tell it to us.

/∴3. So and so is the case.*

Obviously, if both of the premises of an argument having this form are true, then its conclusion must be true. So the argument is deductively valid. But *are* both of its premises true? That is usually the crucial question when evaluating appeals to authority in everyday life. To answer it, we need to bring to bear our relevant background beliefs. Do we have reason to believe that the authority appealed to has the required knowledge? Might this authority have a reason for concealment? Do other authorities offer contrary opinions? Is this really the sort of thing that anyone now knows?

Before moving on to other matters, let's now state the three criteria of cogent reasoning and argument in one place for handy reference. To be cogent, reasoning must (1) move from believable or warranted premises (2) by way of

---

*The symbol /∴ is commonly used to indicate that a conclusion follows.

valid reasoning (3) without passing over relevant reasons or evidence, in particular not neglecting contrary evidence. Remember, though, that in everyday life premises are often *implied*, not explicitly stated.

When writing arguments, we want to be sure that we satisfy all three of these criteria; otherwise our arguments will not be cogent and readers will be justified in rejecting them.

EXERCISE 1-2

Evaluate the arguments in Exercise 1-1. In doing so, indicate whether the reasons offered in support of a given conclusion are acceptable to you, in view of your background beliefs (whatever you believe that is relevant); whether the reasons satisfactorily support that conclusion (whether the argument is valid); and whether other relevant reasons that you already know can be added to the argument (perhaps to make it valid, if it is invalid as it stands).

SAMPLE ARGUMENT ANALYSIS:

Reason: Pain is subjective.

Reason: Animals cannot talk.

Conclusion: It's difficult to gauge the pain felt by other animals.

1. Both reasons are acceptable (believable). Pain *is* subjective, and everyone knows that nonhuman animals cannot talk.

2. While not conclusive, the reasons given do support the conclusion because they give reasons for believing that it's hard to know when a nonhuman animal is in pain.

3. But, as pet lovers know very well, although animals can't talk, they can and often do indicate that they are in pain by whimpering, wailing, and so on. When this background information is brought forward, the argument can be seen to be less than completely cogent, and we would not be justified in accepting its conclusion.

World Views

The most fundamental theoretical and evaluative background beliefs constitute a person's **world view,** or **philosophy.** World views grow out of family values, religious training, peer group attitudes, formal education, and cultural heritage. They tend to be so deeply engrained that we often appeal to them without noticing that we have done so. Indeed, they are so closely woven into the fabric of our belief systems that we often find it difficult to extricate a strand and examine it. And when we do so, our natural tendency is to reaffirm biases and beliefs that we find comfortable for one reason or another. It isn't easy to become more aware of our unconscious attitudes but doing so will enable us to become more effective in evaluating and writing argumentative essays.

However, it isn't just our own world views that need to be brought into consciousness when writing argumentative essays. We also need to have at least some understanding of the world views of our intended audience. Otherwise, we will have no way of deciding what information should be included in an argumentative essay, or what claims need to be supported by further evidence, in order to convince our intended audience.

Socrates is said to have claimed that the unexamined life is not worth living. By the same token, an unexamined world view is not worth having because it may well contain little more than the passive accumulation of the ideas and prejudices of others. Having an examined world view requires that we take control of our lives by actively sorting out our fundamental beliefs, testing them against newly acquired information, and revising them in the light of what we have learned.

In the next chapter we will discuss a sample essay whose thesis is that our society has an obligation to reduce illiteracy in this country by educating those people we now fail to educate. This thesis grows out of certain fundamental background beliefs of the author: that the continued freedom we enjoy in this country depends on the education of all our people; that those who are well off have an obligation to those who are not; that governments in a democracy should make sure all citizens have an equal education; and so on.

But readers of this essay might well ask whether those who are well off really do owe something to those who are not. Many successful people have worked very hard to accumulate their knowledge, wealth, and power. Why should they be expected to give to people who haven't made the same effort? After all, everyone has an equal opportunity to do well in this country. These questions reflect a somewhat different world view, a view that the writer should take into consideration when developing the argument. In fact, taking into account the world views of those in our intended audience is just as important as is the examination of our own background beliefs. Fundamental to every argument, after all, is *persuasion*. There is an etiquette to persuasive argument that involves a healthy respect for the reader. When shown that respect, an audience is more likely to pay attention and to be convinced by what we write.

EXERCISE 1-3

Choose one of the following topics and ask yourself, first, what your view is on that topic, and, second, how your world view—your most general beliefs and convictions—supports your position on the specific topic you have chosen. Then write a short explanation of the connection between specific and general beliefs so that other students can understand it. There is no need to defend your position at this time. Be brief and to the point.

1. Abortion
2. Capital Punishment
3. Vegetarianism
4. Pornography

Preparing to Write Arguments

THINKING ABOUT THE TOPIC

Recalling and examining relevant background beliefs, in particular those fundamental beliefs that constitute our world views, is an obvious way to begin the writing process. Doing so not only helps us sort out our attitudes on the topic at hand, it also compels us to think in depth about it.

But it isn't always easy to bring what we have experienced or concluded in the past into our conscious minds. It's no secret in this post-Freudian age that the unconscious mind hedges what it allows into consciousness and tries to steer the conscious mind along well-worn paths when the topic at hand is psychologically touchy. Once we have told others our position on a topic, for instance, we tend to think of reasons in favor of that position and to "forget" reasons supporting the other side. But some of this repressed information remains close to consciousness and can be recalled in various ways.

FREE WRITING   We can dredge up a great deal of material from memory simply by writing down everything that comes to mind on a subject. One thought opens into another, and then another, as memory yields up its secrets. Free writing is a kind of internal monologue that enables us to prod our memory for background information. For example, I might want to argue against driving under the influence of alcohol and might free write as follows:

> Driving under the influence of alcohol. Well, some people can do it but it's tricky. Remember what happened to David. He was hauled away by the police on graduation night. Didn't even make it to the ceremony. And Eric—killed in a car accident on his seventeenth birthday. He wasn't even the driver. It was some drunken jerk who got away without a scratch. No wonder insurance rates are so high for teenagers. What was it I read? 80 percent of all car accidents are caused by drunk driving—something like that. Better check that statistic.

Note that not every sentence in this example is grammatically correct. This is perfectly all right, since free writing involves a product intended only for our own use. Shorthand notations, abbreviations, and any other devices that may help our fingers catch up with our more quickly moving minds may also be used.

MAPPING   Knowledge is stored in long-term memory in a systematic way. Current theory postulates two types of memory: episodic and semantic.* Episodic memory stores sequences of events that occur in particular places at a particular time. Memories of a specific experience, perhaps our first day in kindergarten, or the moment we first heard that President Kennedy had been shot and killed, are episodic memory events. Semantic memory, on the other hand, is more abstract and stores concepts and information within hierarchically organized groupings. For example, information about Mencken, Dreiser, Poe, and Hawthorne might be stored under the category of American authors.

The technique of *mapping* seems to draw principally on semantic memory but may use episodic memory as well in recounting anecdotes or examples. In mapping, we indicate the main idea, say, driving under the influence of alcohol, in a circle and then string related thoughts outward from the circle to develop a "map" of the idea. A typical map might look like this:

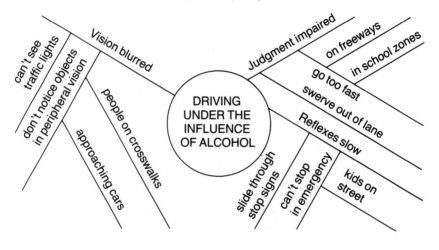

TALKING TO OTHERS

Sometimes we rack our brains for ideas on a topic but just can't get started or become locked into a particular way of thinking about that topic and reach a dead end. When this happens, it often helps to sit down and discuss it with someone else.

BRAINSTORMING   Brainstorming involves generating ideas on a topic in a group setting. The key to this technique is to start with *any* ideas that occur to us, without passing judgment on them. Brainstorming has long been used to elicit creative thinking on a problem—thinking that is divergent, that takes risks

*Edel Tulving, "Episodic and Semantic Memory," in E. Tulving and W. Donaldson (eds.), *Organization of Memory* (New York: Academic Press, 1972) p. 197.

in order to find fresh solutions or new ways of approaching an idea. The important thing to remember is that all members of the group should be allowed to express their ideas freely. No criticism should be permitted until everyone has contributed ideas that have been recorded by a member of the group. Only then should the ideas be evaluated. Evaluation during the brainstorming process itself makes group members more likely to revert to "correct" responses rather than to creative ones that might offer a fresh approach to the problem.

DIALOGUING   Dialoguing involves trying ideas out on another person who asks questions and makes comments designed to help us sharpen our thinking. In addition to helping us develop our ideas on a particular topic, this technique sharpens analytic skills and makes us more aware of audience response. A typical dialogue might go like this:

HE: I don't see anything wrong with pornography. It seems to me we should have the right to read whatever books we want to and to go to porno films if we feel like it.

SHE: Why should we have that right?

HE: The Declaration of Independence says we have the right to life, liberty, and the pursuit of happiness. Seeing or reading pornography involves the pursuit of happiness for some people.

SHE: What if hurting other people made some weirdo happy? Is that okay, too?

HE: Don't be silly.

SHE: I'm not being silly. Should children be allowed to see porno movies because it makes them happy?

HE: Of course not.

SHE: Well, maybe you need to qualify your reason. It doesn't seem very convincing to argue for pornography on the grounds that it makes people happy—even if the Declaration of Independence says we have that right. Surely certain restraints are implied.

HE: I don't think one person's happiness should cause someone else's harm. But pornography doesn't really do that. Seeing a porno film is a voluntary act that doesn't involve anyone else.

SHE: What about kids who don't know any better?

HE: Well, maybe there should be an age of consent, like eighteen.

Trying out our ideas on other people in this way helps us to think more clearly because it forces us to take audience responses into consideration, especially by making us aware of possible counterarguments that need to be addressed.

READING ABOUT A TOPIC

Some arguments can be written simply by drawing on personal experiences or the experiences of acquaintances. But we usually have to do a bit of reading about the subject. Reading, however, should not mean merely passively accepting knowledge, unless we are reading material as undemanding as a recipe or a train schedule, or relaying technical and noncontroversial information gleaned from an authoritative source. Reading effectively about a topic generally requires that our minds be actively engaged in evaluating the material.

It is tempting, when doing research on a topic, to become sidetracked onto interesting tangential subjects. Indeed, many students manage to do this so effectively that they delay the actual writing of a paper until the last minute, when it is too late to do an effective job. Careful readers try to stay on track when doing their reading research. They also draw on a variety of sources and tend to concentrate on the writings of authorities in the field. Readers are more likely to be convinced by citations to authoritative sources, and when several sources are cited, instead of just one, they have the opportunity to compare and contrast different points of view and to gather a wider range of information.

Finally, researchers who are careful thinkers take care not to succumb to the opinions of others merely because those opinions are popular. Rather, they develop their own views and cogent arguments. They read to clarify their ideas, to develop their own arguments, and to find sufficient evidence to support those arguments. Of course, they adopt the opinions or reasons of others when they judge that those ideas are correct.

With these guidelines in mind, let's look at two techniques useful in culling information from material—keeping a reading log and keeping notecards.

KEEPING A READING LOG   Studies of poor and skilled readers have revealed that poor readers do not skim or scan, reread for comprehension, take notes on the material, or make inferences as often as skilled readers do. Poor readers have trouble evaluating texts and often don't realize that they have failed to comprehend the material. Skilled readers, on the other hand, make sure that they understand the text by focusing on important content rather than on minor details, by noticing and taking account of ambiguities and vague passages and— most important of all—by rereading a difficult passage until they are sure they understand its content. Unlike unskilled readers, they usually realize when they fail to comprehend the text, and they take corrective action.*

Keeping a **reading log** improves text comprehension by helping us to distinguish main ideas from subordinate points and minor details. When keeping this kind of log, jot down the main points and pertinent supporting details of the text, add your own thoughts on the matter, note questions you might have, points of agreement or disagreement, and other related ideas that come to mind. This will help you gain a better understanding of the subject and provide a record of information to refer to when writing. To clarify that record further, include bibliographical information and jot down the page numbers of notes in the margin.

*Thomas L. Good and Jere E. Brophy, *Educational Psychology* (New York: Longman, 1986), p. 272.

KEEPING NOTECARDS   Another way to keep track of reading material is to take notes on index cards. Typically each card contains a significant item of information, page numbers, and bibliographic information (to be used for footnoting if the information is used in the paper). Although this method doesn't usually include an overall summary of the material and our responses to it, this method has the advantage of flexibility. We can organize the cards in whatever order seems appropriate to the task, combine cards from various sources, and eliminate those that seem unnecessary.

EXERCISE 1-4

Prepare to write an argument on one of these topics:

1. Animal Liberation
2. Affirmative Action
3. Mandatory Drug Testing in the Workplace

Use at least one of the methods suggested in each of the following categories:

1. Thinking about a topic to write on:
   a. Mapping
   b. Free writing

2. Talking about a topic to write on:
   a. Brainstorming
   b. Dialoguing

3. Reading about a topic to write on:
   a. Keeping a reading log
   b. Keeping notecards

Use this material when doing the exercises assigned in Chapter 2.

⚜ CHAPTER TWO ⚜

Writing Argumentative Essays

A great deal of research has been done on the writing process in recent years. In one typical case,* writers were asked to "think aloud" as they wrote—to talk their thoughts into a tape recorder. The resulting transcripts were then analyzed, along with working notes, drafts, and final papers. This investigation led researchers to draw some broad conclusions that seem to apply to all kinds of writing, including argumentation.

The Writing Process

Experienced writers, according to these investigators, keep their basic goals firmly in mind as they write, and, indeed, as they prepare to write. Typically they develop a plan of attack designed to meet the goals they have set and a method of organization to structure their ideas. But they don't just march relentlessly from one idea to the next. Rather they frequently revise their original plans as they think of new ideas or encounter unexpected difficulties.

When a new plan is devised, or an old one altered, care is taken to make all of the changes necessary to integrate the new material and ideas with the old. What was central before may now be seen as tangential and thus expendable. The overall tone of a completed essay may need to be softened in the light of new thoughts about the nature of the intended audience. A whole section written in the singular may need to be changed into the plural.

But these tasks typically are not performed in a linear manner. One process may interrupt another. Interestingly, editing seems to have a higher priority than any other writing task and tends to interrupt the others at any time. Having used the wrong word, for instance, writers tend to put aside whatever they are doing and search for a more accurate word.

*John R. Hayes and Linda S. Flower, "Writing as Problem Solving," *Visible Language* 14:396–398.

These general conclusions confirm what most experienced writers have believed all along—that writing is a convoluted process, not a straightforward, linear one. A writer may think of an idea, write about it a while, and find that it suggests another, different idea. So the first one is scrapped or modified, and the second is explored. In this way, the writing process itself leads to discovery. By exploring a subject, writers gather information and develop ideas that deepen their understanding and enrich what they write.

Note that skilled writers constantly rework their *ideas* as they write; they don't just edit sentence-level problems. They generate new ideas and modify major and minor ones as they go along. Writing, after all, is a dynamic, recursive process.

For reasons of clarity, however, the guidelines that follow are set down in a linear manner, starting with pointers on narrowing the topic and working through the development of the essay from beginning to end.

The Argumentative Essay

There are two reasons for writing an argumentative essay: the first is to arrive at our own reasoned judgment concerning the subject of the essay; the second is to persuade others to accept our point of view and, often, to take action on it. Sometimes, of course, we already have carefully thought out the thesis we will argue for and are more concerned with convincing others than with examining our own position. But even then, we may be surprised to find that the process of writing down our opinion and reasons may lead us to change our mind. Putting thoughts down on paper often reveals their logical deficiencies as well as their strengths.

Attempts to persuade others, and ourselves for that matter, divide into those that appeal to the rational and to the nonrational side of human nature. In this text our main concern is *rational persuasion by means of cogent arguments*. Of course, this does not mean neglecting the attitudes, beliefs, and interests of those in our intended audience, as we shall see.

NARROW THE TOPIC

Students are often asked to write short argumentative essays on specific topics, such as requiring children under sixteen to attend school or making English the official language of the United States. These topics are narrow enough to suggest the sorts of reasons that will be appropriate. Sometimes, however, the assignment is to write an argument on a general topic, such as education, religion, or animal rights. These assignments are more difficult because the topic needs to be focused before it can be dealt with in a relatively short paper. Education and religion, for instance, are such broad categories that entire libraries are devoted to books on these subjects. Your job when given such a broad assignment is to focus on a narrower aspect of the subject. The general topic of education, for example, might be narrowed to any of the following:

College education

Liberal arts education

Computer education

Course in calculus

Each of these categories is more focused than the one preceding it.

Having narrowed the topic, you now need to give it further focus by taking a *position* on the subject. This requires careful thought about what you believe or don't believe and about what can or can't be supported with good reasons and convincing evidence. Here are two examples:

TOPIC	POSITION
Computer education	Should be required of all high school students
Liberal arts education	Prepares students to succeed in the business world

In each instance, the general topic (education) has been focused on a workable position to be argued for. Your *thesis statement*, or conclusion, should then be formulated so as to state that position accurately.

DEVELOP REASONS FOR YOUR THESIS

Let's suppose you have decided to defend the thesis that a course in computer education should be required of all high school students. You now need to develop reasons justifying acceptance of that thesis. Of course, the reasons must themselves be believable, or, if they aren't likely to be accepted straight off, they must be supported by convincing evidence. Otherwise, readers aren't likely to be persuaded by your essay.

If possible, provide reasons readers can be expected to believe already or that can be supported by providing additional evidence. Draw on your own experiences—those in your audience may have had similar experiences—and on what you have learned from magazines, newspapers, books, and other people. If your first reason is that a high school computer education course will prepare students for college, you may want to support it by drawing on what teachers have told you, what you have read in college catalogues, and what you have heard from friends who have gone on to college. Readers are likely to find this sort of support convincing and thus find the first reason believable.

When you know little or nothing about a topic, research is obviously in order. For instance, most students could not argue effectively either for or against requiring a course in the ethics of genetic engineering without doing a fair amount of research on that topic. But even when the topic is one that you know quite well, additional investigation may be useful. None of us knows everything—we can always profit from additional research.

Most argumentative essays present at least two or three reasons in favor of their thesis. Reasons that are obvious, or at least likely to be accepted by readers, need not be supported further, but any reasons that readers cannot be expected to accept straight off should be supported in turn by additional reasons or evidence. (Sometimes a thesis also needs to be defended by replying to likely counterarguments, a point discussed later.) A well-reasoned argument favoring high school computer education courses might be structured as follows:

> *Thesis:* Computer education should be a required course in high school.
>
> *First Reason:* It prepares students for college.
>
> *Second Reason:* It prepares them for the business world.
>
> *Third Reason:* It prepares them to use computers in their personal lives.

MAKE SURE YOUR ARGUMENT IS VALID

The most believable reasons in the world are worthless unless they genuinely support your argument's thesis. Do the premises of the argument that computer education should be required in high school validly lead to that conclusion? This argument constitutes a proposal, and, as with most proposals, it has an implied premise, in this case that whatever courses will prepare students for college, the business world, and private life should be taught in high school. When this implied reason is added to the argument, its structure becomes something like this:

> *First Reason:* Computer education prepares students for college.
>
> *Second Reason:* It prepares students for the business world.
>
> *Third Reason:* It prepares students for their private lives.
>
> *Implied Reason:* Whatever courses prepare students for college, the business world, and private life should be required in high school.

Restructured this way, the argument is deductively valid. It is also rather tiresome, to say the least, one reason why in daily life arguments are usually not presented in strictly logical form and implied premises generally remain implied.

Nevertheless, going through this process is helpful in clarifying your reasoning and in noticing any weaknesses in the reasons presented that otherwise might be missed. Suppose, for instance, you had supported the computer education argument with the slightly different reasons that (1) it prepares students for college, (2) it prepares them for the business world, and (3) many families now own computers. The first two reasons dovetail nicely with the implied premise that high schools should require courses that prepare students for later life, but the last one does not. Actually stating the implied premise brings out this error and thus makes it clear that revision of some kind is in order.

INCLUDE ALL SIGNIFICANT RELEVANT INFORMATION

Writing the best reasoned and most convincing arguments that you can requires consideration of all the relevant information you can think of. Dredging up this information from your stock of background knowledge is important in several different ways. First, it assures the presentation of the strongest possible reasons for your conclusion. Omitting good reasons from an argument is not the best way to be convincing. Second, it assures that those reasons have been supported where necessary to the best of your ability. Having good support for reasons in the back of your mind is of no help in convincing an audience. Third, in the case of inductive reasoning, it assures that no negative evidence has been suppressed. Knowing that a few people are allergic to aspirin, it would be wrong to argue that aspirin is a completely safe drug since millions of (other) people have used it safely. And, finally, failure to include relevant but negative information leaves an argument open to counterarguments by perceptive and knowledgeable readers. Audiences cannot be counted on to neglect facts that may overturn your conclusion.

This last point is particularly important, since more arguments are rejected because readers bring relevant contrary evidence to bear than for any other reason. We saw that this was true in Chapter 1 with respect to the rejection of the argument about presidents elected every twenty years dying in office. Although all of its stated premises were true and its reasoning valid, the argument neglected all sorts of relevant higher level background information. In the case of the argument about computer education courses, someone might challenge the implied premise that those skills useful in later life should be taught in high school by pointing out that there are hundreds, perhaps thousands of such skills, and all of them cannot be covered, showing at the very least that additional arguing needs to be done to make the argument cogent.

More will be said later in the chapter about bringing relevant background knowledge to bear when writing argumentative essays.

EXERCISE 2-1   CONSTRUCTING ARGUMENTS

1. Develop a thesis concerning one of the following topics (by narrowing the topic) and present two or three good reasons supporting that thesis. (Note that you were asked to do prewriting exercises on one of these topics in the last chapter, page 13. You may want to use the same topic for this assignment.)
   a. Pornography
   b. Abortion

    c. Animal Liberation
    d. Legal Drinking Age
    e. Affirmative Action
2. Evaluate your argument for cogency.
    a. Are the reasons believable?
    b. Is the argument valid?
    c. Has relevant information been suppressed?

Organizing the Essay

An argumentative essay is typically divided into three parts: the introduction, which usually includes the thesis; the body; and the conclusion. Each section serves a rhetorical function in building, organizing, and supporting the argument.

THE INTRODUCTION

The **introduction** engages attention and prepares the reader for the thesis. In fact, an effective introduction may lay the groundwork so well that the reader begins to be persuaded of the thesis before it is even stated. For instance, an essay on literacy might begin with the following quotation:

> "Twenty-five million American adults cannot read the poison warnings on a can of pesticide, a letter from their child's teacher, or the front page of a daily paper. An additional 35 million read only on a level which is less than equal to the full survival needs of our society. Together 60 million people represent more than one-third of the entire adult population." [Jonathan Kozol, *Illiterate America* (New York: Anchor Books/Doubleday, 1985), p.4.]

Such alarming statistics may well begin to persuade the reader of the thesis to follow: that we ought to eradicate illiteracy in this country.

As indicated below, the reasons (premises) that develop the argument are usually stated either after the thesis or in logical order throughout the essay. But when just beginning to learn how to write arguments, it is advisable to state the thesis and reasons in the introduction so as to ensure a firm hold on the argument. Elaboration and justification can come later.

THE BODY

The **body** of an essay develops the reasons offered in support of the thesis. Reasons should be stated in logical order to build and organize the argument. And reasons that a typical reader might challenge have to be supported by convincing evidence, perhaps even by explanations of why the evidence is relevant, and (when appropriate) by refutations of persuasive counterarguments.

Suppose one of the reasons you want to offer in favor of the thesis that society has an obligation to eradicate illiteracy is that illiterate people are unable to deal effectively with everyday life. Perhaps the best way to support this reason is by providing examples of illiterates who are unable to fill out job applications or to understand warning labels on packages. Further support might trace the fates of illiterates in America or provide statistics on the immense number who fail to gain regular employment, become easy prey to con artists, and in general suffer as victims of an impersonal computerized society. Evidence of this kind builds convincing support for the premise that illiterates suffer because of their inability to read.

To further consolidate the argument, potentially persuasive counterarguments may need to be refuted. Some people might contend that since illiterates have been given the opportunity to learn, and have failed to do so, society has no further obligation to them. A persuasive essay might consider this counterargument and then refute it, perhaps by pointing out that if society doesn't take stringent preventative measures to ensure more widespread literacy, it may face other, more serious consequences, such as swollen welfare lists and an inadequate work force. Of course, only those reasons likely to give rise to serious counterarguments need to be defended against in this way.

Once all relevant support for the first reason has been presented, it is time to give the second reason and its supporting evidence, then the third, and so on, until all of the reasons requiring defense have been discussed.

THE CONCLUSION

The **conclusion** of an argumentative essay often restates the thesis—with emphasis. If the argument is particularly long or complex, the main points may be summarized in order to clarify and reinforce them in the mind of the reader. If the essay is short, the reader probably has the reasons firmly in mind, and they need not be repeated.

Various methods of introducing, developing, and concluding essays are discussed in the next chapter.

Supporting Reasons

Perhaps the most difficult part of writing an argument is to provide convincing evidence. It's not enough to have sensible reasons to begin with. You need to convince the reader that those reasons are worth believing. Here are a few guidelines:

ASK QUESTIONS ABOUT YOUR REASONS

Pertinent questions will help you to develop convincing answers. Look again at the thesis that society has an obligation to reduce illiteracy in this country. One reason in favor of this thesis might be that society suffers because of the enormous cost of maintaining an illiterate population. On the face of it, this seems a sensible premise, but alert readers will immediately ask, "Why should we believe you?" And that leads to questions like these:

How do you know the cost is great?

Why is the cost great?

In what ways are illiterates costly?

What exactly are the costs?

These are legitimate questions that deserve carefully reasoned answers. So when you have trouble thinking of ways to support your reasons, try to think of the kinds of questions readers are likely to ask. The answers to these questions will usually provide the evidence necessary for support.

SUPPORT REASONS WITH CONCRETE EVIDENCE

When possible, provide evidence that is *specific*. Use examples, cite statistics, compare or contrast relevant material, draw on factual information. Reasons are more likely to be convincing when they can be verified by specific information than when they are explained in terms of generalities. Information about the costs of illiteracy is a case in point. In *Illiterate America*, Jonathan Kozol estimates on the basis of convincing evidence that the cost of maintaining an illiterate population is about $20 billion a year. He then breaks this figure down into the amounts used to support illiterates on welfare, in prison, on medical aid, and so on. This information makes it clear to the reader how costly it really is to maintain an illiterate population.

Specific information of this kind is usually drawn from these three sources:

1. *Personal experiences.* Suppose your thesis is that the food served at school should be improved or that parking facilities should be expanded on campus. In each instance you, yourself, have had personal experiences that can be used to support your position. Every time you have eaten lunch in the cafeteria the food has been terrible: the bread is rock hard, the spaghetti tastes like rubber, and the coffee is old and strong. Parking spaces tend to be filled by 6:00 A.M. Citing these personal experiences provides good support for your reasons.

2. *The experiences of others.* Another source of evidence is the experiences of other people. But you should try to make sure that their information is accurate. You *know* what your own experiences are because you went through them yourself, but judgment is required in evaluating what others claim has happened to them. Do they usually tell the truth or are they prone to exaggerate? It's helpful, of course, to have two or more accounts of the same situation to check for accuracy, but since that isn't always possible, you may have to rely on a careful assessment of what one person says.

3. *Authoritative sources.* Authoritative sources include reference books, journals, and people who have extensive knowledge about a subject. But here, too, judgment must be exercised. Reputable encyclopedias, dictionaries, and handbooks on specific subjects can usually be relied on, but you have to be more careful with magazines, newspapers, and television programs. Assuming, however, that you have a reasonably accurate source, the information gleaned from authorities can provide invaluable evidence. For instance, an essay whose thesis is that the drinking age in your state should be raised to twenty-one will undoubtedly be improved by a comparison of statistics on teenage accidents in states that allow eighteen-year-olds to drink with those in states that prohibit the sale of alcohol to anyone under twenty-one.

Note this important point: *Authoritative sources must always be credited,* either in a footnote or in the text itself. And *direct quotation must always be indicated by the use of quotation marks.* Using someone else's material without acknowledging the source constitutes **plagiarism,** an extremely serious offense.

EXPLAIN THE CONNECTION BETWEEN EVIDENCE AND REASONS

The evidence introduced in support of a reason often needs to be explained. Exactly how does it support the reason? Suppose one of your reasons is that raising the drinking age to twenty-one will reduce the number of accidents among teenage drivers and that you have supported this reason by giving examples of accidents you or your friends caused while driving under the influence of alcohol. These examples lend credibility to the argument, but they are not enough. You need to explain their connection to the reason, perhaps by explaining why the number of accidents would be reduced if the drinking age were raised. You might say, for instance, that if nineteen-year-olds had been prohibited by law from buying alcoholic beverages, you probably wouldn't have had a few drinks before taking the fateful drive that resulted in an accident. It's true that friends might have provided some alcohol, but it would have been less accessible if illegal, so you would have been less likely to have had an accident. Such an explanation may seem so obvious that you may be inclined not to provide it. But keep in mind that what is obvious to the writer isn't necessarily clear to the reader. The reader needs an explanation of your reasoning to make sense of the evidence.

Addressing the Audience

Writers who seriously intend to influence others have to keep their audience firmly in mind. It's all too easy to forget the audience as we sit alone at a desk, scribbling away. But experienced writers learn that they must always write with the intended readers in mind. Past failures—having had manuscripts rejected, severely criticized, or simply not read by anyone else—motivate them to figure out who they are writing *for* and how best to engage the interest of that particular audience. In fact, most writers have gone through much the same process that you will be going through now—first consciously recognizing who is in the audience and then internalizing that knowledge so that it is applied automatically during the writing process.

One investigator* discovered in her research on the writing process that ineffective writers tend to produce **writer-based prose**,—verbal expressions written by writers to themselves, for themselves. Effective writers, on the other hand, do not simply express their thoughts for their own edification; they also transform them so as to produce **reader-based prose** satisfying the needs of their audience.

Writer-based prose records the thoughts that enable a writer to confront and work through a topic. It is structured in an associative, narrative form, and its language includes privately loaded terms, vague statements, and unexpressed contexts. In contrast, reader-based prose is centered on issues and structured to reflect the writer's purpose, not the discovery process.**

One way to develop a sense of audience is to have one immediately at hand. Much has been written about the importance of writing with an audience in mind, but this advice needs to be augmented by actually having others respond to your work. In college, papers are usually directed to an audience of one—the teacher who evaluates your work and provides valuable advice intended to improve your writing ability.

But what do you do in the hazy prewriting stage when you have the glimmer of an idea but aren't sure if it will work, or when you have thought of a thesis and reasons, but don't know if they are convincing? In this stage of the writing process, it is helpful to try your ideas out on other people. Their feedback will give you a sense of audience response. Some teachers divide their classes into response groups so that students can discuss their ideas and read drafts aloud to each other. Some schools have tutors who can act as an expert audience. And, of course, you can always bring your friends together to form your own response group. The point is to use whatever resources happen to be available so as to become accustomed to addressing a real audience.

Here are some questions to ask about the audience:

1. *Who is in the intended audience?* Most college writing is intended to be read by teachers or classmates, but you may want to write letters to the editor of a local newspaper or to your senator, or you may be assigned a hypothetical audience, such as the National Rifle Association (on gun control). If you have entered the business world, you may need to write to supervisors, coworkers, or clients.

In any case, writers often need to consider the age, sex, level of education, economic status, and ethnic background of their intended audience. If the audience has a vested interest in an issue, that interest *must* be taken into

*Linda Flower, "Writer-Based Prose: A Cognitive Basis for Problems in Writing." *College English* 41 (September 1979):2.
**Flower, pp. 34–35.

account. For example, if you are trying to persuade power-plant managers to cancel construction of a nuclear power facility, you would probably be wise to concentrate on legal problems and economic disadvantages (compared to oil-fired plants). But to convince townspeople living near by, you might want to stress the dangers to local inhabitants. Remember, though, that the degree to which your argument will convince a rational person still depends on how clearly and logically your evidence supports the argument's conclusion.

2. *What is your purpose?* The primary purpose in writing an argumentative essay is to convince readers that your position is worth holding, but you may have other purposes as well. One is to refute an argument that you disagree with. If so, be sure to explain the opposition's point of view so that readers will understand it, before presenting your rebuttal. Another is to inform, as well as to argue a point. This approach is particularly important if readers are likely to need background information on the topic under discussion. Still another purpose is to galvanize readers into action. You may want them not merely to agree with your position but to take action on the matter. Convincing students that campus crime is on the rise is one thing; getting them to do something about it—for instance, petitioning the college president to take active steps to fight crime—is another.

3. *What are the background beliefs of the audience?* When people start reading an argument, they usually bring their own views to bear immediately, before they get through the first paragraph. If their background beliefs are in accord with the writer's, they may be relatively uncritical of the argument; if not, they may be more difficult to persuade. For instance, the Civil War was commonly justified (though, in fact, fought for other reasons as well) on the grounds that all men are created equal, including blacks, and that blacks should enjoy the same freedom and rights as whites. However, since a large number of whites did not share this view, they vehemently opposed giving blacks their freedom. Furthermore, since such views also served to protect economic interests, even the most closely reasoned arguments tended to fall on deaf ears.

But opposing views need not remain irreconcilable. It may be possible to convince opponents by taking into account *their* point of view. Suppose their view on the illiteracy question is based on a larger background belief that the survival of our society is based on the survival of the fittest and that those who have the intelligence and ambition to succeed in life should and will dominate the country and raise children to follow in their footsteps, thus ensuring the survival of society. Keeping this point of view in mind, you might stress the idea that reducing illiteracy has advantages for everyone, not just illiterates themselves, and emphasize the idea that the fittest members of society may have to pay a heavy price, both economically and politically, if they refuse to address the problems of illiterates. A well-documented argument of this kind has a reasonable chance to be convincing with this (rather difficult) audience.

In addition, trying to convince opponents from the perspective of their own world views has an interesting side benefit. Paying close attention to other points of view may help you gain greater insight into the issue as a whole.

4. *What tone is appropriate for the intended audience?* The tone of an essay reflects the writer's attitudes and feelings toward the subject and, to some extent, toward the audience. The possible tones are as varied as the personalities of the writers. Compassion, tranquility, urgency, anger, contempt, cynicism, humor, indifference—these are but a few of the attitudes revealed by writers. A serious argument on a subject such as nuclear disarmament usually takes on a serious tone and a rather formal style. Flippant remarks, humorous asides, and colloquialisms generally would be out of place. On the other hand, an essay suggesting that a pool hall be added to the student center might be written in a more humorous vein, even tongue in cheek, using an informal style and occasional slang to make the point.

Experienced writers control the tone of their arguments so well that tone itself becomes a major persuasive device. Consider, for instance, this droll passage by Adlai Stevenson (then governor of Illinois) arguing against a bill that would protect insectivorous birds by restraining cats:

> We are all interested in protecting certain varieties of birds. That cats destroy some birds, I well know, but I believe this legislation would further but little the worthy cause to which its proponents give such unselfish effort. The problem of the cat versus bird is as old as time. If we attempt to resolve it by legislation who knows but what we may be called upon to take sides as well in the age-old problems of dog versus cat, bird versus bird, or even bird versus worm. In my opinion, the State of Illinois and its local governing bodies already have enough to do without trying to control feline delinquency.

By using elevated language to explain a prosaic matter and by carrying the consequences of the legislation to ridiculous extremes, Stevenson manages to undermine the opposition through gentle humor, without really offending anyone.

Now look at this example by a writer not quite in control of tone. This passage is from a letter to a Volkswagen dealer arguing for a reduction in the $2,000 repair bill to replace the engine on a VW Rabbit:

> Though I realize the one-year warranty on the rebuilt engine you installed in my car expired last month, I nonetheless think you should stretch a point and give me a reduction in rate. That engine was built to last 100,000 miles. The fact that it lasted only 14,000 miles suggests something is seriously wrong with your product. It is your obligation to stand behind that product. And frankly, if you don't, you can take the car and shove it. I've had it with you and your lousy workmanship.

What starts out as a reasonable appeal dissolves in a sputter of anger. The anger may well be justified, since the car does sound like a lemon, but the tone is unlikely to be persuasive.

Whatever tone you assume, write with due respect for your audience. Avoid putting readers down by implying that they are ill informed, by using offensive language, by using technical terms or colloquialisms that they may not understand (unless they are carefully explained), by talking down to them, or by making sarcastic comments at their expense. An offended reader will not be inclined to read on, let alone come to agree with your position.

Some people think that taking audiences into account in this way constitutes persuasion by propaganda, not by rational persuasion. But that definitely is not the case. Human beings are a complicated mixture of rational and nonrational (chiefly emotional) elements; there is no reason for writers to gratuitously anger, offend, or in any way irritate their readers. The point is to allow reason its best chance of success, to make it least likely that reason will be swayed by prejudice, emotion, or ingrained ways of thinking.

EXERCISE 2-2   ADDRESSING YOUR AUDIENCE

1. a. Develop a thesis and three or four supporting reasons either for or against raising the driving age to eighteen. *Briefly* suggest supporting evidence you might use to convince the reader. Your audience is a group of sixteen-year-olds.
   b. Using the same thesis, develop reasons with supporting evidence that might convince the *parents* of the sixteen-year-olds.

2. a. Develop a thesis and three or four supporting reasons either for or against using animals for medical research, and, again, briefly suggest supporting evidence. Your audience is a group of pet owners.
   b. Using the same thesis, develop reasons and supporting evidence that might convince research scientists who use animals in experiments.

EXERCISE 2-3   WRITING AN ARGUMENTATIVE ESSAY

1. Write a draft of an argumentative essay on one of these topics (arguing either for or against):

   Permitting children with AIDS to attend public schools

   Abolishing the tenure system in colleges and universities

   Disobeying a particular law (specify which law)

   Permitting people to own handguns

   Abolishing intercollegiate (not intramural) athletic events

2. Check your thesis and reasons for cogency.
   a. Are the reasons believable?
   b. Is the argument valid?
   c. Is sufficient relevant information included?

3. Evaluate supporting evidence.
   a. Is the evidence convincing?
   b. Is sufficient relevant evidence included?

   c. Have you explained the logical connection between your evidence and reasons?

4. Read your essay to an audience.
   a. Do they think your premises are believable?
   b. Do they find your evidence convincing?
   c. Are they comfortable with the tone of your essay?

5. Revise the essay on the basis of your own evaluation and your audience's response.

EXERCISE 2-4   DEVELOPING TONE IN
                        ARGUMENTATION

Complete one of the following assignments, *paying particular attention to argument tone:*

1. Write a letter to a company that has sold you a faulty product. Argue that the company should replace the product even though it broke down after the warranty expired.

2. Write a letter to a good friend who is presently attending another school. Either urge your friend to transfer to your college or argue against this move if he or she has expressed an interest in your school.

3. Write a letter to the president of your college arguing that a particular condition on your campus should be changed.

An Example of an Argumentative Essay

As must be apparent by now, argument is not a simple matter but rather an intricate web of reasoning, evidence, and refutation that martials all available, pertinent resources to persuade readers that a particular thesis is cogent. Many professional essays contain not only complex reasoning but sophisticated formats as well, thus making them difficult to use as models. The thesis is sometimes implied rather than stated, or the reasons are buried in extended examples. But argumentative essays may have a rather straightforward structure. Here is an example. (Several features are discussed in the next chapter.)

Literacy: A Necessity Not a Privilege

Twenty-five million American adults cannot read the poison warnings on a can of pesticide, a letter from their child's teacher, or the front page of a daily paper. An additional 35 million read only on a level which is less than equal to the full survival needs of our society. Together 60 million people represent more than one-third of our entire population. [Jonathan Kozol, *Illiterate America* (New York: Anchor Books/Doubleday, 1985), p. 4.]

These alarming statistics, compiled from convincing evidence, suggest that there is something drastically wrong with a system of education that turns out so many students who cannot read well enough to function adequately in daily life. Indeed, some students never learn to read at all; others, termed functional illiterates, cannot read well enough to understand the demands society places on them. It is a tragedy that a country claiming to be among the most advanced nations in the world should allow one-third of its adult population to remain illiterate. In light of these statistics, it should come as no surprise to learn that the United States ranks forty-ninth in literacy levels among the 158 member nations of the United Nations (Kozol, p. 5).

Illiteracy is so widespread that it has become a problem of major proportions, one that compels us to agree with the National Commission on Excellence in Education that we are indeed a nation at risk. As such, it is imperative that we as a nation right this wrong by doing what is necessary to ensure a literate citizenry. This resolve is based not only on the need to improve the lot of those who suffer from illiteracy, though that certainly is reason enough, but on the necessity of reducing the costs to our society and of providing a genuine opportunity, not just a token gesture, for disadvantaged people to succeed.

The humane argument for a completely literate population is quite simply that illiterate people suffer a great deal because of their affliction. They suffer on a psychological level and on a practical level. Consider the man who is so embarrassed at being unable to read that he *pretends* to read books on buses and in restaurants, just to save face, or the woman who is ashamed to ask directions when in a strange part of town because she can't read a map or street signs. These examples may seem farfetched unless you have met people who suffer these embarrassments. I knew a young man when I was in high school, who suffered much anxiety and humiliation as a result of his inability to read. Around friends, he pretended he *could* read, for fear of ridicule, though he had to be constantly on guard to avoid the printed page. At work, he had to memorize signs to learn his job. He was a gas station attendant, one of the few positions he applied for that didn't test his ability to read. Because he was too embarrassed to ask his boss for help, his sister showed him how to fill in credit card forms and translated gas pump signs until he memorized them. Much of his life he lived in fear of being discovered by his friends, boss, and casual acquaintances.

Personal humiliation is only one consequence of illiteracy, however. Perhaps even more important are the ways in which the lives of functional illiterates are severely restricted. It doesn't take much imagination to conjure up all the things they cannot do because they cannot read such simple things as product labels, road signs, poison labels, telephone books, prescriptions, street signs, and danger signs. Failure to read such basic information interferes with buying food, taking medicine, traveling beyond the neighborhood or into new territory, looking up phone numbers, and avoiding dangerous situations. If such basic skills are beyond the ken of illiterates, consider the more complicated tasks of reading letters, bank statements, product warranties, insurance forms, and legal documents. An inability to process such essential information makes illiterates more likely to suffer the consequences of bank error, defective merchandise, and fraud, and less likely to obtain what is due them through insurance policies and legal documents.

Finally, failure to read seriously jeopardizes their ability to get employment. As Robert Dentler and Mary Ellen Warshauer point out in *Big City Dropouts* (New York: Center for Urban Education, 1965), a young person's ability to gain employment depends more and more on his or her schooling. This is partly due to the fact that our economy is less dependent on factory and farm workers, who typically needed less education, and more dependent on skilled or trainable service-producing workers (pp. 61–62). It is a rare job that requires no reading ability whatsoever. Even street cleaners have to read road signs, janitors have to read notes telling them what to do, stock boys have to read labels on merchandise. Nonreaders are threatened at every turn. Their lives would be much easier and more satisfying were they at least marginally literate.

It may be argued that the expense of tracking down and stamping out illiteracy is more than our pocketbooks can bear. But that argument fails to take into account how much we as a society have to pay for the illiteracy of a third of our people. To begin with we pay in actual dollars and cents. In *Illiterate America*, Jonathan Kozol cites innumerable facts to support this contention. He estimates from convincing evidence that direct costs to businesses and taxpayers are about $20 billion a year. Costs to taxpayers include state aid to people on welfare, approximately one-third of whom are illiterate; support of 260,000 prisoners whose imprisonment has been directly linked to functional illiteracy, at a cost of $6.6 billion a year (a mid-1970s estimate); extensive health expenditures to people who don't have the literacy skills to understand preventive care measures that reduce such conditions as unwanted pregnancies, cardiac disease, or cancer; and swollen court costs and law enforcement budgets in urban areas in which a large percentage of adults are unemployable because they lack literacy skills (Kozol, pp. 13–14). Taxpayers already heavily burdened can ill afford the additional cost of an illiterate population.

The private sector suffers as well. Because illiterate workers cannot read safety warnings, chemical-content explanations, and instructions for operating machinery, accidents occur that result in several billion dollars a year in workmen's compensation, damage to equipment, and insurance costs. Hundreds of thousands of entry-level jobs go unfilled because applicants don't have the skills necessary to do the work. One New York insurance firm indicated that 70% of its dictated correspondence had to be retyped because secretaries did not know how to spell or punctuate correctly (Kozol, p. 14). Though they had a degree of literacy, it wasn't sufficient for the jobs they were supposed to perform, and thus their companies paid dearly.

In sum, everyone will benefit from the eradication of functional illiteracy. Certainly the illiterate one-third of our adult population has a great deal to gain by learning to read. They will be better able to cope with such simple, practical tasks as shopping for food and following written directions; they will improve their chances for finding employment, and perhaps even more important, they will build confidence and self-esteem that will help them to lead more successful, fulfilling lives. Those of us who enjoy the advantages of literacy will also benefit because the expense of supporting illiterates will be considerably reduced, and we will have a more reliable work force. We thus have everything to gain and nothing to lose by helping these people, and we will have done a good deed in the bargain.

BIBLIOGRAPHY

Dentler, Robert A., and Mary Ellen Warshauer. *Big City Dropouts*. New York: Center for Urban Education, 1965.

Kozol, Jonathan. *Illiterate America*. New York: Anchor Books/Doubleday, 1985.

EXERCISE 2-5   WRITING AN ARGUMENTATIVE ESSAY

Using the notes you gathered for Exercise 1-4 (Chapter 1), write an argumentative essay supporting your position.

EXERCISE 2-6   WRITING AN ARGUMENTATIVE ESSAY

Write a three-to-five page argumentative essay on one of the following topics. Include outside sources when appropriate to develop the reasons you provide. Be sure to acknowledge all sources either in the text or in footnotes, and include a bibliography.

Argue for or against:

1. Providing welfare benefits to unemployed people
2. Raising the driving age to eighteen
3. Abolishing grading in college
4. Providing medical care for all Americans
5. Abolishing nuclear power plants
6. Allowing eighteen-year-olds to buy alcohol
7. Saving endangered species, such as whales or peregrine falcons
8. Censoring pornography
9. Using animals for medical experiments
10. Permitting businesses and government agencies to use drug-detection tests

---

EXERCISE 2-7   ARGUING FROM THE OPPOSITE
                POINT OF VIEW

Either write an argument that takes the opposite side of the issue you argued in exercise 2-6 or, using the list of topics in Exercise 2-6, develop an argument containing good reasons and support for a thesis you strongly believe in. Then do the same for an opposing point of view on the same issue.

Panel Debates: An Exercise in Argumentation

An excellent way to sharpen your argumentative skills is to debate an issue with other members of your class. In a debate, one team argues the affirmative side of an issue; the other team takes the negative position. For example, Team A argues that mandatory drug testing should be permitted in the work place, and Team B argues against this position.

Classroom debates provide an opportunity to brainstorm ideas with other students and to share research on a given topic, making it easier to develop supporting reasons for a thesis and to anticipate opposing arguments. In fact, going through the debating process is an interesting way to accomplish the prewriting, organizing, and development necessary to produce an effective argumentative essay. It prepares you to write clearly reasoned arguments, is quite enjoyable in itself, and provides an opportunity to become better acquainted with classmates.

The following exercise offers a format to help you organize classroom debates so that all students share the workload and no one is too intimidated by the process. The end result is a written argument. (You may want to change the format somewhat to fit the particular needs of your class.)

EXERCISE 2-8   DEBATING AN ISSUE

In a class of twenty-five or thirty students, two issues may be debated. Half the class will argue the pros and cons of one issue, the other half will argue the second issue.

1. The first step is to decide which issues the class wants to debate. This can be done quickly by asking students to suggest various topics, then by taking a vote. Debates might address topics of broad interest, such as:

   Mandatory drug testing

   Compulsory school attendance

   Legalizing prostitution

   Or they might address certain local issues under discussion at your college, or in your community or state.

2. Next, the class breaks into teams of six or seven students on the affirmative and the same number on the negative team.
3. The teams then meet in groups during class time or outside of class and do the following activities:

FIRST GROUP MEETING

   a. Select a captain who will coordinate the discussion and summarize the initial position during the debate.
   b. Determine who will argue the position and who will rebut the opposition. Three students should argue the supporting reasons, each presenting one point. Three other students should rebut the opposition, each refuting one point.
   c. Brainstorm your argument.
   d. Homework: Do some research on the topic of debate and bring to the next class meeting.

SECOND GROUP MEETING

   a. Develop your major reasons and suggest evidence to support those reasons.
   b. Take into account the opposition by anticipating their arguments and developing counter arguments.
   c. Homework: Continue to do research. Organize your argument on notecards.

THIRD GROUP MEETING

   a. Present your completed argument to the members of your team in order to rehearse the debate.
   b. Rebut your argument to anticipate the opposition and to sharpen your own argument.
   c. Homework: Complete notecards for use in the debate.

Use the following debate procedure as your guide. Each debate takes one class period.

THE DEBATE PROCEDURE

1. The class is polled for opinion on the subject of debate before the exchange.
2. The captain of the affirmative side presents a brief summary of the position to be argued.
3. The affirmative team presents its arguments.
4. The captain of the negative team presents a brief summary of the position to be argued.
5. The negative team presents its arguments.
6. The negative team refutes the arguments of the affirmative team.

7. The affirmative team refutes the arguments of the negative team.

8. Each team makes a summary statement; the affirmative team goes first.

9. The class is polled by secret ballot to determine which team has presented the most convincing argument.

10. The class discusses the strengths and weaknesses of the debates.

Note: Team members should take notes during the debates in order to recall points for rebuttal. At no time should the debates be interrupted by members of the class or members of the debate teams.

EXERCISE 2-9   WRITING THE ARGUMENT
                 UNDER DEBATE

Write the argument that your team presented in the debate, revising when necessary to clarify the reasoning and to develop convincing evidence.

Methods of Developing Arguments

Certain kinds of *rhetorical devices*—methods of persuasion—are used by virtually all writers when developing support for their arguments. Of course, all of these methods are rarely used in a given essay; some lend themselves better to one sort of argument than to others. The examples provided below illustrate what are perhaps the most commonly used of these devices.

Rhetorical Devices

EXAMPLE

An **example** serves as an illustration, a model, or an instance. Examples are drawn from personal experiences or from outside sources such as textbooks, magazines, or films. Examples may include facts and statistics, which are of particular importance in argumentative writing. The essay on illiteracy in Chapter 2, for instance, provides readers with examples of items that illiterates cannot read—product labels, road signs, poison warnings, and so on.

Sometimes examples are so apt that they become the principal form of supporting evidence. For instance, in his essay "No Allusions in the Classroom," Jaime M. O'Neill supports his contention that students lack sufficient knowledge of our common heritage by providing examples of the answers to items on a "general knowledge" test he gave his English composition students—all of whom had completed at least one quarter of college:

> Ralph Nader is a baseball player. Charles Darwin invented gravity. Christ was born in the 16th century. J. Edgar Hoover was a 19th-century president. Neil Simon wrote "One Flew Over the Cuckoo's Nest"; "The Great Gatsby" was a magician in the 1930s. Franz Joseph Haydn was a songwriter during the same decade. Sid Caesar was an early Roman emperor. Mark Twain invented the cotton gin. Heinrich Himmler invented the Heimlich maneuver. Jefferson Davis was a guitar player for the Jefferson Airplane. Benito Mussolini was a

Russian leader of the 18th century; Dwight D. Eisenhower came earlier, serving as a president during the 17th century. William Faulkner made his name as a 17th-century scientist. All of these people must have appreciated the work of Pablo Picasso, who painted masterpieces in the 12th century.

These examples illustrate the appalling ignorance of some of O'Neill's students and dramatically support his claim that they are deficient in the kind of general background knowledge needed to keep our heritage alive. Examples are perhaps the most important rhetorical device available when composing argumentative essays.

DESCRIPTION

A **description** gives sensory information, usually about how an object looks, but also about how it sounds, smells, tastes, or feels. It is not used extensively in argumentation but occasionally it is added to provide graphic details. In a humorous argument, "The Baldness Experiment," George Deleon argues that fewer winos are bald than are respectable, middle-class men and supports this contention by briefly describing the derelicts he has observed:

> Black, white, old, young, short, tall, all of them had a full mop. And hair that wouldn't quit. It leaped up as if it were electrified, or shagged down in complete asocial indifference, or zoomed back absurdly neat, gray-black and glued. Inexplicably, it seemed that boozing burned out the guts but grew hair.

This exaggerated description underscores the writer's belief that derelicts are a hairy lot, though it is, of course, drawn from personal observation and is intended to provide humorous support, not factual evidence.

Since argumentation is concerned principally with developing believable reasons accompanied by supporting evidence, description is usually best kept to a minimum. Sometimes, however, a lengthy descriptive passage can be deliberately argumentative in itself, as is this description of Ronald Reagan, then governor of California, by Gore Vidal:

> Ronald Reagan is a well-preserved not young man. Close to, the painted face is webbed with delicate lines while the dyed hair, eyebrows, and eyelashes contrast oddly with the sagging muscle beneath the as yet unlifted chin, soft earnest of wattle soon-to-be. The effect, in repose, suggests the work of a skillful em- balmer. Animated, the face is quite attractive and at a distance youthful; partic- ularly engaging is the crooked smile full of large porcelain-capped teeth. The eyes are the only interesting feature: small, narrow, apparently dark, they glitter in the hot light, alert to every move, for this is enemy country—the liberal Eastern press who are so notoriously immune to that warm and folksy perfor- mance which Reagan quite deliberately projects over their heads to some leg- endary constituency at the far end of the tube, some shining Carverville where good Lewis Stone forever lectures Andy Hardy on the virtues of thrift and the wisdom of the contract system at Metro-Goldwyn-Mayer.

NARRATION

A **narration** is a story. Like description, narration is generally not used extensively in argumentation, but occasionally it is useful in making a point.

Narration can be thought of as a type of extended example. In the essay on illiteracy, for instance, the writer tells a brief story about a young man who lived across the street, in order to illustrate on a personal level the suffering that illiterates experience.

Narration may be used in a variety of ways, not the least of which is to emphasize a point through humor. In a satiric article ridiculing the National Rifle Association's excessive zeal in defending a citizen's right to carry guns, Mike Royko tells a brief tale about the NRA's efforts to defeat an ordinance that would make it illegal to wear a gun in a tavern in the town of Pinedale, Wyoming. He explains that the mayor thought people should remove their weapons when they went into one of the town's three taverns because "liquor and guns don't mix."

> When the NRA heard about the proposed ordinance, they sent one of their field representatives into action.
>
> He raced about town, warning folks that if they ever lost the right to carry a gun into a tavern, the next step might be total disarmament. As he put it, keeping guns out of taverns was just a way for the anti-gun forces to "get their foot in the door." . . .
>
> Thanks to the NRA field representative, the right to wear a gun into a tavern was revealed to the people of Pinedale to be one of their most precious rights.
>
> So when the town board met this week to consider the ordinance, about half the people in town jammed into the hall.
>
> The owner of the Cowboy Bar testified that it was OK with him if somebody packed a pistol in his bar.
>
> The NRA field rep warned them of the dangers to their liberties if a fella couldn't wear his six-shooter while having a beer or two. . . .
>
> Finally, it came time for the town board to vote. . . .
>
> Just about every arm went straight up.
>
> So the tavern gun ban was defeated. . . .
>
> This is another example of the kind of good works that the much-maligned NRA engages in.

This humorous tale makes Royko's point—that the NRA goes to extreme lengths to defeat gun control measures. The story dramatizes the ridiculous situation better than would a terse explanation of the facts, and thus is more effective in persuading the reader to the writer's point of view.

DEFINITION

Definitions explain what words mean. Since a surprising number of misunderstandings arise when people fail to define the terms they use, definitions should always be given for terms important to the argument that the reader may not understand. For instance, the term *functional illiterate,* used throughout the essay on American illiteracy, is defined in the introduction as a person who reads at a level that is unequal to the demands of society.

Sometimes definitions are of minor importance, included to clarify a point, perhaps, or to acquaint the reader with a new term. At other times they may be essential to the argument. In the following example from "The Penalty of Death," H. L. Mencken defines the term *katharsis* in order to emphasize a major premise, that capital punishment should be legal because it brings relief to the immediate victims and to society at large. (Note that his definition is followed by an example.)

> I borrow a better term from the late Aristotle: *katharsis. Katharsis,* so used, means a salubrious discharge of emotions, a healthy letting off of steam. A school boy, disliking his teacher, deposits a tack upon the pedagogical chair; the teacher jumps and the boy laughs. This is *katharsis.* What I contend is that one of the prime objects of all judicial punishments is to afford the same grateful relief *(a)* to the immediate victims of the criminal punished, and *(b)* to the general body of moral and timorous men.

Since katharsis is a term many readers already know, Mencken defines the word not simply to clarify its meaning but to call attention to it and thus emphasize its importance in his argument.

ANALYSIS

An **analysis** takes apart an idea or argument and explains how it works. Analysis in argumentation is often used in rebutting the opposition. For example, Charles Hartshorne, in his essay "Concerning Abortion: An Attempt at a Rational View," uses analysis to refute the view held by his opponents that the fertilized egg, in its early stage, is a human being:

> The fertilized egg is an individual egg, but not an individual human being. For such a being is, in its body, a multicellular organism, a *metazoan*—to use the scientific Greek—and the egg is a single cell. The first thing the egg cell does is to begin dividing into many cells. For some weeks the fetus is not a single individual at all, but a colony of cells. During its first weeks there seems to be no ground for regarding the fetus as comparable to an individual animal. Only in possible or probable destiny is it an individual. Otherwise it is an organized society of single-celled individuals.

By analyzing the function of the egg during the first several weeks after fertilization, Hartshorne provides a good reason for thinking that the egg should not be considered a human being, namely, that it is not yet a multicellular organism.

CAUSAL ANALYSIS

A **causal analysis** explains the cause and effect relationship of certain acts or events. This form of analysis is used rather extensively in argumentation and appears several times in the essay on illiteracy. For instance, the third and fourth paragraphs explain how illiterates suffer (the effects) because they cannot read (the cause). They suffer embarrassment and pretend to be able to read; they suffer on a practical level because they cannot read the labels of cans, danger signs, bank statements, and so forth. The next two paragraphs explain the price that society pays (the effect) to support illiterates (the cause).

In his argument "A Statement on Nuclear Energy," Benjamin Spock uses causal analysis to emphasize the dangers (possible effects) of large-scale employment of nuclear power (the possible cause). He sees five serious dangers (effects) of such use, including these two:

> There are five distinct dangers in nuclear power; the most horrible would be a complete "meltdown" caused by a failure of the cooling system. Highly lethal radioactive materials would melt through the containing walls and be dispersed into the ground and into the atmosphere. This might promptly kill 50,000 people downwind from the plant from radiation sickness, and many more in the succeeding 30 years from leukemia and cancer, especially in children. And the irradiation of the germ cells in the ovaries and testicles of exposed adults, children and unborn babies would produce mental and physical defects for endless generations. For when mutations are produced in the germ cells, they are passed on forever. . . .
>
> A second danger from nuclear power plants is the regular leakage of low-level radiation into the atmosphere and into the water in the ground. It is now known that low levels of radiation are harmful to at least small percentages of the exposed population, depending on the intensity of the exposure. Thousands of cases of leukemia and cancer are calculated to have been caused in the past by diagnostic x-rays and by atomic weapons tests. Whether the radiation leaking from power plants has already caused an increase in leukemia and cancer in downwind areas is still a matter of controversy among scientists. . . .

Spock mounts a powerful argument against using nuclear power by explaining the devastating effects it will have.

COMPARISON AND CONTRAST

A **comparison** explains the similarities among ideas, experiences, people, or objects. **Contrast** explains the differences. The two techniques are often used together to explain both the similarities and differences of a particular subject.

Clarence Darrow does this quite effectively in "The Futility of the Death Penalty," when he contrasts the punishment of criminals in England to their treatment in the United States:

> It seems to be a general impression that there are fewer homicides in Great Britain than in America because in England punishment is more certain, more prompt, and more severe. As a matter of fact, the reverse is true. In England the average term for burglary is eighteen months; with us it is probably four or five years. In England, imprisonment for life means twenty years. Prison sentences in the United States are harder than in any country in the world that could be classed as civilized.

Darrow uses contrasting methods of punishment as evidence to support his argument that neither the death penalty, nor any harsh punishment, will deter crime. By explaining that though England is more lenient in punishing criminals than is the United States, it has fewer homicides, Darrow undermines the widely held belief that severe punishment is a deterrent to crime, and thus he advances his argument against the death penalty.

HISTORICAL BACKGROUND

Although not, strictly speaking, a rhetorical device, **historical background** is sometimes needed in argumentative essays to provide perspective, indicate context, and so on. Margaret Mead, for instance, introduces historical background in her essay "A Life for a Life: What It Means Today" in the service of a rather interesting purpose:

> The struggle for and against the abolition of capital punishment has been going on in our country and among enlightened peoples everywhere for well over a century. In the years before the Civil War the fight to end the death penalty was led in America by men like Horace Greeley, who also was fighting strongly to abolish slavery, and by a tiny handful of active women like New England's Dorothea Dix, who was fighting for prison reform. In those years three states— Michigan in 1847, Rhode Island in 1852 and Wisconsin in 1853—renounced the use of capital punishment, the first jurisdictions in the modern world to do so.

Here Mead recalls historical figures known for their humane concerns as a way of showing that enlightened people have fought capital punishment for over a century and thus, by implication, enlightened people should do so today.

These are the most common ways of developing arguments. In other types of writing, such as exposition or fiction, an entire piece may use only one or two methods. There are, for instance, essays of definition, analysis, or comparison and contrast, and short stories rely almost entirely on narration and description. In argumentation, however, these methods are always used in the service of a larger idea—the thesis or the reasons that support the thesis. Not all methods are used in every argument, but those that are used should make a point that advances the argument.

EXERCISE 3–1   USING RHETORICAL DEVICES TO SUPPORT REASONS

Think of one good reason for accepting one of the following statements. Then write a short passage in support of that reason, using one of the rhetorical methods discussed in this chapter.

1. Students do not work as hard in pass/fail classes as they do in courses that assign letter grades.

2. Falling in love is an illness.
3. The state should retest drivers older than sixty-five every year.

Introductions

An argument may be won or lost on the basis of the introduction alone. An introduction that strikes just the right note starts drawing readers into agreement with the thesis. On the other hand, a strident introduction that offends readers may deter them from accepting a perfectly sensible thesis. And an introduction that fails to engage their interest whatsoever may lose them altogether—before they even get to the thesis.

Although there are dozens of ways to introduce an essay, some are more commonly used than others. The following examples may help you in developing introductions to essays.

PERSONAL EXPERIENCE

One very good way to start an argumentative essay is to describe an engaging personal experience of your own. The advantage of this method is that the reader may identify with you and come to the same conclusion as you do in the thesis. Noel Perrin uses this method in the introduction to his article "The Androgynous Man." He describes a personal experience that led him to examine his masculine identity and to conclude that men who are spiritually androgynous have more freedom than traditionally masculine men:

> The summer I was 16, I took a train from New York to Steamboat Springs, Colo., where I was going to be assistant horse wrangler at a camp. The trip took three days, and since I was much too shy to talk to strangers, I had quite a lot of time for reading. I read all of *Gone With the Wind*. I read all the interesting articles in a couple of magazines I had, and then I went back and read all the dull stuff. I also took all the quizzes, a thing of which magazines were even fuller then than now.
>
> The one that held my undivided attention was called "How Masculine/ Feminine Are You?" It consisted of a large number of inkblots. The reader was supposed to decide which of four objects each blot most resembled. The choices might be a cloud, a steam engine, a caterpillar and a sofa.
>
> When I finished the test, I was shocked to find that I was barely masculine at all. On a scale of 1 to 10, I was about 1.2. Me, the horse wrangler? (And not just wrangler, either. That summer, I had to skin a couple of horses that died— the camp owner wanted the hides.)
>
> The results of that test were so terrifying to me that for the first time in my life I did a piece of original analysis. Having unlimited time on the train, I looked at the "masculine" answers over and over, trying to find what it was that distinguished real men from people like me—and eventually I discovered two very simple patterns. It was "masculine" to think the blots looked like man-

made objects, and "feminine" to think they looked like natural objects. It was masculine to think they looked like things capable of causing harm, and feminine to think of innocent things.

Even at 16, I had the sense to see that the compilers of the test were using rather limited criteria—maleness and femaleness are both more complicated than *that*—and I breathed a huge sigh of relief. I wasn't necessarily a wimp, after all.

Perrin's introduction strikes just the right note because it reveals the same doubts about masculinity that most young men have at age sixteen. Male readers will thus identify with him in the introduction and so want to read on; women, too, in this era of heightened consciousness about male and female roles, should be intrigued and sympathize with the sensitive young man portrayed. Thus the introduction gets readers on Perrin's side right away and prepares them for the thesis.

EXAMPLES GLEANED FROM OTHER SOURCES

Not all examples are personal; as often as not they are drawn from other sources. In "TV Violence: The Shocking New Evidence," Eugene H. Methvin gives a series of startling examples dramatizing the harmful effects of violence on television. His introduction graphically leads the reader to the thesis that watching too much television—violent programs in particular—can be harmful to a viewer's health:

- San Diego: A high-school honor student watches a lurid ABC-TV fictionalization of the 1890s Lizzie Borden ax murder case; then chops his own parents and sister to death and leaves his brother a quadriplegic.
- Denver: *The Deer Hunter* is telecast and a 17-year-old kills himself with a revolver, acting out the movie's climactic game of Russian roulette. He is the 25th viewer in two years to kill himself that way after watching the drama on TV.
- Decatur, Ill.: A 12-year-old overdoses on sleeping pills after her mother forbids her to date a 16-year-old boy. "What gave you the idea of suicide?" an investigating psychiatrist asks. The answer: A little girl tried it on a TV show, was quickly revived and welcomed back by her parents with open arms.

These examples clearly were chosen for their shock value—to startle readers out of their complacency and prepare them for a thesis that is of considerable importance today. Another advantage, of course, is that the examples engage the attention of readers immediately and impel them to read on.

QUOTATION

Henry David Thoreau, in his classic essay "Civil Disobedience," begins his introduction with a *motto*, a brief statement used to express a principle or ideal. He then explores the implications of this motto as a way of leading up to his defense of civil disobedience:

I heartily accept the motto,—"That government is best which governs least"; and I should like to see it acted up to more rapidly and systematically. Carried out, it finally amounts to this, which also I believe,—"That government is best which governs not at all"; and when men are prepared for it, that will be the kind of government which they will have. Government is at best but an expedient; but most governments are usually, and all governments are sometimes, inexpedient. The objections which have been brought against a standing army, and they are many and weighty, and deserve to prevail, may also at last be brought against a standing government. The standing army is only an arm of the standing government. The government itself, which is only the mode which the people have chosen to execute their will, is equally liable to be abused and perverted before the people can act through it.

Notice that Thoreau does not let his quotation stand alone, unexplained, but makes it an integral part of his discussion on government. Quotations should function that way. They are well-phrased, apt sayings that catch the attention of readers and provide the writer with an idea to explore as a way of leading into the thesis. Note that you need not cite the author when using a motto that has become part of the vernacular (indeed, the author may be unknown) but you *must* cite the author of any other quotation.

COMPARISON AND CONTRAST

Introductions using comparison or contrast draw attention to an item or an idea by setting it off against something else. **Comparison** shows how similar things are alike and thus develops our understanding of each more fully. For instance, the notion that consumerism is as old as civilization itself becomes more understandable when the modern supermarket is compared to the ancient bazaar. **Contrast,** on the other hand, sets unlike items off against each other and thus intensifies the qualities of each. A black bowl seems blacker on a white table-cloth than it does on a gray one. In the following introduction from "The New Equality," Peregrine Worsthorne compares and contrasts an aristocracy to a meritocracy in such a manner as to suggest her conclusion that meritocracy is just as unfair to the mass of people as is aristocracy:

> To most of us it now seems very strange, almost incomprehensible, that for centuries gross hereditary inequalities of wealth, status and power were universally accepted as a divinely ordained fact of life. The lord in his castle, like the peasant at his gate, both believed that this was where God wished them to remain. If anybody had then suggested that such an arrangement was manifestly unfair he would have been dismissed as a little crazed, not to say blasphemous.
>
> Modern man, as I say, finds this awfully difficult to understand. To him it seems absolutely axiomatic that each individual ought to be allowed to make his grade according to merit, regardless of the accident of birth. All positions of power, wealth and status should be open to talent. To the extent that this ideal is achieved a society is deemed to be just.

If our feudal forebears thought it perfectly fair that the lord should be in his castle and the peasant at his gate, their liberal successors—which means most of us—have tended to believe it to be fair enough that the man of merit should be on top and the man without merit should be underneath. Anybody who challenged this assumption was thought a little crazed.

Much of the current political and social malaise springs, in my view, from the increasing evidence that this assumption should be challenged. The ideal of a meritocracy no longer commands such universal assent.

CAUSAL ANALYSIS

Causal analysis, in which we explain cause and effect relationships, can be very effective in demonstrating the consequences of an action. In a memorable essay, "The Nuclear Winter," Carl Sagan explains the devastating consequences we can expect if we fail to prevent a nuclear war:

> Except for fools and madmen, everyone knows that nuclear war would be an unprecedented human catastrophe. A more or less typical strategic warhead has a yield of 2 megatons, the explosive equivalent of 2 million tons of TNT . . . about the same as all the bombs exploded in World War II. . . .
>
> In a 2-megaton explosion over a fairly large city, buildings would be vaporized, people reduced to atoms and shadows, outlying structures blown down like matchsticks and raging fires ignited. And if the bomb were exploded on the ground, an enormous crater, like those that can be seen through a telescope on the surface of the Moon, would be all that remained where midtown once had been. There are now more than 50,000 nuclear weapons, more than 13,000 megatons of yield, deployed in the arsenals of the United States and the Soviet Union—enough to obliterate a million Hiroshimas. . . .
>
> Thus, there are vastly more nuclear weapons than are needed for any plausible deterrence of a potential adversary.

The introduction thus sets forth the immediate effects of a nuclear war, drawing the reader into reading further while supporting the conclusion that we must avoid all-out nuclear war at all cost. What better way could there be, after all, to convince readers of the folly of such a war than by describing the effects it would cause? We need only read the first few paragraphs to be drawn into a subject of such immediate concern to everyone. One good reason, then, to use this method of introduction is to give readers concrete evidence of what will happen if they either take, or fail to take, an action the author proposes.

CONSIDERING THE OPPOSITION

In his classic essay on capital punishment, "The Penalty of Death," Mencken starts right off with the opposing point of view, which he then goes on to refute, before presenting his own reasons for supporting the death penalty:

> Of the arguments against capital punishment that issue from uplifters, two are commonly heard most often, to wit:

1. That hanging a man (or frying him or gassing him) is a dreadful business, degrading to those who have to do it and revolting to those who have to witness it.
2. That it is useless, for it does not deter others from the same crime.

The first of these arguments, it seems to me, is plainly too weak to need serious refutation. All it says, in brief, is that the work of the hangman is unpleasant. Granted. But suppose it is? It may be quite necessary to society for all that. There are, indeed, many other jobs that are unpleasant, and yet no one thinks of abolishing them—that of the plumber, that of the soldier, that of the garbage-man, that of the priest hearing confessions, that of the sand-hog, and so on. Moreover, what evidence is there that any actual hangman complains of his work? I have heard none. On the contrary, I have known many who delighted in their ancient art, and practiced it proudly.

In the second argument of the abolitionists there is rather more force, but even here, I believe, the ground under them is shaky. Their fundamental error consists in assuming that the whole aim of punishing criminals is to deter other (potential) criminals—that we hang or electrocute A simply in order to so alarm B that he will not kill C. This, I believe, is an assumption which confuses a part with the whole. Deterrence, obviously, is *one* of the aims of punishment, but it is surely not the only one.

Considering the opposition's point of view first is particularly effective when there are strong counterarguments to your position that must be dealt with. The success of this method, of course, depends on the writer's ability to refute the opposition successfully. Note that Mencken uses humor as well as logic to undermine the opposition. In the hands of a master like Mencken, humor can be a powerful technique, but most of us lack his talent and are probably better off relying on clear reasoning—no mean feat in itself—to persuade the reader.

These sample introductions suggest ways to begin an essay, but you need not be limited to them. You may have other ideas that will work better for the essay you have in mind. Whatever method you use, however, remember that the introduction of an essay has to engage the interest of readers and if possible draw them to your side so that they are open to the position you are about to argue. Remember also that introductions should be written with your own voice, reflecting who you are and what you believe.

Conclusions

The conclusion of an argumentative essay effectively emphasizes the writer's position, either directly, by restating the thesis and summarizing the main points, or indirectly, by using various techniques that appeal to the readers' reason and emotion.

There are as many ways to end an argument as there are to begin one, but they all should be designed to persuade the reader one last time that the position argued for is the right one. Let's now consider some of the common ways to conclude an argumentative essay.

PERSONAL EXAMPLE

Personal experiences can be molded into an effective conclusion to an essay just as into a successful beginning. In "KILL 'EM! CRUSH 'EM! EAT 'EM RAW!" John McMurtney reveals the brutality of football in a series of devastating examples drawn from his years as a professional football player in Canada. His conclusion explains the incident that finally led him to quit the game and take up another profession:

> I got out of football in 1962. I had asked to be traded after Calgary had offered me a $25-a-week-plus-commissions off-season job as a clothing-store salesman. ("Dear Mr. Finks:" I wrote. [Jim Finks was then the Stampeders' general manager.] "Somehow I do not think the dialectical subtleties of Hegel, Marx and Plato would be suitably oriented amidst the environmental stimuli of jockey shorts and herringbone suits. I hope you make a profitable sale or trade of my contract to the East.") So the Stampeders traded me to Montreal. In a preseason intersquad game with the Alouettes I ripped the cartilages in my ribs on the hardest block I'd ever thrown. I had trouble breathing and I had to shuffle-walk with my torso on a tilt. The doctor in the local hospital said three weeks rest, the coach said scrimmage in two days. Three days later I was back home reading philosophy.

CONCLUSION BY CAUSAL ANALYSIS

An argument that emphasizes the consequences of taking a particular action, or failing to take it, may end with a causal analysis that discusses the cumulative effects of such an action. In "The Damnation of a Canyon," Edward Abbey argues for shutting down the Glen Canyon power plant that lies at the heart of the Colorado canyonlands, draining off the reservoir, and allowing this wilderness area to regenerate itself. He concludes by explaining the effects of such an action:

> All of the foregoing would be nothing but a futile exercise in nostalgia (so much water over the dam) if I had nothing constructive and concrete to offer. But I do. As alternate methods of power generation are developed, such as solar, and as the nation establishes a way of life adapted to actual resources and basic needs, so that the demand for electrical power begins to diminish, we can shut down the Glen Canyon power plant, open the diversion tunnels, and drain the reservoir.
>
> This will no doubt expose a dreary and hideous scene: immense mud flats and whole plateaus of sodden garbage strewn with dead trees, sunken boats, the skeletons of long-forgotten, decomposing water-skiers. But to those who find the prospect too appalling, I say give nature a little time. In five years, at most in ten, the sun and wind and storms will cleanse and sterilize the repellent mess. The inevitable floods will soon remove all that does not belong within the canyons. Fresh green willow, box elder and redbud will reappear; and the

ancient drowned cottonwoods (noble monuments to themselves) will be re-placed by young of their own kind. With the renewal of plant life will come the insects, the birds, the lizards and snakes, the mammals. Within a generation—thirty years—I predict the river and canyons will bear a decent resemblance to their former selves. Within the lifetime of our children Glen Canyon and the living river, heart of the canyonlands, will be restored to us. The wilderness will again belong to God, the people and the wild things that call it home.

APPEALS TO A SPECIFIC AUDIENCE

Argumentative essays generally are aimed at a specific audience—college students, senior citizens, the business world, or members of a labor union—and may conclude by appealing directly to that audience. In "Where College Fails Us," Caroline Bird argues against the notion that college is beneficial to all those who attend. Her audience is prospective college students and, presumably, their parents, and so the conclusion is directed to both of these groups:

> College is an ideal place for those young adults who love learning for its own sake, who would rather read than eat, and who like nothing better than writing research papers. But they are a minority, even at the prestigious colleges, which recruit and attract the intellectually oriented.
>
> The rest of our high school graduates need to look at college more closely and critically, to examine it as a consumer product, and decide if the cost in dollars, in time, in continued dependency, and in future returns, is worth the very large investment each student—and his family—must make.

APPEALS TO A GENERAL AUDIENCE

Whereas some arguments are aimed at a specific audience, others embrace a much wider readership—the citizens of our country, for example, or the members of the human race. Generally these arguments address national or international concerns, such as ecological imbalances, immigration policies, or nuclear disarmament. In *Silent Spring*, Rachel Carson argued against the use of pesticides so convincingly that she persuaded both the public and government that change was necessary. The conclusion of "The Obligation to Endure," a chapter from that book, addresses a concern that citizens of the nation at large must share. Note also that it ends with a quote that drives her point home.

> There is still very limited awareness of the nature of the threat. This is an era of specialists, each of whom sees his own problem and is unaware of or intolerant of the larger frame into which it fits. It is also an era dominated by industry, in which the right to make a dollar at whatever cost is seldom challenged. When the public protests, confronted with some obvious evidence of damaging results of pesticide applications, it is fed little tranquilizing pills of half truth. We urgently need an end to these false assurances, to the sugar coating of unpalatable facts. It is the public that is being asked to assume the risks that the insect controllers calculate. The public must decide whether it wishes to continue on the present road, and it can do so only when in full possession of the facts. In

the words of Jean Rostand, "The obligation to endure gives us the right to know."

CALLS TO ACTION

Finally, conclusions can urge readers to take action on an issue. They can provide remedies to specific problems, such as recommending that the city council restrict the building of high-rise apartments or urging the university to provide more parking spaces for students. Other conclusions may stir people to action by a more general appeal. In his inspirational 1963 address to 200,000 civil rights supporters, Martin Luther King described his vision of a free America. Fittingly he delivered his sermon on the steps of the Lincoln Memorial. In his conclusion he exhorts the people of this country to "let freedom ring throughout the land" by treating blacks and whites as equals:

> . . . let freedom ring from the prodigious hilltops of New Hampshire! Let freedom ring from the heightening Alleghenies of Pennsylvania!
>
> Let freedom ring from the snowcapped Rockies of Colorado!
>
> Let freedom ring from the curvaceous peaks of California!
>
> But not only that; let freedom ring from Stone Mountain of Georgia!
>
> Let freedom ring from every hill and molehill of Mississippi. From every mountainside, let freedom ring.
>
> When we let freedom ring, when we let it ring from every village and every hamlet, from every state and every city, we will be able to speed up that day when all of God's children, black men and white men, Jews and Gentiles, Protestants and Catholics, will be able to join hands and sing in the words of the old Negro spiritual, "Free at last! free at last! thank God almighty, we are free at last!"

Since the conclusion is your last chance to convince the reader of your position, remember to choose your method carefully. Even the most closely reasoned argument will lose its force if it peters out. But an effective conclusion will drive your point home with emphasis and thus be persuasive.

EXERCISE 3–2   USING RHETORICAL DEVICES IN
ARGUMENTATIVE ESSAYS

Write an argument for or against one of the following statements using several of the rhetorical devices.

1. Older people are just as capable of learning new subjects as younger people.

2. The most important technological development in recent years is the computer.

3. Prostitution should be legalized.

4. Full-time students who work should not have to pay income tax.

5. The federal government should restrict immigration more than it does.

Essay Analysis: Evaluating Argumentative Essays

Argumentative essays may run from a few hundred words to several hundred pages and deal with such major issues as the decline of heavy industry in the United States or such minor matters as the merits of a good restaurant. What distinguishes argumentative essays from other forms of writing is not length or subject matter but purpose: persuading readers to adopt a particular opinion or course of action by providing sufficient *reasons* for doing so.

The other major kind of nonfiction writing, *exposition*, explains or describes something without arguing for a position. Of course, many argumentative essays contain explanatory sections and thus are both argumentative and expository. And even the most neutral exposition may *imply* a claim or urge a course of action. (Fiction, also, is often written with an intent to persuade, by satirizing a situation, as in Swift's "A Modest Proposal," or simply by describing an event, as in George Orwell's "A Hanging.")

Essays that are intended to persuade can be evaluated or analyzed for literary style and quality (word choice, emphasis, grammatical constructions, tone, use of metaphor, and so on) or to determine their logical *cogency*. Our concern in this chapter will be cogency, except insofar as poor writing fosters a lack of cogency, as it frequently does. The crucial questions will always be the same: Does this essay present (or suggest) believable reasons? Are the arguments it contains valid? Is there other relevant evidence that might overturn these arguments? The main reason we read most argumentative essays, after all, is to decide whether or not to accept their theses. No matter how well written in other respects, an essay is likely to be persuasive only if the arguments it presents in support of its thesis are cogent (or if we can add additional support from our stock of background beliefs to make them cogent).

Evaluating Arguments in Preparation for Writing

Since much of the reading in college is done in preparation for writing essays, students often need to work with that end in mind. Careful readers read actively in order to clearly comprehend the author's meaning and to evaluate the material. When writing an essay, they evaluate what they read and try to develop their own viewpoint on the subject. Various studies on strategic reading reveal that critical readers identify the implicit and explicit purpose of the text (the two often are different), draw on relevant background information for both comprehension and assessment, concentrate on major points rather than on minor details, evaluate the internal consistency of the material, and determine how it fits with background knowledge and common sense. *

Reading for accurate comprehension is the first step in evaluating an argument. At times, though, our background beliefs and world views lead us to distort or oversimplify an argument in the process of reading it. Our minds work in such a way that when we take in new information, we try to make it fit our existing understanding of the subject. If our prior knowledge is distorted or oversimplified, the new information we gain can be distorted as well, to fit our previous understanding without correcting it. The careful reader, therefore, guards against this tendency by first trying to understand the argument without distorting it in any way. What follows is a discussion of this process.

The Basic Tasks

The difference between the evaluation of an essay and the assessment of a single argument is primarily one of complexity, given that a typical argumentative essay is constructed out of several related arguments and may contain counter-arguments, arguments pro and con, and so on. In reading and evaluating an essay for cogency, several fundamental tasks need to be accomplished (although exactly in what order is a matter of individual taste).

FIND THE THESIS

The basic question is whether or not to accept the argument's thesis, so we have to figure out *accurately* just what the thesis is, and then keep it in the back of our mind as we read the essay. The sooner we discover what the thesis is, the better.

FIND THE REASONS SUPPORTING THE THESIS

Once we see what the thesis is, we can begin to figure out the essay's logical structure. Our first task, obviously, is to find the reasons given for accepting the thesis.

Most reasons will be explicitly stated and perhaps even labeled as reasons, but some will just be implied by what is said. Our task is to find both of these

*Thomas L. Good and Jere E. Brophy, *Educational Psychology* 3rd edition/New York and London (Longman, 1986), p. 279.

kinds of reasons. In particular, we don't want to fault an argument for neglecting to state a premise that is obvious or that readers can be expected to believe anyway. Fair evaluation requires that we consider the strongest version of an argument, not the weakest (as those who are prejudiced are inclined to do).

Some reasons are presented without justification—the reader is expected to accept them on sight, as it were. But well-written essays provide additional *support* for reasons readers cannot be expected to accept straight off. This process of justifying reasons occasionally goes on for several "layers," but usually it ends after just one or two. Here is the beginning of an argument presenting a reason for its thesis and one layer of support for that reason:

> We ought to legalize the use of marijuana as a recreational drug [*thesis*]. For one thing, contrary to what many people believe, marijuana is a relatively harmless substance when compared to legal drugs such as alcohol and cigarettes [*reason*]. Cigarette smoking causes cancer, heart disease, and all sorts of other ailments, resulting in untold thousands of deaths, and alcohol is implicated in over 20,000 deaths resulting from auto accidents every year, while not a single death has conclusively been attributed to marijuana smoking [*support for reason*].

Note that from the point of view of logic, supporting a reason for a thesis is the same sort of process as supporting the thesis itself. That is, the *kinds* of reasons that can support a thesis may in some cases support a reason offered in favor of that thesis.

One of the most important kinds of reasons is supporting *evidence*, including statistical evidence. Suppose the thesis of an essay is that there should be capital punishment for certain heinous crimes. One reason commonly proposed in favor of this thesis is that the threat of capital punishment is a better deterrent than, say, life imprisonment. Legitimate statistics indicating that capital punishment does indeed deter better than a life term in jail would constitute good support for that reason—just how good will depend on the quality of the statistics offered (as well as the possible existence of counterstatistics indicating that at least sometimes it is not a better deterrent).

Examples are another very common type of support for reasons, as we have seen. Consider an essay whose thesis is that patients in a hospital should have a legal right to see their own medical records (in most places in the United States they do not have this right, although certain others do, for instance, insurance companies, the police, and government agencies). An important reason that might be offered for this conclusion is that the interests of patients sometimes are seriously harmed because they are refused permission to see their own medical records. Since most readers of an essay on a topic such as this one cannot be expected to know *how* patients could be harmed by having such information withheld, furnishing examples may be the most effective way to prove the point. This was done, for instance, in a magazine article that described someone accidentally recorded as schizophrenic who thereafter had great difficulty obtaining medical attention and was consistently passed over for job advancement. *

IDENTIFY OTHER ARGUMENTATIVE STRUCTURES

The simplest argumentative essay structure consists of just a thesis and reasons for the thesis. The next simplest adds support for some of its reasons. But most argumentative essays are more complicated than this. Full-blown essays also support their theses by raising and refuting possible or likely counterarguments or by arguing against alternative proposals, and so on. In laying bare an argumentative essay's logical structure, we want to be sure to take into account these other kinds of argumentative devices so that the entire relevant structure of the essay is revealed. (This is illustrated by the analysis of Paul Goodman's essay on abolishing grades that follows soon.)

PASS OVER IRRELEVANT MATERIAL

Good writers tend not to include irrelevant remarks in their essays. They stick to the point and, in particular, don't provide readers with allegedly relevant reasons that are in fact irrelevant. (See page 80 in Chapter 5, where the related fallacies *invalid reason* and *non sequitur* are discussed.) Anything not truly relevant to the thesis, however informative or enjoyable a tidbit it may be, has to be disregarded for purposes of critical analysis.

BRING RELEVANT BACKGROUND INFORMATION TO BEAR

Everything needed to prove a thesis is never—that means *never*—included in an essay, no matter how long. To do that would require dragging in big chunks of a writer's background beliefs and would mean proving things that everyone already believes anyway. Good writers try to provide just the information their audience will need. Someone writing about baseball for a big city American newspaper doesn't need to tell readers that Hank Aaron hit a lot of home runs or that Sandy Koufax was a exceptionally great pitcher, although for some audiences—in Outer Mongolia or Upper Volta—this might be brand-new information. We should add supporting background information of this kind, and whatever information may be implied but not stated, before coming to an evaluation. And, of course, we should add any information or evidence contrary to the argument's thesis that we can think of.

Note also that the point of an essay analysis should determine in part what sort of background information we bring to bear. If our concern is whether or not to accept an essay's thesis, clearly we should bring to bear all relevant background information that we can think of, even including reasons totally

*See "Double Indignity," *The Washington Monthly*, October 1986.

different from those mentioned in the essay. But if we are concerned with the quality of the essay as an essay, with how well the essay argues for its thesis, and not primarily with whether or not to accept that thesis, then clearly we should not add entirely new reasons that the author did not think to include in the essay, although even in this case we should include obvious things that readers can be expected to know. In most cases, our main concern is the believability of the thesis, but occasionally we will be more interested in the question of how well an essay argues for its thesis. (The classic instance of this, no doubt, occurs when instructors evalute student essays.)

COME TO AN EVALUATION

While evaluation is logically the last thing we need to do in argument analysis, good critical thinkers tend to start evaluating as soon as they discover what the thesis is. They keep in mind questions such as: Does this thesis fit well with what I already know or believe? If not, what sort of reasons or support might change my mind? And they continue to evaluate as they go along, asking such questions as: Is this reason acceptable without further argument? Does that reason defend the actual thesis or something a bit different? Do the facts referred to seem plausible, given my background beliefs? Is there some serious counterargument the writer seems to have forgotten?

Of course, a completely confident judgment can't be reached until the structure of the whole essay has been figured out. When this has been done, the relevant passages will divide into those that are argued for within the essay and those that are not. The latter are the writer's basic "starting points." When evaluating an essay, we need to ask and answer three basic questions corresponding to the three basic requirements of cogent reasoning introduced in Chapter 1: (1) Are the reasons provided justified by what we already believe or by arguments within the essay? (2) Do we know other relevant reasons or support? (If so, they should be added if our purpose is to decide on the truth of the writer's thesis.) (3) Is the reasoning in the essay valid?

If there is a statement relevant to the thesis that is neither argued for within the essay nor already justified by our own background beliefs, or if we know relevant information that refutes or casts doubt on the thesis, or if the reasoning is not completely valid, then clearly we should not be persuaded to accept the essay's thesis.

It's important to remember that the reasons given in an argument may not be premises of the kind given in formal logic textbooks. In particular, it should be noted again that supporting *evidence* of various sorts (statistics on drunk-driving deaths when the thesis concerns drunk-driving laws), *expert opinion* (Einstein writing to President Roosevelt to tell him that atomic weapons were feasible), and *examples* (patients who are harmed by not being allowed to see their medical records) may all count as legitimate reasons under some circumstances.

The Margin Note and Summary Method

Most essay analysis in everyday life is done informally. We read the essay, see what appears to be the thesis and main reasons, and evaluate in our heads as we go along. Some readers like to give themselves little prompts to keep better track of things, perhaps by drawing a line in the margin next to significant passages or by circling the thesis and underlining reasons that support it.

In addition, a good many critical thinkers try to figure out what it would take to convince themselves to accept the thesis and what holds them back from already believing it. There often is a key point that keeps us from agreeing with the other side on an issue, and it makes sense when reading a particular essay to be on the lookout for reasons pro or con that point. In the case of capital punishment, for instance, the sticking point for many is whether taking a person's life deters more than does life imprisonment; for legalized abortions, it is whether an aborted fetus is indeed a human being. Knowing what to look for greatly increases our ability to wade through a mass of material and catch what is most important to us.

Informal methods of evaluation can be very effective in the hands of a skilled practitioner with a good stock of reasonably accurate background beliefs. But when we absolutely must be right, most of us need to use a more time-consuming method, such as the **margin note and summary method.** Although this is in part a matter of taste, a great many critical reasoners find that the margin note and summary method is a very effective way to go about the business of thesis evaluation.

There are four basic steps in this method:

1. Read the essay to be evaluated, to get its general drift.

2. Read it through again, this time roughly indicating content in the margins next to the important passages. Margin notes need not be full sentences, grammatically correct, or easily understood by anyone except yourself. And they may contain abbreviations or other shorthand devices whenever you wish.

3. Use the margin notes to construct a summary of the arguments in the essay, showing how they hang together. To do this, you obviously have to figure out the logical structure of the essay: what the thesis is, what reasons are given in its support, what supporting evidence is given for doubtful reasons, and so on. Different people will tend to make different summaries because we all bring to bear different background beliefs and thus sometimes find different parts of the same passage to be relevant to accepting or rejecting the essay's thesis. Indeed, one evaluator may completely pass over whole paragraphs that others with different background beliefs consider vital.

4. Evaluate the original essay by reviewing your summary, checking to make sure there are no relevant changes from the original. The temptation, of course, is to overlook relevant differences that might make you change your mind—always a painful process most of us are loath to go through.

Several things need to be said about this method. First, when we skip part of an essay, we make a value judgment that the skipped material is not even indirectly relevant to the thesis of the essay in question. It takes practice to acquire the skill needed to do this *fairly*. Second, margin notes and summaries are supposed to be shorthand devices. A good summary should therefore be a good deal shorter than the essay itself. (A very few essays are so tightly written that they cannot effectively be summarized, although they can often be rearranged so as to better reveal their logical structure. In any case, it usually pays to put the arguments into our own words.) And, third, it has to be mentioned that sometimes (often?), if we would only admit it to ourselves, we don't have enough background information to evaluate an essay, so that a bit of investigation is in order. This may mean resorting to fairly drastic measures, such as going over to the library.

Suppose, for instance, that you are required to evaluate Gore Vidal's claim in his essay on drugs that marijuana is not addictive. You may already have good background knowledge on this issue, in which case you may be able to evaluate his arguments without further research. But if not, you may become sufficiently interested in this point to do some investigating on this topic—over at the library.

Critical Essay Evaluation: An Example

Here is a short essay excerpted from the book *Compulsory Miseducation*, by Paul Goodman (New York: Horizon Press, 1964) with margin notes attached to save time and space:

ABOLISH GRADES AT TOP COLLEGES

Let half a dozen of the prestigious Universities—Chicago, Stanford, the Ivy League—abolish grading, and use testing only and entirely for pedagogic purposes as teachers see fit.

Thesis: Abolish grades at Ivy type schools and use tests only for pedagogic purposes.

Anyone who knows the frantic temper of the present schools will understand the transvaluation of values that would be effected by this modest innovation. For most of the students, the competitive grade has come to be the essence. The naive teacher points to the beauty of the subject and the ingenuity of the research; the shrewd student asks if he is responsible for that on the final exam.

Reason: Grades, not learning, are students' chief concern under current policy.

Let me at once dispose of an objection whose unanimity is quite fascinating. I think that the great majority of professors agree that grading hinders teaching and creates a bad spirit, going as far as cheating and plagiarizing. I have before me the collection of essays, *Examining in Harvard College*, and this is the consensus. It is uniformly asserted, however, that the grading is inevita-

Reason: Grading hinders teaching & fosters cheating & plagiarism.

Objection: Without grading, how will

ble; for how else will the graduate schools, the foundations, the corporations *know* whom to accept, reward, hire? How will the talent scouts know whom to tap?

By testing the applicants, of course, according to the specific task-requirements of the inducting institution, just as applicants for the Civil Service or for licenses in medicine, law, and architecture are tested. Why should Harvard professors do the testing *for* corporations and graduate schools?

The objection is ludicrous. Dean Whitla, of the Harvard Office of Tests, points out that the scholastic-aptitude and achievement tests used for *admission* to Harvard are a super-excellent index for all-around Harvard performance, better than high-school grades or particular Harvard course-grades. Presumably, these college-entrance tests are tailored for what Harvard and similar institutions want. By the same logic, would not an employer do far better to apply his own job-aptitude test rather than to rely on the vagaries of Harvard sectionmen? Indeed, I doubt that many employers bother to look at such grades; they are more likely to be interested merely in the fact of a Harvard diploma, whatever that connotes to them. The grades have most of their weight with the graduate schools—here, or elsewhere, the system runs mainly for its own sake. . . .

Perhaps the chief objectors to abolishing grading would be the students and their parents. The parents should be simply disregarded; their anxiety has done enough damage already. For the students, it seems to me that a primary duty of the university is to deprive them of their props, their dependence on extrinsic valuation and motivation, and to force them to confront the difficult enterprise itself and finally lose themselves in it.

A miserable effect of grading is to nullify the various uses of testing. Testing, for both student and teacher, is a means of structuring, and also of finding out what is blank or wrong and what has been assimilated and can be taken for granted. Review—including high-pressure review—is a means of bringing together the fragments, so that there are flashes of synoptic insight. [The authors agree with Goodman that testing for grades has harmful effects and should be avoided in the absence of compelling reasons to the contrary. So the important question for us is whether or not there are such compelling reasons. Consequently, we have omitted most of the support Goodman gives for his claim that testing for grades has harmful consequences.]

There are several good reasons for testing, and kinds of test. But if the aim is to discover weakness, what is the point of down-grading and punishing it, and thereby in-

grad schools and others know whom to accept?

Replies to objection: 1. They'll test applicants, as others do.

2. Why should Harvard test for others?

3. Employers can do this better for themselves.

4. Not many employers look at grades anyway; they're more interested just in who granted the diploma.

Objection: Students and parents want grades. Replies: 1. Disregard parents. 2. It is schools' duty to deprive students of props & force them to learn w/o grades.

Reason: Grading nullifies good uses of testing.

viting the student to conceal his weakness, by faking and bulling, if not cheating? The natural conclusion of synthesis is the insight itself, not a grade for having had it. For the important purpose of placement, if one can establish in the student the belief that one is testing *not* to grade and to make invidious comparisons but for his own advantage, the student should normally seek his own level, where he is challenged and yet capable, rather than trying to get by. If the student dares to accept himself as he is, a teacher's grade is a crude instrument compared with a student's self-awareness. But it is rare in our universities that students are encouraged to notice objectively their vast confusion. Unlike Socrates, our teachers rely on power-drives rather than shame and ingenuous idealism.

Support for reason: Testing for grades invites students to fake & cheat, nullifying good effects of testing for placement.

Support for reason: Testing for grades does not encourage students to notice their own "vast confusion."
Support for reason: (So?) Teachers rely on power rather than shame & idealism.

Many students are lazy, so teachers try to goad or threaten them by grading. In the long run this must do more harm than good. Laziness is a character-defense. It may be a way of avoiding learning, in order to protect the conceit that one is already perfect (deeper, the despair that one *never* can be). It may be a way of avoiding just the risk of failing and being down-graded. Sometimes it is a way of politely saying, "I won't." But since it is the authoritarian grown-up demands that have created such attitudes in the first place, why repeat the trauma? There comes a time when we must treat people as adult, laziness and all. It is one thing courageously to fire a do-nothing out of your class; it is quite another thing to evaluate him with a lordly F.

Support for reason: Goading lazy students into learning does more harm than good.

Most important of all, it is often obvious that balking in doing the work, especially among bright young people who get to great universities, means exactly what it says: The work does not suit me, not this subject, or not at this time, or not in this school, or not in school altogether. The student might not be bookish; he might be school-tired; perhaps his development ought now to take another direction. Yet unfortunately, if such a student is intelligent and is not sure of himself, he *can* be bullied into passing, and this obscures everything. My hunch is that I am describing a common situation. What a grim waste of young life and teacherly effort! Such a student will retain nothing of what he has "passed" in. Sometimes he must get mononucleosis to tell his story and be believed.

Support for reason: Although they can be bullied into passing by a grading system, they won't retain what they learned.

And ironically, the converse is also probably commonly true. A student flunks and is mechanically weeded out, who is really ready and eager to learn in a scholastic setting, but he has not quite caught on. A good teacher can recognize the situation, but the computer wreaks its will.

Reason: Some students who are now ready to learn are mechanically weeded out by the grading system.

We now need to construct a summary from our margin notes. The point of making a summary is to be able to evaluate a more succinct version of the essay than the original. So the summary must be as short as possible. This poses problems with respect to including material offered in support of premises. How much support, if any, should be included? The answer is, first, that there is no reason to include support for premises that you already accept or that are common knowledge. And, second, some critical thinkers prefer to include support for premises that are questionable without it, while others like to go back to the original passage and examine the evidence there. Either way, support that might otherwise convince us *cannot* be ignored, if we are to come to a sensible and fair appraisal.

In some essays, emotively charged language is used in a way that constitutes *unfair* argument. In a typical case of this kind, emotive language is used at least partly in place of reasons and genuine argument. We should be on our guard against this kind of illicit use of emotively loaded language. Goodman does use emotively charged language in his essay, but not in place of reasons and genuine argument.

Similarly, some essays employ irony, often quite subtle. In constructing a summary it sometimes is best to translate into a more literal form if there is any possibility of confusion. In the case of the Goodman essay, this problem does not arise, although he does employ a tiny bit of irony.

In any case, here is our summary of the Goodman essay, intended primarily to capture and elucidate the logical structure of the essay (numbers in parentheses indicate the paragraph in which the thesis or reason occurred in the essay):

Thesis: To improve education, we should abolish grades at top-notch schools and test only for pedagogical purposes. (1)

First Reason: Students have come to concentrate on exams and grades to the detriment of learning. (2)

Second Reason: Grading creates a bad spirit and hinders education, even fostering cheating and plagiarizing. (3)

Third Reason: Grading "nullifies" good uses of testing, including the discovery of what a student has and has not learned. (7)

Support #1 (for third reason):   Testing for grades invites students to conceal weaknesses, unlike testing for pedagogic purposes, and doesn't encourage them to realize what they haven't learned. (8)

Support #2 (for third reason):   Grading allows teachers to rely on power rather than on shame and idealism (8), and this goading of students into learning does more harm than good. (9)

Support #3 (for third reason):   They won't retain what they learn in that way. (10)

Fourth Reason: A grading system may automatically flunk out students who were slow to catch on but now may be ready and eager to learn. (11)

Objection #1 (to the thesis):   We must have grades; otherwise how will graduate schools and others know whom to accept or hire? (3)

Replies to objection #1:   1. They'll test their own applicants, as others do. (4) 2. Why should Harvard test for others? (4) 3. Others can better test for themselves. (5) 4. Not many employers look at grades anyway, but just at who granted the diploma. (5)

Objection #2 (to the thesis):   Parents and students would object. (6)

Replies to objection #2:   1. Parental anxiety has done enough damage already. (6) [In all fairness to Goodman, we have to add that he said a great deal more on this topic in other parts of his book.] 2. The primary duty of the university is to force students "to confront the difficult enterprise itself and finally lose themselves in it." So we should overrule student objections. (6)

Once we have summarized an argument we need to come to an evaluation. Although experienced readers tend to evaluate as they go along, the final evaluation cannot be made until we accurately understand the writer's argument. Otherwise we risk being unfair to the writer of the essay and may indeed continue to believe what is false.

Evaluating arguments is an excellent way to sharpen our thinking on the subject we plan to write about. To begin with we draw on our background beliefs and knowledge to help us clarify our ideas on the subject.

USING BACKGROUND BELIEFS AND KNOWLEDGE

Our summary of Goodman's essay indicates that he presented four reasons (premises) in support of his thesis. The background beliefs of the two authors of this textbook support the opinion that the first two reasons have a good deal of truth in them and do lend good support to Goodman's thesis. We have seen many students respond to the grading system as Goodman indicated, in particular by concentrating on what they think will be asked on exams, and we conclude by induction that this is likely to be generally true.

Similarly, our experiences support Goodman's view expressed in his third reason that the important task of testing for placement is harmed by testing for grades. His first item of support for this idea seems right on target. But supports #2 and #3 are a different matter. Our experience indicates that teachers have plenty of power over students if they can toss them out of class for not studying and can award or withhold degrees; whatever evils flow from the power granted to teachers under the grading system very likely would remain under Goodman's system. And we don't believe that shaming students into learning is all that much better than using power to force them into it. Furthermore, while there is some truth to the idea that students retain less when forced to learn for grades, our experience indicates that they retain a good deal of what they learn under the current system, and in any event psychologists are in agreement that we are likely to forget much of what we learn no matter what system is used. (This doesn't mean that it was a waste of time to learn it in the first place! For one thing, it is generally easier to relearn than to learn the first time, and for another, even though we may forget specific points, general impressions may remain.) Nevertheless, we think Goodman's third reason is a modestly good one; students are unlikely to admit ignorance when they will be graded down for doing so.

On the other hand, Goodman's fourth point seems open to strong counterargument. Any system can be used mechanically and thus not work completely well. There is nothing about testing for grades that requires schools to flunk out late bloomers who are now ready and willing to learn.

As for the first objection raised and answered by Goodman, we agree that other institutions can test for themselves and indeed believe they will when others don't do it for them. One support for this belief is the fact that industries unable to rely on college evaluations do in fact test for themselves in one way or another. We deny, however, that employers care only where a degree is from and not what grades have been received, and we think experience is on our side. Goodman is right, of course, that degrees from prestigious institutions count for more in the marketplace than degrees from other schools. But he himself admits that graduate schools do indeed look carefully at grades when deciding which students they will admit.

DEVELOPING COUNTERARGUMENTS

It isn't enough just to point out the reasoning errors in an essay. That the reasons given do not adequately support an essay's thesis does not prove that the thesis is false; it just proves that the thesis has not been justified. To refute the thesis, we need to present counterarguments.

If the relatively small objections to Goodman's thesis just raised were our only objections to his thesis, we might be inclined to accept it, in particular because of his first two reasons. Unfortunately, we see two serious flaws in his position. The first concerns his treatment of the likely objections of parents and students. Parental objections, no matter how irrelevant they may seem, cannot be passed over so lightly, since it is parents who in most cases pay all or part of the bill. Nor can student desires be so easily disregarded. They, along with their parents, decide which schools will be applied to. If graduate schools and employers look to grades as well as degrees, and they will if they can, then students will tend to apply to schools that give grades. The fact that very few American schools have survived giving degrees but no grades is evidence that Goodman is mistaken on this. (There are a few successful institutions that do not give formal grades, for example, the University of California at Santa Cruz, but they do give indications of class performance on transcripts and this amounts to giving grades.) It may well be true that in an ideal world parents and students would attend colleges that did not give grades, but presumably Goodman's proposal was a serious one suggesting that we change the system actually in use, not just a blueprint for an ideal but unattainable society. The point is that, in our opinion, his proposal would not work better than the present system because students would tend to gravitate to more traditional institutions.

The other flaw in Goodman's proposal, less serious than the first, is that tossing lazy students out of classes and awarding degrees on the completion of a program themselves amount to a kind of grading, although only in terms of no credit (given to those thrown out of class), pass, and fail, not A, B, C, D, F. His proposal thus is not really to abolish the grading system but merely to reduce the number of grading categories from five to two (or three, depending on whether no credit is counted as a grade).

But even this neglects a feature of grading that many find desirable, namely, the awarding of honors to exceptional students. Doing so provides the recognition better students deserve and acts as a strong study incentive. (Granting honors constitutes a positive incentive as compared to the negative incentive of shame. Psychologists are unanimous in agreeing that positive incentives work much better than negative ones.) If we add awards for honors to Goodman's proposal, we get three categories instead of the usual four or five, and with this idea we are in sympathy, for one thing because of the difficulty of distinguishing so many levels of performance. But our background beliefs lead us to conclude that parent and student resistance, not to mention that of many faculty members and administrators, make this impractical.

Note that our evaluation of Goodman's essay centered on the first and third criteria of cogent reasoning—believable premises and relevant evidence. This is usually the case when a course of action is being proposed. As mentioned in Chapter 1, in these cases there is always an easy way to make the argument as a whole valid, namely, by adding an implied premise stating that the reasons provided are good enough to warrant taking the suggested course of action and there are no sufficiently weighty reasons against doing so. Our objections to Goodman's proposal grew out of background beliefs that moved us to reject one of his stated premises as well as his implied premise. This is the typical way proposals are argued against.

As must be apparent, by the time we have finished analyzing another person's argument we have come a long way in clarifying our own ideas on the subject. Analyzing several arguments offering different points of view on the same topic would give us an even wider range of material to work with. As we come to understand the complexity of an issue, we often experience a conceptual change in our attitudes. Beliefs we already possess are stretched and deepened by our new knowledge, and we begin to have a much more comprehensive understanding of the issue we plan to address in writing.

EXERCISE 4-1   WRITING ARGUMENTS

Complete one of the following assignments:

1. Write an argument in favor of continuing the standard grading system. As part of your support, refute premises in Goodman's argument that seem unconvincing.

2. Write an argument against the current grading system. Develop your own ideas on the matter but when appropriate cite convincing evidence from Goodman's argument, taking care to document your source in footnotes.

⧖ GORE VIDAL

Drugs

Gore Vidal (1925–   ), well-known novelist and essayist, wrote this short piece in favor of legalizing marijuana and other illegal drugs at a time when the counterculture "hippie" movement was strong in the United States, marijuana use had become widespread here for the first time, and government efforts to suppress use of the drug were increasing.

It is possible to stop most drug addiction in the United States within a very short time. Simply make all drugs available and sell them at cost. Label each drug with a precise description of what effect—good and bad—the drug will   1 have on the taker. This will require heroic honesty. Don't say that marijuana is addictive or dangerous when it is neither, as millions of people know—unlike "speed," which kills most unpleasantly, or heroin, which is addictive and diffi-cult to kick.

For the record, I have tried—once—almost every drug and liked none, disproving the popular Fu Manchu theory that a single whiff of opium will enslave the mind. Nevertheless many drugs are bad for certain people to take   2 and they should be told why in a sensible way.

Along with exhortation and warning, it might be good for our citizens to recall (or learn for the first time) that the United States was the creation of men who believed that each man has the right to do what he wants with his own life   3 as long as he does not interfere with his neighbor's pursuit of happiness (that his neighbor's idea of happiness is persecuting others does confuse matters a bit).

This is a startling notion to the current generation of Americans. They reflect a system of public education which has made the Bill of Rights, literally, unacceptable to a majority of high school graduates (see the annual Purdue   4 reports) who now form the "silent majority"—a phrase which that underesti-mated wit Richard Nixon took from Homer who used it to describe the dead.

Now one can hear the warning rumble begin: if everyone is allowed to   5 take drugs everyone will and the GNP will decrease, the Commies will stop us from making everyone free, and we shall end up a race of zombies, passively murmuring "groovy" to one another. Alarming thought. Yet it seems most unlikely that any reasonably sane person will become a drug addict if he knows in advance what addiction is going to be like.

Is everyone reasonably sane? Some people will always become drug addicts   6 just as some people will always become alcoholics, and it is just too bad. Every man, however, has the power (and should have the legal right) to kill himself if he chooses. But since most men don't, they won't be mainliners either. Never-theless, forbidding people things they like or think they might enjoy only makes them want those things all the more. This psychological insight is, for some mysterious reason, perennially denied our governors.

It is a lucky thing for the American moralist that our country has always 7 existed in a kind of time-vacuum: we have no public memory of anything that happened before last Tuesday. No one in Washington today recalls what happened during the years alcohol was forbidden to the people by a Congress that thought it had a divine mission to stamp out Demon Rum—launching, in the process, the greatest crime wave in the country's history, causing thousands of deaths from bad alcohol, and creating a general (and persisting) contempt among the citizenry for the laws of the United States.

The same thing is happening today. But the government has learned 8 nothing from past attempts at prohibition, not to mention repression.

Last year when the supply of Mexican marijuana was slightly curtailed by 9 the Feds, the pushers got the kids hooked on heroin and deaths increased dramatically, particularly in New York. Whose fault? Evil men like the Mafiosi? Permissive Dr. Spock? Wild-eyed Dr. Leary? No.

The Government of the United States was responsible for those deaths. 10 The bureacratic machine has a vested interest in playing cops and robbers. Both the Bureau of Narcotics and the Mafia want strong laws against the sale and use of drugs because if drugs are sold at cost there would be no money in it for anyone.

If there was no money in it for the Mafia, there would be no friendly 11 playground pushers, and addicts would not commit crimes to pay for the next fix. Finally, if there was no money in it, the Bureau of Narcotics would wither away, something they are not about to do without a struggle.

Will anything sensible be done? Of course not. The American people are 12 as devoted to the idea of sin and its punishment as they are to making money—and fighting drugs is nearly as big a business as pushing them. Since the combination of sin and money is irresistible (particularly to the professional politician), the situation will only grow worse.

EXERCISE 4–2

1. Read the above Gore Vidal essay carefully and summarize it, using the margin note and summary method.

2. Identify its thesis and reasons, evaluate each reason—bringing your background knowledge and beliefs to bear—and refute any reason you consider faulty.

3. Develop your own position on the issue, and write an argument defending your point of view.

Cogent and Fallacious Arguments

As pointed out in Chapter 1, all good arguments—all arguments that are *cogent*—have three things in common: they present believable reasons in support of a thesis or conclusion; the reasons really do support that conclusion—the reasoning is valid or correct; and the conclusion is not contradicted by relevant background beliefs. Arguments that lack one or more of these qualities are said to be *fallacious*.

We also said in Chapter 1 that cogent arguments divide into those that are *deductively valid* and those that are *inductively correct*, or *inductively valid*. The conclusion of a deductively valid argument is already contained in its premises, although usually only implicitly, so that if the premises of such an argument are true, then its conclusion also must be true. On the other hand, the conclusion of an inductively valid argument is not contained in its premises, explicitly or implicitly. In valid induction there is an "inductive leap" from premises to conclusion, which is why it may happen that the premises of a correct induction are all true and yet its conclusion turns out to be false.* Let's now discuss a few details concerning these two kinds of reasoning or argument.

Deductively Valid Arguments

Different arguments may have the same **form,** or **structure.** Here are two deductively valid arguments that share the same form:

1. If the national debt is paid off with inflated money, then borrowers will benefit and lenders be harmed.

2. The national debt *will* be paid off with inflated money.

/∴3. Debtors will benefit and lenders be harmed.

---

*The terms *deduction* and *induction* are also used in other, related, ways in everyday life. In Sherlock Holmes stories, for instance, what are called *deductions* are generally a combination of deductions (in our sense) and inductions (also in our sense).

1. If Shakespeare wrote great plays, everybody should read them.
2. Shakespeare did write great plays.
/∴3. Everybody should read them.

And here is the form or structure that they share:

1. If [some proposition] then [a second proposition].
2. [The first proposition.]
/∴3. [The second proposition.]

Or, using A and B to stand for the two propositions:

1. If A, then B.
2. A.
/∴3. B.

This form traditionally has been called *modus ponens*.

Below are several other commonly used and intuitively valid argument forms, accompanied by a traditional name and illustrated by an example:

MODUS TOLLENS

FORM:	EXAMPLE:
1. If A, then B.	1. If he ran for office successfully, then he wasn't fit to hold it.*
2. Not B.	2. But he was fit to hold that office. (That is, it's false that he was unfit.)
/∴3. Not A.	/∴3. He didn't run successfully.

DISJUNCTIVE SYLLOGISM

FORM:	EXAMPLE:
1. A or B.	1. Either Mondale won in 1984 or Reagan did.
2. Not A.	2. Mondale sure didn't win.
/∴3. B.	/∴3. Reagan did.

*A takeoff on Adlai Stevenson's famous remark that the hardest thing to do is win an election without proving oneself unfit to hold the office won.

HYPOTHETICAL SYLLOGISM

FORM:	EXAMPLE:
/∴1. If A, then B.	1. If the Reds win the playoffs, they'll win the pennant.
2. If B, then C.	2. If they win the pennant, they'll play in the World Series.
/∴3. If A, then C.	/∴3. If the Reds win the playoffs, they'll play in the World Series.

Now here are some deductively valid argument forms of a slightly different nature.* All but the first of these are called **syllogisms.****

FORM:	EXAMPLE:
1. No Fs are Gs.	1. No saints are successful in politics.
/∴2. It's false that some Fs are Gs.	/∴2. It's false that some saints are successful in politics.

FORM:	EXAMPLE:
1. All Fs are Gs.	1. All TV evangelists have high moral standards.
2. All Gs are Hs.	2. All who have high moral standards live up to those standards.
/∴3. All Fs are Hs.	/∴3. All TV evangelists live up to high moral standards.

FORM:	EXAMPLE:
1. All Fs are Gs.	1. Elected officials always tell the truth. (All elected officials are truth tellers.)
2. This is an F.	2. Ted Kennedy is an elected official.
/∴3. This is a G.	/∴3. Ted Kennedy always tells the truth.

---

*See Howard Kahane's *Logic and Philosophy*, 5th ed. (Belmont, Calif.: Wadsworth, 1986) for more on this difference.
**In spite of their names, disjunctive syllogism and hypothetical syllogism are not syllogisms.

FORM:	EXAMPLE:
1. All Fs are Gs.	1. All males are chauvinist pigs.
2. No Gs are Hs.	2. No chauvinist pigs are likeable.
/∴3. No Fs are Hs.	/∴3. No males are likeable.

FORM:	EXAMPLE:
1. No Fs are Gs.	1. No Russians can be trusted.
2. Some Hs are Fs.	2. Some newborn babies are Russians.
/∴3. Some Hs are not Gs.	/∴3. There must be some newborn babies that can't be trusted.

Inductively Valid Arguments

As stated in Chapter 1, the key idea in valid induction is that of *learning from experience* (unlike valid deductions whose mark is learning from what we already know). A valid induction projects observed regularities noticed in experience onto specified other possible experiences. Let's now look at some of the species of induction commonly encountered in everyday life.

INDUCTION BY ENUMERATION

When reasoning according to the form called **induction by enumeration,** we infer from the fact that all items of a certain kind in our sample have a certain property to the conclusion that all things of that kind have that property. (This kind of induction is much beloved by philosophers.) We reason this way when we conclude from the premise that all of the fifteen secondary school social studies (civics) texts we examined play down the gap between American ideals and actual everyday practice to the conclusion that probably all social studies texts do the same thing (an actual case in which the conclusion turned out to be true).

REASONING BY ANALOGY

Induction by analogy is very much like induction by enumeration. The difference is that in induction by enumeration we project an observed regularity onto the whole "population" from which the sample was drawn, whereas in induction by analogy, we typically project the observed regularity onto just one additional item. For instance, having heard several pieces of music by Mozart, all of which were first rate, we may conclude by analogy that the next piece we hear by him will be first rate (definitely an actual case). Or we may conclude by analogy that American veterans of the fighting in Vietnam should be given the same sorts of benefits as those received by veterans of officially declared wars since the Vietnam encounter was like a war in virtually every respect except that it was never officially declared by Congress.

Inductions by analogy are on the whole more probable than corresponding inductions by enumeration because they make weaker claims. Consider the following pair of inductively valid arguments:

1. So far, everything I've ever listened to by Mozart has been first rate. I conclude that the next work I hear by Mozart will be first rate.

2. So far, everything I've ever listened to by Mozart has been first rate. I conclude that everything I'll ever hear written by Mozart will be first rate.

Clearly, if the conclusion of argument 2 turns out to be true, then the conclusion of 1 will also have to be true.* However, the conclusion of 1 might turn out to be true when the conclusion of 2 is false. This would be the case, for instance, if Mozart wrote a few klinkers in addition to all those gems. The point is that stronger claims, by virtue of their greater strength, run a greater risk of being false than do weaker ones and so are less probable than corresponding weaker claims.

STATISTICAL INDUCTION

When drawing a sample from a population, we often find that not all As we examine have some common property B, so that we cannot draw a valid induction by enumeration connecting As to Bs. But having found that a certain percentage of As in our sample have the property B, we can conclude that the same percentage of As in the population as a whole have the property B. An induction of this kind is said to be **statistical induction.** An example is the conclusion that a large majority of people like chocolate based on the fact that in our sample a large majority liked that addicting confection.

Obviously, some inductions are better than others, in particular those based on better samples. Thus, other things being equal, the greater the *sample size,* and the more *representative* it is of the population from which it was drawn, the more probable is the resulting induction. That is the point of the advice about not sampling just the top of a barrel full of apples to determine if any are rotten.

---

*This is the case because the argument: "Everything I'll ever hear written by Mozart will be first rate" [the conclusion of the stronger argument 2]; "therefore the next Mozart work I hear will be first rate" [the conclusion of the weaker argument 1] is deductively valid.

HIGHER LEVEL INDUCTION

Induction of a broader, more general, nature can be used to evaluate (support or correct) lower level inductions. Using a low-level induction all by itself is risky. Lots of people concluded that John Kennedy would not win the 1960 presidential election because he was Catholic and all presidents up to that time had been Protestant. These people based their conclusion on a low-level induction when higher level theories (based on complicated higher level inductions) were available about what motivates people to vote for one candidate rather than another and about the changes that were occurring in the United States concerning racial, religious, and ethnic tolerance and acceptance. Of course, in most cases in everyday life, we can't evaluate lower level inductions by means of higher unless we already have the results of relevant higher level inductions in our stock of background beliefs.

CAUSAL CONNECTIONS

When we reason inductively, we are often looking for explanations, or **causes.** Early investigators of the connection between cigarette smoking and lung cancer, emphysema, strokes, and heart disease wanted to determine by means of statistical inductions whether smoking **causes** these death-dealing diseases. They found that smokers get these diseases much more often than nonsmokers do, and heavy smokers more than light. Having discovered this statistical connection between smoking cigarettes and contracting these diseases, and finding no higher level evidence to the contrary, they concluded that cigarette smoking does indeed cause these life-threatening illnesses. (More precisely, they concluded that smoking was part of the cause, since many smokers never come down with any of these diseases.)

It is important to remember, however, that merely finding a statistical connection is not sufficient to claim a causal connection, even if the connection is 100%, and even if we believe the connection will continue indefinitely. It all depends on what other inductively arrived at beliefs we have that are relevant.

To take a famous example, before Newton most scientists believed that the earth would circle the sun forever, revolving on its axis every twenty-four hours. They thus believed in a constant connection, a one-to-one correlation, between occurrences of night and of day. That is, they believed that every time one occurred it would be followed by the other. But they did not believe night *causes* day, nor day night. For they know that *if* the earth stopped rotating on its axis (of course, they believed this would never happen), then night would not follow day, nor day night. Thus, for them, night could not be the cause of day, nor day the cause of night.

By way of contrast, we assume that the constant conjunction between, say, connecting a copper wire to an electric current and having the current flow through the wire *is* a causal connection because (unlike the day/night case) we have no higher level theories that show how this constant connection might be broken.

EXERCISE 5–1

Answer each of the following, making sure to explain and defend your answers, in particular by providing examples (original if possible).

1. Can an inductively valid argument that has all true premises have a false conclusion?

2. How about a deductively valid argument?

3. Carefully explain the difference between induction by enumeration and induction by analogy.

4. Why say that, all other things being equal, the conclusion of an induction by analogy is more probable than an analogous conclusion drawn by means of induction by enumeration?

5. What is the difference between an induction by enumeration and a higher level induction?

6. Can a valid induction have all true premises and yet not be cogent?

7. How about a valid deduction?

8. What does it mean to increase the size and representativeness of a sample on which an inductive inference is based? Is that good or bad? Why?

9. Imagine that you are working on cancer research way back before there was any proof that tobacco smoking causes lung cancer and you find that the results of a ten-year study show that those in the survey who smoked at least a pack a day suffer from a far higher incidence of lung cancer than those who did not smoke. Carefully explain why it would have been wrong to conclude that smoking cigarettes causes lung cancer.

10. Now suppose you discover that every time the bells in an old London church strike, the bells in an equally old church in Manchester strike also, exactly a tenth of a second later. Consulting records, you find that this correlation between the ringing of one set of bells and the other has been going on since the two churches were constructed, at least so far as anyone can tell. Explain why, in this case, it would be wrong to conclude that striking the bells in London causes the bells to strike in Manchester.

◈ THOMAS H. HUXLEY

The Method of Scientific Investigation*

Thomas H. Huxley (1825–1895), British scientist, writer, and lecturer, is per-
haps best remembered as an early, ardent, and quite effective supporter of the
theories of Charles Darwin concerning evolution and natural selection. In this
essay, he writes on a different sort of subject than evolution, namely the methods
of reasoning used by scientists and the rest of us in our everyday lives.

The method of scientific investigation is nothing but the expression of the   1
necessary mode of working of the human mind. It is simply the mode at which
all phenomena are reasoned about, rendered precise and exact. There is no
more difference, but there is just the same kind of difference, between the
mental operations of a man of science and those of an ordinary person, as there
is between the operations and methods of a baker or of a butcher weighing out
his goods in common scales, and the operations of a chemist in performing a
difficult and complex analysis by means of his balance and finely-graduated
weights. It is not that the action of the scales in the one case, and the balance
in the other, differ in the principles of their construction or manner of working;
but the beam of one is set on an infinitely finer axis than the other, and of
course turns by the addition of a much smaller weight.

You will understand this better, perhaps, if I give you some familiar ex-   2
ample. You have all heard it repeated, I dare say, that men of science work by
means of induction and deduction, and that by the help of these operations,
they, in a sort of sense, wring from Nature certain other things, which are called
natural laws, and causes, and that out of these, by some cunning skill of their
own, they build up hypotheses and theories. And it is imagined by many, that
the operations of the common mind can be by no means compared with these
processes, and that they have to be acquired by a sort of special apprenticeship
to the craft. To hear all these large words, you would think that the mind of a
man of science must be constituted differently from that of his fellow men; but
if you will not be frightened by terms, you will discover that you are quite
wrong, and that all these terrible apparatus are being used by yourselves every
day and every hour of your lives.

There is a well-known incident in one of Molière's plays, where the author   3
makes the hero express unbounded delight on being told that he had been
talking prose during the whole of his life. In the same way, I trust, that you will
take comfort, and be delighted with yourselves, on the discovery that you have
been acting on the principles of inductive and deductive philosophy during the

*Taken from the third of the 1862 lectures "On Our Knowledge of the Causes of the Phenom-
ena of Organic Nature."

same period. Probably there is not one here who has not in the course of the day had occasion to set in motion a complex train of reasoning, of the very same kind, though differing of course in degree, as that which a scientific man goes through in tracing the causes of natural phenomena.

A very trivial circumstance will serve to exemplify this. Suppose you go 4 into a fruiterer's shop, wanting an apple,—you take up one, and, on biting it, you find it is sour; you look at it, and see that it is hard and green. You take up another one, and that too is hard, green, and sour. The shopman offers you a third; but, before biting it, you examine it, and find that it is hard and green, and you immediately say that you will not have it, as it must be sour, like those that you have already tried.

Nothing can be more simple than that, you think; but if you will take the 5 trouble to analyse and trace out into its logical elements what has been done by the mind, you will be greatly surprised. In the first place, you have performed the operation of induction. You found that, in two experiences, hardness and greenness in apples went together with sourness. It was so in the first case, and it was confirmed by the second. True, it is a very small basis, but still it is enough to make an induction from; you generalise the facts, and you expect to find sourness in apples where you get hardness and greenness. You found upon that a general law, that all hard and green apples are sour; and that, so far as it goes, is a perfect induction. Well, having got your natural law in this way, when you are offered another apple which you find is hard and green, you say, "All hard and green apples are sour; this apple is hard and green, therefore this apple is sour." That train of reasoning is what logicians call a syllogism, and has all its various parts and terms,—its major premiss, its minor premiss, and its conclusion. And, by the help of further reasoning, which, if drawn out, would have to be exhibited in two or three other syllogisms, you arrive at your final determination, "I will not have that apple." So that, you see, you have, in the first place, established a law by induction, and upon that you have founded a deduction, and reasoned out the special conclusion of the particular case. Well now, suppose, having got your law, that at some time afterwards, you are discussing the qualities of apples with a friend: you will say to him, "It is a very curious thing,—but I find that all hard and green apples are sour!" Your friend says to you, "But how do you know that?" You at once reply, "Oh, because I have tried them over and over again, and have always found them to be so." Well, if we were talking science instead of common sense, we should call that an experimental verification. And, if still opposed, you go further, and say, "I have heard from the people in Somersetshire and Devonshire, where a large number of apples are grown, that they have observed the same thing. It is also found to be the case in Normandy, and in North America. In short, I find it to be the universal experience of mankind wherever attention has been directed to the subject." Whereupon, your friend, unless he is a very unreasonable man, agrees with you, and is convinced that you are quite right in the conclusion you have drawn. He believes, although perhaps he does not know he believes it, that the more extensive verifications are,—that the more frequently experiments have been made, and results of the same kind arrived at,—that the more varied the conditions under which the same results are attained, the more certain is the ultimate conclusion, and he disputes the question no further. He sees that the experiment has been tried under all sorts of conditions, as to time, place, and people, with the same result; and he says with you, therefore, that the law you have laid down must be a good one, and he must believe it.

In science we do the same thing;—the philosopher exercises precisely the 6
same faculties, though in a much more delicate manner. In scientific inquiry it becomes a matter of duty to expose a supposed law to every possible kind of verification, and to take care, moreover, that this is done intentionally, and not left to a mere accident, as in the case of the apples. And in science, as in common life, our confidence in a law is in exact proportion to the absence of variation in the result of our experimental verifications. For instance, if you let go your grasp of an article you may have in your hand, it will immediately fall to the ground. That is a very common verification of one of the best established laws of nature—that of gravitation. The method by which men of science establish the existence of that law is exactly the same as that by which we have established the trivial proposition about the sourness of hard and green apples. But we believe it in such an extensive, thorough, and unhesitating manner because the universal experience of mankind verifies it, and we can verify it ourselves at any time; and that is the strongest possible foundation on which any natural law can rest.

So much, then, by way of proof that the method of establishing laws in 7
science is exactly the same as that pursued in common life. Let us now turn to another matter (though really it is but another phase of the same question), and that is, the method by which, from the relations of certain phenomena, we prove that some stand in the position of causes towards the others.

I want to put the case clearly before you, and I will therefore show you 8
what I mean by another familiar example. I will suppose that one of you, on coming down in the morning to the parlour of your house, finds that a teapot and some spoons which had been left in the room on the previous evening are gone,—the window is open, and you observe the mark of a dirty hand on the window-frame, and perhaps, in addition to that, you notice the impress of a hob-nailed shoe on the gravel outside. All these phenomena have struck your attention instantly, and before two seconds have passed you say, "Oh somebody has broken open the window, entered the room, and run off with the spoons and the tea-pot!" That speech is out of your mouth in a moment. And you will probably add, "I know there has; I am quite sure of it!" You mean to say exactly what you know; but in reality you are giving expression to what is, in all essential particulars, an hypothesis. You do not *know* it at all; it is nothing but an hypothesis rapidly framed in your own mind. And it is an hypothesis founded on a long train of inductions and deductions.

What are those inductions and deductions, and how have you got at this 9
hypothesis? You have observed, in the first place, that the window is open; but by a train of reasoning involving many inductions and deductions, you have probably arrived long before at the general law—and a very good one it is—that

windows do not open of themselves; and you therefore conclude that something has opened the window. A second general law that you have arrived at in the same way is, that tea-pots and spoons do not go out of a window spontaneously, and you are satisfied that, as they are not now where you left them, they have been removed. In the third place, you look at the marks on the window-sill, and the shoe-marks outside, and you say that in all previous experience the former kind of mark has never been produced by anything else but the hand of a human being; and the same experience shows that no other animal but man at present wears shoes with hob-nails in them such as would produce the marks in the gravel. I do not know, even if we could discover any of those "missing links" that are talked about, that they would help us to any other conclusion! At any rate the law which states our present experience is strong enough for my present purpose. You next reach the conclusion, that as these kinds of marks have not been left by any other animals than men, or are liable to be formed in any other way than by a man's hand and shoe, the marks in question have been formed by a man in that way. You have, further, a general law, founded on observation and experience, and that, too, is, I am sorry to say, a very universal and unimpeachable one,—that some men are thieves; and you assume at once from all these premises—and that is what constitutes your hypothesis—that the man who made the marks outside and on the window-sill, opened the window, got into the room, and stole your tea-pot and spoons. You have now arrived at a *vera causa;*—you have assumed a cause which, it is plain, is competent to produce all the phenomena you have observed. You can explain all these phenomena only by the hypothesis of a thief. But that is a hypothetical conclusion, of the justice of which you have no absolute proof at all; it is only rendered highly probable by a series of inductive and deductive reasonings.

I suppose your first action, assuming that you are a man of ordinary 10 common sense, and that you have established this hypothesis to your own satisfaction, will very likely be to go off for the police, and set them on the track of the burglar, with the view to the recovery of your property. But just as you are starting with this object, some person comes in, and on learning what you are about, says, "My good friend, you are going on a great deal too fast. How do you know that the man who really made the marks took the spoons? It might have been a monkey that took them, and the man may have merely looked in afterwards." You would probably reply, "Well, that is all very well, but you see it is contrary to all experience of the way teapots and spoons are abstracted; so that, at any rate, your hypothesis is less probable than mine." While you are talking the thing over in this way, another friend arrives, one of that good kind of people that I was talking of a little while ago. And he might say, "Oh, my dear sir, you are certainly going on a great deal too fast. You are most presumptuous. You admit that all these occurrences took place when you were fast asleep, at a time when you could not possibly have know anything about what was taking place. How do you know that the laws of Nature are not suspended during the night? It may be that there has been some kind of supernatural interference in this case." In point of fact, he declares that your hypothesis is one of which you cannot at all demonstrate the truth, and that you are by no means sure that the laws of Nature are the same when you are asleep as when you are awake.

Well, now, you cannot at the moment answer that kind of reasoning. You 11 feel that your worthy friend has you somewhat at a disadvantage. You will feel perfectly convinced in your own mind, however, that you are quite right, and you say to him, "My good friend, I can only be guided by the natural probabilities of the case, and if you will be kind enough to stand aside and permit me to pass, I will go and fetch the police." Well, we will suppose that your journey is successful, and that by good luck you meet with a policeman; that eventually the burglar is found with your property on his person, and the marks correspond to his hand and to his boots. Probably any jury would consider those facts a very good experimental verification of your hypothesis, touching the cause of the abnormal phenomena observed in your parlour, and would act accordingly.

Now, in this suppositious case, I have taken phenomena of a very common 12 kind, in order that you might see what are the different steps in an ordinary process of reasoning, if you will only take the trouble to analyse it carefully. All the operations I have described, you will see, are involved in the mind of any man of sense in leading him to a conclusion as to the course he should take in order to make good a robbery and punish the offender. I say that you are led, in that case, to your conclusion by exactly the same train of reasoning as that which a man of science pursues when he is endeavouring to discover the origin and laws of the most occult phenomena. The process is, and always must be, the same; and precisely the same mode of reasoning was employed by Newton and Laplace in their endeavours to discover and define the causes of the movements of the heavenly bodies, as you, with your own common sense, would employ to detect a burglar. The only difference is, that the nature of the inquiry being more abstruse, every step has to be most carefully watched, so that there may not be a single crack or flaw in your hypothesis. A flaw or crack in many of the hypotheses of daily life may be of little or no moment as affecting the general correctness of the conclusions at which we may arrive; but, in a scientific inquiry, a fallacy, great or small, is always of importance, and is sure to be in the long run constantly productive of mischievous, if not fatal results.

Do not allow yourselves to be misled by the common notion that an 13 hypothesis is untrustworthy simply because it is a hypothesis. It is often urged, in respect to some scientific conclusion, that, after all, it is only an hypothesis. But what more have we to guide us in nine-tenths of the most important affairs of daily life than hypotheses, and often very ill-based ones? So that in science, where the evidence of an hypothesis is subjected to the most rigid examination, we may rightly pursue the same course. You may have hypotheses and hypotheses. A man may say, if he likes, that the moon is made of green cheese: that is an hypothesis. But another man, who has devoted a great deal of time and attention to the subject, and availed himself of the most powerful telescopes and the results of the observations of others, declares that in his opinion it is probably composed of materials very similar to those of which our own earth is made up: and that is also only an hypothesis. But I need not tell you that there is an enormous difference in the value of the two hypotheses. That one which is based on sound scientific knowledge is sure to have a corresponding value; and that which is a mere hasty random guess is likely to have but little value. Every great step in our progress in discovering causes has been made in exactly the same way as that which I have detailed to you. A person observing the occurrence of certain facts and phenomena asks, naturally enough, what process, what kind of operation known to occur in Nature applied to the particular case, will unravel and explain the mystery? Hence you have the scientific hypothesis; and its value will be proportionate to the care and completeness with which its basis had been tested and verified. It is in these matters as in the commonest affairs of practical life: the guess of the fool will be folly, while the guess of the wise man will contain wisdom. In all cases, you see that the value of the result depends on the patience and faithfulness with which the investigator applies to his hypothesis every possible kind of verification.

Fallacious Arguments

Becoming familiar with the more frequently encountered fallacies is of use not just when evaluating the arguments of others but also when writing our own argumentative essays. We want to avoid being taken in by the fallacious arguments of others and equally avoid this kind of shoddy reasoning in our own writings. Restraining ourselves to cogent reasoning is more effective in the long run, not to mention having a greater air of honesty about it. Indeed, that we need to resort to fallacious reasoning to "prove" a point is a sign that we haven't thought through our position with sufficient care, or perhaps even are arguing the wrong side of the issue.

As stated in Chapter 1, arguments that do not satisfy all three of the requirements of cogent reasoning are said to be **fallacious**. This means that we reason fallaciously whenever we (1) reason from questionable premises, (2) reason invalidly, or (3) fail to use relevant background information. The basic fallacy categories from the point of view of logic are thus *questionable premise*, *suppressed* or *neglected evidence*, and *invalid reasoning*, corresponding to the three fundamental ways just mentioned in which reasoning may go wrong.

But experience has shown that fallacy categories based primarily on other factors tend to be more useful in everyday life, and it is these that have received the lion's share of attention in the literature. Unfortunately, the standard fallacy categories crosscut or overlap each other, tend to be vague and ambiguous, and don't even cover the entire field (there is no guarantee that taken all together they exhaust every possibility of fallacious reasoning). Yet experience has shown that they are of greater practical use than the three basic categories just mentioned.

Nevertheless, in the last analysis, to prove that an argument is fallacious, it won't do simply to place it in one of these standard fallacy categories or label it with a standard name. Take the very important fallacy called *appeal to authority* (discussed below). The logical structure of an argument based on appeal to an authority is that the authority says such and such (premise), the authority can be believed (premise), and so such and such is the case (conclusion). An appeal to an authority is fallacious only when there is not sufficient reason to believe either the first or the second premise of this argument structure. This means that fallacious appeals to authority are a species of the broader logical category *questionable premise*. And it also means that when we judge a particular argument to make a *fallacious* appeal to an authority, we need to specify what is wrong with this particular appeal this particular time, *why* we should not believe this authority *this time*. Appealing to the authority, say, of highly regarded, licensed physicians on medical questions is not fallacious because we have reason to believe that they know a good deal about the topic, will not tell us they know when they don't, and in general can be expected to furnish honest answers. Appealing to the authority of a *National Enquirer* "famed psychic," on the other hand, is fallacious because there is very good reason to believe that the *Enquirer's* alleged psychics don't have any knowledge not available to the rest of us, and, in particular, that the overwhelming number of their predictions have not come true.

Bearing all this in mind, here is a list of some of the more frequently encountered fallacies, with examples:

• The fallacy of **ad hominem argument** (*argumentum ad hominem*) consists in irrelevantly attacking opponents rather than their arguments. *Example:* Senator Jennings Randolph responded to women who argued for passage of the Equal Rights Amendment (ERA) to the Constitution by calling them a "small band of bra-less bubbleheads."

• The fallacy **appeal to authority** applies chiefly to *improper* appeals to an authority. Appeals are improper, among other cases, when there is good reason to doubt that the authorities have the information needed, or there is evidence of special interests or the like that might prejudice authoritative wisdom, or when the subject itself is controversial and competent authorities may differ on the matter. *Examples:* Taking the word of lawyers who say that no-fault insurance will raise rates and lower the quality of insurance (lawyers have an interest in insurance litigation); believing star quarterback Joe Montana when he touts Nissan autos in a TV commercial (football is his field of expertise, not autos, and he is paid handsomely for his endorsements); accepting the claim of President Reagan—because he is president of the United States—that his "Star Wars" program has a good chance of success in the near future (The matter was, and is, controversial in the extreme and a large majority of experts have always been on the other side of the issue.)

• The mistake in the case of the fallacy of **affirming the consequent** consists in reasoning from statements of the form "If A, then B" and "B" to the analogous conclusion "A." *Example:* "If it rained last night (A), then the streets were wet this morning (B). The streets were wet this morning (B). So it must have rained last night (A)." This argument overlooks other possibilities— it may have snowed and the snow melted.

The point is that an argument having this form is not deductively valid since its conclusion might be false even if both of its premises are true.

• The fallacy of **appeal to ignorance** (*argumentum ad ignorantiam*) consists in arguing from the absence of proof that one's position is false to the contrary conclusion that it therefore must be correct. *Example:* "Until someone has proved that ESP is impossible, we are entitled to believe it is true."

• The fallacy of **begging the question** (*petitio principii*) is committed when someone uses as a premise some form of the very thesis at issue. *Example:* Arguing that socialism is replacing capitalism because the private ownership of the means of production has become obsolete.

• Although not strictly speaking a fallacy, the linguistic device generally referred to as the fallacy of the **complex question** consists in asking a question that presupposes an incriminating answer to some other question that in fact is not asked. *Classic example:* "When did you stop beating your wife?" This implies that you once did beat your wife without explicitly saying so, making it hard to deny.

• The fallacy of **composition** (*salesman's fallacy*) is committed when someone assumes that a whole must have some particular property because all of its parts have it. *Example:* Since each monthly payment is small, the whole price of, say, a new car is small.

• The fallacy of **denying the antecedent** is committed by those who reason from statements of the form "If A, then B" and "Not-A" to a conclusion having the analogous form "Not-B." *Example:* "If today is Monday, then liquor stores are open. But today isn't Monday, so liquor stores are not open. Liquor stores are open on other days in addition to Monday."

• The fallacy of **division** consists in assuming that all of the parts of some item have a certain property since the whole has that property. *Example:* Arguing that since a Mercedes Benz car is expensive, each part of the car is expensive.

• The fallacy of **double standard** is committed when we judge the arguments or conduct of some according to higher standards than we apply in the case of others. *Example:* Holding Israel to a higher standard of conduct in the Middle East than the Palestinians, PLO, Lebanese, or Syrians.

• A term or expression is used *ambiguously* or *equivocally* in an argument when it is used in one sense in one place and in another sense in another. When we fail to notice a shift in meaning of this kind and are led to accept a conclusion that we otherwise would have denied, then we are victims of the fallacy of **equivocation.** *Example:* The sugar advertisement that argued for increased consumption of sugar on the grounds that "Sugar is an essential component of the body . . . a key material in all sorts of metabolic processes."

The sugar that is essential to the body is glucose (blood sugar), while the sugar being touted in the ad was refined table sugar.

• A **false charge of fallacy** consists in accusing someone of fallacy without having good reason to do so. *Example:* Bertrand Russell was charged with *inconsistency* because soon after World War II he argued that we should nuke the Russians if they didn't behave but later argued that we had to get along with the Russians no matter what. Since he explained his mind change as due to the fact that the Soviets now also had the bomb, he was *not* guilty of inconsistency. *Related fallacy: Quibbling.*

• The fallacy of **false dilemma** is committed by arguing from the premise that there are just two plausible solutions to a problem or issue when, in fact, there is at least one other. *Example:* Arguing that differences in behavior between the sexes are due either to heredity or to environment, neglecting the likely possibility that both of these factors play a role.

• The foolish belief that the less frequently a gambling outcome has occurred in the recent past, the more likely it is to occur now is called the **gambler's fallacy** (although in truth it should be mentioned that there are one or two other strong candidates for that honorific title). *Example:* Betting on seven at a dice table in Atlantic City because seven hasn't shown up for, say, seven tosses in a row at that table.

• Those who are convinced by relevant but insufficient evidence in support of a theory are guilty of the fallacy called **hasty conclusion.** *Example:* Sherlock Holmes concluding from meager clues on first meeting Dr. Watson that he was an English army doctor just back from Afghanistan. (Watson turns out to fit that description exactly, which just proves that in fiction you don't need to be smart, or even lucky, just in control of the pen!) *Variation: Small sample.*

• The fallacy of **inconsistency** consists in arguing from contradictory premises or to a contradictory conclusion. In everyday life this fallacy is often broadened to cover cases where there is no contradiction within the argument itself but there is a contradiction when commonly known and relevant facts are added. *Example:* The politician who promises all sorts of new and expensive programs in addition to the ones we already have, and then also promises to balance the budget without raising taxes. Similarly, we can extend the fallacy to cover contradictions between words and actions—between what a person says and what that person does. *Example:* Someone sitting at a bar guzzling booze and drinking to the idea of a drug-free society.

• The traditional name given to the fallacy now sometimes called **invalid reasoning** is *non sequitur* (literally "it does not follow")—reasoning in a way that is both deductively and inductively invalid, that is, in a way so that the reasons of our argument do not lend adequate, or even any, support to its conclusion. *Example:* Fallacies of the species *affirming the consequent* and *denying the antecedent.*

• A much overlooked fallacy is that of **lack of proportion**—failing to put things in proper perspective or proportion. *Example:* The great emphasis placed on the drug problem in the United States by the Reagan administration compared to its relative silence on the vastly more serious AIDS epidemic. *Variation:* *Tokenism:* Accepting a token gesture as though it were the genuine article.

• The device of **persuasive definition** (often discussed with fallacies, whether or not it is one) consists in defining oneself into victory. *Example:* The statement "Socialism is theft by the poor and the lazy from the rich and the industrious" is often used to argue against socialism.

• In the case of **poisoning the well** (often discussed with fallacies), the trick is to use emotively charged negative language to trash an argument before attempting to truly argue against it. *Example:* "What can we say about such a mean-spirited, selfish, inhuman system as capitalism?"

• **Provincialism** results from overstressing the importance of one's own society to the point of overlooking what is going on elsewhere that is relevant to what is at issue, or (worse) deciding what is true or false on the basis of loyalty. *Examples:* Calling the American baseball championships the *World Series* even though no Cuban, Japanese, or other teams are allowed to take part; claiming that American soldiers in Vietnam did not commit the atrocities that the evidence clearly proved they did, on the grounds that "Our boys couldn't do such things."

• The fallacy **questionable analogy**, or *faulty comparison*, consists in "comparing apples with oranges," that is, in reasoning by analogy when there is not a sufficient or relevant similarity between the items compared. *Humorous (and questionable?) example:* "If we have to teach the Bible account of creation along with evolution theory, we ought to have to teach the stork theory of creation along with the biological theory."

• The fallacy **questionable cause** (traditional name *post hoc, ergo propter hoc*) is committed when someone argues that something is the cause of something else without sufficient reason, usually on the basis that the first thing preceded the second in time (*post hoc, ergo propter hoc* means "after this, therefore because of this"). *Famous and no doubt apocryphal example:* Arguing that an observed correlation between fluctuations in stock prices and Olympic elk populations indicate a causal connection.

• The fallacy **questionable premise** consists in arguing from premises that should not be accepted without further justification. *Example:* Jimmy Carter: "You can trust me because I will never lie to you."

• Arguing that if a certain course of action is taken, it will start a slide all the way down to some horror lurking at the bottom of a slippery slope is often called, not surprisingly, the fallacy of **slippery slope**. In another variation, the fallacy is committed when someone argues that whatever would justify taking the first step along a course of action would justify every other one, but since the last step isn't justified the first one isn't either. *Example:*   Arguing that an increase in Medicare will lead to socialized medicine and eventually therefore to a completely socialistic system. *Variation:*   The *domino theory,* popular during the Vietnam War, when it was argued that if we lost in Vietnam then many other countries would fall like dominoes to the communists. This has recently been revived and applied to Central America.

• Arguing from relevant but insufficient evidence makes one guilty of the fallacy of **small sample**. *Example:*   Predicting the outcome of a senatorial campaign on the basis of a poll of fifty-six voters.

• The fallacy **straw man** is committed when someone attacks a weakened version of an opponent's position rather than the genuine article, or attacks a weaker opponent while ignoring a stronger one. *Example:*   Richard Nixon attacked his opponents, for example, Helen Gahagan Douglas, by charging them with being pinko, or "soft on communism," when they were liberals. *Variation:*   *Exaggeration.* But note that exaggeration is not fallacious when it is used for emphasis or in other ways in which it is not to be taken literally. *Example of a nonfallacious use:*   "Jose Canseco and Mark McGwire are going to hit a million home runs before they're through playing baseball."

• The fallacy of **suppressed evidence** consists in the failure to apply known and relevant information to an argument. *Example:*   Ex-governor of Texas John Connally in answering a question before a congressional committee stated that he had no significant personal interest in the oil and gas industry and cited the fact that he had made only a total of $7,240 profit from that industry, while neglecting to mention that he had received $750,000 for legal services to the foundation set up by Texas oil millionaire Sid Richardson. (Political payoffs are often disguised as other sorts of payments.) Connally's statement is said to be an "error of omission," as compared to an "error of commission," which is an outright lie.

• The fallacy **two wrongs make a right** is committed when we try to justify an apparently wrong action by charging our accusers with a similar wrong. *Example:*   South Africans who answer American charges that their country is a racist society by pointing to the American treatment of blacks. Our sins don't excuse theirs. *Related fallacies:*   *Many wrongs make a right, common practice, traditional wisdom, popularity.*

• One of the more easily fallen for statistical fallacies is that of the **unrepresentative sample** *(biased sample),* committed when we reason from a sample to the population from which it was drawn when there is doubt that the sample is representative of the population as a whole. *Classic examples:*   Sampling only the top apples from a barrel full of apples; the *Literary Digest* poll in 1936 which predicted Alf Landon would defeat Franklin Roosevelt. (The poll was based on a sample drawn from auto registration and telephone subscriber lists at a time when most Americans could not afford to own a car or a telephone.)

EXERCISE 5–2

Here are several very short passages. In each case, determine whether the reasoning is cogent or fallacious, and if fallacious, explain what the error consists in and provide a standard fallacy label if you know one that is appropriate.

EXAMPLE

Passage: In March 1986, a Reagan administration spokesperson discussing the alleged dangers of "a communist base" in Nicaragua told members of Congress that they had to either "stand with Ronald Reagan and the resistance (the Contras) or with Daniel Ortega and the Communists."

Evaluation: The implication of this passage is that we shouldn't stand with Ortega and the Communists, so we should stand with Ronald Reagan. This reasoning is fallacious because one of its premises is questionable, namely, that we either have to support the Contras or Ortega. There are many other possibilities, including just ignoring the whole mess.

1. A woman whose husband dropped evidence here and there indicating he was having an affair (which he denied) asked "Dear Abby": "Is this man a saint or a sinner?" Abby's reply was, "If your suspicions are correct, he's a sinner."

2. Newspaper article entitled "Reagan's Remedy for His 'Woman Problem' ". The Reagan administration has launched a campaign to close the political "gender gap" by attempting to improve its negative image to women. In recent days the administration has appointed two women to Cabinet positions, filed a brief supporting women's pension benefits and is hinting at taking further initiatives.

     At the same time, there is no indication that President Reagan plans to change his opposition to many fundamental rights that would strengthen women—from abortion to equal pay.

3. *Village Voice* article (October 18, 1976) by Howard Smith and Brian Van der Horst: Sri Swami Swanandashram, Hindu holy man from India, after criticizing other Hindu swamis [for instance, Maharishi Mahesh Yogi of Transcendental Meditation fame, Swami Muktananda, and Sri Chinmoy] for making lots of money in the United States from their teaching: "They should have no house, no foundation, no bank accounts. . . . Our laws strictly forbid selling spirituality. But that's what they're doing." When asked what will happen when *he* starts making money, his chosen ally, the Divine Mother Swami Lakshmy Devyashram Mahamandaleshwari, responded: "Money itself is not bad. It's how it's used. Money should all be given away to schools, hospitals, and needy children, or something. It shouldn't be held on to." When asked if it wasn't against their own rules to criticize anyone else's spiritual path, that each must find his or her own way, Swami Swanandashram answered: "Oh, yes, it's true. Nobody is sup-

posed to do it. But I'm in America. In India we wouldn't criticize. But we are not actually criticizing here. When they are deviating from the real path, we are just telling the truth."

4. Pope Pius XII (in 1944): "If the exclusive aim of nature [for sexual intercourse] or at least its primary intent had been the mutual giving and possessing of husband and wife in pleasure and delight; if nature had arranged that act only to make their personal experience joyous in the highest degree, and not as an incentive in the service of life, then the Creator would have made use of another plan in the formation of the marital act."

5. Shirley MacLaine (*Time*, 7 December 1987) answering charges that she and others were "getting rich" on the New Age spiritual revival: "That seems to be a concern of many journalists. But I would say we all have to decide what we're worth. . . . I think journalists who are investigating belief in the unseen have to adjust the way they are judging the issue of materialism in relation to spirituality. Anything you want to learn costs money in this world."

6. William Safire, *American Heritage*, December 1987: "The greatness of Lincoln was his purposefulness. He saw something that few others saw: that the democratic experiment centered on the Union and that majority rule was everything. The minute you allowed secession, you made democracy an absurdity—because what would happen would be continued subdivision."

7. Bob Schwabach, "On Computers," *San Francisco Chronicle*, February 24, 1986: "There aren't just a couple of brands [of IBM compatibles] for those 'very low' prices; there are dozens. Do they work? Someone I know has been running one continuously for five months, and it's never missed a beat."

8. Thomas O. Enders, Reagan administration official (late 1981): "There is no question that the decisive battle for Central America is under way in El Salvador. . . . If after Nicaragua El Salvador is captured by a violent minority, who in Central America would not live in fear? How long would it be before major strategic United States interests—the Panama Canal, sea lanes, oil supplies—were at risk?"

9. Richard H. Rovere, in his *Senator Joe McCarthy*: "On the Senate floor in 1950, [Senator] Joe McCarthy announced that he had penetrated 'Truman's iron curtain of secrecy.' He had 81 case histories of persons whom he considered to be Communists in the State Department. Of case 40, he said, 'I do not have much information on this except the general statement of the agency that there is nothing in the files to disprove his Communist connections.' "

10. Plato, in his *Timaeus*: ". . . we must accept the traditions of the men of old time who affirm themselves to be the offspring of the gods—that is

what they say—and they must surely have known their own ancestors. How can we doubt the word of the children of the gods?"

11. Peter Singer in his *Animal Liberation:* "The racist violates the principle of equality by giving greater weight to the interests of members of his own race when there is a clash between their interests and the interests of those of another race. The sexist violates the principle of equality by favoring the interests of his own sex. Similarly the speciesist allows the interests of his own species to override the greater interests of members of other species. The pattern is identical in each case."

12. *Detroit Free Press* article by Ronald Kotulak: "If surgeons performed fewer operations more people would still be alive.

"This controversial conclusion, by a public health expert from the University of California at Los Angeles, is the latest and perhaps most serious attack on the surgical field. . . .

"The newest charge was made by Dr. Milton I. Roemer, professor of health-care administration at UCLA, after studying the effects of a five-week doctor strike in Los Angeles in 1976.

"Roemer and Dr. Jerome L. Schwartz from the California State Department of Health found that the death rate in Los Angeles County declined significantly during the strike.

"They said that fewer people had non-emergency surgery, so there was less risk of dying.

" 'These findings . . . lend support to the mounting evidence that people might benefit if less elective [non-emergency] surgery were performed in the United States,' said Roemer. 'It would appear, therefore, that greater restraint in the performance of elective surgical operations may well improve U.S. life expectancy.' "

EXERCISE 5–3

1. Carefully explain when appeals to authority are legitimate and when fallacious. Give examples of each, original if possible, to illustrate your explanations.

2. What do you think of the following argument: The alleged fallacy of *two wrongs make a right* is not a fallacy. Suppose you strike me and I then retaliate. While it's true that striking someone is normally a wrong, so that in that sense two wrongs have been committed, in this case the second wrong is justified by reason of self-defense and so in this case two wrongs do indeed make a right. The point is that there is nothing wrong with fighting fire with fire, and so no such fallacy as two wrongs make a right.

Responding to Political Rhetoric

A distinction has always been drawn between rhetoric that appeals to reason and rhetoric that is directed to the nonrational side of human nature. The first kind is sometimes referred to as *argumentation* and the second as *persuasion*, or even as *propaganda*. So far in this text we have concentrated on argumentation, the writing and evaluation of rational arguments. This does not mean that we have ignored the nonrational side of human nature. We've taken pains, for instance, to point out that good essay writers always take account of audience interests and foibles. But we have not advised clever appeals designed to *take advantage* of widespread human foibles—prejudices, superstitions, rationalizations—in lieu of cogent argument. Indeed, the point of the fallacy discussion in Chapter 5 was to sound the alarm against fallacious rhetoric, not to urge its employment in the manipulation of audiences.

It must be admitted, however, that a good deal of everyday rhetoric leans in the direction of nonrational persuasion and even of propaganda. Political rhetoric intended for a mass audience is an important case in point.

Political Rhetoric as Advertisement

In a representative system of government, the primary function of political rhetoric intended for a mass audience is to persuade large numbers of people to vote for a particular political candidate or to support a particular policy. It thus resembles all other kinds of advertising in its purpose, which may explain why it uses the same sorts of devices that are employed when selling toothpastes, the latest movies, or fancy automobiles. In any case, selling candidates and policies, it turns out, is very much like selling any other kinds of products.

Advertising in general tends to use a mixture of rational and emotional ploys, illustrated by the auto commercial that depicted a vivacious young woman happily driving the product while the voice-over talked about 3.9% financing. Advertising may flatter, cajole, amuse, or even inform listeners or

87

readers as a way of getting them to favor the product, or at least to remember it. It may employ questionable analogies and use jargon, humor, slogans, or catch phrases. It frequently plays on audience fears or dreams, and on occasion even makes use of cogent arguments.

While there are several different advertising theories, one way to divide the field is to notice that virtually all ads either *promise* listeners or readers something (use Tide for cleaner clothes; a vote for Jesse Jackson is a vote for civil rights) or try to get them to *identify* with a candidate, corporation, or political party (AT&T—the right choice; Jimmy Carter—a man of the people). In non-political advertising, promise advertising predominates, although most ads contain a mixture of the two elements. But in politics, especially in this age of television, image is the more important ingredient, a fact driven home to the skeptical by the phenomenon of Ronald Reagan. (Of course, in the political arena an *aura* of rationality is part of the required persona. That is one reason why revelations about how Nancy Reagan's astrological consultations influenced her husband's conduct as president were damaging to his reputation.)

Exactly what sort of rhetoric a politican is likely to use depends on many factors, the most important of which is the nature of the intended audience (which should come as no surprise at this point). An effective address to a large audience cannot be complicated, detailed, or too logically rigorous. Large masses of people cannot, or at least will not follow such reasoning or evaluate it on its logical merits and demerits. But an article in a prestigious journal such as *Foreign Affairs* needs to provide at least the pretense of cogent argument while avoiding strident language and overt appeals to prejudice or self-interest. (Covert appeals are another matter.) A speech delivered to an audience of senior citizens cannot as vigorously attack the Social Security system or Medicare as one addressed to an audience of yuppies. When dealing with the pronouncements of political candidates and elected officials, we need to remember these basic facts about what sorts of rhetoric move masses of people.

While persuasion is the chief function performed by political rhetoric, it is by no means the only one. Ceremony and ritual, for instance, often play an important role, as in an acceptance speech by a newly nominated candidate or an address by a newly sworn in U.S. president. Indeed, a single political speech may perform several different functions, and most do. For instance, the "mea culpa" speech given by President Reagan in 1987 at the height of the Irangate scandal contains portions that are primarily ceremonial, a section that on the whole is argumentative, and several paragraphs whose very enunciation on national television amounted to the performance of a ritual act of contrition. (This speech will be examined in more detail shortly.)

Nonargumentative portions of political addresses—ceremonial remarks, symbolic gestures, flattery—serve very important functions. They signal friendliness on the part of the speaker, put an audience at ease, unite members of a group behind shared values and myths, and bid the audience to give a fair hearing to the politician and his or her point of view.

All of this is to the good. Indeed, it is hard to imagine a large democratic society and its political system functioning well without this kind of political rhetoric. The trouble is that gracious compliments, gestures of solidarity, bows to the hometown audience, and the like invite soft-headedness rather than a fair hearing when the time comes to evaluate the more substantive portions of a political speech or commercial. Overcoming the unfortunately almost universal human tendency to be taken in by such rhetorical devices takes a good deal of self-awareness (of actual cases when we mentally shoot ourselves in the foot in this way) combined with persistent efforts at reform.

A Close Look at an Important Political Address

Let's now take a close look at the Ronald Reagan speech just mentioned. It was delivered on March 4, 1987, when the Irangate mess threatened to topple the Reagan administration or at least hamstring its last two years in office.

The television audience for this speech was extremely large. Americans wanted to know whether their aging president could still be trusted with the power and duties of his office. They wondered if his performance up to that point had been as bad as the Tower Commission report of the week before had indicated, and, in particular, they wanted Reagan to stop stonewalling and admit his share of guilt in this fiasco. (This demand for atonement on Reagan's part is not something to be dismissed lightly. Failure to own up was an important reason why Richard Nixon had been driven from office only a dozen years before. Every one of Reagan's advisors had for some time been telling him that he had to do this.)

The crafting of a speech that would satisfy the demands and allay the fears of the general public posed serious problems for the president, his advisors, and in particular his speechwriters. * The Tower Commission report had fanned the flames of suspicion. *Time* magazine (March 9, 1987) wrote that Reagan "stands exposed as a President *willfully* ignorant of what his aides were doing, *myopically* unaware of the glaring contradictions between his public and secret policies, *complacently* dependent on advisors who never once, from start to finish, presented him with any systematic analysis of aims, means, risks and alternatives. And in the end, as a President *unable* to recall when, how or even whether he had reached the key decision that started the whole arms-to-Iran affair" [italics added]. Any president who could be treated so roughly by the press had to be in serious trouble. To get out of it, Reagan needed to accept the damning charges of the Tower Commission report, or at least accept its main

---

*Many people have the quaint idea that presidents still compose their own orations, as Lincoln composed his famous Gettysburg Address. But, in fact, the last president to do so was Woodrow Wilson. Of course, presidents still control the general content and tone of their speeches, but that is another matter.

thrust, while at the same satisfying doubts concerning his ability to manage the executive branch of the government and to tell truth from falsehood.

The address composed by his speechwriters can conveniently be divided into thirty-four paragraphs. The first two consist primarily of introductory ceremonial remarks, much like saying "How do you do?" to the audience. While custom and indeed common courtesy require an introduction of this kind, by its very nature this introductory bow to the audience was not relevant to the substantive questions at issue (for example, whether the president authorized or even knew what was going on).

In this case, the introductory remarks were salted with a nice compliment designed to warm up the audience for the more serious business ahead. Here are the first two paragraphs—printed without margin notes because there is nothing in them relevant to the main question concerning Reagan's guilt and his ability to run the government.

> My fellow Americans, I've spoken to you from this 1   *[Nothing relevant*
> historic office on many occasions about many things.   *here, and so nothing*
> The power of the presidency is often thought to reside   *we need to keep track*
> within this Oval Office. Yet it doesn't rest here; it   *of or put into a*
> rests in you, the American people, and in your trust.   *summary.]*
>
> Your trust is what gives a president his powers of 2
> leadership and his personal strength, and it's what I
> want to talk to you about this evening.

The third paragraph asked and the fourth then answered a question that must have occurred to many citizens:

> For the past three months, I've been silent on the 3   *Q: Why hasn't the*
> revelations about Iran. You must have been thinking.   *president spoken to*
> "Well, why doesn't he just speak to us as he has in   *us on the Iran busi-*
> the past when we've faced troubles or tragedies?"   *ness during the past*
> Others of you, I guess, were thinking, "What's he   *three months?*
> doing hiding out in the White House?"
>
> I've paid a price for my silence in terms of your 4   *A: B/C he had to*
> trust and confidence. But I have had to wait, as have   *wait for the Tower*
> you, for the complete story. That's why I appointed   *Commission report.*
> Ambassador David Abshire as my special counselor
> to help get out the thousands of documents to the
> various investigations. And I appointed a special re-
> view board, the Tower board, which took on a chore
> of pulling the truth together for me and getting to the
> bottom of things. It has now issued its findings.

Note that in asking and answering this question right after flattering his audience, the president continued the process of softening audience resistance to the important message to follow, that he could be trusted to continue running the government.

Now the president had to speak to the report and its charges of incompetence and unconcern. The speech allowed him to jump in gingerly by starting out with the one point in the report favorable to Ronald Reagan:

> I'm often accused of being an optimist, and it's true   5
> I had to hunt pretty hard to find any good news in
> the board's report. As you know, it's well stocked with
> criticisms, which I'll discuss in a moment, but I was
> very relieved to read this sentence, ". . . the board is
> convinced that the president does indeed want the
> full story to be told." And that will continue to be
> my pledge to you as the other investigations go
> forward.

The report affirms that RR wanted the full story told.

The sixth paragraph contained more ceremonial material irrelevant to the main questions about Reagan's part in the fiasco or his ability to run the government:

> I want to thank the members of the panel—former   6
> Senator John Tower, former Secretary of State Ed-
> mund Muskie, and former National Security Adviser
> Brent Scowcroft. They have done the nation, as well
> as me personally, a great service by submitting a re-
> port of such integrity and depth. They have my gen-
> uine and enduring gratitude.

[Nothing relevant here.]

Finally, Reagan had to come to the point—his admission of guilt and act of contrition (paragraphs 7 through 11):

> I've studied the board's report. Its findings are honest,   7
> convincing, and highly critical, and I accept them.
> Tonight I want to share with you my thoughts on
> these findings and report to you on the actions I'm
> taking to implement the board's recommendations.
>
>   First let me say I take full responsibility for my   8
> own actions and for those of my Administration. As
> angry as I may be about activities taken without my
> knowledge, I am still accountable for those activities.
> As disappointed as I may be in some who served me,
> I am still the one who must answer to the American
> people for this behavior. And as personally distasteful
> as I find secret bank accounts and diverted funds, as
> the Navy would say, this happened on my watch.

RR accepts the Tower findings, critical as they are.

RR takes "full responsibility" and admits there were "secret bank accounts and diverted funds."

Note the quick switch from his taking "full responsibility" to his anger at subordinates who acted without his knowledge. This tends to shift responsibility from Reagan to his staff. It also masks the contradiction in his acceptance of the Tower Commission's assertion that he authorized his staff to engage in this activity while now saying that they acted without his knowledge. The implication of this paragraph is that it happened on his watch so he was responsible, but he did not know what they were doing.

Notice also that Reagan accepted the commission's report but did not enumerate its negative contents. Saying that the report was "highly critical" does not convey the flavor of that report's damning picture of an uncaring and incompetent president. Of course, he could not be expected to wallow in the sordid details; the point is that he softened the blow as much as he could while still doing what he had to do: accept the report and admit that he was guilty.

Let's start with the part that is the most controversial. A few months ago I told the American people I did not trade arms for hostages. My heart and my best intentions still tell me that is true, but the facts and the evidence tell me it is not.	9	*RR doesn't remember (authorizing) an arms trade for hostages, but admits the facts show he did so.*
As the Tower Board reported, what began as a strategic opening to Iran deteriorated in its implementation into trading arms for hostages. This runs counter to my own beliefs, to administration policy, and to the original strategy we had in mind. There are reasons why it happened, but no excuses. It was a mistake.	10	*TB report: what began as "strategic opening" to Iran "deteriorated" into trade for hostages. RR didn't want that, but it happened and was mistaken—no excuses.*
I undertook the original Iran initiative in order to develop relations with those who might assume leadership in a post-Khomeini government. It's clear from the board's report, however, that I let my personal concern for the hostages spill over into the geopolitical strategy of reaching out to Iran. I asked so many questions about the hostages' welfare that I didn't ask enough about the specifics of the total Iran plan.	11	*RR authorized the Iran approach to develop post-K. relations. But his concern for hostages led him to ask too much about them and not enough about the specific plan.*

Having ruffled feathers by admitting he may have been too concerned about the hostages, he then had to placate those who may have been offended:

Let me say to the hostage families, we have not given up. We never will. And I promise you we'll use every legitimate means to free your loved ones from captivity. But I must also caution that those Americans who freely remain in such dangerous areas must know that they're responsible for their own safety.	12	*[Nothing relevant here.]*

Since the Tower report did not settle the question of the transfer of funds to the Nicaraguan Contras, it apparently was felt that the president had to say something about this, and he did in the next paragraph, where he again adopted the mea culpa tone of paragraphs 7 through 11 (the tone of the first half of the speech):

Now, another major aspect of the board's findings regards the transfer of funds to the Nicaraguan Contras. The Tower board was not able to find out what	13	*RR didn't know of funds "diverted" to the Contras, but*

happened to this money, so the facts here will be left to the continuing investigation of the court-appointed independent counsel and the two congressional investigating committees. As I told the Tower Board, I didn't know about any diversion of funds to the Contras. But as president I cannot escape responsibility.

takes responsibility.

Next the president turned to his management style and admitted that it didn't work in this case while at the same time claiming it was a good and successful style:

Much has been said about my management style, a style that has worked successfully for me during eight years as governor of California and for most of my presidency. The way I work is to identify the problem, find the right individuals to do the job, and then let them go to it. I have found this invariably brings out the best in people. They seem to rise to their full capability and in the long run you get more done.

14 *RR's management style was to identify a problem, find the right people to solve it, and "then let them go to it." This style had been successful in the past.*

Reagan could expect that most people would not see this for the simple-minded theory of management that it is and in particular, would not notice that it says nothing about checking up on subordinates to see that they carry out their work correctly.

When it came to managing the NSC staff, let's face it, my style didn't match its previous track record. I have already begun correcting this. As a start, yesterday I met with the entire professional staff of the National Security Council. I defined for them the values I want to guide the national security policies of this country. I told them that I wanted a policy that was as justifiable and understandable in public as it was in secret. I wanted a policy that reflected the will of the Congress as well as the White House. And I told them that there'll be no more free-lancing by individuals when it comes to our national security.

15 *RR's style didn't work managing the NSC in the Iran business, but he's already begun to correct that by meeting with the NSC staff and telling them what to do now.*

Notice how "my style didn't match its previous track record" was used here as a euphemism for "I mismanaged."

This last paragraph introduced a new tone and a new subject into the president's speech. The mea culpa protestations went into the background and we were shown a new Ronald Reagan who was in charge again and could be trusted to run the government, having learned from experience. This is the theme of the rest of the speech after ceremonial paragraph 16:

You have heard a lot about the staff of the National Security Council in recent months. I can tell you, they are good and dedicated government employees,

16 *[Nothing relevant.]*

who put in long hours for the nation's benefit. They
are eager and anxious to serve their country.

In paragraphs 17 through 31, Reagan listed the changes and actions he
had accomplished to get the ship of state back on course again, indicating that
he still could be trusted with the power of the presidency. Since they said simply
that Reagan endorsed the Tower commission's recommendations and had appointed several new people to replace those who were discredited, let's omit
margin notes at this point, remembering, of course, that we'll have to include
something on these paragraphs in any summary we happen to make.

> One thing still upsetting me, however, is that no one   17
> kept proper records of meetings or decisions. This led
> to my failure to recollect whether I approved an arms
> shipment before or after the fact. I did approve it; I
> just can't say specifically when. Rest assured, there's
> plenty of record-keeping now going on at 1600 Penn-
> sylvania Avenue.

Reagan here glossed over his inability to remember even the most basic facts in
the case. In paragraph 9 he had said he did not remember *whether* he had
approved the shipments, but at this point he said that he could not remember
when, a much less serious matter. This passage also is interesting in its employment of a standard mea culpa device: admitting error in the context of announcing its correction. (Reagan also passed over all sorts of inconvenient evidence
indicating that he was not on top of the situation, for instance, his failure to act
with sufficient promptness to prevent Lieutenant Colonel North and his secretary from shredding relevant evidence well after the scandal had broken.)

> For nearly a week now, I have been studying the   18
> board's report. I want the American people to know
> this wrenching ordeal of recent months has not been
> in vain. I endorse every one of the Tower board's
> recommendations. In fact, I'm going beyond its rec-
> ommendations so as to put the house in even better
> order.
>
> I'm taking action in three basic areas—person-   19
> nel, national security policy, and the process for mak-
> ing sure that the system works.
>
> First, personnel. I've brought in an accom-   20
> plished and highly respected new team here at the
> White House. They bring new blood, new energy,
> and new credibility and experience.
>
> Former Senator Howard Baker, my new chief of   21
> staff, possesses a breadth of legislative and foreign
> affairs skills that's impossible to match. I'm hopeful
> that his experience as minority and majority leader
> of the Senate can help us forge a new partnership
> with the Congress, especially on foreign and national

security policies. I'm genuinely honored that he has given up his own presidential aspirations to serve the country as my chief of staff.

Frank Carlucci, my new national security ad- 22 viser, is respected for his experience in government and trusted for his judgment and counsel. Under him, the NSC staff is being rebuilt with proper management discipline. Already, almost half the NSC professional staff is comprised of new people.

Yesterday I nominated William Webster, a man 23 of sterling reputation, to be director of the Central Intelligence Agency. Mr. Webster has served as director of the FBI and as a U.S. district court judge. He understands the meaning of "rule of law."

So that his knowledge of national security mat- 24 ters can be available to me on a continuing basis, I will also appoint John Tower to serve as a member of my Foreign Intelligence Advisory Board.

I am considering other changes in personnel and 25 I will move more furniture as I see fit in the weeks and months ahead.

Second, in the area of national security policy, I 26 have ordered the NSC to begin a comprehensive review of all covert operations. I have also directed that any covert activity be in support of clear policy objectives and in compliance with American values. I expect a covert policy that if Americans saw it on the front page of their newspaper, they'd say, "That makes sense."

I have had issued a directive prohibiting the 27 NSC staff itself from undertaking covert operations—no ifs, ands, or buts.

I have asked Vice President Bush to reconvene 28 his task force on terrorism to review our terrorist policy in light of the events that have occurred.

Third, in terms of the process of reaching na- 29 tional security decisions, I am adopting in total the Tower report's model of how the NSC process and staff should work. I am directing Mr. Carlucci to take the necessary steps to make that happen. He will report back to me on further reforms that might be needed.

I've created the post of NSC legal adviser to as- 30 sure a greater sensitivity to matters of law.

I am also determined to make the congressional 31 oversight process work. Proper procedures for consultation with the Congress will be followed, not only in letter but in spirit. Before the end of March, I will

report to the Congress on all the steps I've taken in
line with the Tower Commission's conclusions.

Having been told about the host of changes he had instituted in his
administration, the audience was now ready for the president's socko ending,
tying together his admission of mistakes in the past with his current forthright
actions—he had learned from his past mistakes and was better able to lead now
because of what he had learned:

> Now what should happen when you make a mistake   32   *[Nothing relevant.]*
> is this: You take your knocks, you learn your lessons
> and then you move on. That's the healthiest way to
> deal with a problem. This in no way diminishes the
> importance of the other continuing investigations but
> the business of our country and our people must pro-
> ceed. I have gotten this message from Republicans
> and Democrats in Congress, from allies around the
> world—and if we're reading the signals right, even
> from the Soviets. And, of course, I have heard the
> message from you, the American people.
>
> You know, by the time you reach my age, you've   33   *[Nothing relevant.]*
> made plenty of mistakes if you've lived your life prop-
> erly. So you learn. You put things in perspective. You
> pull your energies together. You change. You go
> forward.
>
> My fellow Americans, I have a great deal that I   34   *[Nothing relevant.]*
> want to accomplish with you and for you over the
> next two years. And, the Lord willing, that's exactly
> what I intend to do.

Judged in terms of persuasive power, President Reagan's speech was an
excellent one. It allowed him to admit his guilt while at the same time presenting himself in as positive a light as possible. It allowed him to own up to
past errors while appearing to have regained control. Here is a summary taken
from margin notes of the relevant remarks in the president's speech (put into
the first person, as though said by President Reagan himself):

1. The Tower Commission affirmed that I want the whole story to be told.

2. The report was very critical of me, but I accept it and take full
responsibility.

3. I don't remember trading arms for hostages, but admit that the facts
show this to be the case.

4. The Tower report said that the Iran business began as a strategic opening to Iran but turned into a trade, which was wrong, and I admit this is so.

5. My concern for the hostages led me to skew my monitoring of the
situation from developing post-Khomeini relations to swapping arms for
hostages.

6. I have moved to correct the situation and to prevent further difficulties from arising by appointing new people and instructing them to obey the law and do only what the American people will approve of.

What is there in this summary either favorable or unfavorable to the president?

FAVORABLE TO PRESIDENT REAGAN

1. He wanted the Tower Commission to find and reveal the truth (that is, unlike Richard Nixon, he didn't want a cover-up).

2. He admitted his guilt and took full responsibility for what had happened.

3. He moved to correct the situation and to make things work right in the future by appointing new people.

UNFAVORABLE TO PRESIDENT REAGAN

1. He admitted that he can't remember vital matters of state with which he was concerned.

2. He admitted that he was unable in this case to keep his mind on his own plan of action and became diverted to a disastrous course of action contrary to his own stated policy.

3. He accepted the Tower Commission report conclusion that he had bungled.

At the time the speech was being delivered, audiences also were influenced by factors pro and con that lay outside the content of the speech itself. Favorable to the president was that he seemed in complete control of himself, delivered his speech in an absolutely first rate manner, and displayed no signs of senility.

Unfavorable to him was the actual content of the Tower Commission's report. That report was not just critical of the president, as his speech indicated, but rather was *damning* in its criticism and described a president who was not competent to hold the office. (Very few people had actually read the report, but most Americans at the time had a pretty good idea of what it said because the mass media had given it a great deal of coverage.)

In addition, there was the fact that for over three months President Reagan had denied guilt in this matter before finally coming clean in this speech. The obvious implication of this delay was that either he had lied to the people for over three months or else he himself did not know and for three months was unable to determine what he had authorized or how his staff had carried out his orders.

In any case, the upshot of this speech was a small but significant change in the national mood of disappointment. Large numbers of people seemed to become more willing to give the Reagan administration another chance to do something effective and to regain some of its lost power and respect.

But should this speech have convinced rational people to again trust the president? Did it present convincing reasons for doing so? How many people would have retained confidence in an accountant, doctor, or lawyer who could say no more in self-defense than Reagan was able to? Analogy: Imagine the president of a large bank saying to the board of directors and depositors: "Trust me to remain as president of this bank. I take full responsibility for the foolish and illegal loans that I authorized, as the facts show although I've forgotten myself. I admit to being carried away in my zeal to make money to the point of authorizing secret and, it turns out, bad loans made contrary to my own publicly announced policy, and admit that this caused damage to the bank's solvency. However, I've now appointed new people to run the bank and instructed them not to do these bad things any more." Who would be moved by such remarks to put their money back into a bank whose president had found it necessary to own up in this way? Yet Reagan's speech convinced masses of Americans, even if only tentatively, to give him another chance.

The focus of this book has been on *rational* persuasion via cogent argument, but it must be admitted that human beings are not always rational animals, whatever Aristotle may have said on the matter.

☒ PATRICK J. BUCHANAN

Never Strike a King

Political columnist Patrick J. Buchanan, former director of communications for President Reagan and before that special assistant and speechwriter for Richard Nixon when he was president, wrote this article shortly after Lieutenant Colonel Oliver North had concluded his testimony before the congressional Iran-Contra committee. So we read it now with a good deal of hindsight.

Noon Wednesday, suddenly, it was over; and everyone knew it. The coup 1 d'état had failed. Ronald Reagan would survive . . . .

In November, when it was first revealed that Ronald Reagan had autho- 2 rized weapons sales to mullahs—in contravention of stated policy—the anger, the anguish, the outrage—even among the president's own—were genuine, legitimate. Today, they are synthetic, feigned, and transparently so. . . .

In a single week Ollie (Lt. Col. Oliver North) not only put God and 3 Country and the Constitution, and all the splendid values he represents, back on the side of the president and the Nicaraguan resistance; he held up a mirror to the ugly face of the inquisition.

How, when Colonel North admitted to setting up secret bank accounts, to deceiving Congress, to shredding documents, can the American people consider him a national hero . . . ?

The answer is simple. What the American people saw was genuine drama: 4 A patriotic son of the Republic who, confronted with a grave moral dilemma—whether to betray his comrades and causes, or to deceive members of Congress—chose the lesser of two evils, the path of honor. It was magnificent. The American people watched daily the anguish and pain of a genuinely moral man; and contrasted that with the stuffy self-righteousness of the pharisees putting him through his ordeal. . . .

Colonel North speaks the language of duty, honor, country; his is a faith 5 deeply rooted in Christian tradition. He did not, and would not, proclaim some amoral "right to lie"; he was forced into a moral dilemma by an immoral act of Congress.

With the Boland Amendment, the Congress of the United States passed a 6 death sentence upon the embattled friends of Colonel North; and then it instructed men like Colonel North to carry it out. Instead, the colonel built a new and ingenious lifeline to keep the Contras alive; and when Congress came to close that down as well, Colonel North protected it, at risk of his own career.

He deceived Congress, to save his friends on a field of battle. That is what 7 the American people, deeply moved, were applauding. That is why American people laughed out loud, when Colonel North volunteered that even as Justice Department lawyers were seizing documents in one room, he was shredding documents in the next.

"They were doing their jobs, and I was doing mine," Ollie said; and every 8 American knew in his heart that Colonel North had done a brave and beautiful thing. For all this moralizing about "the end does not justify the means," the truth is the colonel's ends were noble and his means—secrecy and shredding documents—licit or not, were not inherently immoral.

There is another reason America took Colonel North into her heart. That 9 is because they believe that the Left, the Sam Donaldsons of the world, lack the moral standing to sit in judgment on anyone—especially Colonel North.

Men who have proclaimed it a great advance for human freedom, when 10 4,000 unborn children are daily shredded in abortuaries of the United States, are to be laughed at when they profess moral horror over the shredding of documents. . . .

The Boland Amendment did not forbid Iranian contributions to the Con- 11 tras; it did not forbid private aid to the Contras; it did not apply to the NSC [National Security Council]. It was a civil statute with no criminal penalities. And there is no hard evidence either man [Colonel North and NSC presidential advisor Admiral John Poindexter] violated that amendment. . . .

But if the letter of the Boland Amendment was not violated, its "spirit" 12 merited contempt. For the Boland Amendment was rooted in malice; it was a calculated, cold-blooded congressional act to abandon to their communist enemies thousands of Nicaraguan patriots who had taken up arms, at the urging of the United States, to expel Moscow's Quislings from Central America.

The Boland Amendment was rooted in the same malevolence that motivated an earlier Congress to disarm and desert to its communist enemies a South Vietnamese army that had fought for seven years alongside our own. . . .

It is not Poindexter and North who belong in a court of law; but Congress that belongs in the court of public opinion explaining why, for three years, it has actively sought a Contra defeat—and its natural concomitant, a communist victory in Central America.

In 1985 and 1986, while Fidel Castro moved 3,000 combat advisers into   14
Nicaragua, while Gorbachev pumped in a billion dollars in military hardware, the Congress did its damndest to discredit, defund and defeat the army of peasants fighting on the side of freedom and the United States. The Boland Amendment was nothing less than the American corollary to the Brezhnev Doctrine. . . .

No more no-win wars, Mr. President. Did not you tell us, sir, that this   15
was the central lesson of Vietnam?

And should the Democratic Party in Congress, with no policy of its own   16
for dealing with the beachhead of the Warsaw Pact on the mainland of North America, choose to pursue its dog-in-the-manger tactics and defund the Contras, the president should find the supplies, ship them openly, and challenge the Congress to impeach him. As Colonel North demonstrated, they haven't got the cohones. . . .

Any indictment of Colonel North or Admiral Poindexter would be an   17
offense against justice that ought not to be permitted by the president, whom they served honorably, faithfully and well. And the president should so state, publicly. . . .

Never strike a king unless you kill him. That was among the first things   18
taught us by Richard M. Nixon when I hooked up with him more than two decades ago. For the last six months, the left wing of the Democratic Party, and its auxiliaries in the press, have sought to use the Iran-Contra affair to cripple and kill the presidency of Ronald Reagan as they used Watergate to kill the presidency of Richard Nixon.

They failed, Mr. President; they are retreating in disarray; and now is the   19
time to let the jackal pack know what it means to strike a king.

EXERCISE 6-1   QUESTIONS FOR FURTHER THOUGHT
                 AND RESEARCH

1. Buchanan says that "For all this moralizing about 'the end does not justify the means,' the truth is the colonel's ends were noble and his means— secrecy and shredding documents—licit or not, were not inherently immoral." What is your judgment of this statement, and why do you think so? Do noble ends in general justify immoral means?

2. Does Buchanan say that North's actions violated the Boland Amendment? Did his actions violate the Boland Amendment?

3. Buchanan does say that North "did not, and would not, proclaim some amoral 'right to lie'; he was forced into a moral dilemma by an immoral act of Congress." What is your judgment of this statement, and why do you think so?

4. Underlying this essay is the fundamental question as to whether we're ever justified in breaking the law just because we disagree with it. A fundamental idea of the theory of democratic governments is that decisions are to be made according to a set rule, such as majority rule, and that those who are outvoted are obligated to obey the law anyway. There seem to be exceptions, for example, cases of systematic legal unfairness that, it has been argued, justify certain kinds of civil disobedience. But was North's case an exception? And were his actions, which did not in the least resemble typical acts of civil disobedience, justified under the circumstances?

5. Using the margin note and summary method, or whatever method works best for you, compose and evaluate a summary of Buchanan's article.

EXERCISE 6-2   SUGGESTIONS FOR WRITING

1. Write an essay either defending or attacking President Reagan's role in the Iran-Contra affair.

2. Write an essay either defending or attacking Oliver North's role in the Iran-Contra affair.

3. If you have already composed a summary of Buchanan's article, you have already done a good deal of the work involved in writing a short evaluation—an analysis—of Buchanan's essay.

READINGS

The readings that follow are intended to serve as models and information sources, or, in other words, to stimulate the thought required to write effective and cogent argumentative essays.

Although most of the readings are themselves argumentative essays of one kind or another, a few are not, for instance, George Orwell's short story "A Hanging," which speaks against capital punishment by describing someone being hanged. These nonargumentative readings have been included to illustrate how other devices can be used to persuade.

The readings divide into sections according to topics, starting with those that present parts of several quite diverse world views.

WORLD VIEWS

Background beliefs, in particular those most fundamental beliefs called *world views* or *philosophies*, are crucial in the evaluation of arguments and argumentative essays. When Socrates said that the unexamined life is not worth living, he meant a life in which one's world views are not examined and evaluated—the sort of life that most people lead who unquestioningly accept the beliefs and values of their culture and of those around them.

The readings that follow in this section divide roughly into those concerning fundamental beliefs various people have held concerning politics, religion, human nature, evolution and race.

☒ **THOMAS JEFFERSON**

The Declaration of Independence

Thomas Jefferson (1743–1826), the third president of the United States (1801–1809), wrote the basic draft of the statement declaring American independence in 1776. In it, he espouses equality for all men and the right to life, liberty, and the pursuit of happiness. He also lists the colonies' grievances that moved them to absolve their allegiance to the British crown.

When in the Course of human events, it becomes necessary for one people to 1 dissolve the political bands which have connected them with another, and to assume among the powers of the earth, the separate and equal station to which the Laws of Nature and of Nature's God entitle them, a decent respect to the opinions of mankind requires that they should declare the causes which impel them to the separation.

We hold these truths to be self-evident, that all men are created equal, 2 that they are endowed by their Creator with certain unalienable Rights, that among these are Life, Liberty and the pursuit of Happiness. That to secure these rights, Governments are instituted among Men, deriving their just powers from the consent of the governed, That whenever any Form of Government becomes destructive of these ends it is the Right of the People to alter or to abolish it, and to institute new Government, laying its foundation on such principles and organizing its powers in such form, as to them shall seem most likely to effect their Safety and Happiness. Prudence, indeed, will dictate that Governments long established should not be changed for light and transient causes; and accordingly all experience has shewn, that mankind are more disposed to suffer, while evils are sufferable, than to right themselves by abolishing the forms to which they are accustomed. But when a long train of abuses and usurpations, pursuing invariably the same Object evinces a design to reduce them under absolute Despotism, it is their right, it is their duty, to throw off such Government, and to provide new Guards for their future security. Such has been the patient sufferance of these Colonies; and such is now the necessity which constrains them to alter their former Systems of Government. The history of the present King of Great Britain is a history of repeated injuries and usurpations, all having in direct object the establishment of an absolute Tyranny over these States. To prove this, let Facts be submitted to a candid world.

He has refused his Assent to Laws, the most wholesome and necessary for 3
the public good.

He has forbidden his Governors to pass Laws of immediate and pressing 4
importance, unless suspended in their operation till his Assent should be obtained; and when so suspended, he has utterly neglected to attend to them. He has refused to pass other Laws for the accommodation of large districts of people, unless those people would relinquish the right of Representation in the Legislature, a right inestimable to them and formidable to tyrants only.

He has called together legislative bodies at places unusual, uncomfortable, 5
and distant from the depository of their public Records, for the sole purpose of fatiguing them into compliance with his measures.

He has dissolved Representative Houses repeatedly, for opposing with 6
manly firmness his invasions on the rights of the people.

He has refused for a long time, after such dissolutions, to cause others to 7
be elected; whereby the Legislative powers, incapable of Annihilation, have returned to the People at large for their exercise, the State remaining in the mean time exposed to all the dangers of invasion from without, and convulsions within.

He has endeavoured to prevent the population of these States; for that 8
purpose obstructing the Laws for Naturalization of Foreigners; refusing to pass others to encourage their migrations hither, and raising the conditions of new Appropriations of Lands.

He has obstructed the Administration of Justice, by refusing his Assent to 9
Laws for establishing Judiciary powers.

He has made Judges dependent on his Will alone, for the tenure of their 10
offices, and the amount and payment of their salaries.

He has erected a multitude of New Offices, and sent hither swarms of 11
Officers to harass our People, and eat out their substance.

He has kept among us, in times of peace, standing Armies without the 12 Consent of our legislatures.

He has affected to render the Military independent of and superior to the 13 Civil power.

He has combined with others to subject us to a jurisdiction foreign to our 14 constitution, and unacknowledged by our laws; giving his Assent to their Acts of pretended Legislation:

For Quartering large bodies of armed troops among us: 15

For protecting them, by a mock Trial, from punishment for any Murders 16 which they should commit on the Inhabitants of these States:

For cutting off our Trade with all parts of the world: 17

For imposing Taxes on us without our Consent: 18

For depriving us in many cases of the benefits of Trial by Jury: 19

For transporting us beyond Seas to be tried for pretended offences: 20

For abolishing the free System of English Laws in a neighbouring Prov- 21 ince, establishing therein an Arbitrary government, and enlarging its Boundaries so as to render it at once an example and fit instrument for introducing the same absolute rule into these Colonies:

For taking away our Charters, abolishing our most valuable Laws, and 22 altering fundamentally the Forms of our Governments:

For suspending our own Legislatures, and declaring themselves invested 23 with power to legislate for us in all cases whatsoever.

He has abdicated Government here, by declaring us out of his Protection 24 and waging War against us.

He has plundered our seas, ravaged our Coasts, burnt our towns, and 25 destroyed the Lives of our people.

He is at this time transporting large Armies of foreign Mercenaries to 26 compleat the works of death, desolation and tyranny, already begun with circumstances of Cruelty & perfidy scarcely paralleled in the most barbarous ages, and totally unworthy the Head of a civilized nation.

He has constrained our fellow Citizens taken Captive on the high Seas to 27 bear Arms against their Country, to become the executioners of their friends and Brethren, or to fall themselves by their Hands.

He has excited domestic insurrections amongst us, and has endeavoured 28 to bring on the inhabitants of our frontiers, merciless Indian Savages, whose known rule of warfare, is an undistinguished destruction of all ages, sexes and conditions.

In every stage of these Oppressions We have Petitioned for Redress in the 29 most humble terms: Our repeated Petitions have been answered only by repeated injury. A Prince, whose character is thus marked by every act which may define a Tyrant, is unfit to be the ruler of a free people.

Nor have We been wanting in attentions to our Brittish brethren. We have 30 warned them from time to time of attempts by their legislature to extend an unwarrantable jurisdiction over us. We have reminded them of the circumstances of our emigration and settlement here. We have appealed to their native justice and magnanimity, and we have conjured them by the ties of our common kindred to disavow these usurpations, which would inevitably interrupt our connections and correspondence. They too have been deaf to the voice of Justice and of consanguinity. We must, therefore, acquiesce in the necessity, which denounces our Separation, and hold them, as we hold the rest of mankind, Enemies in War, in Peace Friends.

We, therefore, the Representatives of the united States of America, in 31 General Congress, Assembled, appealing to the Supreme Judge of the world for the rectitude of our intentions, do, in the Name, and by Authority of the good People of these Colonies, solemnly publish and declare, That these United Colonies are, and of Right ought to be Free and Independent States; that they are absolved from all Allegiance to the British Crown, and that all political connection between them and the State of Great Britain, is and ought to be totally dissolved; and that as Free and Independent States, they have full Power to levy War, conclude Peace, contract Alliances, establish Commerce, and to do all other Acts and Things which Independent States may of right do. And for the support of this Declaration, with a firm reliance on the protection of divine Providence, we mutually pledge to each other our Lives, our Fortunes and our sacred Honor.

⊠ KARL MARX AND FRIEDRICH ENGELS

The Communist Manifesto

Karl Marx (1818–1883) formulated the view that history is determined principally by economic factors and predicted that capitalism would give way to socialism and, eventually, to the "withering away of the state" into communism. His book, Das Kapital (Capital), *is the bible of present-day Marxists and Marxist countries such as the Soviet Union (although Marx certainly would not have approved of most of the policies adopted in his name). The following has been excerpted from* The Communist Manifesto, *written with Friedrich Engels (1820–1895), and* Critique of the Gotha Program.

A specter is haunting Europe—the specter of Communism. All the Powers of 1 old Europe have entered into a holy alliance to exorcise this specter; Pope and Czar, Metternich and Guizot, French Radicals and German police-spies.

Where is the party in opposition that has not been decried as communistic 2 by its opponents in power? Where the Opposition that has not hurled back the branding reproach of Communism against the more advanced opposition parties, as well as against its reactionary adversaries?

Two things result from this fact. 3

I. Communism is already acknowledged by all European Powers to be 4
itself a Power.

II. It is high time that Communists should openly, in the face of the whole 5
world, publish their views, their aims, their tendencies, and meet this nursery
tale of the specter of Communism with a Manifesto of the party itself.

To this end, Communists of various nationalities have assembled in Lon- 6
don and sketched the following Manifesto, to be published in the English,
French, German, Italian, Flemish and Danish languages.

BOURGEOIS AND PROLETARIANS

The history of all hitherto existing society is the history of class struggles. 7

Freeman and slave, patrician and plebeian, lord and serf, guildmaster and 8
journeyman, in a word, oppressor and oppressed, stood in constant opposition
to one another, carried on an uninterrupted, now hidden, now open fight, a
fight that each time ended, either in a revolutionary re-constitution of society
at large, or in the common ruin of the contending classes . . . .

The modern bourgeois society that has sprouted from the ruins of feudal 9
society, has not done away with class antagonisms. It has but established new
classes, new conditions of oppression, new forms of struggle in place of the
old ones.

Our epoch, the epoch of the bourgeoisie, possesses, however, this distinc- 10
tive feature; it has simplified the class antagonisms. Society as a whole is more
and more splitting up into two great hostile camps, into two great classes directly
facing each other: Bourgeoisie and Proletariat . . . .

The bourgeoisie, wherever it has got the upper hand, has put an end to all 11
feudal, patriarchal, idyllic relations. It has pitilessly torn asunder the motley
feudal ties that bound man to his "natural superiors," and has left remaining
no other nexus between man and man than naked self-interest, than callous
"cash payment." It has drowned the most heavenly ecstasies of religious fervor,
of chivalrous enthusiasm, of philistine sentimentalism, in the icy water of
egotistical calculation. It has resolved personal worth into exchange value, and
in place of the numberless indefeasible chartered freedoms, has set up that
single, unconscionable freedom—Free Trade. In one word, for exploitation,
veiled by religious and political illusions, it has substituted naked, shameless,
direct, brutal exploitation.

The bourgeoisie has stripped of its halo every occupation hitherto honored 12
and looked up to with reverent awe. It has converted the physician, the lawyer,
the priest, the poet, the man of science, into its paid wage-laborers.

The bourgeoisie has torn away from the family its sentimental veil, and 13
has reduced the family relation to a mere money relation . . . .

The weapons with which the bourgeoisie felled feudalism to the ground 14
are now turned against the bourgeoisie itself . . . .

The essential condition for the existence, and for the sway of the bourgeois 15
class, is the formation and augmentation of capital; the condition for capital is

wage-labor. Wage-labor rests exclusively on competition between the laborers. The advance of industry, whose involuntary promoter is the bourgeoisie, re-places the isolation of the laborers, due to competition, by their revolutionary combination, due to association. The development of Modern Industry, there-fore, cuts from under its feet the very foundation on which the bourgeoisie therefore produces, and appropriates products. What the bourgeoisie therefore produces, above all, are its own grave-diggers. Its fall and the victory of the proletariat are equally inevitable.

WHAT IS "A FAIR DISTRIBUTION"?

Do not the bourgeois assert that the present-day distribution is "fair"? And is it 16
not, in fact, the only "fair" distribution on the basis of the present-day mode of production? . . .

   What we have to deal with here is a communist society, not as it has 17
developed on its own foundations, but, on the contrary, just as it *emerges* from capitalist society, which is thus in every respect, economically, morally, and intellectually, still stamped with the birthmarks of the old society from whose womb it emerges. Accordingly, the individual producer receives back from society—after the deductions have been made—exactly what he gives to it. What he has given to it is his individual quantum of labor. For example, the social working day consists of the sum of the individual hours of work; the individual labor time of the individual producer is the part of the social working day contributed by him, his share in it. He receives a certificate from society that he has furnished such and such an amount of labor (after deducting his labor for the common funds), and with this certificate he draws from the social stock of means of consumption as much as costs the same amount of labor. The same amount of labor which he has given to society in one form he receives back in another.

   Here obviously the same principle prevails as that which regulates the 18
exchange of commodities, as far as this is exchange of equal values. Content and form are changed because under the altered circumstances no one can give anything except his labor, and because, on the other hand, nothing can pass to the ownership of individuals except individual means of consumption. But, as far as the distribution of the latter among the individual producers is concerned, the same principle prevails as in the exchange of commodity equivalents: a given amount of labor in one form is exchanged for an equal amount of labor in another form.

   Hence *equal right* here is still in principle—*bourgeois right*, although 19
principle and practice are no longer at loggerheads, while the exchange of equivalents in commodity exchange exists only *on the average* and not in the individual case.

   In spite of this advance this *equal right* is still constantly stigmatized by a 20
bourgeois limitation. The right of the producers is *proportional* to the labor they supply; the equality consists in the fact that measurement is made with an *equal standard*, labor.

But one man is superior to another physically or mentally, and so supplies   21
more labor in the same time, or can labor for a longer time; and labor, to serve
as a measure, must be defined by its duration or intensity; otherwise, it ceases
to be a standard of measurement. This *equal* right is an unequal right for
unequal labor. It recognizes no class differences because everyone is only a
worker like everyone else, but it tacitly recognizes unequal individual endowment and thus productive capacity as natural privileges. *It is, therefore, a right
of inequality, in its content, like every right.* Right by its very nature can consist
only in the application of an equal standard; but unequal individuals (and they
would not be different individuals if these were not unequal) are measurable
only by an equal point of view, are taken from one *definite* side only, for
instance, in the present case, are regarded *only as workers*, and nothing more is
seen in them, everything else being ignored. Further, one worker is married,
another not; one has more children than another, and so on and so forth. Thus,
with an equal performance of labor, and hence an equal share in the social
consumption fund, one will in fact receive more than another, one will be
richer than another, and so on. To avoid all these defects, right instead of being
equal would have to be unequal.

But these defects are inevitable in the first phase of communist society as   22
it is when it has just emerged after prolonged birth pangs from capitalist society.
Right can never be higher than the economic structure of society and the
cultural development conditioned by it.

In a higher phase of communist society, after the enslaving subordination   23
of the individual to the division of labor, and therewith also the antithesis
between mental and physical labor, has vanished; after labor has become not
only a means of life but life's prime want; after the productive forces have also
increased with the all-round development of the individual, and all the springs
of cooperative wealth flow more abundantly—only then can the narrow horizon
of bourgeois right be crossed in its entirety and society inscribe on its banners:
"From each according to his ability, to each according to his needs!"

⊠ ADAM SMITH

Benefits of the Profit Motive

*Wealth of Nations by Adam Smith (1723–1790), is often referred to as the bible
of capitalism. In the following excerpt, he discusses the value of the division of
labor and the advantages of the capitalist system. Compare his ideas with those
of Karl Marx.*

The greatest improvement in the productive powers of labor, and the greater 1
part of the skill, dexterity, and judgment with which it is anywhere directed, or
applied, seem to have been the effects of the division of labor . . . .

To take an example, therefore, from a very trifling manufacture; but one 2
in which the division of labor has been very often taken notice of, the trade of
the pin-maker; a workman not educated to this business (which the division of
labor has rendered a distinct trade), nor acquainted with the use of the machinery employed in it (to the invention of which the same division of labor has
probably given occasion), could scarce, perhaps, with his utmost industry, make
one pin a day, and certainly could not make twenty. But in the way in which
this business is now carried on, not only the whole work is a peculiar trade, but
it is divided into a number of branches, of which the greater part are likewise
peculiar trades. One man draws out the wire, another straights it, a third cuts
it, a fourth points it, a fifth grinds it at the top for receiving the head; to make
the head requires two or three distinct operations; to put it on is a peculiar
business, to whiten the pins is another; it is even a trade by itself to put them
into the paper; and the important business of making a pin is, in this manner,
divided into about eighteen distinct operations, which, in some manufactories,
are all performed by distinct hands, though in others the same man will sometimes perform two or three of them. I have seen a small manufactory of this
kind where ten men only were employed, and where some of them consequently performed two or three distinct operations. But though they were very
poor, and therefore but indifferently accommodated with the necessary machinery, they could, when they exerted themselves, make among them about twelve
pounds of pins in a day. There are in a pound upwards of four thousand pins of
a middling size. Those ten persons, therefore, could make among them upwards of forty-eight thousands pins in a day. Each person, therefore, making a
tenth part of forty-eight thousand pins, might be considered as making four
thousand eight hundred pins in a day. But if they had all wrought separately
and independently, and without any of them having been educated to this
peculiar business, they certainly could not each of them have made twenty,
perhaps not one pin in a day; that is, certainly, not the two hundred and fortieth,
perhaps not the four thousand eight hundredth part, of what they are at present
capable of performing in consequence of a proper division and combination of
their different operations.

In every other art and manufacture, the effects of the division of labor are 3
similar to what they are in this very trifling one; though in many of them, the
labor can neither be so much subdivided, nor reduced to so great a simplicity
of operation. The division of labor, however, so far as it can be introduced,
occasions, in every art, a proportionable increase of the productive powers of
labor . . . .

This great increase of the quantity of work, which, in consequence of the 4
division of labor, the same number of people are capable of performing, is
owing to three different circumstances: first, to the increase of dexterity in every
particular workman; secondly, to the saving of the time which is commonly lost

in passing from one species of work to another; and lastly, to the invention of a great number of machines which facilitate and abridge labor, and enable one man to do the work of many.

First, the improvement of the dexterity of the workman necessarily in- 5 creases the quantity of the work he can perform; and the division of labor, by reducing every man's business to some one simple operation and by making this operation the sole employment of his life, necessarily increases very much the dexterity of the workman. A common smith, who, though accustomed to handle the hammer, has never been used to make nails, if upon some particular occasion he is obliged to attempt it, will scarce, I am assured, be able to make about two or three hundred nails in a day, and those too very bad ones. A smith who has been accustomed to make nails, but whose sole or principal business has not been that of a nailer, can seldom with his utmost diligence make more than eight hundred or a thousand nails in a day. I have seen several boys under twenty years of age who had never exercised any other trade but that of making nails, and who, when they exerted themselves, could make, each of them, upwards of two thousand three hundred nails in a day. The making of a nail, however, is by no means one of the simplest operations. The same person blows the bellows, stirs or mends the fire as there is occasion, heats the iron, and forges every part of the nail: In forging the head too he is obliged to change his tools. The different operations into which the making of a pin or of a metal button is subdivided, are all of them much more simple; and the dexterity of the person, of whose life it has been the sole business to perform them, is usually much greater. The rapidity with which some of the operations of those manufactures are performed exceeds what the human hand could, by those who had never seen them, be supposed capable of acquiring.

Secondly, the advantage which is gained by saving the time commonly 6 lost in passing from one sort of work to another is much greater than we should at first view be apt to imagine it. It is impossible to pass very quickly from one kind of work to another, that is carried on in a different place, and with quite different tools. A country weaver who cultivates a small farm must lose a good deal of time in passing from his loom to the field, and from the field to his loom. When the two trades can be carried on in the same workhouse, the loss of time is no doubt much less. It is even in this case, however, very consider-able . . . .

Thirdly, and lastly, every body must be sensible how much labor is facili- 7 tated and abridged by the application of proper machinery . . . .

. . . A great part of the machines made use of in those manufactures in 8 which labor is most subdivided were originally the inventions of common workmen, who, being each of them employed in some very simple operation, naturally turned their thoughts toward finding out easier and readier methods of performing it. Whoever has been much accustomed to visit such manufac-turers must frequently have been shown very pretty machines which were the inventions of such workmen in order to facilitate and quicken their own partic-ular part of the work. In the first fire-engines, a boy was constantly employed to open and shut alternately the communication between the boiler and the cylinder, according as the piston either ascended or descended. One of those boys, who loved to play with his companions, observed that, by tying a string from the handle of the valve which opened this communication to another part of the machine, the valve would open and shut without his assistance, and leave him at liberty to divert himself with his play-fellows. One of the greatest improvements that has been made upon this machine, since it was first invented, was in this manner the discovery of a boy who wanted to save his own labor . . . .

It is the great multiplication of the productions of all the different arts, in consequence of the division of labor, which occasions, in a well-governed society, that universal opulence which extends itself to the lowest ranks of people. Every workman has a great quantity of his own work to dispose of beyond what he himself has occasion for; and every other workman being exactly in the same situation, he is enabled to exchange a great quantity of his own goods for a great quantity, or, what comes to the same thing, for the price of a great quantity of theirs. He supplies them abundantly with what they have occasion for, and they accommodate him as amply with what he has occasion for, and a general plenty diffuses itself through all the different ranks of the society . . . .

This division of labor, from which so many advantages are derived, is not originally the effect of any human wisdom which foresees and intends that general opulence to which it gives occasion. It is the necessary, though very slow and gradual, consequence of a certain propensity in human nature which has in view no such extensive utility: the propensity to truck, barter, and exchange one thing for another.

. . . In almost every other race of animals each individual, when it is grown up to maturity, is entirely independent, and in its natural state has occasion for the assistance of no other living creature. But man has almost constant occasion for the help of his brethren, and it is in vain for him to expect it from their benevolence only. He will be more likely to prevail if he can interest their self-love in his favor, and show them that it is for their own advantage to do for him what he requires of them. Whoever offers to another a bargain of any kind, proposes to do this. Give me that which I want, and you shall have this which you want, is the meaning of every such offer; and it is in this manner that we obtain from one another the far greater part of those good offices which we stand in need of. It is not from the benevolence of the butcher, the brewer, or the baker, that we expect our dinner, but from their regard to their own interest. We address ourselves, not to their humanity but to their self-love, and never talk to them of our own necessities but of their advantages. Nobody but a beggar chooses to depend chiefly upon the benevolence of his fellow-citizens. Even a beggar does not depend on it entirely. The charity of well-disposed people, indeed, supplies him with the whole fund of his subsistence. But though this principle ultimately provides him with all the necessaries of life which he has occasion for, it neither does nor can provide him with them as he has occasion for them. The greater part of his occasional wants are supplied in the same manner as those of other people, by treaty, by barter, and by purchase. With the money which one man gives him he purchases food. The old clothes which another bestows upon him he exchanges for other old clothes which suit him better, or for lodging, or for food, or for money, with which he can buy either food, clothes, or lodging, as he has occasion.

As it is by treaty, by barter, and by purchase that we obtain from one 12 another the greater part of those mutual good offices which we stand in need of, so it is this same trucking disposition which originally gives occasion to the division of labor. In a tribe of hunters or shepherds a particular person makes bows and arrows, for example, with more readiness and dexterity than any other. He frequently exchanges them for cattle or for venison with his companions; and he finds at last that he can in this manner get more cattle and venison than if he himself went to the field to catch them. From a regard to his own interest, therefore, the making of bows and arrows grows to be his chief business, and he becomes a sort of armorer. Another excels in making the frames and covers of their little huts or movable houses. He is accustomed to be of use in this way to his neighbors, who reward him in the same manner with cattle and with venison till at last he finds it his interest to dedicate himself entirely to this employment, and to become a sort of house carpenter. In the same manner a third becomes a smith or a brazier; a fourth a tanner or dresser of hides or skins, the principal part of the clothing of savages. And thus the certainty of being able to exchange all that surplus part of the produce of his own labor, which is over and above his own consumption, for such parts of the produce of other men's labor as he may have occasion for, encourages every man to apply himself to a particular occupation, and to cultivate and bring to perfection whatever talent or genius he may possess for that particular species of business.

The difference of natural talents in different men is, in reality, much less 13 than we are aware of; and the very different genius which appears to distinguish men of different professions, when grown up to maturity, is not upon many occasions so much the cause as the effect of the division of labor. The difference between the most dissimilar characters, between a philosopher and a common street porter, for example, seems to arise not so much from nature as from habit, custom, and education. When they came into the world, and for the first six or eight years of their existence, they were, perhaps, very much alike, and neither their parents nor play-fellows could perceive any remarkable difference. About that age, or soon after, they come to be employed in very different occupations. The difference of talents comes then to be taken notice of, and widens by degrees, till at last the vanity of the philosopher is willing to acknowledge scarce any resemblance. But without the disposition to truck, barter, and exchange, every man must have procured to himself every necessary and conveniency of life which he wanted. All must have had the same duties to perform, and the same work to do, and there could have been no such difference of employment as could alone give occasion to any great difference of talents . . . .

Every individual is continually exerting himself to find out the most ad- 14 vantageous employment for whatever capital he can command. It is his own advantage, indeed, and not that of the society, which he has in view. But the study of his own advantage, naturally, or rather necessarily, leads him to prefer that employment which is most advantageous to the society . . . .

As every individual, therefore, endeavors as much as he can both to em- 15 ploy his capital in the support of domestic industry, and so to direct that industry that its produce may be of the greatest value, every individual necessarily labors to render the annual revenue of the society as great as he can. He generally, indeed, neither intends to promote the public interest, nor knows how much he is promoting it. By preferring the support of domestic to that of foreign industry, he intends only his own security: and by directing that industry in such a manner as its produce may be of the greatest value, he intends only his own gain, and he is in this, as in many other cases, led by an invisible hand to promote an end which was no part of his intention. Nor is it always the worse for the society that it was no part of it. By pursuing his own interest he frequently promotes that of the society more effectually than when he really intends to promote it. I have never known much good done by those who affected to trade for the public good. It is an affectation, indeed, not very common among merchants, and very few words need be employed in dissuading them from it . . . .

If we examine, I say, all those things . . . we shall be sensible that without 16 the assistance and cooperation of many thousands, the very meanest person in a civilized country could not be provided, even according to what we very falsely imagine, the easy and simple manner in which he is commonly accommodated. Compared indeed with the more extravagant luxury of the great, his accommodation must no doubt appear extremely simple and easy; and yet it may be true, perhaps, that the accommodation of a European prince does not always so much exceed that of an industrious and frugal peasant, as the accommodation of the latter exceeds that of many an African king, the absolute master of the lives and liberties of ten thousand naked savages.

※ **ADOLF HITLER**

Nation and Race

Adolf Hitler (1889–1945), the infamous Austrian-born leader of Nazi Germany who plunged Europe into World War II and came close to conquering all of Europe, held and acted on very strong views concerning the superiority of the "Aryan" or "Nordic" race and the inferiority of untermenschen *such as Russians, Jews, and Gypsies. The following passage, taken from the chapter titled "Nation and Race" in Hitler's* Mein Kampf *(written in prison in the early 1920s), provides the gist of his views concerning the "unnaturalness" of the mating of "higher" and "lower" races, the superiority of the Aryan race, its right to dominate, and so on.*

There are some truths which are so obvious that for this very reason they are   1
not seen or at least not recognized by ordinary people. They sometimes pass by
such truisms as though blind and are most astonished when someone suddenly
discovers what everyone really ought to know. Columbus's eggs lie around by
the hundreds of thousands, but Columbuses are met with less frequently.

Thus men without exception wander about in the garden of Nature; they   2
imagine that they know practically everything and yet with few exceptions pass
blindly by one of the most patent principles of Nature's rule: the inner segregation of the species of all living beings on this earth.

Even the most superficial observation shows that Nature's restricted form   3
of propagation and increase is an almost rigid basic law of all the innumerable
forms of expression of her vital urge. Every animal mates only with a member
of the same species. The titmouse seeks the titmouse, the finch the finch, the
stork the stork, the field mouse the field mouse, the dormouse the dormouse,
the wolf the she-wolf, etc . . . .

Any crossing of two beings not at exactly the same level produces a me-   4
dium between the level of the two parents. This means: the offspring will
probably stand higher than the racially lower parent, but not as high as the
higher one. Consequently, it will later succumb in the struggle against the
higher level. Such mating is contrary to the will of Nature for a higher breeding
of all life. The precondition for this does not lie in associating superior and
inferior, but in the total victory of the former. The stronger must dominate and
not blend with the weaker, thus sacrificing his own greatness. Only the born
weakling can view this as cruel, but he after all is only a weak and limited man;
for if this law did not prevail, any conceivable higher development of organic
living beings would be unthinkable.

The consequence of this urge toward racial purity, universally valid in   5
Nature, is not only the sharp outward delimitation of the various races, but
their uniform character in themselves. The fox is always a fox, the goose a

goose, the tiger a tiger, etc., and the difference can lie at most in the varying measure of force, strength, intelligence, dexterity, endurance, etc., of the individual specimens. But you will never find a fox who in his inner attitude might, for example, show humanitarian tendencies toward geese, as similarly there is no cat with a friendly inclination toward mice.

Therefore, here, too, the struggle among themselves arises less from inner 6 aversion than from hunger and love. In both cases, Nature looks on calmly, with satisfaction, in fact. In the struggle for daily bread all those who are weak and sickly or less determined succumb, while the struggle of the males for the female grants the right or opportunity to propagate only to the healthiest. And struggle is always a means for improving a species' health and power of resistance and, therefore, a cause of its higher development.

If the process were different, all further and higher development would 7 cease and the opposite would occur. For, since the inferior always predominates numerically over the best, if both had the same possiblity of preserving life and propagating, the inferior would multiply so much more rapidly that in the end the best would inevitably be driven into the background, unless a correction of this state of affairs were undertaken. Nature does just this by subjecting the weaker part to such severe living conditions that by them alone the number is limited, and by not permitting the remainder to increase promiscuously, but making a new and ruthless choice according to strength and health.

No more than Nature desires the mating of weaker with stronger individ- 8 uals, even less does she desire the blending of a higher with a lower race, since, if she did, her whole work of higher breeding, over perhaps hundreds of thousands of years, might be ruined with one blow.

Historical experience offers countless proofs of this. It shows with terrifying 9 clarity that in every mingling of Aryan blood with that of lower peoples the result was the end of the cultured people. North America, whose population consists in by far the largest part of Germanic elements who mixed but little with the lower colored peoples, shows a different humanity and culture from Central and South America, where the predominantly Latin immigrants often mixed with the aborigines on a large scale. By this one example, we can clearly and distinctly recognize the effect of racial mixture. The Germanic inhabitant of the American continent, who has remained racially pure and unmixed, rose to be master of the continent; he will remain the master as long as he does not fall a victim to defilement of the blood.

The result of all racial crossing is therefore in brief always the following: 10
(a) Lowering of the level of the higher race;   11
(b) Physical and intellectual regression and hence the beginning of a slowly 12 but surely progressing sickness.

To bring about such a development is, then, nothing else but to sin against 13 the will of the eternal creator.

And as a sin this act is rewarded.   14

When man attempts to rebel against the iron logic of Nature, he comes 15 into struggle with the principles to which he himself owes his existence as a man. And so his action against Nature must lead to his own doom . . . .

Everything we admire on this earth today—science and art, technology 16 and inventions—is only the creative product of a few peoples and originally perhaps of *one* race. On them depends the existence of this whole culture. If they perish, the beauty of this earth will sink into the grave with them.

However much the soil, for example, can influence men, the result of the 17 influence will always be different depending on the races in question. The low fertility of a living space may spur the one race to the highest achievements; in others it will only be the cause of bitterest poverty and final undernourishment with all its consequences. The inner nature of peoples is always determining for the manner in which outward influences will be effective. What leads the one to starvation trains the other to hard work.

All great cultures of the past perished only because the originally creative 18 race died out from blood poisoning.

The ultimate cause of such a decline was their forgetting that all culture 19 depends on men and not conversely; hence that to preserve a certain culture the man who creates it must be preserved. This preservation is bound up with the rigid law of necessity and the right to victory of the best and stronger . . . .

Those who want to live, let them fight, and those who do not want to fight 20 in this world of eternal struggle do not deserve to live.

Even if this were hard—that is how it is! Assuredly, however, by far the 21 harder fate is that which strikes the man who thinks he can overcome Nature, but in the last analysis only mocks her. Distress, misfortune, and diseases are her answer.

The man who misjudges and disregards the racial laws actually forfeits the 22 happiness that seems destined to be his. He thwarts the triumphal march of the best race and hence also the precondition for all human progress, and remains, in consequence, burdened with all the sensibility of man, in the animal realm of helpless misery . . . .

It is idle to argue which race or races were the original representative of 23 human culture and hence the real founders of all that we sum up under the word "humanity." It is simpler to raise this question with regard to the present, and here an easy, clear answer results. All the human culture, all the results of art, science, and technology that we see before us today, are almost exclusively the creative product of the Aryan. This very fact admits of the not unfounded inference that he alone was the founder of all higher humanity, therefore representing the prototype of all that we understand by the word "man." He is the Prometheus of mankind from whose bright forehead the divine spark of genius has sprung at all times, forever kindling anew that fire of knowledge which illumined the night of silent mysteries and thus caused man to climb the path to mastery over the other beings of this earth. Exclude him—and perhaps after a few thousand years darkness will again descend on the earth, human culture will pass, and the world turn to a desert . . . .

⊠ NICCOLÒ MACHIAVELLI

Concerning the Way in Which Princes Should Keep Faith

The Italian Niccolò Machiavelli (1469–1527) is perhaps the best-known writer on the topic of acquiring and wielding political power. (The term Machiavellian *is defined by one dictionary as ". . . characterized by the principles of expediency attributed to Machiavelli.") In this excerpt from his celebrated work,* The Prince, *Machiavelli explains why it is best for a ruler to lie under certain circumstances if he is to rule effectively.*

Every one admits how praiseworthy it is in a prince to keep faith, and to live   1
with integrity and not with craft. Nevertheless our experience has been that those princes who have done great things have held good faith of little account, and have known how to circumvent the intellect of men by craft, and in the end have overcome those who have relied on their word. You must know there are two ways of contesting, the one by the law, the other by force; the first method is proper to men, the second to beasts; but because the first is frequently not sufficient, it is necessary to have recourse to the second. Therefore it is necessary for a prince to understand how to avail himself of the beast and the man. This has been figuratively taught to princes by ancient writers, who describe how Achilles and many other princes of old were given to the centaur Chiron to nurse, who brought them up in his discipline; which means solely that, as they had for a teacher one who was half beast and half man, so it is necessary for a prince to know how to make use of both natures, and that one without the other is not durable. A prince, therefore, being compelled knowingly to adopt the beast, ought to choose the fox and the lion; because the lion cannot defend himself against snares and the fox cannot defend himself against wolves. Therefore, it is necessary to be a fox to discover the snares and a lion to terrify the wolves. Those who rely simply on the lion do not understand what they are about. Therefore a wise lord cannot, nor ought he to, keep faith when such observance may be turned against him, and when the reasons that caused him to pledge it exist no longer. If men were entirely good this precept would not hold, but because they are bad, and will not keep faith with you, you too are not bound to observe it with them. Nor will there ever be wanting to a prince legitimate reasons to excuse this non-observance. Of this endless modern examples could be given, showing how many treaties and engagements have been made void and of no effect through the faithlessness of princes; and he who has known best how to employ the fox has succeeded best.

But it is necessary to know well how to disguise this characteristic, and to   2
be a great pretender and dissembler; and men are so simple, and so subject to
present necessities, that he who seeks to deceive will always find someone who
will allow himself to be deceived. One recent example I cannot pass over in
silence. Alexander the Sixth did nothing else but deceive men, nor ever thought
of doing otherwise, and he always found victims; for there never was a man
who had greater power in asserting, or who with greater oaths would affirm a
thing, yet would observe it less; nevertheless his deceits always succeeded according to his wishes, because he well understood this side of mankind.

Therefore it is unnecessary for a prince to have all the good qualities I   3
have enumerated, but it is very necessary to appear to have them. And I shall
dare to say this also, that to have them and always to observe them is injurious,
and that to appear to have them is useful; to appear merciful, faithful, humane,
religious, upright, and to be so, but with a mind so framed that should you
require not to be so, you may be able and know how to change to the opposite.

And you have to understand this, that a prince, especially a new one,   4
cannot observe all those things for which men are esteemed, being often forced,
in order to maintain the state, to act contrary to fidelity, friendship, humanity,
and religion. Therefore it is necessary for him to have a mind ready to run itself
accordingly as the winds and variations of fortune force it, yet, as I have said
above, not to diverge from the good if he can avoid doing so, but, if compelled,
then to know how to set about it.

For this reason a prince ought to take care that he never lets anything slip   5
from his lips that is not replete with the above-named five qualities, that he
may appear to him who sees and hears him altogether merciful, faithful, humane, upright, and religious. There is nothing more necessary to appear to
have than this last quality, inasmuch as men judge generally more by the eye
than by the hand, because it belongs to everybody to see you, to few to come
in touch with you. Every one sees what you appear to be, few really know what
you are, and those few dare not oppose themselves to the opinion of the many,
who have the majesty of the state to defend them; and in the actions of all men,
and especially of princes, which it is not prudent to challenge, one judges by
the result.

For that reason, let a prince have the credit of conquering and holding his   6
state, the means will always be considered honest, and he will be praised by
everybody; because the vulgar are always taken by what a thing seems to be and
by what comes of it; and in the world there are only the vulgar, for the few find
a place there only when the many have no ground to rest on.

One prince [Ferdinand of Aragon] of the present time, whom it is not well   7
to name, never preaches anything else but peace and good faith, and to both
he is most hostile, and either, if he had kept it, would have deprived him of
reputation and kingdom many a time.

⊠ SIGMUND FREUD

Consciousness and What Is Unconscious

Sigmund Freud (1856–1939), probably the most important figure in modern psychology, will be remembered for dozens of insightful ideas, but perhaps the most important and enduring will turn out to be his theory of unconsciously motivated behavior. In the following excerpt from Chapter 1 of The Ego and the Id, *he explains how the "division into what is conscious and what is unconscious is the fundamental premise of psychoanalysis."*

. . . The division of the psychical into what is conscious and what is uncon-   1
scious is the fundamental premiss of psycho-analysis; and it alone makes it possible for psycho-analysis to understand the pathological processes in mental life, which are as common as they are important, and to find a place for them in the framework of science. To put it once more, in a different way: psycho-analysis cannot situate the essence of the psychical in consciousness, but is obliged to regard consciousness as a quality of the psychical, which may be present in addition to other qualities or may be absent.

If I could suppose that everyone interested in psychology would read this   2
book, I should also be prepared to find that at this point some of my readers would already stop short and would go no further; for here we have the first shibboleth of psycho-analysis. To most people who have been educated in philosophy the idea of anything psychical which is not also conscious is so inconceivable that it seems to them absurd and refutable simply by logic. I believe this is only because they have never studied the relevant phenomena of hypnosis and dreams, which—quite apart from pathological manifestations— necessitate this view. Their psychology of consciousness is incapable of solving the problems of dreams and hypnosis.

"Being conscious" is in the first place a purely descriptive term, resting on   3
perception of the most immediate and certain character. Experience goes on to show that a psychical element (for instance, an idea) is not as a rule conscious for a protracted length of time. On the contrary, a state of consciousness is characteristically very transitory; an idea that is conscious now is no longer so a moment later, although it can become so again under certain conditions that are easily brought about. In the interval the idea was—we do not know what. We can say that it was *latent*, and by this we mean that it was *capable of becoming conscious* at any time. Or, if we say that is was *unconscious*, we shall also be giving a correct description of it. Here "unconscious" coincides with "latent and capable of becoming conscious." The philosophers would no doubt object: "No, the term unconscious is not applicable here; so long as the idea was in a state of latency it was not anything psychical at all." To contradict them at this point would lead to nothing more profitable than a verbal dispute.

But we have arrived at the term or concept of the unconscious along   4
another path, by considering certain experiences in which mental *dynamics*
play a part. We have found—that is, we have been obliged to assume—that
very powerful mental processes or ideas exist (and here a quantitative or *economic* factor comes into question for the first time) which can produce all the
effects in mental life that ordinary ideas do (including effects that can in their
turn become conscious as ideas), though they themselves do not become conscious. It is unnecessary to repeat in detail here what has been explained so
often before. It is enough to say that at this point psycho-analytic theory steps
in and asserts that the reason why such ideas cannot become conscious is that
a certain force opposes them, that otherwise they could become conscious, and
that it would then be apparent how little they differ from other elements which
are admittedly psychical. The fact that in the technique of psycho-analysis a
means has been found by which the opposing force can be removed and the
ideas in question made conscious renders this theory irrefutable. The state in
which the ideas existed before being made conscious is called by us *repression*,
and we assert that the force which instituted the repression and maintains it is
perceived as *resistance* during the work of analysis.

Thus we obtain our concept of the unconscious from the theory of repres-   5
sion. The repressed is the prototype of the unconscious for us. We see, however,
that we have two kinds of unconscious—the one which is latent but capable of
becoming conscious, and the one which is repressed and which is not, in itself
and without more ado, capable of becoming conscious. This piece of insight
into psychical dynamics cannot fail to affect terminology and description. The
latent, which is unconscious only descriptively, not in the dynamic sense, we
call *preconscious*; we restrict the term *unconscious* to the dynamically unconscious repressed; so that now we have three terms, conscious (Cs.), preconscious
(Pcs.), and unconscious (Ucs.), whose sense is no longer purely descriptive.
The *Pcs.* is presumably a great deal closer to the *Cs.* than is the *Ucs.*, and since
we have called the *Ucs.* psychical we shall with even less hesitation call the
latent *Pcs.* psychical. But why do we not rather, instead of this, remain in
agreement with the philosophers and, in a consistent way, distinguish the *Pcs.*
as well as the *Ucs.* from the conscious psychical? The philosophers would then
propose that the *Pcs.* and the *Ucs.* should be described as two species or stages
of the "psychoid" and harmony would be established. But endless difficulties
in exposition would follow; and the one important fact, that these two kinds of
"psychoid" coincide in almost every other respect with what is admittedly psychical, would be forced into the background in the interests of a prejudice dating
from a period in which these psychoids, or the most important part of them,
were still unknown.

We can now play about comfortably with our three terms, *Cs.*, *Pcs.*, and   6
Ucs., so long as we do not forget that in the descriptive sense there are two
kinds of unconscious, but in the dynamic sense only one. For purposes of
exposition this distinction can in some cases be ignored, but in others it is of
course indispensable. At the same time, we have become more or less accus-

tomed to this ambiguity of the unconscious and have managed pretty well with it. As far as I can see, it is impossible to avoid this ambiguity; the distinction between conscious and unconscious is in the last resort a question of perception, which must be answered "yes" or "no" and the act of perception itself tells us nothing of the reason why a thing is or is not perceived. No one has a right to complain because the actual phenomenon expresses the dynamic factor ambiguously. . . .

In the further course of psycho-analytic work, however, even these distinc- 7 tions have proved to be inadequate and, for practical purposes, insufficient. This has become clear in more ways than one; but the decisive instance is as follows. We have formed the idea that in each individual there is a coherent organization of mental processes; and we call this his *ego*. It is to this ego that consciousness is attached; the ego controls the approaches to motility—that is, to the discharge of excitations into the external world; it is the mental agency which supervises all its own constituent processes, and which goes to sleep at night, though even then it exercises the censorship on dreams. From this ego proceed the repressions, too, by means of which it is sought to exclude certain trends in the mind not merely from consciousness but also from other forms of effectiveness and activity. In analysis these trends which have been shut out stand in opposition to the ego, and the analysis is faced with the task of removing the resistances which the ego displays against concerning itself with the repressed. Now we find during analysis that, when we put certain tasks before the patient, he gets into difficulties; his associations fail when they should be coming near the repressed. We then tell him that he is dominated by a resistance; but he is quite unaware of the fact, and, even if he guesses from his unpleasurable feelings that a resistance is now at work in him, he does not know what it is or how to describe it. Since, however, there can be no question but that this resistance emanates from his ego and belongs to it, we find ourselves in an unforeseen situation. We have come upon something in the ego itself which is also unconscious, which behaves exactly like the repressed—that is, which produces powerful effects without itself being conscious and which requires special work before it can be made conscious. From the point of view of analytic practice, the consequence of this discovery is that we land in endless obscurities and difficulties if we keep to our habitual forms of expression and try, for instance, to derive neuroses from a conflict between the conscious and the unconscious. We shall have to substitute for this antithesis another, taken from our insight into the structural conditions of the mind—the antithesis between the coherent ego and the repressed which is split off from it.

For our conception of the unconscious, however, the consequences of our 8 discovery are even more important. Dynamic considerations caused us to make our first correction; our insight into the structure of the mind leads to the second. We recognize that the Ucs. does not coincide with the repressed; it is still true that all that is repressed is Ucs., but not all that is Ucs. is repressed. A part of the ego, too—and Heaven knows how important a part—may be Ucs., undoubtedly is Ucs. And this Ucs. belonging to the ego is not latent like the

Pcs.; for if it were, it could not be activated without becoming Cs., and the process of making it conscious would not encounter such great difficulties. When we find ourselves thus confronted by the necessity of postulating a third Ucs., which is not repressed, we must admit that the characteristic of being unconscious begins to lose significance for us. It becomes a quality which can have many meanings, a quality which we are unable to make, as we should have hoped to do, the basis of far-reaching and inevitable conclusions. Nevertheless we must beware of ignoring this characteristic, for the property of being conscious or not is in the last resort our one beacon-light in the darkness of depth-psychology.

⌇ WILLIAM JAMES

The Will to Believe

William James (1842–1910), brother of writer Henry James, is an important figure in early twentieth century psychology and philosophy. He is one of the founders of what is perhaps the only truly American philosophical movement, namely, pragmatism. In the following excerpt, he presents a rather novel argument for the rationality of belief in God in the absence of direct evidence one way or another. "Better risk loss of truth than chance of error" he says in rejecting the skeptic's position, and instead asks: "Dupery for dupery, what proof is there that dupery through hope [that there is a God] is so much worse than dupery through fear [of being wrong]?"

. . . I have brought with me tonight . . . a defense of our right to adopt a   1
believing attitude in religious matters, in spite of the fact that our merely logical intellect may not have been coerced . . . . The thesis I defend is, briefly stated, this: *Our passional nature not only lawfully may, but must, decide an option between propositions, whenever it is a genuine option that cannot by its nature be decided on intellectual grounds; for to say, under such circumstances, "Do not decide, but leave the question open," is itself a passional decision—just like deciding yes or no—and is attended with the same risk of losing the truth.*
    . . . [Religion] says that the best things are the more eternal things, the overlapping things, the things in the universe that throw the last stone, so to speak, and say the final word. "Perfection is eternal,"—this phrase of Charles Secrétan seems a good way of putting this first affirmation of religion, which obviously cannot yet be verified scientifically at all.

The second affirmation of religion is that we are better off even now if we 2
believe her first affirmation to be true.

Now, let us consider what the logical elements of this situation are *in case* 3
the religious hypothesis in both its branches be really true . . . . We see, first,
that religion offers itself as a *momentous* option. We are supposed to gain, even
now, by our belief, and to lose by our non-belief, a certain vital good. Secondly,
religion is a *forced* option, so far as that good goes. We cannot escape the issue
by remaining sceptical and waiting for more light, because, although we do
avoid error in that way *if religion be untrue*, we lose the good, *if it be true*, just
as certainly as if we positively chose to disbelieve . . . . Scepticism, then, is not
avoidance of option; it is option of a certain particular kind of risk. *Better risk
loss of truth than chance of error,*—that is your faith-vetoers exact position.
. . . To preach scepticism to us as a duty until "sufficient evidence" for religion
be found, is tantamount therefore to telling us, when in the presence of the
religious hypothesis, that to yield to our fear of its being error is wiser and better
than to yield to our hope that it may be true. It is not intellect against all
passions, then; it is only intellect with one passion laying down its law. And by
what, forsooth, is the supreme wisdom of this passion warranted? Dupery for
dupery, what proof is there that dupery through hope is so much worse than
dupery through fear? I, for one, can see no proof; and I simply refuse obedience
to the scientist's command to imitate his kind of option, in a case where my
own stake is important enough to give me the right to choose my own form of
risk. If religion be true and the evidence for it be still insufficient, I do not
wish, by putting your extinguisher upon my nature . . . to forfeit my sole
chance in life of getting upon the winning side,—that chance depending, of
course, on my willingness to run the risk of acting as if my passional need of
taking the world religiously might be prophetic and right . . . . One who should
shut himself up in snarling logicality and try to make the gods extort his
recognition willy-nilly, or not get it at all, might cut himself off forever from his
only opportunity of making the gods' acquaintance. This feeling, forced on us
we know not whence, that by obstinately believing that there are gods (although
not to do so would be so easy both for our logic and our life) we are doing the
universe the deepest service we can, seems part of the living essence of the
religious hypothesis. If the hypothesis *were* true in all its parts, including this
one, then pure intellectualism, with its veto on our making willing advances,
would be an absurdity; and some participation of our sympathetic nature would
be logically required. I, therefore, for one, cannot see my way to accepting the
agnostic rules for truth-seeking, or wilfully agree to keep my willing nature out
of the game. I cannot do so for this plain reason, that a *rule of thinking which
would absolutely prevent me from acknowledging certain kinds of truth if those
kinds of truth were really there, would be an irrational rule.* That for me is the
long and short of the formal logic of the situation, no matter what the kinds of
truth might materially be . . . . Let me end by a quotation from [Fitz-James]
Stephen. In all important transactions of life we have to take a leap in the dark.
. . . If we decide to leave the riddles unanswered, that is a choice; if we waver

in our answer, that, too, is a choice: but whatever choice we make, we make it at our peril. If a man chooses to turn his back altogether on God and the future, no one can prevent him; no one can show beyond reasonable doubt that he is mistaken. If a man thinks otherwise and acts as he thinks, I do not see that anyone can prove that *he* is mistaken. Each must act as he thinks best; and if he is wrong, so much the worse for him. We stand on a mountain pass in the midst of whirling snow and blinding mist, through which we get glimpses now and then of paths which may be deceptive. If we stand still we shall be frozen to death. If we take the wrong road we shall be dashed to pieces. We do not certainly know whether there is any right one. What must we do? "Be strong and of a good courage. Act for the best, hope for the best, and take what comes. . . . If death ends all, we cannot meet death better."

⊠ SØREN KIERKEGAARD

The Eternal Happiness Promised by Christianity

The Danish theologian Søren Kierkegaard (1813–1855) has had perhaps more influence on twentieth century Protestant theologians than any other modern writer. Here are excerpts from his Concluding Unscientific Postscript *in which he shouts the superiority of Christian belief over the faith of Socrates on the grounds that Socrates believed that which is not known, that which is objectively uncertain, while Kierkegaard believes that which is objectively absurd. "If I am capable of grasping God objectively, I do not believe, but precisely because I cannot do this I must believe."*

The objective problem consists of an inquiry into the truth of Christianity. The   1 subjective problem concerns the relationship of the individual to Christianity. To put it quite simply: How may I, Johannes Climacus [Kierkegaard], partici-pate in the happiness promised by Christianity? . . .

Everything being assumed in order with respect to the Scriptures—what   2 follows? Has anyone who previously did not have faith been brought a single step nearer to its acquisition? No, not a single step. Faith does not result simply from a scientific inquiry; it does not come directly at all. On the contrary, in this objectivity one tends to lose that infinite personal interestedness in passion which is the condition of faith, the *ubique et musquam* in which faith can come into being. Has anyone who previously had faith gained anything with respect to its strength and power? No, not in the least. Rather is it the case that in this voluminous knowledge, this certainty that lurks at the door of faith and threatens to devour it, he is in so dangerous a situation that he will need to put forth much effort in great fear and trembling, lest he fall a victim to the temptation to confuse knowledge with faith. While faith has hitherto had a profitable schoolmaster in the existing uncertainty, it would have in the new certainty its most dangerous enemy. For if passion is eliminated, faith no longer exists, and certainty and passion do not go together. Whoever believes that there is a God and an over-ruling providence finds it easier to preserve his faith, easier to acquire something that definitely is faith and not an illusion, in an imperfect world where passion is kept alive, than in an absolutely perfect world. In such a world faith is . . . unthinkable.

I assume now the opposite, that the opponents have succeeded in proving   3 what they desire about the Scriptures, with a certainty transcending the most ardent wish of the most passionate hostility—what then? Have the opponents thereby abolished Christianity? By no means. Has the believer been harmed? By no means, not in the least. Has the opponent made good a right to be relieved of responsibility for not being a believer? By no means. Because these books are not written by these authors, . . . are not inspired, it does not follow . . . that Christ has not existed. In so far, the believer is equally free to assume it . . . .

Here is the crux of the matter, and I come back to the case of the learned   4 theology. For whose sake is it that the proof is sought? Faith does not need it: aye, it must even regard the proof as its enemy. But when faith begins to feel embarrassed and ashamed, like a young woman for whom her love is no longer sufficient, but who secretly feels ashamed of her lover and must therefore have it established that there is something remarkable about him—when faith thus begins to lose its passion, when faith begins to cease to be faith, then proof becomes necessary so as to command respect from the side of unbelief . . . . Philosophy teaches that the way is to become objective, while Christianity teaches that the way is to become subjective, i.e., to become a subject in truth . . . Christianity wishes to intensify passion to its highest pitch; but passion is subjectivity, and does not exist objectively . . . .

The task of becoming subjective, then, may be presumed to be the highest   5 task, and one that is proposed to every human being; just as, correspondingly, the highest reward, an eternal happiness, exists only for those who are subjective; or rather, comes into being for the individual who becomes subjective.

When the question of truth is raised in an objective manner, reflection is   6 directed objectively to the truth, as an object to which the knower is related. Reflection is not focused upon the relationship, however, but upon the question of whether it is the truth to which the knower is related. If only the object to which he is related is the truth, the subject is accounted to be in the truth. When the question of the truth is raised subjectively, reflection is directed subjectively to the nature of the individual's relationship; if only the mode of this relationship is in the truth, the individual is in the truth even if he should happen to be thus related to what is not true. Let us take as an example the knowledge of God. Objectively, reflection is directed to the problem of whether this object is the true God; subjectively, reflection is directed to the question whether the individual is related to a something in such a manner that his relationship is in truth a God-relationship. . . . The existing individual who chooses to pursue the objective way enters upon the entire approximation-process by which it is proposed to bring God to light objectively. But this is in all eternity impossible, because God is a subject, and therefore exists only for subjectivity in inwardness. The objective accent falls on WHAT is said, the subjective accent on HOW it is said. This distinction holds even in the aesthetic realm, and receives definite expression in the principle that what is in itself true may in the mouth of such and such a person become untrue. . . . Objectively the interest is focused merely on the thought-content, subjectively on the inwardness. At its maximum this inward "how" is the passion of the infinite, and the passion of the infinite is the truth. But the passion of the infinite is precisely subjectivity, and thus subjectivity becomes the truth . . . . Only in subjectivity is there decisiveness, to seek factor and not its content, for its content is precisely itself. In this manner subjectivity and the subjective "how" constitute the truth . . . . Here is such a definition of truth: An objective uncertainty held fast in an appropriation-process of the most passionate inwardness is the truth, the highest truth attainable for an existing individual. . . .

But the above definition of truth is an equivalent expression for faith. 7 Without risk there is no faith. Faith is precisely the contradiction between the infinite passion of the individual's inwardness and the objective uncertainty. If I am capable of grasping God objectively, I do not believe, but precisely because I cannot do this I must believe . . . . Without risk there is no faith, and the greater the risk the greater the faith; the more objective security the less inwardness (for inwardness is precisely subjectivity), and the less objective security the more profound the possible inwardness. When the paradox is paradoxical in itself, it repels the individual by virtue of its absurdity, and the corresponding passion of the inwardness is faith.

When Socrates believed that there was a God, he held fast to the objective 8 uncertainty with the whole passion of his inwardness, and it is precisely in this contradiction and in this risk, that [his] faith is rooted. Now it is otherwise. Instead of the objective uncertainty, there is here a certainty, namely, that objectively it is absurd; and this absurdity, held fast in the passion of inwardness, is faith. The Socratic ignorance is as a witty jest in comparison with the earnestness of facing the absurd; and the Socratic existential inwardness is as Greek light-mindedness in comparison with the grave strenuosity of faith. The absurd is precisely by its objective repulsion the measure of the intensity of faith in inwardness. Suppose a man who wishes to acquire faith; let the comedy begin. He wishes to have faith, but he wishes also to safeguard himself by means of an objective inquiry and its approximation-process. What happens? With the help of the approximation-process the absurd becomes something different; it becomes probable, it becomes increasingly probable, it becomes extremely and emphatically probable. Now he is ready to believe it, and he ventures to claim for himself that he does not believe as shoemakers and tailors and simple folk believe, but only after long deliberation. Now he is ready to believe it; and lo, now it has become precisely impossible to believe it. Anything that is almost probable, or probable, or extremely and emphatically probable, is something he can almost know, or as good as know, or extremely and emphatically almost know—but it is impossible to believe . . . .

⊠ BERTRAND RUSSELL

The Scientific Outlook

The English philosopher Bertrand Russell (1872–1970) is perhaps the most cele-brated philosopher of the last century in the English-speaking world. He is the principal inventor of the modern predicate or quantifier logic that has replaced the much narrower Aristotelian syllogistic logic, and many would say he is the greatest logician since that ancient Greek. But his works have been influential in virtually every area of philosophy as well as in the social/political arena. In this essay against the view that evolution is evidence of a divine plan, Russell argues that there is no reason to suppose evolution points to a godlike purpose and counsels against "slothful relapses into infantile fantasies."

Evolution, when it was new, was regarded as hostile to religion, and is still so 1 considered by fundamentalists. But a whole school of apologists has grown up who see in evolution evidence of a Divine Plan slowly unfolding through the ages. . . . From a cosmic point of view, life is a very unimportant phenomenon: very few stars have planets; very few planets can support life. Life, even on the earth, belongs to only a very small proportion of the matter close to the earth's surface. During the greater part of the past existence of the earth, it was too hot to support life; during the greater part of its future existence, it will be too cold. It is by no means impossible that there is, at this moment, no life anywhere in the universe except on earth; but even if, taking a very liberal estimate, we suppose that there are scattered through space some hundred thousand other planets on which life exists, it must still be admitted that living matter makes rather a poor show if considered as the purpose of the whole creation. There are some old gentlemen who are fond of prosy anecdotes leading at last to a "point"; imagine an anecdote longer than any you have ever heard, and the "point" shorter, and you will have a fair picture of the activities of the Creator according to the biologists. Moreover, the "point" of the anecdote, even when it is reached, appears hardly worthy of so long a preface. I am willing to admit that there is merit in the tail of the fox, the song of the thrush, or the horns of the ibex. But it is not to these things that the evolutionary theologian points with pride: it is to the soul of man. Unfortunately, there is no impartial arbiter to decide on the merits of the human race; but for my part, when I consider their poison gases, their researches into bacteriological warfare, their meannesses, cruelties and oppressions, I find them, considered as the crowning gem of the creation, somewhat lacking in lustre.

Is there anything in the process of evolution that demands the hypothesis of a purpose? This is the crucial question. . . . I am . . . quite unable to see why an intelligent Creator should have the purpose which we must attribute to Him if He has really designed all that happens in the world of organic life. Nor does the progress of scientific investigation afford any evidence that the behaviour of living matter is governed by anything other than laws of physics and chemistry.

Or take again reproduction, which though not universal throughout the animal kingdom, is nevertheless one of its most interesting peculiarities. There is now nothing in this process that can rightly be called mysterious. I do not mean to say that it is all fully understood, but that mechanistic principles have explained enough of it to make it probable that, given time, they will explain the whole. . . .

One of the best statements of the point of view of a religiously minded biologist is to be found in Lloyd Morgan's *Emergent Evolution* (1923) and *Life, Mind and Spirit* (1926). Lloyd Morgan believes that there is a Divine Purpose underlying the course of evolution, more particularly of what he calls "emergent evolution." The definition of emergent evolution, if I understand it rightly, is as follows: it sometimes happens that a collection of objects arranged in a suitable pattern will have a new property which does not belong to the objects singly, and which cannot, so far as we can see, be deduced from their several properties together with the way in which they are arranged. He considers that there are examples of the same kind of thing even in the inorganic realm. The atom, the molecule, and the crystal will all have properties which, if I understand Lloyd Morgan aright, he regards as not deducible from the properties of their constituents. The same holds in a higher degree of living organisms, and most of all with those higher organisms which possess what are called minds. Our minds, he would say, are, it is true, associated with the physical organism, but are not deducible from the properties of that organism considered as an arrangement of atoms in space. "Emergent evolution," he says, "is from first to last a revelation and manifestation of that which I speak of as Divine Purpose." Again he says: "Some of us, and I for one, end with a concept of activity, under acknowledgment, as part and parcel of Divine Purpose." . . .

It would be easier to deal with this view if any reasons were advanced in its favour, but so far as I have been able to discover from Professor Lloyd

Morgan's pages he considers that the doctrine is its own recommendation and does not need to be demonstrated by appeals to the mere understanding. I do not pretend to know whether Professor Lloyd Morgan's opinion is false. For aught I know to the contrary, there may be a Being of infinite power who chooses that children should die of meningitis, and older people of cancer; these things occur, and occur as the result of evolution. If, therefore, evolution embodies a Divine Plan, these occurrences must also have been planned. I have been informed that suffering is sent as a purification for sin, but I find it difficult to think that a child of four or five years can be sunk in such black depths of iniquity as to deserve the punishment that befalls not a few of the children whom our optimistic divines might see any day, if they choose, suffering torments in children's hospitals. Again, I am told that though the child himself may not have sinned very deeply, he deserves to suffer on account of his parent's wickedness. I can only repeat that if this is the Divine sense of justice it differs from mine, and that I think mine superior. If indeed the world in which we live has been produced in accordance with a Plan, we shall have to reckon Nero a saint in comparison with the Author of that Plan. Fortunately, however, the evidence of Divine Purpose is non-existent; so at least one must infer from the fact that no evidence is adduced by those who believe in it. We are, therefore, spared the necessity for that attitude of impotent hatred which every brave and humane man would otherwise be called upon to adopt towards the Almighty Tyrant. . . .

We have reviewed . . . a number of different apologies for religion on the part of eminent men of science. We have seen that Eddington and Jeans contradict each other, and that both contradict the biological theologians, but all agree that in the last resort science should abdicate before what is called the religious consciousness. This attitude is regarded by themselves and by their admirers as more optimistic than that of the uncompromising rationalist. It is, in fact, quite the opposite: it is the outcome of discouragement and loss of faith. Time was when religion was believed with wholehearted fervour, when men went on crusades and burned each other at the stake because of the intensity of their convictions. After the wars of religion, theology gradually lost this intense hold on men's minds. So far as anything has taken its place, its place has been taken by science. In the name of science we revolutionize industry, undermine family morals, enslave coloured races, and skilfully exterminate each other with poison gases. Some men of science do not altogether like these uses to which science is being put. In terror and dismay they try to find refuge in the superstitions of an earlier day. 6

But it is not by going backward that we shall find an issue from our troubles. No slothful relapses into infantile fantasies will direct the new power which men have derived from science into the right channels; nor will philosophic scepticism as to the foundations arrest the course of scientific technique in the world of affairs. Men need a faith which is robust and real, not timid and halfhearted. Science is in its essence nothing but the systematic pursuit of knowledge, and knowledge, whatever ill-uses bad men may make of it, is in its 7 essence good. To lose faith in knowledge is to lose faith in the best of man's capacities; and therefore I repeat unhesitatingly that the unyielding rationalist has a better faith and a more unbending optimism than any of the timid seekers after the childish comforts of a less adult age.

⊠ **FRIEDRICH WILHELM NIETZSCHE**

Beyond Good and Evil

The nineteenth century German philosopher Friedrich Nietzsche (1844–1900) believed that the usual moral idea about not harming or exploiting others is "a Will to the denial of life," a "slave morality" almost the opposite of the "master morality" he advocated for a "select class of beings." This excerpt is from Beyond Good and Evil.

Every elevation of the type "man," has hitherto been the work of an aristocratic   1 society—and so will it always be—a society believing in a long scale of gradations of rank and differences of worth among human beings, and requiring slavery in some form or other. . . . Let us acknowledge unprejudicedly how every higher civilization hitherto has *originated*! Men with a still natural nature, barbarians in every terrible sense of the word, men of prey, still in possession of unbroken strength of will and desire for power, threw themselves upon weaker, more moral, more peaceful races. . . .

The essential thing, however, in a good and healthy aristocracy is that it   2 should *not* regard itself as a function either of the kingship or the commonwealth, but as the *significance* and highest justification thereof—that it should therefore accept with a good conscience the sacrifice of a legion of individuals, who, *for its sake*, must be suppressed and reduced to imperfect men, to slaves and instruments. . . .

To refrain mutually from injury, from violence, from exploitation, and put   3 one's will on a par with that of others: this may result in a certain rough sense in good conduct among individuals when the necessary conditions are given (namely, the actual similarity of the individuals in amount of force and degree of worth, and their co-relation within one organization). As soon, however, as one wished to take this principle more generally, and if possible even as *the fundamental principle of society*, it would immediately disclose what it really is—namely, a Will to the *denial* of life, a principle of dissolution and decay.

Here one must think profoundly to the very basis and resist all sentimental weakness: life itself is *essentially* appropriation, injury, conquest of the strange and weak, suppression, severity, obtrusion of peculiar forms, incorporation, and at the least, putting it mildest, exploitation . . . life *is* precisely Will to Power.

In a tour through the many finer and coarser moralities which have hith-   4 erto prevailed or still prevail on the earth, I found certain traits recurring regularly together, and connected with one another, until finally two primary types revealed themselves to me, and a radical distinction was brought to light. There is *master-morality* and *slave-morality*;—I would at once add, however, that in all higher and mixed civilizations, there are also attempts at the reconciliation of the two moralities; but one finds still oftener the confusion and mutual misunderstanding of them, indeed, sometimes their close juxtaposition—even in the same man, within one soul. The distinctions of moral values have either originated in a ruling caste, pleasantly conscious of being different from the ruled—or among the ruled class, the slaves and dependents of all sorts. In the first case, when it is the rulers who determine the conception "good," it is the exalted, proud disposition which is regarded as the distinguishing feature, and that which determines the order of rank. The noble type of man separates from himself the beings in whom the opposite of this exalted, proud disposition displays itself: he despises them. Let it at once be noted that in this first kind of morality the antithesis "good" and "bad" means practically the same as "noble" and "despicable";—the antithesis "good" and "*evil*" is of a different origin. The cowardly, the timid, the insignificant, and those thinking merely of narrow utility are despised; moreover, also, the distrustful, with their constrained glances, the self-abasing, the dog-like kind of men who let themselves be abused, the mendicant flatterers, and above all the liars;—it is a fundamental belief of all aristocrats that the common people are untruthful. "We truthful ones"—the nobility in ancient Greece called themselves. . . . A morality of the ruling class, however, is more especially foreign and irritating to present-day taste in the sternness of its principle that one has duties only to one's equals; that one may act towards beings of a lower rank, towards all that is foreign, just as seems good to one, or "as the heart desires," and in any case "beyond good and evil": it is here that sympathy and similar sentiments can have a place. The ability and obligation to exercise prolonged gratitude and prolonged revenge—both only within the circle of equals—artfulness in retaliation, *raffinement* of the idea in friendship, a certain necessity to have enemies (as outlets for the emotions of envy, quarrelsomeness, arrogance—in fact, in order to be a good *friend*): all these are typical characteristics of the noble morality, which, as has been pointed out, is not the morality of "modern ideas," and is therefore at present difficult to realise, and also to unearth and disclose.— It is otherwise with the second type of morality, *slave-morality*. Supposing that the abused, the oppressed, the suffering, the unemancipated, the weary, and those uncertain of themselves, should moralise, what will be the common element in their moral estimates? Probably a pessimistic suspicion with regard to the entire situation of man will find expression, perhaps a condemnation of man, together with his situation. The slave has an unfavourable eye for the virtues of the powerful; he has a scepticism and distrust, a *refinement* of distrust of everything "good" that is there honoured—he would fain persuade himself that the very happiness there is not genuine. On the other hand, *those* qualities which serve to alleviate the existence of sufferers are brought into prominence and flooded with light; it is here that sympathy, the kind, helping hand, the warm heart, patience, diligence, humility, and friendliness attain to honour; for here these are the most useful qualities, and almost the only means of supporting the burden of existence. Slave-morality is essentially the morality of utility. Here is the seat of the origin of the famous antithesis "good" and "*evil*":— power and dangerousness are assumed to reside in the evil, a certain dreadfulness, subtlety, and strength, which do not admit of being despised. According to slave-morality, therefore, the "evil" man arouses fear; according to master-morality, it is precisely the "good" man who arouses fear and seeks to arouse it, while the bad man is regarded as the despicable being. . . . A last fundamental difference: the desire for *freedom*, the instinct for happiness and the refinements of the feeling of liberty belong as necessarily to slave-morals and morality, as artifice and enthusiasm in reverence and devotion are the regular symptoms of an aristocratic mode of thinking and estimating.—Hence we can understand without further detail why love *as a passion* . . . must absolutely be of noble origin.

At the risk of displeasing innocent ears, I submit that egoism belongs to 5 the essence of a noble soul; I mean the unalterable belief that to a being such as "we," other beings must naturally be in subjection, and have to sacrifice themselves. The noble soul accepts the fact of his egoism without question, and also without consciousness of harshness, constraint, or arbitrariness therein, but rather as something that may have its basis in the primary law of things:—if he sought a designation for it he would say: "It is justice itself." He acknowledges under certain circumstances, which made him hesitate at first, that there are other equally privileged ones; as soon as he has settled this question of rank, he moves among those equals and equally privileged ones with the same assurance, as regards modesty and delicate respect, which he enjoys in intercourse with himself. . . . The noble soul gives as he takes. . . . The notion of "favour" has . . . neither significance nor good repute; there may be a sublime way of letting gifts as it were light upon one from above, and of drinking them thirstily like dewdrops; but for those arts and displays the noble soul has no aptitude. His egoism hinders him here: In general, he looks "aloft" unwillingly—he looks either *forward*, horizontally and deliberately, or downwards—*he knows that he is on a height*. . . .

⊠ RAMAKRISHNA

Many Paths to the Same Summit

*In this little essay, Ramakrishna (1836–1886), one of the best known Hindu
saints of modern times, claims that "Every man should follow his own religion.
A Christian should follow Christianity, a Mohammedan should follow Mohammedanism, and so on."*

God has made different religions to suit different aspirants, times, and coun-   1
tries. All doctrines are only so many paths; but a path is by no means God
Himself. Indeed, one can reach God if one follows any of the paths with
wholehearted devotion. One may eat a cake with icing either straight or side-
wise. It will taste sweet either way.

As one and the same material, water, is called by different names by   2
different peoples, one calling it water, another eau, a third aqua, and another
pani, so the one Everlasting-Intelligent-Bliss is invoked by some as God, by
some as Allah, by some as Jehovah, and by others as Brahman.

As one can ascend to the top of a house by means of a ladder or a bamboo   3
or a staircase or a rope, so diverse are the ways and means to approach God,
and every religion in the world shows one of these ways.

As the young wife in a family shows her love and respect to her father-in-   4
law, mother-in-law, and every other member of the family, and at the same time
loves her husband more than these; similarly, being firm in thy devotion to the
deity of thy own choice, do not despise other deities, but honour them all.

Bow down and worship where others kneel, for where so many have been   5
paying the tribute of adoration the kind Lord must manifest himself, for he is
all mercy.

The devotee who has seen God in one aspect only, knows him in that   6
aspect alone. But he who has seen him in manifold aspects is alone in a position
to say, "All these forms are of one God and God is multiform." He is formless
and with form, and many are his forms which no one knows.

The Saviour is the messenger of God. He is like the viceroy of a mighty   7
monarch. As when there is some disturbance in a far-off province, the king
sends his viceroy to quell it, so wherever there is a decline of religion in any
part of the world, God sends his Saviour there. It is one and the same Saviour
that, having plunged into the ocean of life, rises up in one place and is known
as Krishna (the leading Hindu incarnation of God), and diving down again
rises in another place and is known as Christ.

Every man should follow his own religion. A Christian should follow   8
Christianity, a Mohammedan should follow Mohammedanism, and so on. For
the Hindus, the ancient path, the path of the Aryan sages, is the best.

People partition off their lands by means of boundaries, but no one can 9
partition off the all-embracing sky overhead. The indivisible sky surrounds all
and includes all. So common man in ignorance says, "My religion is the only
one, my religion is the best." But when his heart is illumined by true knowledge, he knows that above all these wars of sects and sectarians presides the one
indivisible, eternal, all-knowing bliss.

As a mother, in nursing her sick children, gives rice and curry to one, and 10
sago arrowroot to another, and bread and butter to a third, so the Lord has laid
out different paths for different men suitable to their natures.

Dispute not. As you rest firmly on your own faith and opinion, allow 11
others also the equal liberty to stand by their own faiths and opinions. By mere
disputation you will never succeed in convincing another of his error. When
the grace of God descends on him, each one will understand his own mistakes.

There was a man who worshipped Shiva but hated all other deities. One 12
day Shiva appeared to him and said, "I shall never be pleased with thee so long
as thou hatest the other gods." But the man was inexorable. After a few days
Shiva again appeared to him and said, "I shall never be pleased with thee so
long as thou hatest." The man kept silent. After a few days Shiva again appeared
to him. This time one side of his body was that of Shiva, and the other side
that of Vishnu. The man was half pleased and half displeased. He laid his
offerings on the side representing Shiva, and did not offer anything to the side
representing Vishnu. Then Shiva said, "Thy bigotry is unconquerable. I, by
assuming this dual aspect, tried to convince thee that all gods and goddesses
are but various aspects of the one Absolute Brahman."

⌇ THE BIBLE

Genesis

The first book of the Bible, Genesis, provides the biblical account of creation.

CHAPTER 1

In the beginning God created the heaven and the earth.   1

And the earth was without form, and void; and darkness *was* upon the face 2
of the deep. And the Spirit of God moved upon the face of the waters.

And God said, Let there be light: and there was light.   3

And God saw the light, that *it was* good: and God divided the light from 4
the darkness.

And God called the light Day, and the darkness he called Night. And the 5
evening and the morning were the first day.

And God said, Let there be a firmament in the midst of the waters, and 6
let it divide the waters from the waters.

And God made the firmament, and divided the waters which *were* under 7
the firmament from the waters which *were* above the firmament: and it was so.

And God called the firmament Heaven. And the evening and the morning 8
were the second day.

And God said, Let the waters under the heaven be gathered together unto 9
one place, and let the dry *land* appear: and it was so.

And God called the dry *land* Earth; and the gathering together of the 10
waters called he Seas: and God saw that *it was* good.

And God said, Let the earth bring forth grass, the herb yielding seed, *and* 11
the fruit tree yielding fruit after his kind, whose seed *is* in itself, upon the earth:
and it was so.

And the earth brought forth grass, *and* herb yielding seed after his kind, 12
and the tree yielding fruit, whose seed *was* in itself, after his kind: and God saw
that *it was* good.

And the evening and the morning were the third day.   13

And God said, Let there be lights in the firmament of the heaven to divide 14
the day from the night; and let them be for signs, and for seasons, and for days,
and years:

And let them be for lights in the firmament of the heaven to give light 15
upon the earth: and it was so.

And God made two great lights; the greater light to rule the day, and the 16
lesser light to rule the night: *he made* the stars also.

And God set them in the firmament of the heaven to give light upon the 17
earth.

And to rule over the day and over the night, and to divide the light from 18
the darkness: and God saw that *it was* good.

And the evening and the morning were the fourth day.   19

And God said, Let the waters bring forth abundantly the moving creature 20
that hath life, and fowl *that* may fly above the earth in the open firmament of
heaven.

And God created great whales, and every living creature that moveth, 21
which the waters brought forth abundantly, after their kind, and every winged
fowl after his kind: and God saw that *it was* good.

And God blessed them, saying, Be fruitful, and mulitply, and fill the 22
waters in the seas, and let fowl multiply in the earth.

And the evening and the morning were the fifth day.   23

And God said, Let the earth bring forth the living creature after his kind, 24
cattle, and creeping thing, and beast of the earth after his kind: and it was so.

And God made the beast of the earth after his kind, and cattle after their 25 kind, and every thing that creepeth upon the earth after his kind: and God saw that *it was* good.

And God said, Let us make man in our image, after our likeness: and let 26 them have dominion over the fish of the sea, and over the fowl of the air, and over the cattle, and over all the earth, and over every creeping thing that creepeth upon the earth.

So God created man in his *own* image, in the image of God created he 27 him; male and female created he them.

And God blessed them, and God said unto them, Be fruitful, and multi- 28 ply, and replenish the earth, and subdue it: and have dominion over the fish of the sea, and over the fowl of the air, and over every living thing that moveth upon the earth.

And God said, Behold, I have given you every herb bearing seed, which 29 *is* upon the face of all the earth, and every tree, in the which *is* the fruit of a tree yielding seed; to you it shall be for meat.

And to every beast of the earth, and to every fowl of the air, and to every 30 thing that creepeth upon the earth, wherein *there is* life, *I have given* every green herb for meat: and it was so.

And God saw every thing that he had made, and, behold, *it was* very 31 good. And the evening and the morning were the sixth day.

CHAPTER 2

Thus the heavens and the earth were finished, and all the host of them.   32

And on the seventh day God ended his work which he had made; and he 33 rested on the seventh day from all his work which he had made.

And God blessed the seventh day, and sanctified it: because that in it he 34 had rested from all his work which God created and made.

These *are* the generations of the heavens and of the earth when they were 35 created, in the day that the Lord God made the earth and the heavens,

And every plant of the field before it was in the earth, and every herb of 36 the field before it grew: for the Lord God had not caused it to rain upon the earth, and *there was* not a man to till the ground.

But there went up a mist from the earth, and watered the whole face of 37 the ground.

And the Lord God formed man *of* the dust of the ground, and breathed 38 into his nostrils the breath of life; and man became a living soul.

And the Lord God planted a garden eastward in Eden; and there he put 39 the man whom he had formed.

And out of the ground made the Lord God to grow every tree that is 40 pleasant to sight, and good for food; the tree of life also in the midst of the garden, and the tree of knowledge of good and evil.

And a river went out of Eden to water the garden; and from thence it was 41 parted, and became into four heads.

The name of the first *is* Pí-son: that *is* it which compasseth the whole land 42
of Haṽ-i-lah, where *there is* gold;

And the gold of that land is good: there *is* bdellium and the onyx stone.   43

And the name of the second river *is* Gíhon: the same *is* it that compasseth 44
the whole land of E-thi-ó-pi-a.

And the name of the third river *is* Hid'-de-kel: that *is* it which goeth 45
toward the east of Assyria. And the fourth river *is* Eu-phrá-tes.

And the Lord God took the man, and put him into the garden of Eden to 46
dress it and to keep it.

And the Lord God commanded the man, saying, Of every tree of the 47
garden thou mayest freely eat:

But of the tree of the knowledge of good and evil, thou shalt not eat of it: 48
for in the day that thou eatest thereof thou shalt surely die.

And the Lord God said, *It is* not good that the man should be alone; I will 49
make him an help meet for him.

And out of the ground the Lord God formed every beast of the field, and 50
every fowl of the air; and brought *them* unto Adam to see what he would call
them: and whatsoever Adam called every living creature, that *was* the name
thereof.

And Adam gave names to all cattle, and to the fowl of the air, and to every 51
beast of the field; but for Adam there was not found an help meet for him.

And the Lord God caused a deep sleep to fall upon Adam, and he slept: 52
and he took one of his ribs, and closed up the flesh instead thereof;

And the rib which the Lord God had taken from man, made he a woman, 53
and brought her unto the man.

And Adam said, This *is* now bone of my bones, and flesh of my flesh: she 54
shall be called Woman, because she was taken out of Man.

Therefore shall a man leave his father and his mother, and shall cleave 55
unto his wife: and they shall be one flesh.

And they were both naked, the man and his wife, and were not ashamed. 56

CLARENCE DARROW AND WILLIAM JENNINGS BRYAN

Scopes "Monkey Trial" Testimony

*Clarence Darrow (1857–1938) was a famous trial lawyer who was involved in
several landmark cases, including the Loeb-Leopold murder trial. The Scopes
trial concerned the teaching of evolution in Tennessee public schools and drew*

national coverage and attention. The high point of the trial was Darrow's cross-examination of William Jennings Bryan (1860–1925), the Democratic party's candidate for president of the United States in 1896, 1900, and 1908. Bryan defended belief in the literal truth of what is said in the Bible, including the Genesis account of creation; Darrow tried to show that the Bible is contradicted by science and common sense. Bryan died soon after testifying at the trial.

MR. DARROW. Do you claim that everything in the Bible should be literally 1 interpreted?

MR. BRYAN. I believe everything in the Bible should be accepted as it is given 2 there. Some of the Bible is given illustratively. For instance: "Ye are the salt of the earth." I would not insist that man was actually salt, or that he had flesh of salt, but it is used in the sense of salt as saving God's people.

MR. DARROW. But when you read that Jonah swallowed the whale—or that 3 the whale swallowed Jonah, excuse me, please—how do you literally interpret that?

MR. BRYAN. When I read that a big fish swallowed Jonah—it does not say 4 whale.

MR. DARROW. Doesn't it? Are you sure? 5

MR. BRYAN. That is my recollection of it, a big fish; and I believe it; and I 6 believe in a God who can make a whale and can make a man, and make both do what He pleases. . . .

MR. DARROW. Have you an opinion as to whether—whoever wrote the book, I 7 believe it was Joshua—the Book of Joshua—thought the sun went around the earth or not?

MR. BRYAN. I believe that he was inspired. . . . I believe that the Bible is 8 inspired, and an inspired author, whether one who wrote as he was directed to write understood the things he was writing about, I don't know.

MR. DARROW. Do you think whoever inspired it believed that the sun went 9 around the earth?

MR. BRYAN. I believe it was inspired by the Almighty, and He may have used language that could be understood at that time.

MR. DARROW. So . . . it might have been subject to construction, might it not?

MR. BRYAN. It might have been used in language that could be understood then.

MR. DARROW. That means it is subject to construction?

MR. BRYAN. That is your construction. I am answering your questions.

MR. DARROW. Is that correct? 10

MR. BRYAN. That is my answer to it.

MR. DARROW. Can you answer?

MR. BRYAN. I might say Isaiah spoke of God sitting upon the circle of the earth.

MR. DARROW. I am not talking about Isaiah.

JUDGE RAULSTON. Let him illustrate, if he wants to, Mr. Darrow. It is your opinion that passage was subject to construction?

MR. BRYAN. Well, I think anybody can put his own construction upon it, but I do not mean necessarily that it is a correct construction. I have answered the question.

MR. DARROW. Don't you believe that in order to lengthen the day it would   11 have been construed that the earth stood still?

MR. BRYAN. I would not attempt to say what would have been necessary, but I   12 know this, that I can take a glass of water that would fall to the ground without the strength of my hand, and to the extent of the glass of water I can overcome the law of gravitation and lift it up; whereas, without my hand, it would fall to the ground. If my puny hand can overcome the law of gravitation, the most universally understood, to that extent, I would not set power to the hand of Almighty God that made the universe.

MR. DARROW. I read that years ago. Can you answer my question directly? If   13 the day was lengthened by stopping, either the earth or the sun, it must have been the earth?

MR. BRYAN. Well, I should say so: yes, but it was language that was understood   14 at that time, and we now know that the sun stood still, as it was, with the earth.

MR. DARROW. We know also the sun does stand still?

MR. BRYAN. Well, it is relatively so, as Mr. Einstein would say.

MR. DARROW. I ask you, if it does stand still?

MR. BRYAN. You know as well as I know.

MR. DARROW. Better. You have no doubt about it?

MR. BRYAN. No, no.

MR. DARROW. And the earth moves around it?

MR. BRYAN. Yes. But I think there is nothing improper if you will protect the Lord against your criticism.

MR. DARROW. I suppose he needs it?   15

MR. BRYAN. He was using language at that time that the people understood.

MR. DARROW. And that you call "interpretative"?

MR. BRYAN. No, sir, I would not call it interpretation.

MR. DARROW. I say, you would call it interpretation at this time, to say it meant something else?

MR. BRYAN. You may use your own language to describe what I have to say, and I will use mine in answering.

MR. DARROW. Now, Mr. Bryan, have you ever pondered what would have happened to the earth if it had stood still?

MR. BRYAN. No.   16

MR. DARROW. You have not?

MR. BRYAN. No. The God I believe in could have taken care of that, Darrow.

MR. DARROW. I see. Have you ever pondered what would naturally happen to the earth if it stood still suddenly?

MR. BRYAN. No.

MR. DARROW. Don't you know it would have been converted into a molten mass of matter?

MR. BRYAN. You testify to that when you get on the stand. I will give you a chance.

MR. DARROW. Don't you believe it?   17

MR. BRYAN. I would want to hear expert testimony on that.

MR. DARROW. You have never investigated that subject?

MR. BRYAN. I don't think I every had the question asked.

MR. DARROW. Or ever thought of it?

MR. BRYAN. I have been too busy on things that I thought were of more importance than that. . . .

MR. DARROW. How long ago was the flood, Mr. Bryan?

MR. BRYAN. Let me see Ussher's calculation about it.

MR. DARROW. Surely. (*Hands a Bible to the witness*) . . .

MR. BRYAN. Genesis. It is given here as 2348 years B.C.   18

MR. DARROW. Well, 2348 years B.C.

MR. DARROW. You believe that all the living things that were not contained in the Ark were destroyed?

MR. BRYAN. I think the fish may have lived.

MR. DARROW. Outside of the fish?

MR. BRYAN. I cannot say.

MR. DARROW. You cannot say?

MR. BRYAN. No. I accept that just as it is. I have no proof to the contrary.

MR. DARROW. I am asking you whether you believe it.   19

MR. BRYAN. I do. I accept that as the Bible gives it, and I have never found any reason for denying, disputing, or rejecting it.

MR. DARROW. Let me make it definite—2348 years?

MR. BRYAN. I didn't say that. That is the time given (*indicating a Bible*), but I don't pretend to say that is exact.

MR. DARROW. You never figured it out, those generations, yourself?

MR. BRYAN. No, sir; not myself.

MR. DARROW. But the Bible you have offered in evidence says 2340 something, so that 4200 years ago there was not a living thing on the earth, excepting the people on the Ark and the animals on the Ark, and the fishes?

MR. BRYAN. There had been living things before that.   20

MR. DARROW. I mean at that time?

MR. BRYAN. After that.

MR. DARROW. Don't you know there are any number of civilizations that are traced back to more than 5000 years?

MR. BRYAN. I know we have people who trace things back according to the number of ciphers they have. But I am not satisfied they are accurate.

MR. DARROW. You are not satisfied there is any civilization that can be traced back 5000 years?

MR. BRYAN. I would not want to say there is, because I have no evidence of it that is satisfactory.

MR. DARROW. Would you say there is not?   21

MR. BRYAN. Well, so far as I know, but when 306,000,000 years is their   22 opinion, as to how long ago life came here, I want them to be nearer, to come nearer together, before they demand of me to give up my belief in the Bible.

MR. DARROW. Do you say that you do not believe that there were any civilizations on this earth that reach back beyond 5000 years?

MR. BRYAN. I am not satisfied by any evidence that I have seen–

MR. DARROW. I didn't ask what you are satisfied with. I asked if you believed it.

MR. BRYAN. Will you let me answer it?

JUDGE RAULSTON. Go right on.

MR. BRYAN. I am satisfied by no evidence that I have found that would justify   23 me in accepting the opinions of these men against what I believe to be the inspired Word of God. . . .

MR. DARROW. . . . You believe that all the various human races on the earth have come into being in the last 4000 years or 4200 years, whatever it is? . . .

MR. BRYAN. According to the Bible there was a civilization before that, destroyed by the flood.

MR. DARROW. Let me make this definite. You believe that every civilization on the earth and every living thing, except possibly the fishes, that came out of the Ark, were wiped out by the flood?

MR. BRYAN. At that time.

MR. DARROW. At that time; and then, whatever human beings, including all   24 the tribes that inhabited the world, and have inhabited the world, and who run their pedigree straight back, and all the animals have come on to the earth since the flood?

MR. BRYAN. Yes.

MR. DARROW. Within 4200 years? Do you know a scientific man on the earth that believes any such thing?

MR. BRYAN. I cannot say, but I know some scientific men who dispute entirely the antiquity of man as testified to by other scientific men.

MR. DARROW. Oh, that does not answer the question. Do you know of a single   25 scientific man on the face of the earth that believes any such thing as you stated, about the antiquity of man?

MR. BRYAN. I don't think I have even asked one the direct question.

MR. DARROW. Quite important, isn't it?

MR. BRYAN. Well, I don't know as it is.

MR. DARROW. It might not be?

MR. BRYAN. If I had nothing else to do except speculate on what our remote   26 ancestors were and what our remote descendants have been, but I have been more interested in Christians going on right now, to make it much more important than speculations on either the past or the future.

MR. DARROW. You do know that there are thousands of people who profess to be Christians who believe the earth is much more ancient and that the human race is much more ancient?

MR. BRYAN. I think there may be.

MR. DARROW. And you never have investigated to find out how long man has been on the earth?

MR. BRYAN. I have never found it necessary. I do not expect to find out all 27 those things. I do not expect to find out about races.

MR. DARROW. I didn't ask you that. Now, I ask you, if you know, if it was interesting enough, or important enough for you, to try to find out, how old these ancient civilizations are?

MR. BRYAN. No. I have not made a study of it.

MR. DARROW. Don't you know that the ancient civilizations of China are six or seven thousand years old, at the very least?

MR. BRYAN. No, but they would not run back beyond the creation, according to the Bible, six thousand years.

MR. DARROW. You don't know how old they are, is that right? 28

MR. BRYAN. I don't know how old they are, but possibly you do. (*Laughter*)

MR. DARROW. Have you any idea how old the Egyptian civilization is.

MR. BRYAN. No.

MR. DARROW. Do you know of any record in the world, outside of the story of the Bible, which conforms to any statement that it is 4300 years ago or thereabouts, that all life was wiped off the face of the earth?

MR. BRYAN. I think they have found records.

MR. DARROW. Do you know of any?

MR. BRYAN. Records reciting the flood, but I am not an authority on the subject.

MR. DARROW. Mr. Bryan, don't you know that there are many old religions 29 that describe the flood?

MR. BRYAN. No, I don't know. The Christian religion has satisfied me and I have never felt it necessary to look up some competing religion. . . .

MR. DARROW. Do you know how old the Confucian religion is?

MR. BRYAN. I can't give you the exact date of it.

MR. DARROW. Do you know how old the religion of Zoroaster is?

MR. BRYAN. No, sir.

MR. DARROW. Do you know they are both more ancient than the Christian religion?

MR. BRYAN. I am not willing to take the opinion of people who are trying to 30 find excuses for rejecting the Christian religion.

MR. DARROW. Are you familiar with James Clark's book on the ten great religions?

MR. BRYAN. No.

MR. DARROW. You don't know how old they are, all these other religions?

MR. BRYAN. I wouldn't attempt to speak correctly, but I think it is much more important to know the difference between them than to know the age.

MR. DARROW. Not for the purpose of this inquiry, Mr. Bryan. Do you know 31 about how many people there were on this earth at the beginning of the Christian Era?

MR. BRYAN. No. I don't think I ever saw a census on that subject.

MR. DARROW. Do you know about how many people there were on this earth 3000 years ago?

MR. BRYAN. No.

MR. DARROW. Did you ever try to find out?

MR. BRYAN. When you display my ignorance, could you not give me the facts so I would not be ignorant any longer?

MR. DARROW. Can you tell me how many people there were when Christ was 32 born? You know, some of us might get the facts and still be ignorant.

MR. BRYAN. Will you please give me that? You ought not to ask me a question that you don't know the answer to.

MR. DARROW. I can make an estimate.

MR. BRYAN. What is your estimate.

MR. DARROW. Wait until you get to me. Do you know anything about how many people there were in Egypt 3500 years ago, or how many people there were in China 5000 years ago?

MR. BRYAN. No. 33

MR. DARROW. Have you ever tried to find out?

MR. BRYAN. No, sir; you are the first man I ever heard of who was interested in it. (*Laughter*)

MR. DARROW. Mr. Bryan, am I the first man you ever heard of who has been interested in the age of human societies and primitive man?

MR. BRYAN. You are the first man I ever heard speak of the number of people at these different periods.

MR. DARROW. Where have you lived all your life?

MR. BRYAN. Not near you. (*Laughter and applause*)

MR. DARROW. Nor near anybody of learning? 34

MR. BRYAN. Oh, don't assume you know it all.

MR. DARROW. Do you know there are thousands of books in your libraries on all those subjects I have been asking you about? . . .

MR. DARROW. You don't care how old the earth is, how old man is, and how long the animals have been here?

MR. BRYAN. I am not so much interested in that.

MR. DARROW. You have never made any investigation to find out?

MR. BRYAN. No, sir, I never have.

MR. DARROW. You have heard of the Tower of Babel, haven't you?

MR. BRYAN. Yes, sir.

MR. DARROW. That tower was built under the ambition that they could build 35 a tower up to heaven, wasn't it? And God saw what they were at and, to prevent their getting into heaven, He confused their tongues?

Mr. Bryan. Something like that. I wouldn't say to prevent their getting into heaven, He confused their tongues . . . I don't think it is necessary to believe that God was afraid they would get to heaven. . . .

Mr. Darrow. . . . Up to 4143 years ago, every human being on earth spoke the same language?

Mr. Bryan. Yes, sir, I think that is the inference that could be drawn from that.

Mr. Darrow. All the different languages of the earth, dating from the Tower 36 of Babel–is that right? Do you know how many languages are spoken on the face of the earth?

Mr. Bryan. No. I know the Bible has been translated into 500, and no other book has been translated into anything like that many.

Mr. Darrow. That is interesting, if true. Do you know all the languages there are?

Mr. Bryan. No, sir, I can't tell you. There may be many dialects besides that and some languages, but those are all the principal languages.

Mr. Darrow. There are a great many that are not principal languages? 37

Mr. Bryan. Yes, sir.

Mr. Darrow. You haven't any idea how many there are?

Mr. Bryan. No, sir.

Mr. Darrow. And you say that all those languages of all the sons of men have come on the earth not over 4150 years ago?

Mr. Bryan. I have seen no evidence that would lead me to put it any farther back than that. . . .

Mr. Darrow. Did you ever discover where Cain got his wife?

Mr. Bryan. No, sir; I leave the agnostics to hunt for her. 38

Mr. Darrow. You have never found out?

Mr. Bryan. I have never tried to find.

Mr. Darrow. You have never tried to find?

Mr. Bryan. No.

Mr. Darrow. The Bible says he got one, doesn't it? Were there other people on the earth at that time?

Mr. Bryan. I cannot say.

Mr. Darrow. You cannot say? Did that never enter into your consideration.

Mr. Bryan. Never bothered me. 39

Mr. Darrow. There were no others recorded, but Cain got a wife. That is 40 what the Bible says. Where she came from, you don't know. All right. Does the statement, "The morning and the evening were the first day" and "The morning and the evening were the second day" mean anything to you?

Mr. Bryan. I do not think it means necessarily a twenty-four-hour day.

Mr. Darrow. You do not?

Mr. Bryan. No.

Mr. Darrow. What do you consider it to be?

Mr. Bryan. I have not attempted to explain it. If you will take the second   41
chapter—let me have the Book. (*Examining the Bible*) The fourth verse of
the second chapter (Genesis) says: "These are the generations of the heavens
and of the earth, when they were created, in the day that the Lord God made
the earth and the heavens." The word "day" there in the very next chapter is
used to describe a period. I do not see that there is necessity for construing
the words, "the evening and the morning," as meaning necessarily a twenty-
four-hour day: "in the day when the Lord made the heaven and the earth."

Mr. Darrow. Then when the Bible said, for instance, "And God called the   42
firmament heaven. And the evening and the morning were the second
day"—that does not necessarily mean twenty-four hours?

Mr. Bryan. I do not think it necessarily does.

Mr. Darrow. Do you think it does or does not?

Mr. Bryan. I know a great many think so.

Mr. Darrow. What do you think?

Mr. Bryan. I do not think it does.

Mr. Darrow. You think these were not literal days?

Mr. Bryan. I do not think they were twenty-four-hour days.

Mr. Darrow. What do you think about it?   43

Mr. Bryan. That is my opinion—I do not know that my opinion is better on
that subject than those who think it does.

Mr. Darrow. Do you not think that?

Mr. Bryan. No. But I think it would be just as easy for the kind of God we
believe in to make the earth in six days as in six years or in six million years
or in six hundred million years. I do not think it important whether we
believe one or the other.

Mr. Darrow. Do you think those were literal days?

Mr. Bryan. My impression is they were periods, but I would not attempt to
argue as against anybody who wanted to believe in literal days.

Mr. Darrow. Have you any idea of the length of the periods?   44

Mr. Bryan. No, I don't.

Mr. Darrow. Do you think the sun was made on the fourth day?

Mr. Bryan. Yes.

Mr. Darrow. And they had evening and morning without the sun?

Mr Bryan. I am simply saying it is a period.

Mr. Darrow. They had evening and morning for four periods without the
sun, do you think?

Mr. Bryan. I believe in creation, as there told, and if I am not able to explain
it, I will accept it.

Mr. Darrow. Then you can explain it to suit yourself. And they had the   45
evening and the morning before that time for three days or three periods. All
right, that settles it. Now, if you call those periods, they may have been a
very long time?

MR. BRYAN. They might have been.

MR. DARROW. The creation might have been going on for a very long time?

MR. BRYAN. It might have continued for millions of years.

MR. DARROW. Yes, all right. Do you believe the story of the temptation of Eve by the serpent?

MR. BRYAN. I do.

MR. DARROW. Do you believe that after Eve ate the apple, or gave it to Adam— 46 whichever way it was—God cursed Eve, and at that time decreed that all womankind thenceforth and forever should suffer the pains of childbirth in the reproduction of the earth?

MR. BRYAN. I believe what it says, and I believe the fact as fully.

MR. DARROW. That is what it says, doesn't it?

MR. BRYAN. Yes.

MR. DARROW. And for that reason, every woman born of woman, who has to 47 carry on the race—the reason they have childbirth pains is because Eve tempted Adam in the Garden of Eden?

MR. BRYAN. I will believe just what the Bible says. I ask to put that in the 48 language of the Bible, for I prefer that to your language. Read the Bible, and I will answer.

MR. DARROW. All right, I will do that: "And I will put enmity between thee and the woman." That is referring to the serpent?

MR. BRYAN. The serpent.

MR. DARROW (*reading*). "And between thy seed and her seed; it shall bruise 49 thy head, and thou shalt bruise his heel. Unto the woman He said, I will greatly multiply thy sorrow and thy conception; in sorrow thou shalt bring forth children; and thy desire shall be to thy husband, and he shall rule over thee." That is right, is it?

MR. BRYAN. I accept it as it is.

MR. DARROW. Do you believe that was because Eve tempted Adam to eat the fruit?

MR. BRYAN. I believe it was just what the Bible said.

MR. DARROW. And you believe that is the reason that God made the serpent to go on his belly after he tempted Eve?

MR. BRYAN. I believe the Bible as it is, and I do not permit you to put your 50 language in the place of the language of the Almighty. You read that Bible and ask me questions, and I will answer them. I will not answer your questions in your language.

MR. DARROW. I will read it to you from the Bible: "And the Lord God said 51 unto the serpent, Because thou hast done this, thou art cursed above all cattle, and above every beast of the field; upon thy belly shalt thou go, and dust shalt thou eat all the days of thy life." Do you think that is why the serpent is compelled to crawl upon its belly?

MR. BRYAN. I believe that.

MR. DARROW. Have you any idea how the snake went before that time?

MR. BRYAN. No, sir.

MR. DARROW. Do you know whether he walked on his tail or not?

MR. BRYAN. No, sir. I have no way to know. *(Laughter)*

MR. DARROW. Now, you refer to the bow that was put in the heaven after the 52
flood, the rainbow. Do you believe in that?

MR. BRYAN. Read it.

MR. DARROW. All right, Mr. Bryan, I will read it for you.

MR. BRYAN. Your Honor, I think I can shorten this testimony. The only pur- 53
pose Mr. Darrow has is to slur at the Bible, but I will answer his questions. I
will answer it all at once, and I have no objection in the world. I want the
world to know that this man, who does not believe in a God, is trying to use
a court in Tennessee . . .

MR. DARROW. I object to that.

MR. BRYAN. To slur at it, and, while it will require time, I am willing to take
it.

MR. DARROW. I object to your statement. I am examining you on your fool 54
ideas that no intelligent Christian on earth believes.

WORLD VIEWS

QUESTIONS AND SUGGESTIONS FOR WRITING

1. Jefferson's political philosophy has become central to our world view. Explain that philosophy and indicate how it has influenced your political
   beliefs.

2. In what ways do the world views expressed in the Communist Manifesto
   and in the Declaration of Independence differ? In what ways are they alike?

3. Hitler draws on the theory of evolution to justify his racial philosophy.
   Explain his misconception of that theory and examine the false evidence
   he provides about racial characteristics and behavior.

4. Machiavelli asserts that a prince should seem to be "merciful, humane,
   sincere and religious," but under certain circumstances he must lie to rule
   effectively. Can you think of any modern rulers who seem to share Machiavelli's conviction? Explain your examples.

5. More than anyone else, Freud is responsible for enlightening us on the
   nature of the unconscious. His influence has had far-reaching effects not
   only in the field of psychology but in politics, philosophy, literature, and
   the arts as well. Equally important is his influence on our daily lives.
   Explain how his theory of the unconscious has deepened our perception
   of ourselves and others.

6. Examine the reasons James gives for his belief in God. Do you consider
   them convincing? Evaluate them in terms of your own beliefs concerning
   God and religion.

7. Russell argues against the view that evolution is evidence of a divine plan. Do you agree or disagree with his reasoning? Why?

8. What world view emerges as Darrow closely questions Bryan on the fine points of the biblical account of creation? What was Darrow's purpose in this cross-examination?

9. Ramakrishna urges people to follow their own religion, arguing that God can be reached by many paths. To make his point he reasons by analogy. Discuss the efficacy of his analogies.

10. Write an essay in which you explain a portion of your world view and present your reasons for believing it. (World views tend to be held, at least in large part, on the basis of a lifetime of experiences. You need mention only a few of them in your essay.)

CAPITAL PUNISHMENT

The most frequently encountered reasons given in favor of capital punishment are deterrence (and its partner rehabilitation) and retribution. In the essays that follow, Clarence Darrow argues against capital punishment on the grounds that it does not deter crime and is inflicted primarily to satisfy the hunger of the crowd for revenge. H. L. Mencken, on the other hand, sees this desire for revenge as a desire for retribution and a need for *katharsis*, "a healthy letting off of steam," satisfying the desire to strike back at transgressors and square accounts. Walter Berns argues that capital punishment is justified because it exacts retribution from the criminal for certain heinous crimes. And George Orwell tries to convince us of the barbaric nature of capital punishment simply by graphically describing a hanging.

⊠ CLARENCE DARROW

The Futility of the Death Penalty

As noted before, Clarence Darrow (1857–1938) was a famous trial lawyer involved in many landmark cases. He wrote the following essay against capital punishment in 1927, just a few years after defending Richard Loeb and Nathan Leopold in their celebrated murder trial. Darrow believed that "capital punishment is no deterrent to crime; . . . [yet] the state continues to kill its victims . . . to appease the mob's emotions of hatred and revenge."

Little more than a century ago, in England, there were over two hundred 1
offenses that were punishable with death. The death sentence was passed upon
children under ten years old. And every time the sentimentalist sought to lessen
the number of crimes punishable by death, the self-righteous said no, that it

would be the destruction of the state; that it would be better to kill for more transgressions rather than for less.

Today, both in England and America, the number of capital offenses has 2 been reduced to a very few, and capital punishment would doubtless be abolished altogether were it not for the self-righteous, who still defend it with the same old arguments. Their major claim is that capital punishment decreases the number of murders, and hence, that the state must retain the institution as its last defense against the criminal.

It is my purpose in this article to prove, first, that capital punishment is 3 no deterrent to crime; and second, that the state continues to kill its victims, not so much to defend society against them—for it could do that equally well by imprisonment—but to appease the mob's emotions of hatred and revenge.

Behind the idea of capital punishment lie false training and crude views 4 of human conduct. People do evil things, say the judges, lawyers, and preachers, because of depraved hearts. Human conduct is not determined by the causes which determine the conduct of other animal and plant life in the universe. For some mysterious reason human beings act as they please; and if they do not please to act in a certain way, it is because, having the power of choice, they deliberately choose to act wrongly. The world once applied this doctrine to disease and insanity in men. It was also applied to animals, and even inanimate things were once tried and condemned to destruction. The world knows better now, but the rule has not yet been extended to human beings.

The simple fact is that every person starts life with a certain physical 5 structure, more or less sensitive, stronger or weaker. He is played upon by everything that reaches him from without, and in this he is like everything else in the universe, inorganic matter as well as organic. How a man will act depends upon the character of his human machine, and the strength of the various stimuli that affect it. Everyone knows that this is so in disease and insanity. Most investigators know that it applies to crime. But the great mass of people still sit in judgment, robed with self-righteousness, and determine the fate of their less fortunate fellows. When this question is studied like any other, we shall then know how to get rid of most of the conduct that we call "criminal," just as we are now getting rid of much of the disease that once afflicted mankind.

If crime were really the result of wilful depravity, we should be ready to 6 concede that capital punishment may serve as a deterrent to the criminally inclined. But it is hardly probable that the great majority of people refrain from killing their neighbors because they are afraid; they refrain because they never had the inclination. Human beings are creatures of habit; and, as a rule, they are not in the habit of killing. The circumstances that lead to killings are manifold, but in a particular individual the inducing cause is not easily found. In one case, homicide may have been induced by indigestion in the killer; in another, it may be traceable to some weakness inherited from a remote ancestor;

but that it results from *something* tangible and understandable, if all the facts were known, must be plain to everyone who believes in cause and effect.

Of course, no one will be converted to this point of view by statistics of 7 crime. In the first place, it is impossible to obtain reliable ones; and in the second place, the conditions to which they apply are never the same. But if one cares to analyze the figures, such as we have, it is easy to trace the more frequent causes of homicide. The greatest number of killings occur during attempted burglaries and robberies. The robber knows that penalties for burglary do not average more than five years in prison. He also knows that the penalty for murder is death or imprisonment. Faced with this alternative, what does the burglar do when he is detected and threatened with arrest? He shoots to kill. He deliberately takes the chance of death to save himself from a five-year term in prison. It is therefore as obvious as anything can be that fear of death has no effect in diminishing homicides of this kind, which are more numerous than any other type.

The next largest number of homicides may be classed as "sex murders." 8 Quarrels between husbands and wives, disappointed love, or love too much requited cause many killings. They are the result of primal emotions so deep that the fear of death has not the slightest effect in preventing them. Spontaneous feelings overflow in criminal acts, and consequences do not count.

Then there are cases of sudden anger, uncontrollable rage. The fear of 9 death never enters into such cases; if the anger is strong enough, consequences are not considered until too late. The old-fashioned stories of men deliberately plotting and committing murder in cold blood have little foundation in real life. Such killings are so rare that they need not concern us here. The point to be emphasized is that practically all homicides are manifestations of well-recognized human emotions, and it is perfectly plain that the fear of excessive punishment does not enter into them.

In addition to these personal forces which overwhelm weak men and lead 10 them to commit murder, there are also many social and economic forces which must be listed among the causes of homicides, and human beings have even less control over these than over their own emotions. It is often said that in America there are more homicides in proportion to population than in England. This is true. There are likewise more in the United States than in Canada. But such comparisons are meaningless until one takes into consideration the social and economic differences in the countries compared. Then it becomes apparent why the homicide rate in the United States is higher. Canada's population is largely rural; that of the United States is crowded into cities whose slums are the natural breeding places of crime. Moreover, the population of England and Canada is homogeneous, while the United States has gathered together people of every color from every nation in the world. Racial differences intensify social, religious, and industrial problems, and the confusion which attends this indiscriminate mixing of races and nationalities is one of the most fertile sources of crime.

Will capital punishment remedy these conditions? Of course it won't; but   11
its advocates argue that the fear of this extreme penalty will hold the victims of
adverse conditions in check. To this piece of sophistry the continuance and
increase of crime in our large cities is a sufficient answer. No, the plea that
capital punishment acts as a deterrent to crime will not stand. The real reason
why this barbarous practice persists in a so-called civilized world is that people
still hold the primitive belief that the taking of one human life can be atoned
for by taking another. It is the age-old obsession with punishment that keeps
the official headsman busy plying his trade.

And it is precisely upon this point that I would build my case against   12
capital punishment. Even if one grants that the idea of punishment is sound,
crime calls for something more—for careful study, for an understanding of
causes, for proper remedies. To attempt to abolish crime by killing the criminal
is the easy and foolish way out of a serious situation. Unless a remedy deals
with the conditions which foster crime, criminals will breed faster than the
hangman can spring his trap. Capital punishment ignores the causes of crime
just as completely as the primitive witch doctor ignored the causes of disease;
and, like the methods of the witch doctor, it is not only ineffective as a remedy,
but is positively vicious in at least two ways. In the first place, the spectacle of
state executions feeds the basest passions of the mob. And in the second place,
so long as the state rests content to deal with crime in this barbaric and futile
manner, society will be lulled by a false sense of security, and effective methods
of dealing with crime will be discouraged.

It seems to be a general impression that there are fewer homicides in Great   13
Britain than in America because in England punishment is more certain, more
prompt, and more severe. As a matter of fact, the reverse is true. In England
the average term for burglary is eighteen months; with us it is probably four or
five years. In England, imprisonment for life means twenty years. Prison sentences in the United States are harder than in any country in the world that
could be classed as civilized. This is true largely because, with us, practically
no official dares to act on his own judgment. The mob is all-powerful and
demands blood for blood. That intangible body of people called "the public"
vents its hatred upon the criminal and enjoys the sensation of having him put
to death by the state—this without any definite idea that it is really necessary.

For the last five or six years, in England and Wales, the homicides reported   14
by the police range from sixty-five to seventy a year. Death sentences meted out
by jurors have averaged about thirty-five, and hangings, fifteen. More than half
of those convicted by juries were saved by appeals to the Home Office. But in
America there is no such percentage of lives saved after conviction. Governors
are afraid to grant clemency. If they did, the newspapers and the populace
would refuse to re-elect them.

It is true that trials are somewhat prompter in England than America, but   15
there no newspaper dares publish the details of any case until after the trial. In
America the accused is often convicted by the public within twenty-four hours
of the time a homicide occurs. The courts sidetrack all other business so that a

homicide that is widely discussed may receive prompt attention. The road to the gallows is not only opened but greased for the opportunity of killing another victim.

Thus, while capital punishment panders to the passions of the mob, no one takes the pains to understand the meaning of crime. People speak of crime or criminals as if the world were divided into the good and the bad. This is not true. All of us have the same emotions, but since the balance of emotions is never the same, nor the inducing causes identical, human conduct presents a wide range of differences, shading by almost imperceptible degrees from that of the saint to that of the murderer. Of those kinds of conduct which are classed as dangerous, by no means all are made criminal offenses. Who can clearly define the difference between certain legal offenses and many kinds of dangerous conduct not singled out by criminal statute? Why are many cases of cheating entirely omitted from the criminal code, such as false and misleading advertisements, selling watered stock, forestalling the market, and all the different ways in which great fortunes are accumulated to the envy and despair of those who would like to have money but do not know how to get it? Why do we kill people for the crime of homicide and administer a lesser penalty for burglary, robbery, and cheating? Can anyone tell which is the greater crime and which is the lesser? 16

Human conduct is by no means so simple as our moralists have led us to believe. There is no sharp line separating good actions from bad. The greed for money, the display of wealth, the despair of those who witness the display, the poverty, oppression, and hopelessness of the unfortunate—all these are factors which enter into human conduct and of which the world takes no account. Many people have learned no other profession but robbery and burglary. The processions moving steadily through our prisons to the gallows are in the main made up of these unfortunates. And how do we dare to consider ourselves civilized creatures when, ignoring the causes of crime, we rest content to mete out harsh punishments to the victims of conditions over which they have no control? 17

Even now, are not all imaginative and humane people shocked at the spectacle of a killing by the state? How many men and women would be willing to act as executioners? How many fathers and mothers would want their children to witness an offical killing? What kind of people read the sensational reports of an execution? If all right-thinking men and women were not ashamed of it, why would it be needful that judges and lawyers and preachers apologize for the barbarity? How can the state censure the cruelty of the man who— moved by strong passions, or acting to save his freedom, or influenced by weakness or fear—takes human life, when everyone knows that the state itself, after long premeditation and settled hatred, not only kills, but first tortures and bedevils its victims for weeks with the impending doom? 18

For the last hundred years the world has shown a gradual tendency to mitigate punishment. We are slowly learning that this way of controlling human beings is both cruel and ineffective. In England the criminal code has 19 consistently grown more humane, until now the offenses punishable by death are reduced to practically one. There is no doubt whatever that the world is growing more humane and more sensitive and more understanding. The time will come when all people will view with horror the light way in which society and its courts of law now take human life; and when that time comes, the way will be clear to devise some better method of dealing with poverty and ignorance and their frequent byproducts, which we call crime.

◁▷ H. L. MENCKEN

The Penalty of Death

H. L. Mencken (1880–1956), author of the monumental work The American Language, *and long-time reporter and columnist for the* Baltimore Sun, *often took a cynical, unpopular position on controversial issues and enjoyed ridiculing popular but (in his opinion) foolish ideas, thus earning the epithet* curmudgeon. *In this essay written in the 1920s, he argues for capital punishment on the grounds that it satisfies our need for* katharsis, *"a healthy letting off of steam."*

Of the arguments against capital punishment that issue from uplifters, two are commonly heard most often, to wit: 1

1. That hanging a man (or frying him or gassing him) is a dreadful business, degrading to those who have to do it and revolting to those who have to witness it.   2

2. That it is useless, for it does not deter others from the same crime.   3

The first of these arguments, it seems to me, is plainly too weak to need serious refutation. All it says, in brief, is that the work of the hangman is unpleasant. Granted. But suppose it is? It may be quite necessary to society for all that. There are, indeed, many other jobs that are unpleasant, and yet no one thinks of abolishing them—that of the plumber, that of the soldier, that of the garbage-man, that of the priest hearing confessions, that of the sand-hog, and so on. Moreover, what evidence is there that any actual hangman complains of his work? I have heard none. On the contrary, I have known many who delighted in their ancient art, and practiced it proudly.   4

In the second argument of the abolitionists there is rather more force, but 5 even here, I believe, the ground under them is shaky. Their fundamental error consists in assuming that the whole aim of punishing criminals is to deter other (potential) criminals—that we hang or electrocute A simply in order to so alarm B that he will not kill C. This, I believe, is an assumption which confuses a part with a whole. Deterrence, obviously, is *one* of the aims of punishment, but it is surely not the only one. On the contrary, there are at least a half dozen, and some are probably quite as important. At least one of them, practically considered, is *more* important. Commonly, it is described as revenge, but revenge is really not the word for it. I borrow a better term from the late Aristotle: *katharsis*. *Katharsis*, so used, means a salubrious discharge of emotions, a healthy letting off of steam. A school-boy, disliking his teacher, deposits a tack upon the pedagogical chair; the teacher jumps and the boy laughs. This is *katharsis*. What I contend is that one of the prime objects of all judicial punishments is to afford the same grateful relief (*a*) to the immediate victims of the criminal punished, and (*b*) to the general body of moral and timorous men.

These persons, and particularly the first group, are concerned only indi- 6 rectly with deterring other criminals. The thing they crave primarily is the satisfaction of seeing the criminal actually before them suffer as he made them suffer. What they want is the peace of mind that goes with the feeling that accounts are squared. Until they get that satisfaction they are in a state of emotional tension, and hence unhappy. The instant they get it they are comfortable. I do not argue that this yearning is noble; I simply argue that it is almost universal among human beings. In the face of injuries that are unimportant and can be borne without damage it may yield to higher impulses; that is to say, it may yield to what is called Christian charity. But when the injury is serious Christianity is adjourned, and even saints reach for their sidearms. It is plainly asking too much of human nature to expect it to conquer so natural an impulse. A keeps a store and has a bookkeeper, B. B steals $700, employs it in playing at dice or bingo, and is cleaned out. What is A to do? Let B go? If he does so he will be unable to sleep at night. The sense of injury, of injustice, of frustration will haunt him like pruritus. So he turns B over to the police, and they hustle B to prison. Thereafter A can sleep. More, he has pleasant dreams. He pictures B chained to the wall of a dungeon a hundred feet underground, devoured by rats and scorpions. It is so agreeable that it makes him forget his $700. He has got his *katharsis*.

The same thing precisely takes place on a larger scale when there is a 7 crime which destroys a whole community's sense of security. Every law-abiding citizen feels menaced and frustrated until the criminals have been struck down—until the communal capacity to get even with them, and more than even, has been dramatically demonstrated. Here, manifestly, the business of deterring others is no more than an afterthought. The main thing is to destroy the concrete scoundrels whose act has alarmed everyone, and thus made everyone unhappy. Until they are brought to book that unhappiness continues; when the law has been executed upon them there is a sigh of relief. In other words, there is *katharsis*.

I know of no public demand for the death penalty for ordinary crimes, 8 even for ordinary homicides. Its infliction would shock all men of normal decency of feeling. But for crimes involving the deliberate and inexcusable taking of human life, by men openly defiant of all civilized order—for such crimes it seems, to nine men out of ten, a just and proper punishment. Any lesser penalty leaves them feeling that the criminal has got the better of society—that he is free to add insult to injury by laughing. That feeling can be dissipated only by a recourse to *katharsis*, the invention of the aforesaid Aristotle. It is more effectively and economically achieved, as human nature now is, by wafting the criminal to realms of bliss.

The real objection to capital punishment doesn't lie against the actual ex- 9 termination of the condemned, but against our brutal American habit of putting it off so long. After all, every one of us must die soon or late, and a murderer, it must be assumed, is one who makes that sad fact the cornerstone of his metaphysic. But it is one thing to die, and quite another thing to lie for long months and even years under the shadow of death. No sane man would choose such a finish. All of us, despite the Prayer Book, long for a swift and unexpected end. Unhappily, a murderer, under the irrational American system, is tortured for what, to him, must seem a whole series of eternities. For months on end he sits in prison while his lawyers carry on their idiotic buffoonery with writs, injunctions, mandamuses, and appeals. In order to get his money (or that of his friends) they have to feed him with hope. Now and then, by the imbecility of a judge or some trick of juridic science, they actually justify it. But let us say that, his money all gone, they finally throw up their hands. Their client is now ready for the rope or the chair. But he must still wait for months before it fetches him.

That wait, I believe, is horribly cruel. I have seen more than one man 10 sitting in the death-house, and I don't want to see any more. Worse, it is wholly useless. Why should he wait at all? Why not hang him the day after the last court dissipates his last hope? Why torture him as not even cannibals would torture their victims? The common answer is that he must have time to make his peace with God. But how long does that take? It may be accomplished, I believe, in two hours quite as comfortably as in two years. There are, indeed, no temporal limitations upon God. He could forgive a whole herd of murderers in a millionth of a second. More, it has been done.

⊠ **WALTER BERNS**

For Capital Punishment

Walter Berns, a professor in the Department of Government at Georgetown University, has written extensively in his field and in related areas. In the following excerpts from his book, For Capital Punishment, *he argues in favor of the general view called* retributionism, *the idea that those who do wrong deserve to be punished—to be paid back—for what they have done. ". . . the American people are entitled as a people to demand that criminals be paid back, and that the worst of them be made to pay back with their lives."*

It must be one of the oldest jokes in circulation. In the dark of a wild night a 1 ship strikes a rock and sinks, but one of its sailors clings desperately to a piece of wreckage and is eventually cast up exhausted on an unknown and deserted beach. In the morning he struggles to his feet and, rubbing his salt-encrusted eyes, looks around to learn where he is. The only human thing he sees is a gallows. "Thank God," he exclaims, "civilization." There cannot be many of us who have not heard this story or, when we first heard it, laughed at it. The sailor's reaction was, we think, absurd. Yet, however old the story, the fact is that the gallows has not been abolished in the United States even yet, and we count ourselves among the civilized peoples of the world. Moreover, the attempt to have it abolished by the U.S. Supreme Court may only have succeeded in strengthening its structure. . . .

The idea that the presence of a gallows could indicate the presence of a 2 civilized people is, as I indicated at the outset, a joke. I certainly thought so the first time I heard the story; it was only a few years ago that I began to suspect that that sailor may have been right. What led me to change my mind was the phenomenon of Simon Wiesenthal.

Like most Americans, my business did not require me to think about 3 criminals or, more precisely, the punishment of criminals. In a vague way, I was aware that there was some disagreement concerning the purpose of punishment—deterrence, rehabilitation, or retribution—but I had no reason then to decide which was right or to what extent they may all have been right. I did know that retribution was held in ill repute among criminologists. Then I began to reflect on the work of Simon Wiesenthal, who, from a tiny, one-man office in Vienna, has devoted himself since 1945 exclusively to the task of hunting down the Nazis who survived the war and escaped into the world. Why did he hunt them, and what did he hope to accomplish by finding them? And why did I respect him for devoting his life to this singular task? He says that his conscience forces him "to bring the guilty ones to trial." And if they are convicted, then what? Punish them, of course. But why? To rehabilitate them? The very idea is absurd. To incapacitate them? But they represent no present danger. To deter others from doing what they did? That is a hope too extravagant to be indulged. The answer—to me and, I suspect, everyone else who agrees that they should be punished—was clear: *to pay them back*. And how do you pay back SS Obersturmführer Franz Stangl, SS Untersturmführer Wilhelm Rosenbaum, SS Obersturmbannführer Adolf Eichmann, or someday—who knows?—Reichsleiter Martin Bormann? As the world knows, Eichmann was executed, and I suspect that most of the decent, *civilized* world agrees that this was the only way he could be paid back. . . .

The abolitionists condemn [capital punishment] because it springs from   4
revenge, they say, and revenge is the ugliest passion in the human soul. They condemn it because it justifies punishment for the sake of punishment alone, and they are opposed to punishment that serves no purpose beyond inflicting pain on its victims. . . .

They condemn retribution because they see it, rightly or wrongly, as the   5
only basis on which the death penalty can be supported. To kill an offender is not only unnecessary but precludes the possiblity of reforming him, and reformation, they say, is the only civilized response to the criminal. Even murderers—indeed, especially murderers—are capable of being redeemed or of repenting their crimes. Camus tells the story of one Bernard Fallot, a member of a particularly vicious gang that worked for the Gestapo, who admitted having committed many terrible crimes.

> Public opinion and the opinion of his judges certainly classed him among the irremediable, and I should have been tempted to agree if I had not read a surprising testimony. This is what Fallot said . . . after declaring that he wanted to die courageously: "Shall I tell you my greatest regret? Well, it is not having known the Bible I now have here. I assure you that I wouldn't be where I now am."

What is accomplished by killing this man? To kill him may satisfy the public's desire to wreak revenge on him, but no good and much harm is accomplished by giving vent to such passions. Besides, to kill him is to waste another valuable human life, a life that in the future would surely be devoted to good works. Not only should he not be killed, he should not be imprisoned. The elimination of capital punishment must be followed by the elimination of all punishment for the sake of punishment alone; only when the law is purged of the punitive spirit can we solve the crime problem.

> Though capital punishment was a contradiction to the chosen methods of nineteenth-century penology, which had revolted against violence, that penology still accepted the necessity of exacting retribution from criminals. Present-day penology, by contrast, puts its emphasis not on retribution, nor even on deterrence, but on rehabilitation. It combats crime by such reformative and essentially nonpunitive means as probation and psychiatric help in and out of prisons. It seeks eventually to replace the old concept of "the punishment to fit the crime" with a quite new notion: "the treatment to fit the criminal."

Not even a murderer deserves to be *punished*.

The goal of the abolitionists is not merely the elimination of capital pun- 6
ishment but the reform or rehabilitation of the criminal, *even* if he is a murderer. The public that favors capital punishment is of the opinion that the
murderer deserves to be punished, and does not deserve to be treated, even if
by treatment he *could* be rehabilitated.

✻   ✻   ✻

Anger is expressed or manifested on those occasions when someone has 7
acted in a manner that is thought to be unjust, and one of its bases is the
opinion that men are responsible, and should be held responsible, for what
they do. Thus, anger is accompanied not only by the pain caused by him who
is the object of anger, but by the pleasure arising from the expectation of
exacting revenge on someone who is thought to deserve it. We can become
angry with an inanimate object (the door we run into and then kick in return)
only by foolishly attributing responsibility to it, and we cannot do that for long,
which is why we do not think of returning later to revenge ourselves on the
door. For the same reason, we cannot be more than momentarily angry with
an animate creature other than man; only a fool or worse would dream of taking
revenge on a dog. And, finally, we tend to pity rather than to be angry with
men who—because they are insane, for example—are not responsible for their
acts. Anger, then, is a very human passion not only because only a human
being can be angry, but also because it acknowledges the humanity of its objects:
it holds them accountable for what they do. It is an expression of that element
of the soul that is connected with the view that there is responsibility in the
world; and in holding particular men responsible, it pays them that respect
which is due them as men. Anger recognizes that only men have the capacity
to be moral beings and, in so doing, acknowledges the dignity of human beings.
Anger is somehow connected with justice, and it is this that modern penology
has not understood; it tends, on the whole, to regard anger as merely a selfish
passion. . . .

Criminals are properly the objects of anger, and the perpetrators of terrible 8
crimes—for example, Lee Harvey Oswald and James Earl Ray—are properly
the objects of great anger. They have done more than inflict an injury on an
isolated individual; they have violated the foundations of trust and friendship,
the necessary elements of a moral community, the only community worth
living in. A moral community, unlike a hive of bees or a hill of ants, is one
whose members are expected freely to obey the laws and, unlike a tyranny, are
trusted to obey the laws. The criminal has violated that trust, and in so doing
has injured not merely his immediate victim but the community as such. He
has called into question the very possibility of that community by suggesting
that men cannot be trusted freely to respect the property, the person, and the
dignity of those with whom they are associated. If, then, men are not angry
when someone else is robbed, raped, or murdered, the implication is that there
is no moral community because those men do not care for anyone other than
themselves. Anger is an expression of that caring, and society needs men who

care for each other, who share their pleasures and their pains, and do so for the sake of the others. It is the passion that can cause us to act for reasons having nothing to do with selfish or mean calculation; indeed, when educated, it can become a generous passion, the passion that protects the community or country by demanding punishment for its enemies. It is the stuff from which heroes are made.

*   *   *

When abolitionists speak of the barbarity of capital punishment and when   9 Supreme Court justices denounce expatriation in almost identical language, they ought to be reminded that men whose moral sensitivity they would not question have supported both punishments. Lincoln, for example, albeit with a befitting reluctance, authorized the execution of 267 persons during his presidency, and ordered the "Copperhead" Clement L. Vallandigham banished; and it was Shakespeare's sensitivity to the moral issue that required him to have Macbeth killed. They should also be given some pause by the knowledge that the man who originated the opposition to both capital and exilic punishment, Cesare Beccaria, was a man who argued that there is no morality outside the positive law and that it is reasonable to love one's property more than one's country. There is nothing exalted in these opinions, and there is nothing exalted in the versions of them that appear in today's judicial opinions. Capital punishment was said by Justice Brennan to be a denial of human dignity, but in order to reach this conclusion he had to reduce human dignity to the point where it became something possessed by "the vilest criminal." Expatriation is said by the Court to be unconstitutional because it deprives a man of his right to have rights, which *is* his citizenship, and no one, no matter what he does, can be dispossessed of the right to have rights. (Why not a right to the right to have rights?) Any notion of what Justice Frankfurter in dissent referred to as "the communion of our citizens," of a community that can be violated by murderers or traitors, is wholly absent from these opinions; so too is any notion that it is one function of the law to protect that community.

But, contrary to abolitionist hopes and expectations, the Court did not   10 invalidate the death penalty. It upheld it. It upheld it on retributive grounds. In doing so, it recognized, at least implicitly, that the American people are entitled *as a people* to demand that criminals be paid back, and that the worst of them be made to pay back with their lives. In doing this, it gave them the means by which they might strengthen the law that makes them a people, and not a mere aggregation of selfish individuals.

⊠ GEORGE ORWELL

A Hanging

George Orwell (1903–1950), whose real name was Eric Arthur Blair, is well known for his political essays, fiction, and writings on language. His political novels, Animal Farm *and* Nineteen Eighty-Four, *have had a tremendous impact on the political scene, and his essay "Politics and the English Language" is one of the most widely read essays of its kind. In this short story, Orwell argues against capital punishment not by presenting reasons that lead to that conclusion with cold logic but rather by simply describing a hanging and his reaction to it.*

We set out for the gallows. Two warders marched on either side of the 1
prisoner, with their rifles at the slope; two others marched close against him, gripping him by arm and shoulder, as though at once pushing and supporting him. The rest of us, magistrates and the like, followed behind. Suddenly, when we had gone ten yards, the procession stopped short without any order or warning. A dreadful thing had happened—a dog, come goodness knows whence, had appeared in the yard. It came bounding among us with a loud volley of barks, and leapt round us wagging its whole body, wild with glee at finding so many human beings together. It was a large wooly dog, half Airedale, half pariah. For a moment it pranced round us, and then, before anyone could stop it, it had made a dash for the prisoner and, jumping up, tried to lick his face. Everyone stood aghast, too taken aback even to grab at the dog.

"Who let that bloody brute in here?" said the superintendent angrily. 2
"Catch it, someone!"

A warder, detached from the escort, charged clumsily after the dog, but it 3
danced and gamboled just out of his reach, taking everything as part of the game. A young Eurasian jailer picked up a handful of gravel and tried to stone the dog away, but it dodged the stones and came after us again. Its yaps echoed from the jail walls. The prisoner, in the grasp of the two warders, looked on incuriously, as though this was another formality of the hanging. It was several minutes before someone managed to catch the dog. Then we put my handkerchief through its collar and moved off once more, with the dog still straining and whimpering.

It was about forty yards to the gallows. I watched the bare brown back of 4
the prisoner marching in front of me. He walked clumsily with his bound arms, but quite steadily, with that bobbing gait of the Indian who never straightens his knees. At each step his muscles slid neatly into place, the lock of hair on his scalp danced up and down, his feet printed themselves on the wet gravel. And once, in spite of the men who gripped him by each shoulder, he stepped slightly aside to avoid a puddle on the path.

It is curious, but till that moment I had never realized what it means to destroy a healthy, conscious man. When I saw the prisoner step aside to avoid the puddle I saw the mystery, the unspeakable wrongness, of cutting a life short when it is in full tide. This man was not dying, he was alive just as we are alive. All the organs of his body were working—bowels digesting food, skin renewing itself, nails growing, tissues forming—all toiling away in solemn foolery. His nails would still be growing when he stood on the drop, when he was falling through the air with a tenth of a second to live. His eyes saw the yellow gravel and the gray walls, and his brain still remembered, foresaw, reasoned—reasoned even about puddles. He and we were a party of men walking together, seeing, hearing, feeling, understanding the same world; and in two minutes, with a sudden snap, one of us would be gone—one mind less, one world less.

The gallows stood in a small yard, separate from the main grounds of the prison, and overgrown with tall prickly weeds. It was a brick erection like three sides of a shed, with planking on top, and above that two beams and a crossbar with the rope dangling. The hangman, a gray-haired convict in the white uniform of the prison, was waiting beside his machine. He greeted us with a servile crouch as we entered. At a word from Francis the two warders, gripping the prisoner more closely than ever, half led, half pushed him to the gallows and helped him clumsily up the ladder. Then the hangman climbed up and fixed the rope round the prisoner's neck.

We stood waiting, five yards away. The warders had formed in a rough circle round the gallows. And then, when the noose was fixed, the prisoner began crying out to his god. It was a high, reiterated cry of "Ram! Ram! Ram! Ram!" not urgent and fearful like a prayer or cry for help, but steady, rhythmical, almost like the tolling of a bell. The dog answered the sound with a whine. The hangman, still standing on the gallows, produced a small cotton bag like a flour bag and drew it down over the prisoner's face. But the sound, muffled by the cloth, still persisted, over and over again: "Ram! Ram! Ram! Ram! Ram!"

The hangman climbed down and stood ready, holding the lever. Minutes seemed to pass. The steady, muffled crying from the prisoner went on and on, "Ram! Ram! Ram!" never faltering for an instant. The superintendent, his head on his chest, was slowly poking the ground with his stick; perhaps he was counting the cries, allowing the prisoner a fixed number—fifty, perhaps, or a hundred. Everyone had changed color. The Indians had gone gray like bad coffee, and one or two of the bayonets were wavering. We looked at the lashed, hooded man on the drop, and listened to his cries—each cry another second of life; the same thought was in all our minds: oh, kill him quickly, get it over, stop that abominable noise!

Suddenly the superintendent made up his mind. Throwing up his head he made a swift motion with his stick. "Chalo!" he shouted almost fiercely.

There was a clanking noise, and then dead silence. The prisoner had vanished, and the rope was twisting on itself. I let go of the dog, and it galloped immediately to the back of the gallows; but when it got there it stopped short, barked, and then retreated into a corner of the yard, where it stood among the weeds, looking timorously out at us. We went round the gallows to inspect the prisoner's body. He was dangling with his toes pointed straight downward, very slowly revolving, as dead as a stone.

CAPITAL PUNISHMENT

QUESTIONS AND SUGGESTIONS FOR WRITING

1. Darrow, in his argument against capital punishment, asks how we can consider ourselves civilized if we ignore the causes of crime and "mete out harsh punishments" to criminals who are "victims of conditions over which they have no control." Should we take into consideration such factors as the background and upbringing of criminals and the conditions leading to the crime? Or should we ignore these factors and suit the punishment to the crime?

2. Mencken begins his essay by presenting the opposition's reasons, which he then refutes. Write an argument for or against capital punishment using Mencken's method of refutation as an introduction to your own argument.

3. The thesis of Orwell's story is implicit in his description of the hanging and in the narrator's response. Explain the thesis and contrast his method of argument to Mencken's or Darrow's. Which writer do you find most convincing?

4. Do some research on capital punishment by examining arguments for and against the death penalty. Gather statistics on the expense of litigation, the number of convicts on death row, the costs of maintaining prisoners in jail. Find examples of unjust punishments and racial discrimination in the court system. Compare the practices of other countries to those of our own. Then evaluate your material and develop a well-reasoned argument for or against the death penalty.

AIDS

In some parts of Africa, AIDS has started to destroy a whole generation of young people. In the rest of the world, the current AIDS epidemic has as yet struck less harshly, except among a few "at risk" groups. But the potential for disaster exists everywhere, given that there is no known cure and it is believed by many that everyone who is exposed to the AIDS virus eventually contracts and dies from the disease. It is thus no small wonder that AIDS has stirred up a great deal of controversy.

✂ CHARLES KRAUTHAMMER

Ignorance Is Cause but Not Justification for AIDS Bias

Charles Krauthammer is a well-known syndicated columnist. In this essay he argues against what he perceives to be an irrational fear of contagion of AIDS in the workplace.

Two years after the accident at Unit 2 nuclear reactor at Three Mile Island, a court suit was filed to prevent the restarting of the other, undamaged, reactor. The argument was not that this reactor was a health hazard. The Nuclear Regulatory Commission had produced 22,000 pages of hearing transcripts to determine that it was not.

The argument instead was that people believed that it was dangerous. Thus 2 if TMI 1 were reopened it might produce "intense anxiety" (tension and fear, accompanied by physical disorders including skin rashes, aggravated ulcers, and skeletal and muscular problems), and that would be a hazard to the surrounding communities.

A novel idea. Something is safe, but because people think it is dangerous 3 that makes it, well, (psychologically) unsafe. Perception is reality. The U.S.

169

Supreme Court, however, was unimpressed with this novelty. It ruled, unanimously, that the commission did not have to consider imaginary effects.

FEAR IS NOT ENOUGH

Fear is undoubtedly an unpleasant state, but in itself does not create actionable 4
claims. If it did, the line of litigants invoking such claims would be endless. Is there anything, after all, that people do not irrationally fear? If a groundless fear is enough to endow one with legal rights, then there is no piece of nonsense that cannot result in yet another claim on others. Your neighbor has a dog. The dog is harmless. But you are afraid of dogs anyway. Can you impound the dog?

In the case of Three Mile Island, the Reagan Justice Department argued 5
no. Now, another year, another place and another piece of nonsense. The hysteria this time is not about gamma rays but about AIDS, the irradiated irrationality of the 1980s.

DISCRIMINATION LAWS DEBASED

The Justice Department has considered again the question of whether percep- 6
tion is reality. It issued a ruling on what kind of discrimination is permissible against AIDS victims. The Rehabilitation Act of 1973 prohibits discrimination on the basis of handicap. The Justice Department decided that an employer may not fire an AIDS victim if the employer is concerned about the "disabling effect of AIDS." But he may fire the victims if he is concerned about the contagious effects of AIDS.

Of course, in the workplace there are no contagious effects. You have 7
about as much chance of catching AIDS in the workplace as you do of catching cancer or multiple sclerosis. So: Your employee has AIDS or cancer or MS. The employee is harmless. But you are afraid of him anyway. Can you fire him? Says the Justice Department, yes.

The immediate effect of this ruling will be to permit AIDS firings left and 8
right. Is there an easier claim than the claim of irrational fear? The more general effect is to debase the idea underlying the anti-discrimination laws. The whole point of such laws is to say this: It may indeed cause you psychological distress to mix with others whom you irrationally dislike or fear. Too bad. The state has decided that these particular prejudices are destructive and irrational. Therefore the state will prohibit you—even in "private-sector" transactions such as hiring or firing or serving people in your own luncheonette—from acting upon your groundless prejudices.

The point of the Rehabilitation Act was to add another class of irrational- 9
ity—irrationality about the disabled—to the catalogue of those that the state will no longer countenance. Now comes the Justice Department, in essence, to add: "—except for one category of irrationality, fear of contagion. The state will permit you to fire disabled people on that account."

Even as a piece of reasoning this casuistry fails. After all, why in general 10
do people shrink from (and end up discriminating against) disability if not from

fear of contagion? Moreover, if contagion were really the problem, private employers would not have to worry about it at all. The state can handle that. It has more sweeping powers against people with serious contagious diseases than it does against criminals. If you are innocent of all sin but have tuberculosis, the government can lock you away.

The problem of AIDS in the workplace is not contagion. It is, as someone 11 well acquainted with disability once said, fear itself. Fear itself does not deserve special protection in our public life.

There is no greater intellectual laziness than the proposition that percep- 12 tion is reality. The last place that Orwellian slogan ought to find refuge is in the law. The whole point of the law is to determine which perceptions are real and which aren't, and to give legal standing to one and not the other.

It does not matter if people think you murdered. If you didn't you don't go 13 to jail. It does not matter if people think TMI 1 is dangerous. If it isn't, it stays open. It should not matter if people think that you can get AIDS in the Xerox room. You can't. Ignorance is a cause of discrimination. It is not a justification for it.

⊠ **WILLIAM E. DANNEMEYER**

The AIDS Epidemic

California Congressman William E. Dannemeyer, Republican, is a leading congressional advocate of increased federal action to control the spread of AIDS. In this excerpt from congressional testimony, he argues that we have no other choice than to start effective AIDS screening test procedures.

The United States is experiencing a health catastrophe of historic proportions 1 and an ethical crisis of equal magnitude. Approximately 28,000 persons have been diagnosed with Acquired Immune Deficiency Syndrome [AIDS]. Of that number, 13,442 are already dead and the remaining number are expected to die within 5 years. A recent report by the Centers for Disease Control [CDC] projects that by 1991 the cumulative number of AIDS cases will total more than 270,000 and the number of deaths will exceed 179,000.

DEVASTATING SCENARIO

In addition, it is estimated that between 1,000,000 and 1,500,000 persons are 2 infected with the AIDS virus and are capable of transmitting the disease. Until recently it was hoped that only 25 to 30 percent of those infected would become victims of full-blown AIDS. However, recent evidence indicates that more than one-third of those exposed to the virus will progress to the fatal stages of the disease and all of those exposed will experience some substantial impairment of their immune system. If this scenario fails to illustrate the severity of the health crisis at hand, there is more.

The AIDS epidemic will result in a profound loss of life. In the next 5   3 years the number of deaths attributable to AIDS will exceed the number of U.S. military deaths which resulted from World War II. It is a tragedy for any nation to lose so many productive citizens in the prime of life and to bear the societal cost of such a devastating disease. . . .

Perhaps the most disturbing aspect of this bleak projection is that individ-   4 uals who suspect they may be infectious and some of those who know they are infectious continue to engage in highrisk activities proven to spread this disease. Despite the authority of public health officials to halt this type of behavior, they have declined to intervene, saying that isolation orders or restrictions on sexual activities infringe on the civil rights of AIDS victims.

The issue at hand is not the civil rights of any victim nor of any potential   5 victims, it is finding a way of stopping any and all activities that may spread this 100 percent fatal disease. The AIDS virus does not have rights, and the rights of individuals who persist in engaging in certain activities are outweighed by the rights of those unsuspecting persons whose lives are placed at risk. It is blatantly selfish for an individual to reject or ignore knowledge which would assist him in preventing the death of another. Yet we are faced with the unfortunate fact that many AIDS victims refuse to acknowledge that their actions could result in the death of another. Persons who suspect they may have been exposed are refusing to get tested because they are afraid of losing their jobs, their friends, and the support of their families. While denial and disbelief are understandable reactions, AIDS victims and all those who have been exposed must be forced to acknowledge the severity of their condition and take responsibility for the consequences of their actions and inactions.

Although I firmly believe that the U.S. Public Health Service and State   6 medical authorities should be the entities responsible for setting and implementing these vital standards, their failure to act has left a dangerous void in public health policies and protections. For this reason I am introducing an omnibus package of legislative measures aimed at taking hold of this devastating disease before it takes hold of the Nation.

VITAL PREVENTIVE STEPS

The first bill is, I believe, the lynchpin for altering the devastating course of   7 this disease. This bill will make it a crime for Federal employees, members of the armed services, and those in Federal buildings who know they have AIDS or who know they carry the virus, to purposefully engage in activities considered high risk for purposes of transmission. The penalty for engaging in this prohibited conduct will be enforced isolation for a period of 5 years under the supervision of a public health officer or until a cure is found.

Although I anticipate that this legislation will not be widely enforced, I   8
believe it is important that credible standards be set and that individuals be on notice that certain conduct will not be tolerated by our society. . . .

No civil rights cry can overcome the realities of actions which condemn   9
another to die. Whether by action or inaction, such conduct is murder and must be sanctioned as such. Society cannot and must not condone different standards of conduct for AIDS victims because they are fatally ill. We must show compassion while taking the preventive steps necessary to control proliferation of this terrifying disease. In my judgment this bill will encourage such action.

PRUDENT LEGISLATION

The second bill I am introducing is an omnibus resolution expressing the sense   10
of Congress that States should enact the following laws in an attempt to deal with the AIDs problem:

Legislation which would require a blood test for AIDS before a couple   11
may be married;

Legislation which would require that partners of AIDS victims be traced   12
and counseled, as is currently done with partners of victims of syphilis and gonorrhea; . . .

Legislation which would require individuals seeking a license to practice   13
medicine, nursing, or any other health care profession to have a negative test result from a test for AIDS, or a test to determine if an individual is a carrier of the virus; . . .

Legislation which would require that all persons arrested for prostitution   14
and intravenous drug use as well as all persons scheduled to be housed in any prison facility be tested for AIDS or for presence of the virus. It is the intravenous drug user who shares needles and the prostitute with largely unidentified partners who are the major avenues of infection. In addition, States should enact legislation which would require that all persons seeking a marriage license must be tested for AIDS or presence of the virus.

Those persons in any of the above groups who test positive should then be   15
counseled about the necessity of stopping all behaviors which could transmit the virus. Ultimately, it would be appropriate for public health authorities to consider court sanctioned isolation for those HIV positive prostitutes who continue to practice their profession and intravenous drug users who continue intravenous drug use and the sharing of needles.

I introduce this resolution with the hope that States will enact such legis-   16
lation and take these and other prudent steps to curtail the spread of AIDS. Some claim that the States are the only ones with jurisdiction over the health threat of AIDS. While I concur with the assessment that States should retain jurisdiction, I do not agree that States are solely responsible. . . .

PUBLIC HEALTH SERVICE

The third bill in this omnibus package makes it a crime for persons with AIDS,   17
or for those who carry the AIDS virus, to knowingly donate blood, semen, or
organs. Evidence that the Public Health Service is not pursuing policies based
solely on concern for the public health but on political considerations is obvious when one considers the inappropriate handling of our blood supply to
date. Virtually all hemophiliacs in the United States and elsewhere who have
received clotting factor concentrates derived from blood collected in the United
States prior to 1985 have become infected with the AIDS virus. Nine thousand
hemophiliacs and 20,000 transfusion recipients are now permanently infected
with the AIDS virus. The most regrettable part of this reality is that the contam-
ination of our Nation's blood supply could largely have been avoided if the
Public Health Service had appropriately restricted all high risk groups, specifically male homosexuals, from donating blood at the outset of the AIDS
epidemic.

AIDS was recognized as a blood-transmitted disease as early as 1982 and   18
as a disease peculiar to homosexuals, intravenous drug users, and Haitians at
approximately the same time. Despite this evidence, PHS recommended in
1985 that intravenous drug users, which comprise 13 percent of the identified
cases, be prohibited from donating blood, while suggesting that polygamous
male homosexuals, who comprised 73 percent of the known cases, refrain from
donating blood. These initial guidelines served to encourage male homosexuals
who consider themselves monogamous, to donate blood. At the time these
guidelines were issued, PHS knew that the incubation period for AIDS may be
as long as 8 years and that a recent Kinsey report indicated that the longest
relationship between homosexuals averaged 1 to 3 years, and yet the recommendation only requested male homosexuals who had been polygamous in the past
6 years to refrain from donating. Following the release of these guidelines, PHS
admitted that they were a product of compromise between the homosexual
community and public health authorities. . . .

The fourth bill deals with the issue of mandatory testing. My legislation   19
would require all federally funded prisons to institute immediate testing of
inmates for seropositivity to the AIDS virus and testing of all persons seeking to
immigrate to this country. The most serious threat we now face is the large
percentage of HTLV-III positive individuals who do not know they are infectious. These individuals cannot take necessary precautions and stop all high-
risk contact because they do not know that their status demands such conduct.
For this reason we must begin mandatory testing in high-risk situations. . . .

Similarly, testing immigrants for disease has long been the policy of im-   20
migration authorities with respect to such diseases as syphilis, gonorrhea, tuberculosis, and others. No country has an obligation to accept immigrants with
a fatal and communicable disease and the United States should, as a matter of
course, extend exclusion policies to victims of AIDS and those who test positive
for presence of the virus.

The fifth bill I am introducing will require all States which receive Federal 21
money pursuant to the Federal Venereal Disease Prevention and Control Projects and Programs or to be used for AIDS counseling and education to set up a
system in which State public health authorities are responsible for tracing the
partners of AIDS victims, testing these persons and counseling them about the
infectious nature of this disease.

Under current law it is common practice for State public health authorities 22
to trace the partners of patients with syphilis, gonorrhea, and other venereal
diseases. It is absurd and unwise public health policy to trace persons with a
nonfatal, venereal disease and counsel them about the risks of transmission but
to fail to take the same prudent steps with persons who may have acquired, or
carry, a 100-percent fatal disease. Oregon and Colorado currently have a tracking system for AIDS which has generally proven effective and has not resulted
in "driving seropositive individuals underground," as was predicted by
authorities.

BENEFITS TO SOCIETY

In addition to being sound public health policy, the role of testing in the AIDS 23
epidemic has some positive implications which have been largely ignored.
First, testing immediately reassures the unexposed that they are currently un-
infected and provides a time and place where they can be counseled on how to
remain that way. Second, mandatory testing would give public health authorities the opportunity to better define the actual character and spread of the
disease.

At this time there are an estimated 300,000 HIV positive individuals in 24
the State of California, while only 60,000 have been tested. That leaves approximately 240,000 HIV positive people who do not know they are infectious
and therefore continue to infect others. The only way to stop this disease is for
infected people to stop engaging in high-risk activities and the only way to
ensure that these people can be responsible for their conduct is to test them and
inform them of their ethical and legal responsibility to contain this fatal epidemic. . . .

This omnibus package of legislation is aimed at closing the voids left by a 25
lethargic and too political public health system. I believe it is urgent that we
shift from complacency to action in preventing future cases of AIDS. In my
judgment, the best way to accomplish this is to discard the naive assumptions
and simplistic solutions which have hampered our progress to date. We have
avoided these and other options out of fear of being labeled discriminatory.

THE SOBERING REALITY

It is time to explore any and all options which may diminish the portent of this 26
frightening disease. It is most properly the jurisdiction of the Public Health
Service to take these vitally needed actions, but in the absence of prudent

management of this epidemic by the PHS it is vital that Congress and the Nation fill that void and mobilize all available resources and channel them into realistic and immediate solutions. The sobering reality is that AIDS is an epidemic that affects us all, and as a society we must become involved in choosing our options.

This omnibus package represents a number of options which, I believe, 27 are vital to altering the course of this devastating disease. I urge Congress and the Nation to join me in advocating actionable, practical alternatives to the current public health policy which has resulted in no choice and little hope.

※ **WILLIAM F. BUCKLEY, JR.**

Identify All the Carriers

William F. Buckley, Jr., is a very well-known syndicated columnist, novelist, essayist, TV personality, acquaintance of Gore Vidal, and editor of The National Review. *In this essay he urges that strong measures be taken to identify all carriers of the deadly AIDS virus because "we are not talking about a kidding matter. Our society is generally threatened, and in order to fight AIDS, we need the civil equivalent of universal military training."*

I have read and listened, and I think now that I can convincingly crystallize 1 the thoughts chasing about in the minds of, first, those whose concern with AIDS victims is based primarily on a concern for them and for the maintenance of the most rigid standards of civil liberties and personal privacy, and, second, those whose anxiety to protect the public impels them to give subordinate attention to the civil amenities of those who suffer from AIDS and primary attention to the safety of those who do not.

Arguments used by both sides are sometimes utilitarian, sometimes moral, 2 sometimes a little of each—and almost always a little elusive. Most readers will locate their own inclinations and priorities somewhere other than in the polar positions here put forward by design.

School A suspects, in the array of arguments of School B, a venture in 3 ethical opportunism. Look, they say, we have made enormous headway in the matter of civil rights for all, dislodging the straight-laced from mummified positions they inherited through eclectic superstitions ranging from the Bible's to Freud's. A generation ago, homosexuals lived mostly in the closet. Nowadays they take over cities and parade on Halloween and demand equal rights for themselves qua homosexuals, not merely as apparently disinterested civil libertarians.

Along comes AIDS, School A continues, and even though it is well 4 known that the virus can be communicated by infected needles, known also that heterosexuals can transmit the virus, still it is both a fact and the popular perception that AIDS is the special curse of the homosexual, transmitted through anal sex between males. And if you look hard, you will discern that little smirk on the face of the man oh-so-concerned about public health. He is looking for ways to safeguard the public, sure, but he is by no means reluctant, in the course of doing so, to sound an invidious tocsin whose clamor is a call to undo all the understanding so painfully cultivated over a generation by those who have fought for the privacy of their bedroom. What School B is really complaining about is the extension of civil rights to homosexuals.

School A will not say all that in words quite so jut-jawed, but it plainly 5 feels that no laws or regulations should be passed that have the effect of identifying the AIDS carrier. It isn't, School A concedes, as if AIDS were transmitted via public drinking fountains. But any attempt to segregate the AIDS carrier is primarily an act of moral ostracism.

School B does in fact tend to disapprove forcefully of homosexuality, but 6 tends to approach the problem of AIDS empirically. It argues that acquired immune deficiency syndrome is potentially the most serious epidemic to have shown its face in this century. Summarizing currently accepted statistics, *The Economist* recently raised the possibility "that the AIDS virus will have killed more than 250,000 Americans in eight years' time." Moreover, if the epidemic extended to that point, it would burst through existing boundaries. There would then be "no guarantee that the disease will remain largely confined to groups at special risk, such as homosexuals, hemophiliacs, and people who inject drugs intravenously. If AIDS were to spread through the general population, it would become a catastrophe." Accordingly, School B says, we face a utilitarian imperative, and this requires absolutely nothing less than the identification of the million-odd people who, the doctors estimate, are carriers.

How? 7

Well, the military has taken the first concrete step. Two million soldiers 8 will be given the blood test, and those who have AIDS will be discreetly discharged.

Discreetly, you say! 9

Hold on. I'm coming to that. You have the military making the first 10 massive move designed to identify AIDS sufferers—and, bear in mind, an AIDS carrier today is an AIDS carrier on the day of his death, which day, depending on the viral strain, will be two years from now or when he is threescore and 10. The next logical step would be to require of anyone who seeks a marriage license that he present himself not only with a Wassermann test but also an AIDS test.

But if he has AIDS, should he then be free to marry?   11

Only after the intended spouse is advised that her intended husband has   12
AIDS, and agrees to sterilization. We know already of children born with the disease, transmitted by the mother, who contracted it from the father.

What then would School B suggest for those who are not in the military   13
and who do not set out to get a marriage license? Universal testing?

Yes, in stages. But in rapid stages. The next logical enforcer is the insur-   14
ance company. Blue Cross, for instance, can reasonably require of those who wish to join it a physical examination that requires tests. Almost every American, making his way from infancy to maturity, needs to pass by one or another institutional turnstile. Here the lady will spring out, her right hand on a needle, her left on a computer, to capture a blood specimen.

Is it then proposed by School B that AIDS carriers should be publicly   15
identified as such?

The evidence is not completely in as to the communicability of the dis-   16
ease. But while much has been said that is reassuring, the moment has not yet come when men and women of science are unanimously agreed that AIDS cannot be casually communicated. Let us be patient on that score, pending any tilt in the evidence: If the news is progressively reassuring, public identification would not be necessary. If it turns in the other direction and AIDS develops among, say, children who have merely roughhoused with other children who suffer from AIDS, then more drastic segregation measures would be called for.

But if the time has not come, and may never come, for public identification,   17
what then of private identification?

Everyone detected with AIDS should be tattooed in the upper forearm, to   18
protect common-needle users, and on the buttocks, to prevent the victimization of other homosexuals.

You have got to be kidding! That's exactly what we suspected all along! You   19
are calling for the return of the Scarlet Letter, but only for homosexuals!

Answer: The Scarlet Letter was designed to stimulate public obloquy. The   20
AIDS tattoo is designed for private protection. And the whole point of this is that we are not talking about a kidding matter. Our society is generally threatened, and in order to fight AIDS, we need the civil equivalent of universal military training.

⌗ JAMES K. FITZPATRICK

AIDS: It Is Not Just Another Disease

Free-lance writer James K. Fitzpatrick wrote the following essay for The Wanderer, *a conservative Catholic newspaper. Fitzpatrick believes that the AIDS
epidemic constitutes a moral as well as a medical problem and that homosexuals
cannot "thumb their noses at the God revealed to man in the Bible and to
denigrate the moral codes articulated to mankind through the Judeo-Christian
heritage."*

Give them credit. There is one thing at which American liberals excel. They   1
are slick. They have a way of putting proponents of traditional values on the
defensive. Argue against kiddie-porn and you first have to explain away your
hostility to freedom of expression. Try to limit abortions and you are cast as an
enemy of women. If you feel welfare in the United States has done more harm
to blacks than good, you spend half your time trying to explain why you cannot
overcome racial stereotypes. If you supported the invasion of Grenada, you are
scolded for harboring that bullying arrogance that leads superpowers to see
themselves as "policemen to the world." But if you do not support sanctions
against South Africa, you are the modern counterpart of those in the 1930s
who "did nothing" during the Holocaust. (Similarly they tell us we should be
tolerant of Marxist dictatorships because we cannot "ethnocentrically" assume
every society is "ready" for democracy as we define it, even though the government of South Africa is called a genocidal police state because it is not moving
quickly enough to a one man-one vote democracy.). . .

WHAT THE HOMOSEXUALS WANT

Perhaps the cleverest example of this dodge can be seen taking place in the   2
current discussion of AIDS. And it is working. Homosexuals and their spokes-
men have successfully disarmed those who feel there is a need to bring a moral
dimension to the question of how much time and energy and sympathy society
owes to those who contract the virus. It seems as if it is only in private that the
thought comes up that homosexuals have some role to play in preventing the
spread of this disease by changing their behavior. The assumption seems to be
that it is primarily society's responsibility to find a cure so that homosexuals
can go on with their preferred "lifestyle."

Repeatedly we hear the complaint that AIDS has not attracted the same   3
kind of attention as other diseases because there are "stupid, backward people
in our society who think they can see the hand of God in the situation. They
think they can read God's mind." Or, "Imagine, there are people who picture a
God who goes around like some medieval despot afflicting people with pain
and misery and a lingering death. What kind of people would want to worship

a God like that!" Also, "God is not a cruel God, he is a loving God who wants us to love each other too." And how about, "God would not have made homosexuals with this powerful drive if he did not want them to fulfill their sexual identity." (These, by the way, are near-to-exact quotes I have picked up without really trying by listening to a few of New York City's radio call-in shows.)

You have to admit: It is neat. An attack is launched against those who 4 wonder about God's will in this issue by those who *assure* us that God could will no such thing. The critics of those who have the "audacity" to interpret divine injunctions argue by interpreting divine injunctions. God can have a voice in public issues when His comments coincide with the enlightened opinion of the times.

Is my point that Christians ought to see AIDS as the will of God? No, it 5 is hard to see by what standard one might come to such a conclusion. There is such a thing as divine Providence, but there is no orthodox guideline for us to define whether AIDS belongs more in the category of the fire and brimstone that hit Sodom or with things like polio and bubonic plague, where the hand of God is more difficult to see clearly.

ONE THING IS CERTAIN

But one thing is certain: You do not get AIDS the way people got polio. Near 6 to 75 percent of those who get the disease are homosexuals. And the record is clear, the other cases are indirectly related to homosexuals. The drug users used a needle once used by a homosexual. Others receive a blood transfusion from a homosexual, or from someone who received a transfusion from a homosexual. The children who become victims are children of homosexuals or bisexuals or drug users who contracted the disease from a homosexual. The disease is being spread by homosexuals to each other, and, increasingly, to the rest of society.

Those who are responsible for the outbreak are men and women who are 7 continuing to engage with a wide variety of partners in sexual acts that have been defined as deviant and sinful by the Judeo-Christian community for over 2,000 years now. Most other societies have expressed similar opprobrium, certainly the Islamic world. Warnings, punishments, exhortation, ridicule, prayer, repugnance, scorn have been employed—sometimes judiciously, sometimes inexcusably cruelly—to help those afflicted with this temptation to overcome their weakness. And those who have succeeded in overcoming the temptation, or who have practiced their vice in secret with a decent respect for their fellow citizens' deeply felt convictions in the matter, have been able to live as tolerated members of Western society. The prissy music teacher, the fuddy-duddy bachelor, the career military man uneasy out of his barracks world, have all been part of our literature and folklore.

THIS BOTHERSOME VIRUS

Those who are responsible for the epidemic have chosen to ignore all this. For 8
them, the Bible is wrong, the Church is wrong. The nature of the sexual act
taught by these authorities is a quaint moralism, nothing more. Society is
wrong. Their sexual activity is not a sin, not shameful, it is a matter of preference, a positive good, except for this bothersome virus that is temporarily
clouding the picture.

Indeed some members of homosexual groups express displeasure with 9
fellow homosexuals who are alarmed enough to call for an end to "promis-
cuous" homosexuality, an end to the casual bathhouse assignations and "gay"
bar pickups. Limiting themselves to one or two "safe" partners is too great a
price to pay. One New York "gay" activist in a *New York Times* interview
complained that "safe sex is unexciting sex." The man makes an intriguing
demand. It is as if Typhoid Mary insisted upon her religious and civil right to
work in the school cafeteria while at the same time complaining that the local
health authorities were dragging their feet in coming up with a cure for her. If
homosexuals want society to attack this disease like any other disease they
should be reminded that any other communicable disease of comparable seriousness is attacked with quarantine.

A PUNITIVE MESSAGE TO HUMANITY

Homosexuals are demanding the right to proudly thumb their noses at the God 10
revealed to man in the Bible and to denigrate the moral codes articulated to
mankind through the Judeo-Christian heritage. We cannot know if the Creator
would respond in our era in a punitive manner. But it certainly would be
presumptuous to assume that He would not. Whether you are a fundamentalist
or not, the story of Sodom and Gomorrah is meant to communicate *something*
to mankind.

And it is an attempt by patent intellectual intimidation to label as religious 11
bigots those who feel that they cannot help but note that the AIDS flare-up
demonstrates that we cannot simply shrug off the inherited wisdom of Western
man on such a crucial issue without paying a price. Even a man who believed
in nothing more than the patterns of nature symbolized by Mother Nature
would have to conclude that the risk of AIDS and herpes and other venereal
diseases teaches us about proper conduct in sexual activity.

AIDS

QUESTIONS AND SUGGESTIONS FOR WRITING

1. In supporting his argument that fear of catching AIDS in the workplace is
   irrational, Krauthammer compares the Justice Department's interpretation
   of the Rehabilitation Act to the U.S. Supreme Court decision on the use of

the undamaged nuclear reactor at Three Mile Island. What is the point of this analogy? Is it a relevant or faulty comparison?

2. Write an essay arguing for or against testing for AIDS in the workplace.

3. Dannemeyer argues that federal legislation should be enacted to control the spread of AIDS. Evaluate the three bills he proposes and argue for or against such legislation.

4. What do you think of the procedures Buckley suggests to identify all AIDS carriers? Examine each one and decide whether they would be effective.

5. Does Fitzpatrick say or imply that AIDS constitutes just retribution for immoral homosexual activities? Argue for or against this idea.

6. Fitzpatrick says that AIDS is a "disease" being spread by homosexuals to each other, and, increasingly [via transfusion, contaminated needles, etc.], to the rest of society." Is he right about this? If he were, would it make a difference with respect to the rights of homosexuals?

7. Argue for or against prohibiting children with AIDS from attending public schools.

EDUCATION IN CRISIS

American students do not perform as well on academic achievement tests as do students in Japan. Test scores indicate that ability in reading, writing, and arithmetic has declined in the United States since the 1950s. There is a widespread feeling that public school education in general has declined considerably. Most American high school graduates know little or nothing about science. Approximately one-third of adult Americans are functionally illiterate in this technological age. In other words, it is claimed that education in America is in crisis. The question is what to do about it, and the solutions we're likely to accept depend in large part on what we believe has caused the decline (some blame television more than the public school system), or what we believe the decline involves, or even whether we believe there has been a decline.

⧖ JOHN I. GOODLAD

Can We Have Effective Schools?

John I. Goodlad has taught every grade level from first grade through advanced graduate work and has investigated schools at all levels and in several different countries. In this excerpt from his book, A Place Called School, *he argues that American education has problems that won't be cured by trying harder and laying greater stress on the three Rs, and he describes seven "conditions surrounding the conduct of schooling" that make his case.*

The problems confronting American schools are substantial; the resources available to them are in most instances severely limited; the stakes are high, and it is by no means preordained that all will go well for many of them in the end.

Daedalus (summer 1981), p. v

American schools are in trouble. In fact, the problems of schooling are of such   1
crippling proportions that many schools may not survive. It is possible that our
entire public education system is nearing collapse. We will continue to have
schools, no doubt, but the basis of their support and their relationships to
families, communities, and states could be quite different from what we have
known.

To survive, an institution requires from its clients substantial faith in its   2
usefulness and a measure of satisfaction with its performance. For our schools,
this is a complex matter. The primary clients of American public schools—
parents and their school-age children—have become a minority group. Declining birth rates and increased aging of our population during the 1970s increased
the proportion of citizens not directly involved with the schools. And there
appears to be a rather direct relationship between these changed demographics
and the growing difficulty of securing tax dollars for schools. Tax levies in
several parts of the country are failing even as these words are being written.
More than one district is in the process of closing down its schools. Our public
system of schooling requires for its survival, to say nothing of its good health,
the support of many not currently using it, and that support is in doubt.

To the extent that the attainment of a democratic society depends on the   3
existence of schools equally accessible to everyone, we are all their clients. It is
not easy, however, to convince a majority of our citizens that this relationship
exists and that schools require their support because of it. It is especially difficult
to convince them if they perceive the schools to be deficient in regard to their
traditional functions. Unfortunately, the ability of schools to do their traditional
jobs of assuring literacy and eradicating ignorance is at the center of current
criticism, which is intense.

A basic premise underlying what follows is that this nation has not out-   4
grown its need for schools. If schools should suddenly cease to exist, we would
find it necessary to reinvent them. Another premise is that the schools we need
now are not necessarily the schools we have known. And a third premise is that
the current wave of criticism lacks the diagnosis required for the reconstruction
of schooling. This criticism is in part psychologically motivated—a product of
a general lack of faith in ourselves and our institutions—and is not adequately
focused. . . .

The datum that appeared most to give substance to the mood of disen-   5
chantment with schooling was a decline in some standardized achievement test
scores, particularly the SAT taken by many high school juniors and seniors
seeking admission to the better colleges and universities. Analysts and critics
looked to conventional, simple explanations, much as those who write daily
analyses of the stock market look for simple explanations to account for zigs and
zags. The reasons given for falling test scores ranged from "progressive" teaching
practices of the 1960s, to incompetent administrators, to poorly prepared teachers, and to those in teachers' colleges who prepare teachers. . . .

Not surprisingly, the reforms proposed were piecemeal. Indeed, it is fair to   6
say that few reforms were proposed. Rather, pressures were exerted on teachers

and, ultimately, students to do better, particularly in the "basic subjects." States set up procedures for holding teachers accountable for raising reading and mathematics scores from year to year. Some required students to pass proficiency tests in order to graduate from high school, sometimes even to pass from grade to grade.

The apparent assumption that teachers and students only had to concentrate on the 3 Rs and try harder in order for all to be well is a familiar one. But it ignored an array of conditions surrounding the conduct of schooling which, if not entirely new, were far more intense and widespread than was recognized. 7

First, the two traditionally stable institutions, the household and the church, which had done much of the educating for centuries were themselves in seriously weakened condition by the 1970s. Strained in performing their own functions, they could only hope that the school would stand strong in performing its function—and perhaps pick up some of what they found increasingly difficult to do. A minority of families now attended church together. Sunday school had lost much of its appeal to the young. By the end of the decade, a quarter of the mothers with children under the age of seven were working; approximately 55% of all mothers of schoolage children held a job. For large numbers of children and youths, no parent was there to greet them at the end of the school day. Almost 45% of children born today can expect to be living with only one parent before they reach 18 years of age. It is difficult to estimate the impact of these developments on our young people and the increased burden they place on our schools. 8

Second, and closely related, the almost unquestioned supportive relationship between home and school that characterized earlier periods deteriorated substantially. The child spanked in school one hundred or even fifty years ago often was spanked again at home. The child spanked in school in 1975 frequently became the pivotal figure in a suit against the school brought by his parents. Principals and teachers could no longer assume that they stood *in loco parentis*. Obviously, the collaborative strength of school and home working together toward common goals of child rearing and educating was weakened. Not so obviously, the willingness of school personnel to engage in activities that took their students out of the routines of seat-based instruction also was reduced. Even a slight accident on a field trip could trigger a lawsuit. 9

Third, the economics of providing for such essentials as food, clothing, and shelter joined other factors in changing the nature of communities. Small local markets, specialized shops, and gasoline stations where once one met and chatted with neighbors were replaced by supermarkets where one ignored or stared blankly at strangers from other communities. The decline in the ratio of single family homes to apartments and, later, condominiums changed the whole nature of neighborhoods. We continued to use the words "community" and "neighborhood," but the fit between the words and reality became increasingly loose and obscure. Children and youths often knew none or only a few of the families of their classmates. Much of the former power of "being known" by families who knew one's own family was lost to the child-rearing process. 10

When I was growing up, my parents already knew before I got home about my transgressions on the way home from school. What are the implications of this change for the moral education of the young? What additional problems are thrust upon the school by all these changes in communities and decline in our sense of community?

Fourth, a political coalition that had fought extremely successfully for financial and moral support of public education was largely in disarray by the 1970s. The decline in little more than a decade was precipitous . . . we frequently saw school boards and their superintendents working at cross-purposes during the 1970s. We rarely found legislators, parents, educators, and business leaders working in concert toward common goals. It no longer was stylish to work for the schools. The consequences for the schools' welfare now and, unless a new coalition can be built, in the future are inestimable. 11

Fifth, educators themselves became badly divided. The manner in which collective bargaining evolved set administrators against teachers. Superintendents' efforts to build an undivided administrative team frequently separated principals from their teachers. Yet a bond of trust and mutual support between the principal and teachers of a school appears to be basic to school improvement. Teachers of English, mathematics, science, social studies, and the like at the secondary level and various specialists at all levels regard themselves as teachers of subjects of their specializations first and as educators second. They belong to professional organizations that reinforce these affiliations rather than concern for the entire educative process. There is an enormous schism, often verging on distrust, between those who run the schools and those in universities who study the schools. Education is a badly segmented profession. Undoubtedly, this makes it exceedingly difficult for the necessarily collaborative effort of school improvement to occur. 12

Sixth, the very success of our society in moving impressively toward universal elementary and secondary schooling has vastly complicated the tasks of the high school. At the turn of this century, it shared with private schools in the education of a small, elite student population preparing, for the most part, for higher education. Today, it educates an extraordinarily diverse student body from families varying widely in their expectations for education. Many of the boys and girls graduating from elementary schools and moving up into junior and senior high schools are not clients in any sense of the word. They go to school until the age of 16 or more because society requires it—and, of course, their friends are there. Many high school teachers simply were not prepared for what they encountered in their students. 13

Seventh, closely related, today's young people are securing their education, to use the word loosely, from sources other than home, church, and school. Television is such a source, one of great but still little-understood power. The total array of educating forces and their impact are as yet little studied and little understood. Much of what is learned by our children comes to them with no mediation, interpretation, or even discussion by the traditional 14 configuration of educating agencies. There has been little rethinking of the school's role in the new configuration. . . .

By the beginning of the 1980s, many people doubted the school's capacity 15 to contribute to . . . democratic ideals. . . . The argument that parents should choose their children's school appealed to increasingly large numbers of people for a variety of reasons. Proponents of the so-called voucher plan sought support for the concept of putting most of the money required to operate public schools directly into the hands of parents, who would then select among alternative schools, which would be in many ways more private than public. In the 1981 Gallup Poll on public schools, 49% of those sampled said that the increasing number of nonpublic schools is a good thing; 30% said that it is a bad thing. Even when only public school parents were surveyed, 44% said the increase is a good thing, as compared with 36% who said it is a bad thing.

What indeed had happened in so short a time to "the foundation of our 16 freedom . . . the source of our enlightenment, the public school"? And what will happen to it in the future?

MARIE WINN

Television and Reading

Marie Winn has written extensively about parents and children. In this excerpt from her book The Plug In Drug, *she argues that "reading is somehow 'better' than television viewing." Unlike television, reading "trains the mind in concentration skills, develops the powers of imagination and inner visualization . . . but does not hypnotize or seduce the reader. . . ."*

Until the television era a young child's access to symbolic representations of 1 reality was limited. Unable to read, he entered the world of fantasy primarily by way of stories told to him or read to him from a book. But rarely did such "literary" experiences take up a significant proportion of a child's waking time; even when a willing reader or storyteller was available, an hour or so a day was more time than most children spent ensconced in the imagination of others.

And when the pre-television child *did* enter those imaginary worlds, he 2 always had a grown-up escort along to interpret, explain, and comfort, if need be. Before he learned to read, it was difficult for the child to enter the fantasy world alone.

For this reason the impact of television was undoubtedly greater on pre-   3
schoolers and pre-readers than on any other group. By means of television, very
young children were able to enter and spend sizable portions of their waking
time in a secondary world of incorporeal people and intangible things, unac-
companied, in too many cases, by an adult guide or comforter. School-age
children fell into a different category. Because they could read, they had other
opportunities to leave reality behind. For these children television was merely
another imaginary world.

But since reading, once the school child's major imaginative experience,   4
has now been virtually eclipsed by television, the television experience must be
compared with the reading experience to try to discover whether they are,
indeed, similar activities fulfilling similar needs in a child's life.

WHAT HAPPENS WHEN YOU READ

It is not enough to compare television watching and reading from the viewpoint   5
of quality. Although the quality of the material available in each medium varies
enormously, from junky books and shoddy programs to literary masterpieces
and fine, thoughtful television shows, the *nature* of the two experiences is
different and that difference significantly affects the impact of the material taken
in.

Few people besides linguistics students and teachers of reading are aware   6
of the complex mental manipulations involved in the reading process. Shortly
after learning to read, a person assimilates the process into his life so completely
that the words in books seem to acquire an existence almost equal to the objects
or acts they represent. It requires a fresh look at a printed page to recognize that
those symbols that we call letters of the alphabet are completely abstract shapes
bearing no inherent "meaning" of their own. Look at an *o*, for instance, or a *k*.
The *o* is a curved figure; the *k* is an intersection of three straight lines. Yet it is
hard to divorce their familiar figures from their sounds, though there is nothing
"o-ish" about an *o* or "k-ish" about a *k*. A reader unfamiliar with the Russian
alphabet will find it easy to look at the symbol щ and see it as an abstract shape;
a Russian reader will find it harder to detach that symbol from its sound, *shch*.
And even when trying to consider *k* as an abstract symbol, we cannot see it
without the feeling of a *k* sound somewhere between the throat and the ears, a
silent pronunciation of *k* that occurs the instant we see the letter.

That is the beginning of reading; we learn to transform abstract figures into   7
sounds, and groups of symbols into the combined sounds that make up the
words of our language. As the mind transforms the abstract symbols into sounds
and the sounds into words, it "hears" the words, as it were, and thereby invests
them with meanings previously learned in the spoken language. Invariably, as
the skill of reading develops, the meaning of each word begins to seem to dwell
within those symbols that make up the word. The word *dog*, for instance,
comes to bear some relationship with the real animal. Indeed, the word *dog*
seems to *be* a dog in a certain sense, to possess some of the qualities of a dog.

But it is only as a result of a swift and complex series of mental activities that the word *dog* is transformed from a series of meaningless squiggles into an idea of something real. This process goes on smoothly and continuously as we read, and yet it becomes no less complex. The brain must carry out all the steps of decoding and investing with meaning each time we read; but it becomes more adept at it as the skill develops, so that we lose the sense of struggling with symbols and meanings that children have when they first learn to read.

But not merely does the mind *hear* words in the process of reading; it is 8 important to remember that reading involves images as well. For when the reader sees the word *dog* and understands the idea of "dog," an image representing a dog is conjured up as well. The precise nature of this "reading image" is little understood, nor is there agreement about what relation it bears to visual images taken in directly by the eyes. Nevertheless images necessarily color our reading, else we would perceive no meaning, merely empty words. The great difference between these "reading images" and the images we take in when viewing television is this: we *create* our own images when reading, based upon our own life experiences and reflecting our own individual needs, while we must accept what we receive when watching television images. This aspect of reading, which might be called "creative" in the narrow sense of the word, is present during all reading experiences, regardless of *what* is being read. The reader "creates" his own images as he reads, almost as if he were creating his own, small, inner television program. The result is a nourishing experience for the imagination. As Bruno Bettelheim notes, "Television captures the imagination but does not liberate it. A good book at once stimulates and frees the mind."

Television images do not go through a complex symbolic transformation. 9 The mind does not have to decode and manipulate during the television experience. Perhaps this is a reason why the visual images received directly from a television set are strong, stronger, it appears, than the images conjured up mentally while reading. But ultimately they satisfy less. A ten-year-old child reports on the effects of seeing television dramatizations of books he has previously read: "The TV people leave a stronger impression. Once you've seen a character on TV, he'll always look like that in your mind, even if you made a different picture of him in your mind before, when you read the book yourself." And yet, as the same child reports, "the thing about a book is that you have so much freedom. You can make each character look exactly the way you want him to look. You're more in control of things when you read a book than when you see something on TV."

It may be that television-bred children's reduced opportunities to indulge 10 in this "inner picture-making" accounts for the curious inability of so many children today to adjust to nonvisual experiences. This is commonly reported by experienced teachers who bridge the gap between the pretelevision and the television eras.

"When I read them a story without showing them pictures, the children 11 always complain—'I can't see.' Their attention flags," reports a first-grade teacher. "They'll begin to talk or wander off. I have to really work to develop their visualizing skills. I tell them that there's nothing to see, that the story is coming out of my mouth, and that they can make their own pictures in their 'mind's eye.' They get better at visualizing, with practice. But children never needed to learn how to visualize before television, it seems to me."

VIEWING VS. READING: CONCENTRATION

Because reading demands complex mental manipulations, a reader is required 12 to concentrate far more than a television viewer. An audio expert notes that "with the electronic media it is openness [that counts]. Openness permits auditory and visual stimuli more direct access to the brain . . . someone who is taught to concentrate will fail to perceive many patterns of information conveyed by the electronic stimuli."

It may be that a predisposition toward concentration, acquired, perhaps, 13 through one's reading experiences, makes one an inadequate television watcher. But it seems far more likely that the reverse situation obtains: that a predisposition toward "openness" (which may be understood to mean the opposite of focal concentration), acquired through years and years of television viewing, has influenced adversely viewers' ability to concentrate, to read, to write clearly— in short, to demonstrate any of the verbal skills a literate society requires.

A comparison between reading and viewing may be made in respect to the 14 pace of each experience, and the relative control a person has over that pace, for the pace may influence the ways one uses the material received in each experience. In addition, the pace of each experience may determine how much it intrudes upon other aspects of one's life.

The pace of reading, clearly, depends entirely upon the reader. He may 15 read as slowly or as rapidly as he can or wishes to read. If he does not understand something, he may stop and reread it, or go in search of elucidation before continuing. The reader can accelerate his pace when the material is easy or less than interesting, and slow down when it is difficult or enthralling. If what he reads is moving, he can put down the book for a few moments and cope with his emotions without fear of losing anything.

The pace of the television experience cannot be controlled by the viewer; 16 only its beginning and end are within his control as he clicks the knob on and off. He cannot slow down a delightful program or speed up a dreary one. He cannot "turn back" if a word or phrase is not understood. The program moves inexorably forward, and what is lost or misunderstood remains so.

Nor can the television viewer readily transform the material he receives 17 into a form that might suit his particular emotional needs, as he invariably does with material he reads. The images move too quickly. He cannot use his own imagination to invest the people and events portrayed on television with the personal meanings that would help him understand and resolve relationships and conflicts in his own life; he is under the power of the imagination of the show's creators. In the television experience the eyes and ears are overwhelmed with the immediacy of sights and sounds. They flash from the television set just fast enough for the eyes and ears to take them in before moving on quickly to the new pictures and sounds . . . so as *not to lose the thread.*

Not to lose the thread . . . it is this need, occasioned by the irreversible 18 direction and relentless velocity of the television experience, that not only limits the workings of the viewer's imagination, but also causes television to intrude into human affairs far more than reading experiences can ever do. If someone enters the room while one is watching television—a friend, a relative, a child, someone, perhaps, one has not seen for some time—one must continue to watch or one will lose the thread. The greetings must wait, for the television program will not. A book, of course, can be set aside, with a pang of regret, perhaps, but with no sense of permanent loss.

A grandparent describes a situation that is, by all reports, not uncommon: 19

"Sometimes when I come to visit the girls, I'll walk into their room and 20 they're watching a TV program. Well, I know they love me, but it makes me feel *bad* when I tell them hello, and they say, without even looking up, 'Wait a minute . . . we have to see the end of this program.' It hurts me to have them care more about that machine and those little pictures than about being glad to see me. I know that they probably can't help it, but still . . ."

Can they help it? Ultimately the power of a television viewer to release 21 himself from his viewing in order to attend to human demands arising in the course of his viewing is not altogether a function of the pace of the program. After all, the viewer might *choose* to operate according to human priorities rather than electronic dictatorship. He might quickly decide "to hell with this program" and simply stop watching when a friend entered the room or a child needed attention.

He might . . . but the hypnotic power of television makes it difficult to 22 shift one's attention away, makes one desperate not to lose the thread of the program. . . .

THE BASIC BUILDING BLOCKS

There is another difference between reading and television viewing that must 23 affect the response to each experience. This is the relative acquaintance of readers and viewers with the fundamental elements of each medium. While the reader is familiar with the basic building blocks of the reading medium, the television viewer has little acquaintance with those of the television medium.

As a person reads, he has his own writing experience to fall back upon. 24 His understanding of what he reads, and his feelings about it, are necessarily affected, and deepened, by his possession of writing as a means of communicating. As a child begins to learn reading, he begins to acquire the rudiments of writing. That these two skills are always acquired together is important and not coincidental. As the child learns to read words, he needs to understand that a word is something he can write himself, though his muscle control may temporarily prevent him from writing it clearly. That he wields such power over the words he is struggling to decipher makes the reading experience a satisfying one right from the start.

A young child watching television enters a realm of materials completely 25 beyond his control—and understanding. Though the images that appear on the screen may be reflections of familiar people and things, they appear as if by magic. The child cannot create similar images, nor even begin to understand how those flickering, electronic shapes and forms come into being. He takes on a far more powerless and ignorant role in front of the television set than in front of a book.

There is no doubt that many young children have a confused relationship 26 to the television medium. When a group of preschool children were asked, "How do kids get to be on your TV?" only 22 percent of them showed any real comprehension of the nature of the television images. When asked, "Where do the people and kids and things go when your TV is turned off?" only 20 percent of the three-year-olds showed the smallest glimmer of understanding. Although there was an increase in comprehension among the four-year-olds, the authors of the study note that "even among the older children the vast majority still did not grasp the nature of television pictures."

The child's feelings of power and competence are nourished by another 27 feature of the reading experience that does not obtain for television: the non-mechanical, easily accessible, and easily transportable nature of reading matter. The child can always count on a book for pleasure, though the television set may break down at a crucial moment. The child may take a book with him wherever he goes, to his room, to the park, to his friend's house, to school to read under his desk: he can *control* his use of books and reading materials. The television set is stuck in a certain place; it cannot be moved easily. It certainly cannot be casually transported from place to place by a child. The child must not only watch television wherever the set is located, but he must watch certain programs at certain times, and is powerless to change what comes out of the set and when it comes out.

In this comparision of reading and television experiences a picture begins 28 to emerge that quite confirms the commonly held notion that reading is some-how "better" than television viewing. Reading involves a complex form of mental activity, trains the mind in concentration skills, develops the powers of imagination and inner visualization; the flexibility of its pace lends itself to a better and deeper comprehension of the material communicated. Reading en-grosses, but does not hypnotize or seduce the reader from his human reponsi-bilities. Reading is a two-way process: the reader can also write; television viewing is a one-way street; the viewer cannot create television images. And books are ever available, ever controllable. Television controls.

✍ NAT HENTOFF

The Dumbing of America

Nat Hentoff is a well-known writer on jazz and politics, an officer of the American Civil Liberties Union, and a staunch defender of the Bill of Rights. In this Progressive *magazine article written in the early 1980s, he takes the textbook industry to task for their part in "the dumbing of America."*

Among all the rising indictments of American public education—in books, reports, stump speeches by the President and Presidential candidates, television specials—one phrase has become embedded in the national consciousness like an aching tooth. It comes from the National Commission on Excellence in Education, which has declared that much of what is going on in classrooms around the nation is responsible for "a rising tide of mediocrity that threatens our very future as a nation and as a people." 1

The blame for this dismal situation has been widely dispersed—the incompetence of teachers, especially young teachers entering the profession; salary scales too low to attract smart new teachers or hold smart older ones; administrators more suited to work as department store floorwalkers; insufficient funds for education from state legislatures, from Congress, from a President who believes all that's really needed to bring up everybody's spirits is prayer, particularly in the schoolhouse. 2

Remarkably, one group that shares complicity for this mounting tide of mediocrity in the schools has gotten off almost without reprimand. The publishers of America's textbooks, who are often also the publishers of the trade books you and I read, have barely been mentioned in connection with what one weary teacher calls "the dumbing of America." 3

When subjected to pressure by state textbook commissions and other bodies in the business of "purifying" what children learn, such highly respectable publishers as Harper & Row, Holt, Rinehart & Winston, Macmillan, and Houghton Mifflin compromise the intellectual integrity of their products rather than lose a sale. So the kids in the classrooms get damaged goods. 4

The basic credo of the textbook publishing industry has been sounded by Bob Jones, Western regional representative of Holt, Rinehart & Winston: "When you're publishing a book, if there's something that is controversial, it's better to take it out." 5

Consider what happens in Texas, one of seventeen states where education agencies adopt textbooks for the entire state. The Texas State Textbook Committee chooses five titles in each subject area, and the 1,200 individual school districts can select one of the five, but no other. Publishers are desperate to get on the list of approved books because the Texas market is so huge; the state's textbook budget was $64 million in 1983. 6

Indeed, the Lone Star market is so significant that textbooks in other states   7
have a Texas brand on them, though that fact is usually not known to students,
teachers, and parents in those other states. Publishers tailor their textbooks to
what they believe will be accepted in Texas, and if they turn out to be right,
those are the texts they will sell elsewhere in the country; it's too expensive to
print other editions which put back in what was left out for Texas.

For instance, the word *evolution*—let alone the teaching of the theory of   8
that name—is in some disrepute in Texas. Thus, a publisher who wants to play
it safe will follow the example of Laidlaw Publishing, a division of Doubleday:
"Laidlaw Publishing doesn't even mention the word *evolution* in its new nation-
ally distributed biology texts," ABC reporter Ron Miller pointed out last
summer.

Then there is the large Follett Publishing Company, whose Texas repre-   9
sentative, William Wood, has said, "It would be very difficult to write off the
Texas market. If we couldn't sell a book without Creationism in it, I imagine
you'd see it there." And you'd see it in Follett books in classrooms in other
states.

About the only persistent exposer of those who publish diluted—and there-   10
fore distorted—educational materials is Barbara Parker, the passionate and
knowledgeable director of the National Schools and Libraries Project of People
for the American Way, the First Amendment support group Norman Lear
founded a few years ago. Parker has tracked down illustrations of the publishers'
devotion to the intellectual well-being of children, such as this one:

"Publishers deleted Shirley Jackson's classic short story, 'The Lottery,' from   11
the national editions of four literature anthologies because, in 1978, the Texas
State Textbook Committee refused to purchase books that included the story.
In 1981, hoping to make [its already bowdlerized high school edition of] *The
American Heritage Dictionary* acceptable for Texas classrooms, Houghton Mif-
flin offered to drop 'offensive words' from its latest edition."

Not all textbooks and reference publishers have round heels, however.   12
G. & C. Merriam Co. refused to make any deletions in its *Webster's New
Collegiate Dictionary*, thereby forgoing all that Texas gold. Merriam's president,
W. A. Llewellyn, told the Commissioner of Education, "Our responsibility as
lexicographers is not fulfilled by pretending such language does not exist."

The absence of those offensive words in Texas classrooms is not a signifi-   13
cant loss to the children who, if pressed, might admit they have picked them
up elsewhere, though without knowledge of the words' etymologies. Still, the
willingness of a firm as respected as Houghton Mifflin to yield to official
censorship—something to which it would not submit in its trade nonfiction
books and novels—is a disturbing indication of how little respect adults in
publishing, like most adults, have for kids.

Manifest harm is done to students in other areas of learning in which   14
textbooks have been subjected to tampering. As you might imagine, the level
of biology instruction in Texas public schools is more than inadequate after all
the watering down of "acceptable" biology textbooks in recent years. The effect,

says Ronnie Hastings, director of science education at Waxahachie High School in Texas, is that his state's public school students are "woefully unprepared" for college science courses.

If that's the case for Texas high school students—betrayed by their own 15 State Textbook Committee—what of the students in other states where those biology textbooks, watered down for Texas, have also been purchased?

Many of the same spineless publishers produce textbooks for the college 16 market as well. And just as in the lower grades, these merchandisers of learning are eager to please the powers that control the marketplace. Whatever the order, they'll fill it.

Education writers on the staffs of newspapers (few radio and television 17 stations have an education reporter) rarely cover the big dealers in textbooks. A persistent exception is William Trombley of the *Los Angeles Times*. In an interview with Paul Mussen, a professor of psychology at the University of California, Berkeley, and co-author of a widely used introductory text in child development, Trombley noted that Mussen was troubled because his publisher kept after him to "simplify" the book.

"I'm concerned," said Mussen, "about the deterioration of standards. 18 There has been a real 'dumbing down' of the texts."

As he examined the simplifying of college texts in a number of fields, 19 Trombley concluded that books for freshmen and sophomores have generally "declined in difficulty to a level that might have been considered suitable for tenth graders not many years ago."

What's the rationale? In higher education, college departments—not a 20 state textbook commission—usually choose the texts. Clearly, Texas can't be blamed for the deterioration of learning at this level. Those who choose the texts and those who publish them place the blame on today's undergraduates, who don't read well and don't want to read much—and who certainly don't want to read books that make their heads ache.

Students are dumber these days: That, at least, is current conventional 21 wisdom among teachers and publishers. Too much television all these years has turned the students' heads soft. Too many oversimplified textbooks in high school have turned their heads softer. Furthermore, too many youngsters in college now have no business being there: twenty years ago, they would have been pumping gas or working for the telephone company after receiving a high school diploma.

Any day now, a publisher attuned to the market is going to put out a line 22 of history and biology texts with pop-up illustrations: See Lenin having some schnapps at the Finland Station!

Indeed, according to a student at the University of South Alabama, "If a 23 dean had not been overruled, the computer science department here would have switched to a coloring book as its textbook for a sophomore-level programming class."

But is any of this the fault of textbook publishers? They say they are only 24 producing what college teachers want and insist on. "Furthermore," a senior official of one large textbook operation told me, "we also have to prepare more and more material to help the teacher work with these already oversimplified books. Some of them are almost on automatic pilot."

With exceptions, of course, college teachers seem to have a diminished 25 sense of responsibility to their students. If the students' potential was, indeed, maimed in high school, the attitude of many professors, including those who select texts, is that the damage is irreversible. "In most cases, the reading level of introductory textbooks has been reduced," writes William Trombley. "Every effort is made to avoid complex arguments that students either cannot or will not follow. Extensive use is made of graphics."

But not much use, it would appear, is made of teaching. 26

The attitude of both professors and textbook editors is fatalistic. There is 27 also what might be called collusion in letting students sink to their lowest level. A professor at UCLA mourns, "Students today are a lot less tolerant of difficult books than they were when I started teaching." Once the "difficult" books are allowed to disappear altogether, the students may become less tolerant of any books.

An editor at Prentice-Hall sighs, "Today's student won't use the dictionary. 28 They'll skip the word or sometimes the entire paragraph."

That doesn't seem to trouble the textbook people. As Damaris Ames, 29 communications director for Houghton Mifflin, puts it, "Publishers simply reflect the attitudes and demands of the society."

You want dummies, they'll make you dummies. 30

Relatively few teachers and textbook writers insist on bucking the trend. 31 Frederick Crews, an English professor at the University of California, is the author of a composition text, *The Random House Handbook*. Instead of using two-syllable words and a lot of pictures, Crews, in his words, aimed "a little high." The text is selling about 75,000 copies a year at Harvard and Yale as well as at many community colleges.

Other composition texts that aim in the opposite direction sell from 32 200,000 to 400,000 copies a year. But *The Random House Handbook* is out there, moving right along, and the fact that it has been adopted "at all levels," says Crews, "is a very encouraging sign to me. Everyone is saying you have to write in baby talk, but that doesn't seem to be the case."

If you have any self-respect. 33

Self-respect seems to be no problem for those professors, experts in their 34 fields, who earn considerable side income as consultants to textbook publishers. They add their names and prestige to the books printed for secondary school use. Privately, many deplore the appalling quality of certain bowdlerized texts put out by the publishing houses that retain them. But they will never say so publicly, let alone accept the invitations of People for the American Way to testify before state textbook commissions. Concern about being cashiered by the textbook publishers keeps them silent.

Because textbook publishers fear controversy more than they fear the loss 35 of their souls, it is not surprising that they have declined comment during the past four years while the following Oregon law has been under challenge from the American Civil Liberties Union:

". . . No textbook shall be used in the schools which speaks slightingly of 36 the founders of the republic or of those who preserved the union or which belittles or undervalues their work. . . ."

The publishers can't say they don't know about the law (which, among 37 many other things, might forbid mention of the slave quarters on the George Washington and Thomas Jefferson plantations). Since the law's enactment, the State Board of Education has distributed, every two years, a circular to major textbook publishers around the country quoting the statute and making clear that publishers must agree to adhere to it in any contract with the state of Oregon.

There is no evidence that any textbook publisher has refused to abide by 38 this brazenly un-American statute. There is also no record that any publishers' organization—including the Association of American Publishers, which professes to oppose censorship—has delivered a word of protest.

Says Stevie Remington, executive director of the Oregon ACLU, who has 39 led the fight to have the law declared unconstitutional, "We received help from teachers. But not from publishers." Not a single individual publisher offered support.

That desolate fact lends special substance to a comment made last spring 40 by William Morris, who edited the first edition of *The American Heritage Dictionary*. During an "Evening of Forbidden Books" sponsored by PEN and the Harvard Graduate School of Education, Morris warned:

"Beware of a new dimension of censorship: censorship inside the publish- 41 er's office, hidden censorship that only the authors, editors, and the ultimate control, the sales department, know about. This may well be more insidious and dangerous than the work of all the professional censors put together."

◿ **JAIME M. O'NEILL**

No Allusions in the Classroom

Jaime M. O'Neill teaches at California State University, Chico. In this News-week *article he provides overly sufficient evidence of the paucity of background knowledge students have about Western society and their common cultural heritage.*

Josh Billings, a nineteenth-century humorist, wrote that it is better "not to   1
know so much than to know so many things that ain't so." Recently, after fifteen
years of teaching in community colleges, I decided to take a sampling to find
out what my students know that ain't so. I did this out of a growing awareness
that they don't always understand what I say. I suspected that part of their failure
to understand derived from the fact that they did not catch my allusions. An
allusion to a writer, a geographical locality or a historical episode inevitably
produced telltale expressions of bewilderment.

There is a game played by students and teachers everywhere. The game   2
goes like this: the teacher tries to find out what students don't know so that he
can correct those deficiencies; the students, concerned with grades and slippery
self-images, try to hide their ignorance in every way they can. So it is that
students seldom ask pertinent questions. So it is that teachers assume that
students possess basic knowledge which, in fact, they don't possess.

Last semester I broke the rules of this time-honored game when I presented   3
my English-composition students with an 86-question "general knowledge" test
on the first day of class. There were twenty-six people in the class; they ranged
in age from eighteen to fifty-four. They had all completed at least one quarter
of college-level work.

Here is a sampling of what they knew that just ain't so: 4

Creative: Ralph Nader is a baseball player. Charles Darwin invented grav-   5
ity. Christ was born in the sixteenth century. J. Edgar Hoover was a nineteenth-
century president. Neil Simon wrote *One Flew Over the Cuckoo's Nest; The
Great Gatsby* was a magician in the 1930s. Franz Joseph Haydn was a song-
writer during the same decade. Sid Caesar was an early Roman emperor. Mark
Twain invented the cotton gin. Heinrich Himmler invented the Heimlich
maneuver. Jefferson Davis was a guitar player for the Jefferson Airplane. Benito
Mussolini was a Russian leader of the eighteenth century; Dwight D. Eisenhower came earlier, serving as a president during the seventeenth century.
William Faulkner made his name as a seventeenth-century scientist. All of
these people must have appreciated the work of Pablo Picasso, who painted
masterpieces in the twelfth century.

My students were equally creative in their understanding of geography.   6
They knew, for instance, that Managua is the capital of Vietnam, that Cape
Town is in the United States and that Beirut is in Germany. Bogotá, of course,
is in Borneo (unless it is in China). Camp David is in Israel, and Stratford-on-
Avon is in Grenada (or Gernada). Gdansk is in Ireland. Cologne is in the
Virgin Islands. Mazatlán is in Switzerland. Belfast was variously located in
Egypt, Germany, Belgium and Italy. Leningrad was transported to Jamaica;
Montreal to Spain.

And on it went. Most students answered incorrectly far more often than   7
they answered correctly. Several of them meticulously wrote "I don't know" 86
times, or 80 times, or 62 times.

They did not like the test. Although I made it clear that the test would not   8
be graded, they did not like having their ignorance exposed. One of them

dismissed the test by saying, "Oh, I get it; it's like Trivial Pursuit." Imagining a game of Trivial Pursuit among some of today's college students is a frightening thought; such a game could last for years.

But the comment bothered me. What, in this time in our global history,   9 is trivial? And what is essential? Perhaps it no longer matters very much if large numbers of people in the world's oldest democratic republic know little of their own history and even less about the planet they inhabit.

But I expect that it does matter. I also suspect that my students provide a   10 fairly good cross section of the general population. There are 1,274 two-year colleges in the United States that collectively enroll nearly 5 million students. I have taught at four of those colleges in two states, and I doubt that my questionnaire would have produced different results at any of them. My colleagues at universities tell me that they would not be surprised at similar undergraduate answers.

My small sampling is further corroborated by recent polls which disclosed   11 that a significant number of American adults have no idea which side the United States supported in Vietnam and that a majority of the general populace have no idea which side the United States is currently supporting in Nicaragua or El Salvador.

Less importantly, a local marketing survey asked a sampling of young   12 computer whizzes to identify the character in IBM's advertising campaign that is based on an allusion to Charlie Chaplin in *Modern Times*. Few of them had heard of Charlie Chaplin, fewer heard or knew about the movie classic.

Common Heritage: As I write this, the radio is broadcasting the news   13 about the Walker family. Accused of spying for the Soviets, the Walkers, according to a U.S. attorney, will be the Rosenbergs of the '80s. One of my students thought Ethel Rosenberg was a singer from the 1930s. The rest of them didn't know. Communication depends, to some extent, upon the ability to make (and catch) allusions, to share a common understanding and a common heritage. Even preliterate societies can claim this shared assessment of their world. As we enter the postindustrial "information processing" age, what sort of information will be processed? And, as the educational establishment is driven "back to the basics," isn't it time we decided that a common understanding of our history and our planet is most basic of all?

As a teacher, I find myself in the ignorance-and-hope business. Each year   14 hopeful faces confront me, trying to conceal their ignorance. Their hopes ride on the dispelling of that ignorance.

All our hopes do.   15

We should begin servicing that hope more responsibly and dispelling that   16 ignorance with a more systematic approach to imparting essential knowledge.

Socrates, the American Indian chieftain, would have wanted it that way.   17

⋈ **ALAN BLOOM**

The Student and the University

Alan Bloom is a professor of social thought at the University of Chicago whose 1987 book The Closing of the American Mind *caused quite a stir in academic circles. In the following excerpt, he argues that the university today "offers no distinctive visage to the young person . . . [that] there is no vision . . . of what an educated human being is." Students have to navigate among a collection of carnival barkers, each trying to lure him into a particular sideshow. And he claims that "the only serious solution is the one that is almost universally neglected: the good old Great Books approach. . . ."*

LIBERAL EDUCATION

What image does a first-rank college or university present today to a teen-ager 1 leaving home for the first time, off to the adventure of a liberal education? He has four years of freedom to discover himself—a space between the intellectual wasteland he has left behind and the inevitable dreary professional training that awaits him after the baccalaureate. In this short time he must learn that there is a great world beyond the little one he knows, experience the exhilaration of it and digest enough of it to sustain himself in the intellectual deserts he is destined to traverse. He must do this, that is, if he is to have any hope of a higher life. These are the charmed years when he can, if he so chooses, become anything he wishes and when he has the opportunity to survey his alternatives, not merely those current in his time or provided by careers, but those available to him as a human being. The importance of these years for an American cannot be overestimated. They are civilization's only chance to get to him.

In looking at him we are forced to reflect on what he should learn if he is 2 to be called educated; we must speculate on what the human potential to be fulfilled is. In the specialties we can avoid such speculation, and the avoidance of them is one of specialization's charms. But here it is a simple duty. What are we to teach this person? The answer may not be evident, but to attempt to answer the question is already to philosophize and to begin to educate. Such a concern in itself poses the question of the unity of man and the unity of the sciences. It is childishness to say, as some do, that everyone must be allowed to develop freely, that it is authoritarian to impose a point of view on the student. In that case, why have a university? If the response is "to provide an atmosphere for learning," we come back to our original questions at the second remove. Which atmosphere? Choices and reflection on the reasons for those choices are unavoidable. The university has to stand for something. The practical effects of unwillingness to think positively about the contents of a liberal education are, on the one hand, to ensure that all the vulgarities of the world outside the university will flourish within it, and, on the other, to impose a much harsher and more illiberal necessity on the student—the one given by the imperial and imperious demands of the specialized disciplines unfiltered by unifying thought.

The university now offers no distinctive visage to the young person. He 3 finds a democracy of the disciplines—which are there either because they are autochthonous or because they wandered in recently to perform some job that was demanded of the university. This democracy is really an anarchy, because there are no recognized rules for citizenship and no legitimate titles to rule. In short there is no vision, nor is there a set of competing visions, of what an educated human being is. The question has disappeared, for to pose it would be a threat to the peace. There is no organization of the sciences, no tree of knowledge. Out of chaos emerges dispiritedness, because it is impossible to make a reasonable choice. Better to give up on liberal education and get on with a specialty in which there is at least a prescribed curriculum and a pro-spective career. On the way the student can pick up in elective courses a little of whatever is thought to make one cultured. The student gets no intimation that great mysteries might be revealed to him, that new and higher motives of action might be discovered within him, that a different and more human way of life can be harmoniously constructed by what he is going to learn.

Simply, the university is not distinctive. Equality for us seems to culminate 4 in the unwillingness and incapacity to make claims of superiority, particularly in the domains in which such claims have always been made—art, religion, and philosophy. When Weber found that he could not choose between certain high opposites—reason vs. revelation, Buddha vs. Jesus—he did not conclude that all things are equally good, that the distinction between high and low disappears. As a matter of fact he intended to revitalize the consideration of these great alternatives in showing the gravity and danger involved in choosing among them; they were to be heightened in contrast to the trivial considerations of modern life that threatened to overgrow and render indistinguishable the profound problems the confrontation with which makes the bow of the soul taut. The serious intellectual life was for him the battleground of the great decisions, all of which are spiritual or "value" choices. One can no longer present this or that particular view of the educated or civilized man as authori-tative; therefore one must say that education consists in knowing, really know-ing, the small number of such views in their integrity. This distinction between profound and superficial—which takes the place of good and bad, true and false—provided a focus for serious study, but it hardly held out against the naturally relaxed democratic tendency to say, "Oh, what's the use?" The first university disruptions at Berkeley were explicitly directed against the multivers-ity smorgasbord and, I must confess, momentarily and partially engaged my sympathies. It may have even been the case that there was some small element of longing for an education in the motivation of those students. But nothing was done to guide or inform their energy, and the result was merely to add multilife-styles to multidisciplines, the diversity of perversity to the diversity of specialization. What we see so often happening in general happened here too;

the insistent demand for greater community ended in greater isolation. Old agreements, old habits, old traditions were not so easily replaced.

Thus, when a student arrives at the university, he finds a bewildering 5 variety of departments and a bewildering variety of courses. And there is no official guidance, no university-wide agreement, about what he *should* study. Nor does he usually find readily available examples, either among students or professors, of a unified use of the university's resources. it is easiest simply to make a career choice and go about getting prepared for that career. The programs designed for those having made such a choice render their students immune to charms that might lead them out of the conventionally respectable. The sirens sing *sotto voce* these days, and the young already have enough wax in their ears to pass them by without danger. These specialties can provide enough courses to take up most of their time for four years in preparation for the inevitable graduate study. With the few remaining courses they can do what they please, taking a bit of this and a bit of that. No public career these days— not doctor nor lawyer nor politician nor journalist nor businessman nor entertainer—has much to do with humane learning. An education, other than purely professional or technical, can even seem to be an impediment. That is why a countervailing atmosphere in the university would be necessary for the students to gain a taste for intellectual pleasures and learn that they are viable.

The real problem is those students who come hoping to find out what 6 career they want to have, or are simply looking for an adventure with themselves. There are plenty of things for them to do—courses and disciplines enough to spend many a lifetime on. Each department or great division of the university makes a pitch for itself, and each offers a course of study that will make the student an initiate. But how to choose among them? How do they relate to one another? The fact is they do not address one another. They are competing and contradictory, without being aware of it. The problem of the whole is urgently indicated by the very existence of the specialties, but it is never systematically posed. The net effect of the student's encounter with the college catalogue is bewilderment and very often demoralization. It is just a matter of chance whether he finds one or two professors who can give him an insight into one of the great visions of education that have been the distinguishing part of every civilized nation. Most professors are specialists, concerned only with their own fields, interested in the advancement of those fields in their own terms, or in their own personal advancement in a world where all the rewards are on the side of professional distinction. They have been entirely emancipated from the old structure of the university, which at least helped to indicate that they are incomplete, only parts of an unexamined and undiscovered whole. So the student must navigate among a collection of carnival barkers, each trying to lure him into a particular sideshow. This undecided student is an embarrassment to most universities, because he seems to be saying, "I am a whole human being. Help me to form myself in my wholeness and let me develop my real potential," and he is the one to whom they have nothing to say.

Cornell was, as in so many other things, in advance of its time on this   7
issue. The six-year Ph.D. program, richly supported by the Ford Foundation,
was directed specifically to high school students who had already made "a firm
career choice" and was intended to rush them through to the start of those
careers. A sop was given to desolate humanists in the form of money to fund
seminars that these young careerists could take on their way through the College
of Arts and Sciences. For the rest, the educators could devote their energies to
arranging and packaging the program without having to provide it with any
substance. That kept them busy enough to avoid thinking about the nothing-
ness of their endeavor. This has been the preferred mode of not looking the
Beast in the Jungle in the face—structure, not content. The Cornell plan for
dealing with the problem of liberal education was to suppress the students'
longing for liberal education by encouraging their professionalism and their
avarice, providing money and all the prestige the university had available to
make careerism the centerpiece of the university.

The Cornell plan dared not state the radical truth, a well-kept secret: the   8
colleges do not have enough to teach their students, not enough to justify
keeping them four years, probably not even three years. If the focus is careers,
there is hardly one specialty, outside the hardest of the hard natural sciences,
which requires more than two years of preparatory training prior to graduate
studies. The rest is just wasted time, or a period of ripening until the students
are old enough for graduate studies. For many graduate careers, even less is
really necessary. It is amazing how many undergraduates are poking around for
courses to take, without any plan or question to ask, just filling up their college
years. In fact, with rare exceptions, the courses are parts of specialties and not
designed for general cultivation, or to investigate questions important for human beings as such. The so-called knowledge explosion and increasing specialization have not filled up the college years but emptied them. Those years are
impediments; one wants to get beyond them. And in general the persons one
finds in the professions need not have gone to college, if one is to judge by
their tastes, their fund of learning or their interests. They might as well have
spent their college years in the Peace Corps or the like. These great universities—which can split the atom, find cures for the most terrible diseases, conduct surveys of whole populations and produce massive dictionaries of lost
languages—cannot generate a modest program of general education for undergraduate students. This is a parable for our times. . . .

. . . just as in the sixties universities were devoted to removing require-   9
ments, in the eighties they are busy with attempts to put them back in, a much
more difficult task. The word of the day is "core." It is generally agreed that "we
went a bit far in the sixties," and that a little fine-tuning has now become
clearly necessary.

There are two typical responses to the problem. The easiest and most   10
administratively satisfying solution is to make use of what is already there in the
autonomous departments and simply force the students to cover the fields, i.e.,
take one or more courses in each of the general divisions of the university:

natural science, social science and the humanities. The reigning ideology here is *breadth*, as was *openness* in the age of laxity. The courses are almost always the already existing introductory courses, which are of least interest to the major professors and merely assume the worth and reality of that which is to be studied. It is general education, in the sense in which a jack-of-all-trades is a generalist. He knows a bit of everything and is inferior to the specialist in each area. Students may wish to sample a variety of fields, and it may be good to encourage them to look around and see if there is something that attracts them in one of which they have no experience. But this is not a liberal education and does not satisfy any longing they have for one. It just teaches that there is no high-level generalism, and that what they are doing is preliminary to the real stuff and part of the childhood they are leaving behind. Thus they desire to get it over with and get on with what their professors do seriously. Without recognition of important questions of common concern, there cannot be serious liberal education, and attempts to establish it will be but failed gestures.

It is a more or less precise awareness of the inadequacy of this approach to core curricula that motivates the second approach, which consists of what one might call composite courses. These are constructions developed especially for general-education purposes and usually require collaboration of professors drawn from several departments. These courses have titles like "Man in Nature," "War and Moral Responsibility," "The Arts and Creativity," "Culture and the Individual." Everything, of course, depends upon who plans them and who teaches them. They have the clear advantage of requiring some reflection on the general needs of students and force specialized professors to broaden their perspectives, at least for a moment. The dangers are trendiness, mere popularization and lack of substantive rigor. In general, the natural scientists do not collaborate in such endeavors, and hence these courses tend to be unbalanced. In short, they do not point beyond themselves and do not provide the student with independent means to pursue permanent questions independently, as, for example, the study of Aristotle or Kant as wholes once did. They tend to be bits of this and that. Liberal education should give the student the sense that learning must and can be both synoptic and precise. For this, a very small, detailed problem can be the best way, if it is framed so as to open out on the whole. Unless the course has the specific intention to lead to the permanent questions, to make the student aware of them and give him some competence in the important works that treat of them, it tends to be a pleasant diversion and a dead end—because it has nothing to do with any program of further study he can imagine. If such programs engage the best energies of the best people in the university, they can be beneficial and provide some of the missing intellectual excitement for both professors and students. But they rarely do, and they are too cut off from the top, from what the various faculties see as their real business. Where the power is determines the life of the whole body. And the intellectual problems unresolved at the top cannot be resolved administratively below. The problem is the lack of any unity of the sciences and the loss of the will or the means even to discuss the issue. The illness above is the cause of the illness below, to which all the good-willed efforts of honest liberal educationists can at best be palliatives.

Of course, the only serious solution is the one that is almost universally 12 rejected: the good old Great Books approach, in which a liberal education means reading certain generally recognized classic texts, just reading them, letting them dictate what the questions are and the method of approaching them—not forcing them into categories we make up, not treating them as historical products, but trying to read them as their authors wished them to be read. I am perfectly well aware of, and actually agree with, the objections to the Great Books cult. It is amateurish; it encourages an autodidact's self-assurance without competence; one cannot read all of the Great Books carefully; if one only reads Great Books, one can never know what a great, as opposed to an ordinary, book is; there is no way of determining who is to decide what a Great Book or what the canon is; books are made the ends and not the means; the whole movement has a certain coarse evangelistic tone that is the opposite of good taste; it engenders a spurious intimacy with greatness; and so forth. But one thing is certain: wherever the Great Books make up a central part of the curriculum, the students are excited and satisfied, feel they are doing something that is independent and fulfilling, getting something from the university they cannot get elsewhere. The very fact of this special experience, which leads nowhere beyond itself, provides them with a new alternative and a respect for study itself. The advantage they get is an awareness of the classic—particularly important for our innocents; and acquaintance with what big questions were when there were still big questions; models, at the very least, of how to go about answering them; and, perhaps most important of all, a fund of shared experiences and thoughts on which to ground their friendships with one another. Programs based upon judicious use of great texts provide the royal road to students' hearts. Their gratitude at learning of Achilles or the categorical imperative is boundless. Alexandre Koyré, the late historian of science, told me that his appreciation for America was great when—in the first course he taught at the University of Chicago, in 1940 at the beginning of his exile—a student spoke in his paper of Mr. Aristotle, unaware that he was not a contemporary. Koyré said that only an American could have the naive profundity to take Aristotle as living thought, unthinkable for most scholars. A good program of liberal education feeds the student's love of truth and passion to live a good life. It is the easiest thing in the world to devise courses of study, adapted to the particular conditions of each university, which thrill those who take them. The difficulty is in getting them accepted by the faculty.

None of the three great parts of the contemporary university is enthusiastic 13 about the Great Books approach to education. The natural scientists are benevolent toward other fields and toward liberal education, if it does not steal away their students and does not take too much time from their preparatory studies. But they themselves are interested primarily in the solution of the questions now important in their disciplines and are not particularly concerned with discussions of their foundations, inasmuch as they are so evidently successful.

They are indifferent to Newton's conception of time or his disputes with Leibniz about calculus; Aristotle's teleology is an absurdity beneath consideration. Scientific progress, they believe, no longer depends on the kind of comprehensive reflection given to the nature of science by men like Bacon, Descartes, Hume, Kant, and Marx. This is merely historical study, and for a long time now, even the greatest scientists have given up thinking about Galileo and Newton. Progress is undoubted. The difficulties about the truth of science raised by positivism, and those about the goodness of science raised by Rousseau and Nietzsche, have not really penetrated to the center of scientific consciousness. Hence, not Great Books, but incremental progress, is the theme for them.

Social scientists are in general hostile, because the classic texts tend to 14 deal with the human things the social sciences deal with, and they are very proud of having freed themselves from the shackles of such earlier thought to become truly scientific. And, unlike the natural scientists, they are insecure enough about their achievement to feel threatened by the works of earlier thinkers, perhaps a bit afraid that students will be seduced and fall back into the bad old ways. Moreover, with the possible exception of Weber and Freud, there are no social science books that can be said to be classic. This may be interpreted favorably to the social sciences by comparing them to the natural sciences, which can be said to be a living organism developing by the addition of little cells, a veritable body of knowledge proving itself to be such by the very fact of this almost unconscious growth, with thousands of parts oblivious to the whole, nevertheless contributing to it. This is in opposition to a work of imagination or of philosophy, where a single creator makes and surveys an artificial whole. But whether one interprets the absence of the classic in the social sciences in ways flattering or unflattering to them, the fact causes social scientists discomfort. I remember the professor who taught the introductory graduate courses in social science methodology, a famous historian, responding scornfully and angrily to a question I naively put to him about Thucydides with "Thucydides was a fool!"

More difficult to explain is the tepid reaction of humanists to Great Books 15 education, inasmuch as these books now belong almost exclusively to what are called the humanities. One would think that high esteem for the classic would reinforce the spiritual power of the humanities, at a time when their temporal power is at its lowest. And it is true that the most active proponents of liberal education and the study of classic texts are indeed usually humanists. But there is division among them. Some humanities disciplines are just crusty specialties that, although they depend on the status of classic books for their existence, are not really interested in them in their natural state—much philology, for example, is concerned with the languages but not what is said in them—and will and can do nothing to support their own infrastructure. Some humanities disciplines are eager to join the real sciences and transcend their roots in the now overcome mythic past. Some humanists make the legitimate complaints about lack of competence in the teaching and learning of Great Books, although their criticism is frequently undermined by the fact that they are only defending recent scholarly interpretation of the classics rather than a vital, authentic understanding. In their reaction there is a strong element of specialist's jealousy and narrowness. Finally, a large part of the story is just the general debilitation of the humanities, which is both symptom and cause of our present condition.

To repeat, the crisis of liberal education is a reflection of a crisis at the 16 peaks of learning, an incoherence and incompatibility among the first principles with which we interpret the world, an intellectual crisis of the greatest magnitude, which constitutes the crisis of our civilization. But perhaps it would be true to say that the crisis consists not so much in this incoherence but in our incapacity to discuss or even recognize it. Liberal education flourished when it prepared the way for the discussion of a unified view of nature and man's place in it, which the best minds debated on the highest level. It decayed when what lay beyond it were only specialties, the premises of which do not lead to any such vision. The highest is the partial intellect; there is no synopsis.

⚌ JACOB NEUSNER

The Speech the Graduates Didn't Hear

Jacob Neusner is a professor at Brown University and a recognized scholar in Judaic studies. In this very short mock graduation speech, he warns students that the world they are about to enter cannot be expected to be as charitable in its judgments as their college teachers have been.

We the faculty take no pride in our educational achievements with you. We 1 have prepared you for a world that does not exist, indeed, that cannot exist. You have spent four years supposing that failure leaves no record. You have learned at Brown that when your work goes poorly, the painless solution is to drop out. But starting now, in the world to which you go, failure marks you. Confronting difficulty by quitting leaves you changed. Outside Brown, quitters are no heroes.

With us you could argue about why your errors were not errors, why 2 mediocre work really was excellent, why you could take pride in routine and slipshod presentation. Most of you, after all, can look back on honor grades for most of what you have done. So, here grades can have meant little in distinguishing the excellent from the ordinary. But tomorrow, in the world to which you go, you had best not defend errors but learn from them. You will be ill-advised to demand praise for what does not deserve it, and abuse those who do not give it.

For four years we created an altogether forgiving world, in which whatever 3 slight effort you gave was all that was demanded. When you did not keep appointments, we made new ones. When your work came in beyond the deadline, we pretended not to care.

Worse still, when you were boring, we acted as if you were saying some- 4 thing important. When you were garrulous and talked to hear yourself talk, we listened as if it mattered. When you tossed on our desks writing upon which you had not labored, we read it and even responded, as though you earned a response. When you were dull, we pretended you were smart. When you were predictable, unimaginative and routine, we listened as if to new and wonderful things. When you demanded free lunch, we served it. And all this why?

Despite your fantasies, it was not even that we wanted to be liked by you. 5 It was that we did not want to be bothered, and the easy way out was pretense: smiles and easy Bs.

It is conventional to quote in addresses such as these. Let me quote 6 someone you've never heard of: Prof. Carter A. Daniel, Rutgers University (*Chronicle of Higher Education*, May 7, 1979):

"College has spoiled you by reading papers that don't deserve to be read, 7 listening to comments that don't deserve a hearing, paying attention even to the lazy, ill-informed and rude. We had to do it, for the sake of education. But nobody will ever do it again. College has deprived you of adequate preparation for the last 50 years. It has failed you by being easy, free, forgiving, attentive, comfortable, interesting, unchallenging fun. Good luck tomorrow."

That is why, on this commencement day, we have nothing in which to 8 take much pride.

Oh, yes, there is one more thing. Try not to act toward your co-workers 9 and bosses as you have acted toward us. I mean, when they give you what you want but have not earned, don't abuse them, insult them, act out with them your parlous relationships with your parents. This too we have tolerated. It was, as I said, not to be liked. Few professors actually care whether or not they are liked by peer-paralyzed adolescents, fools so shallow as to imagine professors care not about education but about popularity. It was, again, to be rid of you. So go, unlearn the lies we taught you. To Life!

⚊ **CARDINAL NEWMAN**

The Idea of a University

Cardinal (John Henry) Newman (1801–1890), theologean, poet, novelist, is perhaps best remembered for his lectures collected under the title The Idea of a University Defined. *In the following excerpts from that work, he advocates a liberal education, which prepares students to be complete, thinking human beings, rather than a practical education that prepares them to be specialists in a particular field.*

Now bear with me, Gentlemen, if what I am about to say has at first sight a fanciful appearance. Philosophy, then, or science, is related to knowledge in this way: knowledge is called by the name of science or philosophy when it is acted upon, informed, or if I may use a strong figure, impregnated by reason. Reason is the principle of that intrinsic fecundity of knowledge, which, to those who possess it, is its especial value, and which dispenses with the necessity of their looking abroad for any end to rest upon external to itself. Knowledge, indeed, when thus exalted into a scientific form, is also power; not only is it excellent in itself, but whatever such excellence may be, it is something more, it has a result beyond itself. Doubtless; but that is a further consideration, with which I am not concerned. I only say that, prior to its being a power, it is a good; that it is not only an instrument, but an end. I know well it may resolve itself into an art, and terminate in a mechanical process, and in tangible fruit; but it also may fall back upon that reason which informs it, and resolve itself into philosophy. In one case it is called useful knowledge, in the other liberal. The same person may cultivate it in both ways at once; but this again is a matter foreign to my subject; here I do but say that there are two ways of using knowledge, and in matter of fact those who use it in one way are not likely to use it in the other, or at least in a very limited measure. You see, then, here are two methods of education; the end of the one is to be philosophical, of the other to be mechanical; the one rises towards general ideas, the other is exhausted upon what is particular and external. Let me not be thought to deny the necessity, or to decry the benefit, of such attention to what is particular and practical, as belongs to the useful or mechanical arts; life could not go on without them; we owe our daily welfare to them; their exercise is the duty of the many, and we owe to the many a debt of gratitude for fulfilling that duty. I only say that knowledge, in proportion as it tends more and more to be particular, ceases to be knowledge. It is a question whether knowledge can in any proper sense be predicated of the brute creation; without pretending to metaphysical exactness of phraseology, which would be unsuitable to an occasion like this, I say, it seems to me improper to call that passive sensation, or perception of things, which brutes seem to possess, by the name of knowledge. When I speak of knowledge, I mean something intellectual, something which grasps what it perceives through the senses; something which takes a view of things; which sees more than the senses convey; which reasons upon what it sees, and while it sees; which invests it with an idea. It expresses itself, not in a mere enunciation, but by an enthymeme: it is of the nature of science from the first, and in this consists its dignity. The principle of real dignity in knowledge, its worth, its desirableness, considered irrespectively of its results, is this germ within it of a scientific or a philosophical process. This is how it comes to be an end in itself; this is why it admits of being called liberal. Not to know the relative disposition of things is the state of slaves or children; to have mapped out the universe is the boast, or at least the ambition, of philosophy.

Moreoever, such knowledge is not a mere extrinsic or accidental advan- 2 tage, which is ours today and another's tomorrow, which may be got up from a book, and easily forgotten again, which we can command or communicate at our pleasure, which we can borrow for the occasion, carry about in our hand, and take into the market; it is an acquired illumination, it is a habit, a personal possession, and an inward endowment. And this is the reason why it is more correct, as well as more usual, to speak of a university as a place of education, than of instruction, though, when knowledge is concerned, instruction would at first sight have seemed the more appropriate word. We are instructed, for instance, in manual exercises, in the fine and useful arts, in trades, and in ways of business; for these are methods, which have little or no effect upon the mind itself, are contained in rules committed to memory, to tradition, or to use, and bear upon an end external to themselves. But education is a higher word; it implies an action upon our mental nature, and the formation of a character; it is something individual and permanent, and is commonly spoken of in con- nexion with religion and virtue. When, then, we speak of the communication of knowledge as being education, we thereby really imply that that knowledge is a state or condition of mind; and since cultivation of mind is surely worth seeking for its own sake, we are thus brought once more to the conclusion, which the word "liberal" and the word "philosophy" have already suggested, that there is a knowledge which is desirable, though nothing come of it, as being of itself a treasure, and a sufficient remuneration of years of labour.

* * *

I have been insisting, in my two preceding discourses, first, on the culti- 3 vation of the intellect, as an end which may reasonably be pursued for its own sake; and next, on the nature of that cultivation, or what that cultivation consists in. Truth of whatever kind is the proper object of the intellect; its cultivation then lies in fitting it to apprehend and contemplate truth. Now the intellect in its present state, with exceptions which need not here be specified, does not discern truth intuitively, or as a whole. We know, not by a direct and simple vision, not at a glance, but, as it were, by piecemeal and accumulation, by a mental process, by going round an object, by the comparison, the combina- tion, the mutual correction, the continual adaptation, of many partial notions, by the employment, concentration, and joint action of many faculties and exercises of mind. Such a union and concert of the intellectual powers, such an enlargement and development, such a comprehensiveness, is necessarily a matter of training. And again, such a training is a matter of rule; it is not mere application, however exemplary, which introduces the mind to truth, nor the reading many books, nor the getting up many subjects, nor the witnessing many experiments, nor the attending many lectures. All this is short of enough; a man may have done it all, yet be lingering in the vestibule of knowledge: he may not realize what his mouth utters; he may not see with his mental eye what confronts him; he may have no grasp of things as they are; or at least he may have no power at all of advancing one step forward of himself, in conse-quence of what he has already acquired, no power of discriminating between truth and falsehood, of sifting out the grains of truth from the mass, of arranging things according to their real value, and, if I may use the phrase, of building up ideas. Such a power is the result of a scientific formation of mind; it is an acquired faculty of judment, of clear-sightedness, of sagacity, of wisdom, of philosophical reach of mind, and of intellectual self-possession and repose, qualities which do not come of mere acquirement. The bodily eye, the organ for apprehending material objects, is provided by nature; the eye of the mind, of which the object is truth, is the work of discipline and habit.

This process of training, by which the intellect, instead of being formed 4 or sacrificed to some particular or accidental purpose, some specific trade or profession, or study or science, is disciplined for its own sake, for the perception of its own proper object, and for its own highest culture, is called liberal education; and though there is no one in whom it is carried as far as is conceiv-able, or whose intellect would be a pattern of what intellects should be made, yet there is scarcely anyone but may gain an idea of what real training is, and at least look towards it, and make its true scope and result, not something else, his standard of excellence; and numbers there are who may submit themselves to it, and secure it to themselves in good measure. And to set forth the right standard, and to train according to it, and to help forward all students towards it according to their various capacities, this I conceive to be the business of a university.

Now this is what some great men are very slow to allow; they insist that 5 education should be confined to some particular and narrow end, and should issue in some definite work, which can be weighed and measured. They argue as if everything, as well as every person, had its price; and that where there has been a great outlay, they have a right to expect a return in kind. This they call making education and instruction "useful," and "utility" becomes their watch-word. With a fundamental principle of this nature, they very naturally go on to ask, what there is to show for the expense of a university; what is the real worth in the market of the article called "a liberal education," on the supposition that it does not teach us definitely how to advance our manufactures, or to improve our lands, or to better our civil economy; or again, if it does not at once make this man a lawyer, that an engineer, and that a surgeon; or at least if it does not lead to discoveries in chemistry, astronomy, geology, magnetism, and science of every kind.

This is the obvious answer which may be made to those who urge upon us the claims of utility in our plans of education; but I am not going to leave the subject here: I mean to take a wider view of it. Let us take "useful," as Locke takes it, in its proper and popular sense, and then we enter upon a large field of thought, to which I cannot do justice in one discourse, though today's is all the space that I can give to it. I say, let us take "useful" to mean, not what is simply good, but what *tends* to good, or is the *instrument* of good; and in this sense also, Gentlemen, I will show you how a liberal education is truly and fully a useful, though it be not a professional, education. "Good" indeed means one thing, and "useful" means another; but I lay it down as a principle, which will save us a great deal of anxiety, that, though the useful is not always good, the good is always useful. Good is not only good, but reproductive of good; this is one of its attributes; nothing is excellent, beautiful, perfect, desirable for its own sake, but it overflows, and spreads the likeness of itself all around it. Good is prolific; it is not only good to the eye, but to the taste; it not only attracts us, but it communicates itself; it excites first our admiration and love, then our desire and our gratitude, and that, in proportion to its intenseness and fulness in particular instances. A great good will impart great good. If then the intellect is so excellent a portion of us, and its cultivation so excellent, it is not only beautiful, perfect, admirable, and noble in itself, but in a true and high sense it must be useful to the possessor and to all around him; not useful in any low, mechanical, mercantile sense, but as diffusing good, or as a blessing, or a gift, or power, or a treasure, first to the owner, then through him to the world. I say then, if a liberal education be good, it must necessarily be useful too.

You will see what I mean by the parallel of bodily health. Health is a good in itself, though nothing came of it, and is especially worth seeking and cherishing; yet, after all, the blessings which attend its presence are so great, while they are so close to it and so redound back upon it and encircle it, that we never think of it except as useful as well as good, and praise and prize it for what it does, as well as for what it is, though at the same time we cannot point out any definite and distinct work or production which it can be said to effect. And so as regards intellectual culture, I am far from denying utility in this large sense as the end of education, when I lay it down that the culture of the intellect is a good in itself and its own end; I do not exclude from the idea of intellectual culture what it cannot but be, from the very nature of things; I only deny that we must be able to point out, before we have any right to call it useful, some art, or business, or profession, or trade, or work, as resulting from it, and as its real and complete end. The parallel is exact: as the body may be sacrificed to some manual or other toil, whether moderate or oppressive, so may the intellect be devoted to some specific profession; and I do not call *this* the culture of the intellect. Again, as some member or organ of the body may be inordinately used and developed, so may memory, or imagination, or the reasoning faculty;

and *this* again is not intellectual culture. On the other hand, as the body may be tended, cherished, and exercised with a simple view to its general health, so may the intellect also be generally exercised in order to its perfect state; and this *is* its cultivation.

Again, as health ought to precede labour of the body, and as a man in 8 health can do what an unhealthy man cannot do, and as of this health the properties are strength, energy, agility, graceful carriage and action, manual dexterity, and endurance of fatigue, so in like manner general culture of mind is the best aid to professional and scientific study, and educated men can do what illiterate cannot; and the man who has learned to think and to reason and to compare and to discriminate and to analyze, who has refined his taste, and formed his judgment, and sharpened his mental vision, will not indeed at once be a lawyer, or a pleader, or an orator, or a statesman, or a physician, or a good landlord, or a man of business, or a soldier, or an engineer, or a chemist, or a geologist, or an antiquarian, but he will be placed in that state of intellect in which he can take up any one of the sciences or callings I have referred to, or any other for which he has a taste or special talent, with an ease, a grace, a versatility, and a success, to which another is a stranger. In this sense then, and as yet I have said but a very few words on a large subject, mental culture is emphatically *useful*.

If then I am arguing, and shall argue, against professional or scientific 9 knowledge as the sufficient end of a university education, let me not be supposed, Gentlemen, to be disrespectful towards particular studies, or arts, or vocations, and those who are engaged in them. In saying that law or medicine is not the end of a university course, I do not mean to imply that the university does not teach law or medicine. What indeed can it teach at all, if it does not teach something particular? It teaches *all* knowledge by teaching all *branches* of knowledge, and in no other way. I do but say that there will be this distinction as regards a professor of law, or of medicine, or of geology, or of political economy, in a university and out of it, that out of a university he is in danger of being absorbed and narrowed by his pursuit, and of giving lectures which are the lectures of nothing more than a lawyer, physician, geologist, or political economist; whereas in a university he will just know where he and his science stand, he has come to it, as it were, from a height, he has taken a survey of all knowledge, he is kept from extravagance by the very rivalry of other studies, he has gained from them a special illumination and largeness of mind and freedom and self-possession, and he treats his own in consequence with a philosophy and a resource, which belongs not to the study itself, but to his liberal education.

This then is how I should solve the fallacy, for so I must call it, by which 10 Locke and his disciples would frighten us from cultivating the intellect, under the notion that no education is useful which does not teach us some temporal calling, or some mechanical art, or some physical secret. I say that a cultivated intellect, because it is a good in itself, brings with it a power and a grace to every work and occupation which it undertakes, and enables us to be more useful, and to a greater number. There is a duty we owe to human society as such, to the state to which we belong, to the sphere in which we move, to the individuals towards whom we are variously related, and whom we successively encounter in life; and that philosophical or liberal education, as I have called it, which is the proper function of a university, if it refuses the foremost place to professional interests, does but postpone them to the formation of the citizen, and, while it subserves the larger interests of philanthropy, prepares also for the successful prosecution of those merely personal objects, which at first sight it seems to disparage. . . .

But I must bring these extracts to an end. Today I have confined myself to   11 saying that that training of the intellect, which is best for the individual himself, best enables him to discharge his duties to society. The philosopher, indeed, and the man of the world differ in their very notion, but the methods, by which they are respectively formed, are pretty much the same. The philosopher has the same command of matters of thought, which the true citizen and gentleman has of matters of business and conduct. If then a practical end must be assigned to a university course, I say it is that of training good members of society. Its art is the art of social life, and its end is fitness for the world. It neither confines its views to particular professions on the one hand, nor creates heroes or inspires genius on the other. Works indeed of genius fall under no art; heroic minds come under no rule; a university is not a birthplace of poets or of immortal authors, of founders of schools, leaders of colonies, or conquerors of nations. It does not promise a generation of Aristotles or Newtons, of Napoleons or Washingtons, of Raphaels or Shakespeares, though such miracles of nature it has before now contained within its precincts. Nor is it content on the other hand with forming the critic or the experimentalist, the economist or the engineer, though such too it includes within its scope. But a university training is the great ordinary means to a great but ordinary end; it aims at raising the intellectual tone of society, at cultivating the public mind, at purifying the national taste, at supplying true principles to popular enthusiasm and fixed aims to popular aspiration, at giving enlargement and sobriety to the ideas of the age, at facilitating the exercise of political power, and refining the intercourse of private life. It is the education which gives a man a clear conscious view of his own opinions and judgments, a truth in developing them, an eloquence in expressing them, and a force in urging them. It teaches him to see things as they are, to go right to the point, to disentangle a skein of thought, to detect what is sophistical, and to discard what is irrelevant. It prepares him to fill any post with credit, and to master any subject with facility. It shows him how to accommodate himself to others, how to throw himself into their state of mind, how to bring before them his own, how to influence them, how to come to an understanding with them, how to bear with them. He is at home in any society, he has common ground with every class; he knows when to speak and when to be silent; he is able to converse, he is able to listen; he can ask a question pertinently, and gain a lesson seasonably, when he has nothing to impart himself; he is ever ready, yet never in the way; he is a pleasant companion, and a comrade you can depend upon; he knows when to be serious and when to trifle, and he has a sure tact which enables him to trifle with gracefulness and to be serious with effect. He has the repose of a mind which lives in itself, while it lives in the world, and which has resources for its happiness at home when it cannot go abroad. He has a gift which serves him in public, and supports him in retirement, without which good fortune is but vulgar, and with which failure and disappointment have a charm. The art which tends to make a man all this is in the object which it pursues as useful as the art of wealth or the art of health, though it is less susceptible of method, and less tangible, less certain, less complete in its result.

EDUCATION IN CRISIS

QUESTIONS AND SUGGESTIONS FOR WRITING

1. Goodlad discusses seven conditions in our society that make it difficult for schools to achieve the ambitious goals expected of them today. These conditions range from the lack of cooperation between families and schools to dissonance among educators themselves. Review these conditions and think of personal examples that might support Goodlad's position or prove it wrong.

2. According to Winn, reading is somehow "better" than watching television because it involves more complex mental activities. Drawing upon personal experience, explain how either watching television or reading extensively has shaped your way of thinking.

3. Hentoff, in his discussion of the "dumbing down" of textbooks, states that "those who choose texts and those who publish them place the blame on today's undergraduates who don't read well and don't want to read much." Do you agree that college textbooks should be simplified for students who cannot read on a college level, or do you think that students should be expected to master more difficult texts? Did you have difficulty reading the Cardinal Newman excerpt?

4. Do you agree with Neusner that college teachers fail to prepare students for the real world by giving them good grades for mediocre work, taking their slipshod writing seriously, and pretending dull students are smart? Explain how your experience in college either supports or contradicts Neusner's claim.

5. Cardinal Newman argues that the principal work of the university is to provide a liberal education, not merely professional training. A liberal education "gives a man a clear conscious view of his own opinions and judgments, a truth in developing them, an eloquence in expressing them, and a force in urging them . . . it prepares him to fill any post with credit and to master any subject with civility." Do you agree or disagree with this assessment of a liberal education? Why?

6. Write an essay in which you argue for or against this position: the principal aim of a college education should be to train students for a profession.

ARTIFICIAL INTELLIGENCE

We often talk as though computers are conscious and can think somewhat in the way that human beings do. But are computers really conscious? And supposing that today's computers are not conscious, and cannot think as we do, will the more complicated computers of the future be able to? Furthermore, will they ever be able to "reason" as well as human beings do? For instance, will chess computers someday be able to beat the world's chess champion? Or is it true that no mere mechanical device, no matter how complicated, can possibly be conscious or be as creatively intelligent as the smartest human beings? Does it take flesh and blood to generate consciousness and true intelligence?

⊠ **CARL SAGAN**

In Defense of Robots

Carl Sagan, astronomer, is one of a handful of writers who can bring science to life for ordinary readers. He is perhaps best known to the lay world for his writings on the "nuclear winter" that he and his colleagues argue would follow an all-out nuclear war. In this excerpt from his 1979 book, Broca's Brain, *he argues that we should not denigrate computers, that they can, in some sense, accomplish intellectual tasks.*

Each human being is a superbly constructed, astonishingly compact, self-   1
ambulatory computer—capable on occasion of independent decision making and real control of his or her environment. And, as the old joke goes, these computers can be constructed by unskilled labor. But there are serious limita-

217

tions to employing human beings in certain environments. Without a great deal of protection, human beings would be inconvenienced on the ocean floor, the surface of Venus, the deep interior of Jupiter, or even on long space missions. . . . But the minimum interplanetary voyages have characteristic times of a year or two. Because we value human beings highly, we are reluctant to send them on very risky missions. If we do send human beings to exotic environments, we must also send along their food, their air, their water, amenities for entertainment and waste recycling, and companions. By comparison, machines require no elaborate life-support systems, no entertainment, no companionship, and we do not yet feel any strong ethical prohibitions against sending machines on one-way, or suicide, missions. . . .

The powerful abilities of computing machines to do arithmetic—hundreds 2 of millions of times faster than unaided human beings—are legendary. But what about really difficult matters? Can machines in any sense think through a new problem? Can they make discussions of the branched-contingency tree variety which we think of as characteristically human? (That is, I ask Question 1; if the answer is A, I ask Question 2; but if the answer is B, I ask Question 3; and so on.) Some decades ago the English mathematician A. M. Turing described what would be necessary for him to believe in machine intelligence. The condition was simply that he could be in teletype communication with a machine and be unable to tell that it was not a human being. Turing imagined a conversation between a man and a machine of the following quality:

INTERROGATOR: In the first line of your sonnet which reads "Shall I compare 3
    thee to a Summer's day," would not "a Spring day" do as well or better?
WITNESS: It wouldn't scan.
INTERROGATOR: How about "a Winter's day"? That would scan all right.
WITNESS: Yes, but nobody wants to be compared to a Winter's day.
INTERROGATOR: Would you say Mr. Pickwick reminded you of Christmas?
WITNESS: In a way.
INTERROGATOR: Yet Christmas is a Winter's day, and I do not think Mr. Pickwick would mind the comparison.
WITNESS: I don't think you're serious. By a Winter's day one means a typical 4
    Winter's day, rather than a special one like Christmas.

No device of this sophistication has yet been built, although I am not sure 5 how many humans would pass Turing's human test. But the amount of effort and money put into artificial intelligence has been quite limited, and there are only about a half-dozen major centers of such activity in the world. One of the more striking results obtained in a very limited universe of discourse—that of children's blocks—has come from the work of Terry Winograd, then at the Massachusetts Institute of Technology. Here is a dialogue between man and machine, the machine having been programmed by Winograd:

Q: What does the box contain?   6
A: The blue pyramid and the blue box.

Q: How many blocks are not in the box?
A: Four of them.
Q: Is at least one of them narrower than the one which I told you to pick up?
A: Yes, the red cube.
Q: Is there a steeple?
A: Sorry, I don't know the word "steeple."
Q: A steeple is a stack which contains two green cubes and a pyramid, for example.
A: I understand.   7
Q: Are there any steeples now?
A: No.
Q: Build one.

The machine does. It reaches out its mechanical hand, moves the cubes   8
and builds the structure that has just been described.

Q: When did you pick up the pyramid?   9
A: While I was stacking up the red cube, the large red block, and the large green cube.
Q: Why?
A: To get rid of it.
Q: Why did you clear off that cube?
A: To put it on the large green cube. . . .

Another sign of the intellectual accomplishments of machines is in games.   10
Even exceptionally simple computers—those that can be wired by a bright ten-year-old—can be programmed to play perfect tic-tac-toe. Some computers can play world-class checkers. Chess is of course a much more complicated game than tic-tac-toe or checkers. Here programming a machine to win is more difficult, and novel strategies have been used, including several rather successful attempts to have a computer learn from its own experience in playing previous chess games. Computers can learn, for example, empirically the rule that it is better in the beginning game to control the center of the chessboard than the periphery. The ten best chess players in the world still have nothing to fear from any present computer. But the situation is changing. Recently a computer for the first time did well enough to enter the Minnesota State Chess Open. This may be the first time that a nonhuman has entered a major sporting event on the planet Earth (and I cannot help but wonder if robot golfers and designated hitters may be attempted sometime in the next decade, to say nothing of dolphins in free-style competition.) The computer did not win the Chess Open, but this is the first time one has done well enough to enter such a competition. Chess-playing computers are improving extremely rapidly.

I have heard machines demeaned (often with a just audible sigh of relief)   11
for the fact that chess is an area where human beings are still superior. This reminds me very much of the old joke in which a stranger remarks with wonder

on the accomplishments of a checker-playing dog. The dog's owner replies, "Oh, it's not all that remarkable. He loses two games out of three." A machine that plays chess in the middle range of human expertise is a very capable machine; even if there are thousands of better human chess players, there are millions who are worse. To play chess requires strategy, foresight, analytical powers, and the ability to cross-correlate large numbers of variables and to learn from experience. These are excellent qualities in those whose job it is to discover and explore, as well as those who watch the baby and walk the dog.

With this as a more or less representative set of examples of the state of 12 development of machine intelligence, I think it is clear that a major effort over the next decade could produce much more sophisticated examples. This is also the opinion of most of the workers in machine intelligence. . . .

As the field of machine intelligence advances and as increasingly distant 13 objects in the solar system become accessible to exploration, we will see the development of increasingly sophisticated onboard computers, slowly climbing the phylogenetic tree from insect intelligence to crocodile intelligence to squirrel intelligence and—in the not very remote future, I think—to dog intelligence. Any flight to the outer solar system must have a computer capable of determining whether it is working properly. There is no possibility of sending to the Earth for a repairman. The machine must be able to sense when it is sick and skillfully doctor its own illnesses. A computer is needed that is able either to fix or replace failed computer, sensor or structural components. Such a computer, which has been called STAR (self-testing and repairing computer), is on the threshold of development. It employs redundant components, as biology does—we have two lungs and two kidneys partly because each is protection against failure of the other. But a computer can be much more redundant than a human being, who has, for example, but one head and one heart. . . .

We appear to be on the verge of developing a wide variety of intelligent 14 machines capable of performing tasks too dangerous, too expensive, too onerous or too boring for human beings. The development of such machines is, in my mind, one of the few legitimate "spin-offs" of the space program. The efficient exploitation of energy in agriculture—upon which our survival as a species depends—may even be contingent on the development of such machines. The main obstacle seems to be a very human problem, the quiet feeling that comes stealthily and unbidden, and argues that there is something threatening or "inhuman" about machines performing certain tasks as well as or better than human beings; or a sense of loathing for creatures made of silicon and germanium rather than proteins and nucleic acids. But in many respects our survival as a species depends on our transcending such primitive chauvinisms. In part, our adjustment to intelligent machines is a matter of acclimatization. There are already cardiac pacemakers that can sense the beat of the human heart; only when there is the slightest hint of fibrillation does the pacemaker stimulate the heart. This is a mild but very useful sort of machine intelligence. I cannot imagine the wearer of this device resenting its intelligence. I think in a relatively short period of time there will be a very similar sort of acceptance for much more intelligent and sophisticated machines. There is nothing inhuman about an intelligent machine; it is indeed an expression of those superb intellectual capabilities that only human beings, of all the creatures on our planet, now possess.

JOHN R. SEARLE

Minds, Brains, and Programs

John R. Searle is a very well known philosopher who has written on many topics, in particular on the philosophy of language. In this essay he distinguishes between what he calls strong and weak artificial intelligence (AI) and argues against the idea that computers have strong AI, or, more specifically, "that the appropriately programmed computer literally has cognitive status and that the programs thereby explain human cognition."

What psychological and philosophical significance should we attach to recent   1
efforts at computer simulations of human cognitive capacities? In answering this question, I find it useful to distinguish what I will call "strong" AI from "weak" or "cautious" AI (artificial intelligence). According to weak AI, the principal value of the computer in the study of the mind is that it gives us a very powerful tool. For example, it enables us to formulate and test hypotheses in a more rigorous and precise fashion. But according to strong AI, the computer is not merely a tool in the study of the mind; rather, the appropriately programmed computer really *is* a mind, in the sense that computers given the right programs can be literally said to *understand* and have other cognitive states. In strong AI, because the programmed computer has cognitive states, the programs are not mere tools that enable us to test psychological explanations; rather, the programs are themselves the explanations.

I have no objection to the claims of weak AI, at least as far as this article   2
is concerned. My discussion here will be directed at the claims I have defined as those of strong AI, specifically the claim that the appropriately programmed computer literally has cognitive states and that the programs thereby explain human cognition. When I hereafter refer to AI, I have in mind the strong version, as expressed by these two claims.

I will consider the work of Roger Schank and his colleagues at Yale   3
(Schank and Abelson, 1977), because I am more familiar with it than I am with any other similar claims. . . .

Very briefly, and leaving out the various details, one can describe Schank's   4
program as follows: The aim of the program is to simulate the human ability to
understand stories. It is characteristic of human beings' story-understanding
capacity that they can answer questions about the story even though the information that they give was never explicitly stated in the story. Thus, for example,
suppose you are given the following story: "A man went into a restaurant and
ordered a hamburger. When the hamburger arrived it was burned to a crisp,
and the man stormed out of the restaurant angrily, without paying for the
hamburger or leaving a tip." Now, if you are asked "Did the man eat the
hamburger?" you will presumably answer, "No, he did not." Similarly, if you
are given the following story: "A man went into a restaurant and ordered a
hamburger; when the hamburger came he was very pleased with it; and as he
left the restaurant he gave the waitress a large tip before paying his bill," and
you are asked the question, "Did the man eat the hamburger?" you will presumably answer, "Yes, he ate the hamburger." Now Schank's machines can similarly answer questions about restaurants in this fashion. To do this, they have a
"representation" of the sort of information that human beings have about restaurants, which enables them to answer such questions as those above, given
these sorts of stories. When the machine is given the story and then asked the
question, the machine will print out answers of the sort that we would expect
human beings to give if told similar stories. Partisans of strong AI claim that in
this question and answer sequence the machine is not only simulating a human
ability but also (1) that the machine can literally be said to *understand* the story
and provide the answers to questions, and (2) that what the machine and its
program do *explains* the human ability to understand the story and answer
questions about it.

Both claims seem to me to be totally unsupported by Schank's work, as I   5
will attempt to show in what follows. I am not, of course, saying that Schank
himself is committed to these claims.

One way to test any theory of the mind is to ask oneself what it would be   6
like if my mind actually worked on the principles that the theory says all minds
work on. Let us apply this test to the Schank program with the following
Gedankenexperiment. Suppose that I'm locked in a room and given a large
batch of Chinese writing. Suppose furthermore (as is indeed the case) that I
know no Chinese, either written or spoken, and that I'm not even confident
that I could recognize Chinese writing as Chinese writing distinct from, say,
Japanese writing or meaningless squiggles. To me, Chinese writing is just so
many meaningless squiggles. Now suppose further that after this first batch of
Chinese writing I am given a second batch of Chinese script together with a set
of rules for correlating the second batch with the first batch. The rules are in
English, and I understand these rules as well as any other native speaker of
English. They enable me to correlate one set of formal symbols with another
set of formal symbols, and all that "formal" means here is that I can identify
the symbols entirely by their shapes. Now suppose also that I am given a third
batch of Chinese symbols together with some instructions, again in English,

that enable me to correlate elements of this third batch with the first two batches, and these rules instruct me how to give back certain Chinese symbols with certain sorts of shapes in response to certain sorts of shapes given me in the third batch. Unknown to me, the people who are giving me all of these symbols call the first batch a "script," they call the second batch a "story," and they call the third batch "questions." Furthermore, they call the symbols I give them back in response to the third batch "answers to the questions," and the set of rules in English that they gave me, they call the "program." Now just to complicate the story a little, imagine that these people also give me stories in English, which I understand, and they then ask me questions in English about these stories, and I give them back answers in English. Suppose also that after a while I get so good at following the instructions for manipulating the Chinese symbols and the programmers get so good at writing the programs that from the external point of view—that is, from the point of view of somebody outside the room in which I am locked—my answers to the questions are absolutely indistinguishable from those of native Chinese speakers. Nobody just looking at my answers can tell that I don't speak a word of Chinese. Let us also suppose that my answers to the English questions are, as they no doubt would be, indistinguishable from those of other native English speakers, for the simple reason that I am a native English speaker. From the external point of view—from the point of view of someone reading my "answers"—the answers to the Chinese questions and the English questions are equally good. But in the Chinese case, unlike the English case, I produce the answers by manipulating uninterpreted formal symbols. As far as the Chinese is concerned, I simply behave like a computer: I perform computational operations on formally specified elements. For the purposes of the Chinese, I am simply an instantiation of the computer program.

Now the claims made by strong AI are that the programmed computer 7 understands the stories and that the program in some sense explains human understanding. But we are now in a position to examine these claims in light of our thought experiment.

1. As regards the first claim, it seems to me quite obvious in the example 8 that I do not understand a word of the Chinese stories. I have inputs and outputs that are indistinguishable from those of the native Chinese speaker, and I can have any formal program you like, but I still understand nothing. For the same reasons, Schank's computer understands nothing of any stories, whether in Chinese, English, or whatever, since in the Chinese case the computer is me, and in cases where the computer is not me, the computer has nothing more than I have in the case where I understand nothing.

2. As regards the second claim, that the program explains human under- 9 standing, we can see that the computer and its program do not provide sufficient conditions of understanding since the computer and the program are functioning, and there is no understanding. But does it even provide a necessary condition or a significant contribution to understanding? One of the claims made

by the supporters of strong AI is that when I understand a story in English, what I am doing is exactly the same—or perhaps more of the same—as what I was doing in manipulating the Chinese symbols. It is simply more formal symbol manipulation that distinguishes the case in English, where I do understand, from the case in Chinese, where I don't. I have not demonstrated that this claim is false, but it would certainly appear an incredible claim in the example. Such plausibility as the claim has derives from the supposition that we can construct a program that will have the same inputs and outputs as native speakers, and in addition we assume that speakers have some level of description where they are also instantiations of a program. On the basis of these two assumptions we assume that even if Schank's program isn't the whole story about understanding, it may be part of the story. Well, I suppose that is an empirical possibility, but not the slightest reason has so far been given to believe that it is true, since what is suggested—though certainly not demonstrated—by the example is that the computer program is simply irrelevant to my understanding of the story. In the Chinese case I have everything that artificial intelligence can put into me by way of a program, and I understand nothing; in the English case I understand everything, and there is so far no reason at all to suppose that my understanding has anything to do with computer programs, that is, with computational operations on purely formally specified elements. As long as the the program is defined in terms of computational operations on purely formally defined elements, what the example suggests is that these by themselves have no interesting connection with understanding. They are certainly not sufficient conditions, and not the slightest reason has been given to suppose that they are necessary conditions or even that they make a significant contribution to understanding. Notice that the force of the argument is not simply that different machines can have the same input and output while operating on different formal principles—that is not the point at all. Rather, whatever purely formal principles you put into the computer, they will not be sufficient for understanding, since a human will be able to follow the formal principles without understanding anything. No reason whatever has been offered to suppose that such principles are necessary or even contributory, since no reason has been given to suppose that when I understand English I am operating with any formal program at all.

Well, then, what is it that I have in the case of the English sentences that   10
I do not have in the case of the Chinese sentences? The obvious answer is that I know what the former mean, while I haven't the faintest idea what the latter mean. But in what does this consist and why couldn't we give it to a machine, whatever it is? . . .

I see no reason in principle why we couldn't give a machine the capacity   11
to understand English or Chinese, since in an important sense our bodies with our brains are precisely such machines. But I do see very strong arguments for saying that we could not give such a thing to a machine where the operation of the machine is defined solely in terms of computational processes over formally defined elements; that is, where the operation of the machine is defined as an

instantiation of a computer program. It is not because I am the instantiation of a computer program that I am able to understand English and have other forms of intentionality (I am, I suppose, the instantiation of any number of computer programs), but as far as we know it is because I am a certain sort of organism with a certain biological (i.e., chemical and physical) structure, and this structure, under certain conditions, is causally capable of producing perception, action, understanding, learning, and other intentional phenomena. And part of the point of the present argument is that only something that had those causal powers could have the intentionality. Perhaps other physical and chemical processes could produce exactly these effects; perhaps, for example, Martians also have intentionality but their brains are made of different stuff. That is an empirical question, rather like the question whether photosynthesis can be done by something with a chemistry different from that of chlorophyll.

But the main point of the present argument is that no purely formal model 12 will ever be sufficent by itself for intentionality because the formal properties are not by themselves constitutive of intentionality, and they have by themselves no causal powers except the power, when instantiated, to produce the next stage of the formalism when the machine is running. And any other causal properties that particular realizations of the formal model have, are irrelevant to the formal model because we can always put the same formal model in a different realization where those causal properties are obviously absent. Even if, by some miracle, Chinese speakers exactly realize Schank's program, we can put the same program in English speakers, water pipes, or computers, none of which understand Chinese, the program notwithstanding. . . .

Still, there are several reasons why AI must have seemed—and to many 13 people perhaps still does seem—in some way to reproduce and thereby explain mental phenomena, and I believe we will not succeed in removing these illusions until we have fully exposed the reasons that give rise to them.

First, and perhaps most important, is a confusion about the notion of 14 "information processing": many people in cognitive science believe that the human brain, with its mind, does something called "information processing," and analogously the computer with its program does information processing; but fires and rainstorms, on the other hand, don't do information processing at all. Thus, though the computer can simulate the formal features of any process whatever, it stands in a special relation to the mind and brain because when the computer is properly programmed, ideally with the same program as the brain, the information processing is identical in the two cases, and this information processing is really the essence of the mental. But the trouble with this argument is that it rests on an ambiguity in the notion of "information." In the sense in which people "process information" when they reflect, say, on problems in arithmetic or when they read and answer questions about stories, the programmed computer does not do "information processing." Rather, what it does is manipulate formal symbols. The fact that the programmer and the interpreter of the computer output use the symbols to stand for objects in the world is totally beyond the scope of the computer. The computer, to repeat, has a syntax but no semantics. Thus, if you type into the computer "2 plus 2 equals?" it will type out "4." But it has no idea that "4" means 4 or that it means anything at all. And the point is not that it lacks some second-order information about the interpretation of its first-order symbols, but rather that its first-order symbols don't have any interpretations as far as the computer is concerned. All the computer has is more symbols. The introduction of the notion of "information processing" therefore produces a dilemma: either we construe the notion of "information processing" in such a way that it implies intentionality as part of the process or we don't. If the former, then the programmed computer does not do information processing, it only manipulates formal symbols. If the latter, then, though the computer does information processing, it is only doing so in the sense in which adding machines, typewriters, stomachs, thermostats, rainstorms, and hurricanes do information processing; namely, they have a level of description at which we can describe them as taking information in at one end, transforming it, and producing information as output. But in this case it is up to outside observers to interpret the input and output as information in the ordinary sense. And no similarity is established between the computer and the brain in terms of any similarity of information processing.

Second, in much of AI there is a residual behaviorism or operationalism. Since appropriately programmed computers can have input-output patterns similar to those of human beings, we are tempted to postulate mental states in the computer similar to human mental states. But once we see that it is both conceptually and empirically possible for a system to have human capacities in some realm without having any intentionality at all, we should be able to overcome this impulse. My desk adding machine has calculating capacities, but no intentionality, and in this paper I have tried to show that a system could have input and output capabilities that duplicated those of a native Chinese speaker and still not understand Chinese, regardless of how it was programmed. The Turing test is typical of the tradition in being unashamedly behavioristic and operationalistic, and I believe that if AI workers totally repudiated behaviorism and operationalism much of the confusion between simulation and duplication would be eliminated. 15

⚔ **HUBERT DREYFUS**

Why Computers Can't Be Intelligent

Philosophy Professor Hubert Dreyfus gained fame with his 1972 book, What Computers Can't Do: A Critique of Artificial Reason. *In this excerpt, taken from a later revision, he argues that human beings are not just very complicated machines and thus that computers, which are just complicated machines, can never be intelligent in the way that human beings are. (His underlying assumptions are against the philosophical position called mechanism, a kind of determinism.)*

Even the most tough-minded men and women have a sense that, although 1
they are made out of matter, they are not machines; yet lately they are more
and more frequently being told, as if it were obvious, that "each human being
is a superbly constructed . . . computer"[1] and that computers will eventually
behave as intelligently as people do. Some scientists say that computers, like
HAL in *2001*, will be just like people; others claim that intelligent machines
will be better than human beings, since they will not suffer from fatigue,
emotions, self doubt, and the illusion that they are not machines. Each of
these predictions is associated with its own disaster scenario: the emotional
computer loses its cool and destroys everyone in its passionate attempt to save
the mission; the purely intellectual computer coolly turns society into a rational
hell fit only for robots. Since spreading the good news of the imminence of
artificial intelligence as well as prophesying inevitable disaster is becoming a
new media industry, it is high time to look again at our quiet assurance that we
are not computers and that claims that computers can be intelligent must be
nonsense.

Two of the most popularized computer "successes" which seem to support 2
the notion that scientists are making steady progress toward intelligent machines
are Winograd's blocks program (SHRDLU)[2] and the impressive performance of
recent chess machines.

When it was first unveiled ten years ago Winograd's program did, indeed, 3
seem a major advance toward intelligent machines. SHRDLU simulates a robot
arm which can move a set of variously shaped blocks and allows a person to
engage in a dialogue with the computer, asking questions, making statements,
and issuing commands about this simple world of movable blocks. Workers in
AI (artificial intelligence) did not try to cover up the fact that it was SHRDLU's
restricted domain which made apparent understanding possible. They even had
a name for Winograd's method of restricting the domain of discourse. He
was dealing with a "micro-world." Marvin Minsky and Seymour Papert, co-
directors of MIT's "robot project," explain:

> Each model—or "micro-world" as we shall call it—is very schematic; it talks
> about a fairyland in which things are so simplified that almost every statement
> about them would be literally false if asserted about the real world.[3]

---

[1]Carl Sagan, "In Defense of Robots," reprinted on page 217 of this text.
[2]Terry Winograd, "A Procedural Model of Language Understanding," *Computer Models of Thought and Language*, Roger Schank and Kenneth Colby, eds. (San Francisco: Freeman, 1973). (SHRDLU is an anti-acronym whose letters don't stand for anything. It was picked up by Winograd from *Mad Magazine*, which uses this frequent typesetter's error as the name of mythical monsters and the like.)
[3]Marvin Minsky and Symour Papert, Draft, July 1970, of a Proposal to ARPA for Research on Artificial Intelligence at M.I.T., 1970–1971, p. 39.

But they immediately add:

> Nevertheless, we feel that they (the micro-worlds) are so important that we are
> assigning a large portion of our effort toward developing a collection of these
> micro-worlds and finding how to use the suggestive and predictive powers of
> the models without being overcome by their incompatibility with literal truth.

Given the admittedly artificial and arbitrary character of micro-worlds, why did
Minsky and Papert think they provide a promising line of research?

To find the answer we must follow Minsky and Papert's perceptive remarks 4
on the understanding of narrative and their less than perceptive conclusions:

> . . . In a familiar fable, the wily Fox tricks the vain Crow into dropping the
> meat by asking it to sing. The usual test of understanding is the ability of the
> child to answer questions like: "Did the Fox think the Crow had a lovely voice?"
> The topic is sometimes classified as "natural language manipulation" or as
> "deductive logic," etc. These descriptions are badly chosen. For the real prob-
> lem is not to understand English; it is to *understand* at all. The difficulty in
> getting a machine to give the right answer does not at all depend on "disambi-
> guating" the words (at least, not in the usual primitive sense of selecting one
> "meaning" out of a discrete set of "meanings"). And neither does the difficulty
> lie in the need for unusually powerful logical apparatus. The main problem is
> that no one has constructed the elements of a body of knowledge about such
> matters that is adequate for understanding the story. Let us see what is involved.
>
> To begin with, there is never a unique solution to such problems, so we do 5
> not ask what the Understander *must* know. But he will surely gain by having
> the concept of FLATTERY. To provide this knowledge, we imagine a "micro-
> theory" of flattery—an extendible collection of facts or procedures that describe
> conditions under which one might expect to find flattery, what forms it takes,
> what its consequences are, and so on. How complex this theory is depends on
> what is presupposed. Thus it would be very difficult to describe flattery to our
> Understander if he (or it) does not already know that statements can be made
> for purposes other than to convey literally correct, factual information. It would
> be almost impossibly difficult if he does not even have some concept like
> PURPOSE or INTENTION.[4]

The surprising move here is the conclusion that there *could* be a circumscribed
"micro-theory" of flattery—somehow intelligible apart from the rest of human
life—while at the same time the account shows that an understanding of flattery
would depend on a further opening out into the understanding of the rest of
our everyday world, with its complex purposes and intentions.

What characterizes the period of the early seventies, and makes SHRDLU 6
seem an advance toward general intelligence, is the pseudo-scientific concept
of a micro-world—a domain which can be analyzed in isolation.

In our everyday life we are, indeed, involved in various "sub-worlds" such 7
as the world of the theater, of business, or of mathematics, but each of these is

---

[4]Ibid., pp. 42–44.

a "mode" of our shared everyday world.[5] That is, sub-worlds are not related like isolatable physical systems to larger systems they *compose*; rather, they are local elaborations of a whole which they *presuppose*.

Only recently has the illusion that one can generalize work done in nar- 8 rowly constrained domains been diagnosed and laid to rest by Winograd himself:

> The AI programs of the late sixties and early seventies are much too literal. They deal with meaning as if it were a structure to be built up of the bricks and mortar provided by the words. . . . This gives them a "brittle" character, able to deal well with tightly specified areas of meaning in an artificially formal conversation. They are correspondingly weak in dealing with natural utterances, full of bits and fragments, continual (unnoticed) metaphor, and reference to much less easily formalizable areas of knowledge.[6]

While popularizers are still praising SHRDLU, it is now generally acknowledged by serious workers in the field that the micro-world approach to everyday intelligence is a dead end.

Everyday human life turns out to be one interrelated whole, but games 9 are just the sort of totally circumscribed micro-worlds in which computers excel. Thus, while expecting failures in dealing with human language, we should expect game-playing programs to have great success. But we must be on our guard against attributing this success to anything like human intelligence.

Chess, for example, is a perfect micro-world in which relevance is re- 10 stricted to the narrow domain of the kind of chess piece (pawn, knight, etc.), its color, and the position of the piece on the board. The size, weight and temperature of a piece are never relevant. But while the game's circumscribed character makes a world champion chess program possible in principle, there is a great deal of evidence that human beings play chess quite differently from the way computers do. Indeed, computers do not use long-range strategy, learn from experience, or even remember previous moves.

To understand the difference between human and machine play, we must 11 first understand how a chess program works. A chess program uses situation-to-action rules. A situation is characterized in terms of context-free features: the position and color of each piece on the board. All possible legal moves and the positions which result are then defined in terms of these features. To evaluate and compare positions, rules are provided for calculating scores on attributes such as "material balance" (where a numerical value is assigned to each piece on the board and the total score is computed for each player) or "center control" (where the number of pieces bearing on each centrally located square is counted). Finally, there must be a formula for evaluating alternative positions

---

[5]This view is worked out by Martin Heidegger in *Being and Time* (New York: Harper & Row, 1962). See especially p. 93 and all of section 18.
[6]Winograd, "Artificial Intelligence and Language Comprehension," in *Artificial Intelligence and Language Comprehension* (Washington, D.C.: National Institute of Education, 1976), p. 17.

on the basis of these scores. Using this approach and looking at around 3 million possible positions, CHESS 4.5 recently won the 84th Minnesota Open Tournament, but a chess master generally looks at the results of less than 100 possible moves and yet plays a far better game. How can this be?

It seems that by playing over book games chess masters develop the ability 12 to recognize present positions as similar to positions which occurred in classic games. These previous positions have already been analyzed in terms of their significant aspects. Aspects of a chess position include such overall characteristics as "control of the situation" (the extent to which a player's opponent's moves can be forced by making threatening moves), "crampedness of the position" (the amount of freedom of maneuver inherent in both the player's position and the opponent's position), or "overextendedness" (the fact that while the position might be superficially quite strong, one is not in sufficient control of the situation to follow through and, with correct play by the opponent, a massive retreat will be required). The already analyzed remembered positions focus the player's attention on critical areas before he begins to count out specific moves.

The distinction between features and aspects is central here. *Aspects* play 13 a role in an account of human play similar to that of *features* in the computer model, but there is a crucial difference. In the computer model the *situation is* DEFINED IN TERMS OF *the features*, whereas in human play *situational understanding is* PRIOR TO *aspect specification*. For example, the numerical value of a feature such as material balance can be calculated independently of any understanding of the game, whereas an aspect like overextendedness cannot be calculated simply in terms of the position of the pieces, since the same board position can have different aspects depending on its place in the long-range strategy of a game.

No *feature-based* matching of the present position against a stored library 14 of previous positions could account for a master player's ability to use past experience to zero in. It is astronomically unlikely that two positions will ever turn out to be *identical*, so that what has to be compared are *similar* positions. But similarity cannot be defined as having a large number of pieces on identical squares. Two positions which are identical except for one pawn moved to an adjacent square can be totally different, while two positions can be similar although no pieces are on the same square in each. Thus similarity depends on the player's sense of the issues at stake, not merely on the position of the pieces. Seeing two positions as similar is exactly what requires a deep understanding of the game. By thus structuring the current situation in terms of aspects of remembered similar situations the human player is able to avoid the massive counting out required by a computer which can only "recognize" positions characterized in terms of context-free features.

Human intelligence, then, even in games, requires the use of background 15 knowledge; in the everyday world this background knowledge consists of the commonsense understanding of how to do things which we share with other human beings. Recent work in artificial intelligence has been forced to deal directly with this background of everyday practices. Faced with this necessity, researchers have implicitly tried to treat the background as a complex of facts related by rules—sometimes called a "belief system." This assumption that the background of practices can be treated as just another object is the basis of the claim that human beings are just very sophisticated computers. This conviction runs deep in our whole philosophical tradition. Following Martin Heidegger, who is the first to have identified and criticized this view, I will call it the metaphysical assumption.

The obvious question to ask is: Is there any reason besides the persistent 16 difficulties and history of unfulfilled promises in AI for believing that the metaphysical assumption is unjustified? Is there any defense against this subtle version of mechanism? The best argument, I think, is that whenever human behavior is analyzed in terms of facts related by rules, these rules must always contain a *ceteris paribus* condition, that is, they apply "everything else being equal," and what "everything else" and "equal" means in any specific situation can never be fully spelled out. Moreover, this *ceteris paribus* condition is not merely an annoyance which shows that the analysis is not yet complete and might be an "infinite task." Rather the *ceteris paribus* condition points to the background of practices which is the condition of the possibility of all rulelike activity. In explaining our actions we must always sooner or later fall back on our everyday practices and simply say "this is what we do" or "that's what it is to be a human being." Thus in the last analysis all intelligibility and all intelligent behavior must be traced back to our sense of what we *are*, which is something we can never explicitly *know*.

This claim can best be made plausible by means of an example from an 17 MIT story-understanding project. Consider the following story fragment:

> Today was Jack's birthday. Penny and Janet went to the store. They were going to get presents. Janet decided to get a kite. "Don't do that," said Penny. "Jack has a kite. He will make you take *it* back."[7]

The goal is to construct a theory that explains how the reader understands that "*it*" refers to the new kite, not the one Jack already owns. Grammatical tricks (such as assigning the referent of "*it*" to the last mentioned noun) are clearly inadequate, as the result would be to mistakenly understand the last sentence of the story as meaning that Jack will make Janet take back the kite *he already owns*. It is clear that one cannot know "*it*" refers to the new kite without knowledge about the trading habits of our society. One could imagine a different world in which newly bought objects are never returned to the store, but old ones are.

The AI approach dictated by the metaphysical assumption is, of course, 18 to try to make the background practices involved in understanding this story explicit as a set of beliefs. But once games and micro-worlds are left behind, a

---

[7]Ira Goldstein and Seymour Papert, M.I.T. AI Laboratory, AI Memo No. 337 (July 1975, revised March 1976), "Artificial Intelligence, Language and the Study of Knowledge," pp. 29–31.

yawning abyss threatens to swallow up those who try to carry out such a program. As Papert notes:

> . . . The story does not include explicitly all important facts. Look back at the story. Some readers will be surprised to note that the text itself does not state (a) that the presents bought by Penny and Janet were for *Jack*, (b) that the [kite] bought by Janet was intended as a present, and (c) that having an object implies that one does not want another.[8]

Our example turns on the question: How does one store the "facts" mentioned in (c) above about returning presents? To begin with there are perhaps indefinitely many reasons for taking a present back. It may be the wrong size, run on the wrong voltage, be carcinogenic, make too much noise, be considered too childish, too feminine, too masculine, too American, etc. And each of these facts requires further facts to be understood. But we will concentrate on the reason mentioned in (c): that normally, i.e., *everything else being equal*, if one has an object, one does not want another just like it. Of course, this cannot simply be entered as a true proposition. It does not hold for dollar bills, cookies, or marbles. (It is not clear it even holds for kites.) Papert would answer that, of course, once we talk of the norm we must be prepared to deal with exceptions.

But here the desperate hand-waving begins, for the text need not explicitly mention the exceptions at all. If the gift were marbles or cookies the text surely would not mention that these were exceptions to the general rule that one of a kind is enough. So the data base would have to contain *an account of all possible exceptions* to augment the text—if it even makes sense to think of this as a definite list. Worse, even if one listed all the exceptional cases where one would be glad to possess more than one specimen of a certain type of object, there are situations which allow an exception to this exception: already having one cookie is more than enough if the cookie in question is three feet in diameter; one thousand marbles is more than a normal child can handle. Must we then list the situations which lead one to expect exceptions to the exceptions? But these exceptions too can be overridden in the case of, say, a cookie monster or a marble freak, and so it goes. The computer programmer writing a story-understander must try to list all possibly relevant information, and once that information contains appeals to the *normal* or *typical* there is no way to avoid an endless series of qualifications of qualifications for applying that knowledge to a specific situation.

The only "answer" Papert offers is the metaphysical assumption that the background of everyday life is a set of rigidly defined situations in which the relevant facts are as clear as in a game:

> The fundamental frame assumption is the thesis that . . . [m]ost situations in which people find themselves *have sufficient in common* with previously en-

[8]Ibid., p. 33.

countered situations for the salient features to be *pre-analyzed* and stored in a *situation-specific* form.[9]

But this "solution" is untenable for two reasons:

1. Even if the current situation is, indeed, *similar* to a preanalyzed one, we still have the problem of deciding which situation it is similar to. We have already seen that even in games such as chess no two positions are likely to be identical, so a deep understanding of what is going on is required to decide what counts as a similar position in any two games. This should be even more obvious in cases where the problem is to decide which preanalyzed situation a given real-world situation most resembles: for example, whether a situation where there are well-dressed babies and new toys being presented has more in common with a birthday party or a beauty contest.

2. Even if all our lives *were* lived in identical stereotypical situations, we have just seen that any real-world frame must be described in terms of the normal, and that appeal to the normal necessarily leads to a regress when we try to characterize the conditions which determine the applicability of the norm to a specific case. Only our *general* sense of what is typical can decide here, and *that* background understanding by definition cannot be "situation-specific."

Still, to this dilemma the AI researchers might plausibly respond: "Whatever the background of shared interests, feelings, and practices necessary for understanding specific situations, that knowledge *must* somehow be in the human beings who have that understanding. And how else could such knowledge be represented but as some explicit set of facts and beliefs?" Indeed, that kind of computer programming accepted by all workers in AI would require such a data structure, and so would philosophers who hold that all knowledge must be explicitly represented in our minds; but there are two alternatives which, by avoiding the idea that everything we know must be in the form of some explicit description, would avoid contradictions inherent in the information-processing model.

One response, shared by existential phenomenologists such as Maurice Merleau-Ponty[10] and ordinary language philosophers such as Ludwig Wittgenstein, is to say that such "knowledge" of human interests and practices need not be represented at all. As Wittgenstein puts it in *On Certainty*, "Children do not learn that books exist, that armchairs exist, etc., etc.—they learn to fetch books, sit in armchairs, etc., etc."[11] Just as it seems plausible that I can learn to swim by practicing until I develop the necessary patterns of responses which run off automatically without my ever describing my body and muscular movements to myself, so too what I "know" about cultural practices which

[9]Ibid., pp. 30–31. (My italics.)
[10]Maurice Merleau-Ponty, *Phenomenology of Perception* (London: Routledge and Kegan Paul, 1962).
[11]Ludwig Wittgenstein, *On Certainty* (New York: Harper Torch Book, 1972), p. 62.

enables me to recognize and act in specific situations has been gradually acquired through training—against an already meaningful background—although no one every did or could make explicit what was being learned.

Another possible account would allow a place for representations, at least 26 in special cases where I have to stop and reflect, but such a position would stress that these are usually not explicit descriptions but more like images, by means of which I explore what I *am*, not what I *know*. In this view, I don't normally represent to myself that I have desires, or that standing up requires balance, or, to take an example from Schank's pathetic attempt to make explicit a bit of our interpersonal knowledge, that:

> (I)f two people are positively emotionally related, then a negative change in one person's state will cause the other person to develop the goal of causing a positive change in the other's state.[12]

When it is helpful, however, as in understanding a story, I can picture myself in a specific situation and ask myself what I would do or how I would feel—if I were in Jack's place how I would react to being given a second kite—without having to make explicit all that a computer would have to be told to come to a similar conclusion. We thus appeal to *concrete* representation (images or memories) based on our own experience without having to make explicit the strict rules and their spelled out *ceteris paribus* conditions required by *abstract* symbolic descriptions.

Indeed, it is hard to see how the subtle variety of ways things can matter 27 to us could be exhaustively spelled out. We can anticipate and understand Jack's reaction because we remember what it feels like to be amused, amazed, incredulous, disappointed, disgruntled, saddened, annoyed, disgusted, upset, angry, furious, outraged, etc., and we recognize the impulses to action associated with these various degrees and kinds of concerns. A computer model would have to be given a description of each shade of feeling as well as each feeling's normal occasion and likely result.

The idea that feelings, memories, and images *must* be the conscious tip 28 of an unconscious explicit description runs up against both *prima facie* evidence and the problem of explicating the *ceteris paribus* conditions. Moreover, this mechanistic assumption is not supported by one shred of scientific evidence from neurophysiology or psychology, or from the past successes of AI, whose repeated failures required appeal to the metaphysical assumption in the first place. When AI workers finally face and analyze their failures, it might well be the metaphysical/mechanistic assumption that they will find they have to reject.

Looking back over the past ten years of AI research, we might say that the 29 basic point which has emerged is that *since intelligence must be situated it cannot be separated from the rest of human life.* The persistent denial of this

---

[12]Roger Schank and Robert P. Abelson, *Scripts, Plans, Goals and Understanding* (Hillsdale, N.J.: Erlbaum, 1970), p. 144.

seemingly obvious point cannot, however, be laid at the door of AI. It starts with Plato's separation of the intellect or rational soul from the body with its skills, emotions, and appetites. Aristotle continued this unlikely dichotomy when he separated the theoretical from the practical, and defined man as a rational animal—as if one could separate man's rationality from his animal needs and desires. If one thinks of the importance of the sensory-motor skills in the development of our ability to recognize and cope with objects, or of the role of needs and desires in structuring all social situations, or finally of the whole cultural background of human self-interpretation involved in our simply knowing how to pick out and use chairs, the idea that we can ignore this know-how while formalizing our intellectual understanding as a complex system of facts and rules is highly implausible.

However incredible, this dubious dichotomy now pervades our thinking 30 about everything including computers. In the *Star Trek* TV series, the episode entitled "The Return of the Archons" tells of a wise statesman named Landru who programmed a computer to run a society. Unfortunately, he could give the computer only his abstract intelligence, not his concrete wisdom, so the computer turned the society into a plannified hell. No one stops to wonder how, without Landru's embodied skills, feelings, and concerns, the computer could understand everyday situations and so run a society at all.

Great artists have always sensed the truth, stubbornly denied by both 31 philosophers and technologists, that, just because man is material in the special way that he is, he can never have the clarity characteristic of a computer. Artists sense that the basis of human understanding cannot be isolated and explicitly understood. In *Moby Dick*, Melville writes of the tattooed savage, Queequeg, who had "written out on his body a complete theory of the heavens and the earth, and a mystical treatise on the art of attaining truth; so that Queequeg in his own proper person was a riddle to unfold; a wondrous work in one volume; but whose mysteries not even himself could read . . ." The monomaniac philosopher Ahab prefigures AI's insistence that all such cultural know-how be made explicit. One morning turning away from surveying Queequeg, Ahab exclaims, "Oh, devilish tantalization of the gods!" Melville is attracted by the philosopher's demand for explicit, settled knowledge but senses the power that the obscure and endlessly reinterpreted traditional wisdom we each embody has to save us from meaninglessness. The mysterious symbols engraved in Queequeg's flesh are carefully copied onto Queequeg's coffin, which, in the end, saves Ishmael from Ahab's disaster. Yeats expresses even more succinctly the poet's appreciation of our incarnate limitations: "I have found what I wanted— to put it in a phrase, I say, 'Man can embody truth, but he cannot know it.' "

⊠ **HOWARD KAHANE**

Other "Minds"

In the following essay, Howard Kahane agrees with John R. Searle and others that today's computers should not be said to be conscious or to have true under- standing. But he disagrees with the claim of Hubert and Stuart Dreyfus, among others, that computers programmed to determine contexts (situations) in terms of specific aspects via precise rules, cannot be constructed to reach the expert level (in their sense) of human intelligence. Kahane wonders how the Dreyfus brothers, or anyone at the present time, can know things of this factual nature without conducting the tedious experiments and making the countless observa- tions of the sort that scientists employ in determining the correctness of their theories.

The invention of complicated computers that can play chess, calculate the 1 decimal expansion of *pi* out to millions of places, and simulate space flights to Alpha Centauri raises interesting questions that have received a good deal of attention from philosophers and scientists.

Consider the question whether computers now or at some time in the 2 future will have *minds*, or, to put it another way, whether they will be *conscious*, in much the same way that human beings are conscious when awake.

This sounds like a purely factual question answerable by empirical inves- 3 tigation, as, for instance, Galileo answered the question whether Jupiter has moons by observing some of them through a telescope. But observation alone cannot settle the matter, because other "minds," including other human minds, are in principle not open to direct observation. Each of us can experience our own stream of consciousness but not those of others—we cannot crack open the skulls of other people, peer inside, and see their mental life.

Nevertheless, all normal human beings do conclude that other human 4 beings have minds, although this belief is so ingrained in us that we normally don't notice it or see the need for justification. But if challenged, we could argue that just as our own minds are associated with our own bodies, so also there must be minds associated with the bodies of other people, given that these other bodies are made of flesh and blood, as are our own bodies, and exhibit various kinds of behavioral responses to stimuli much as we do.

Although skeptical philosophers have challenged this sort of analogical 5 reasoning about the existence of other minds,* normal human beings, even

---

*Their challenge is based, first, on the general challenge to all inductive reasoning (the so-called "problem of induction") and, second, on the unique nature of analogies to other minds arising from the fact mentioned earlier that, unlike other legitimate analogies, we can't even theoretically check up on their conclusions by direct inspection.

the most skeptical of philosophers when not engaged in philosophical reflection, by their very nature are bound to find it convincing—we can't genuinely
doubt that other people have mental lives no matter how hard we try to do so.

The situation with respect to nonhuman animals is a bit different (and 6
perhaps more instructive). Here the analogical nature of the reasoning about
the existence of other minds becomes more apparent. We are more inclined to
attribute mental activity to other mammals than to other animals, no doubt
because other mammals are reasonably similar to ourselves both in physiology
and in some of their overt behavior (for instance, in their responses to pain
stimuli). As we consider animals less and less like ourselves, both in physiology
and in behavioral responses, we are less and less likely to regard them as
conscious beings.

The knowledge needed to draw analogical inferences of the kind just 7
described has been available to human beings for thousands of years. But in the
past several hundred years, ever-increasing knowledge of the inner workings of
the human body, in particular, of the brain and nervous system, has enabled us
to increase the sophistication of our analogical reasoning about the contents of
other minds. For instance, we now understand the connection between vision
and stimulation of the optic nerve and are beginning to grasp how changes in
the secretions of various chemicals such as the endorphins affect responses to
pain stimuli and determine changes in mood. We know that destruction of
certain portions of the brain renders a person incapable of remembering the
beginnings of long sentences, thus becoming incapable of completing them,
while destruction of other areas of the brain makes it impossible to recognize
even the best of friends. In short, we are beginning to understand the various
connections between brain functioning and different sorts of conscious (and
unconscious) experiences. All of this knowledge is based on what we can
observe *plus* reasoning, including analogical reasoning of the kind earlier
described.

The import of all of this to the question of whether computers are now or 8
ever will be conscious should be obvious. The more that computing machines
are or will be like us in certain ways—for instance, in the ways that their
responses are similar to ours and their "wiring" is similar to that of relevant
portions of the brain—the more we will be inclined to say that they are indeed
conscious.

At the present time, we know relatively little about what goes on in the 9
forest of several trillion nerves we call the brain and nervous system, so that
conclusions drawn now about whether today's computers are conscious must
be somewhat tentative. (We can't be sure what the *relevant* factors should be in
drawing an analogy.) But surely it would be a good supposition that when we
more fully understand how brains produce conscious experiences, we will see
the analogy between how today's computers work and how brains function as
too weak to support a belief that machines of this sort are conscious beings.
(For one thing, they aren't sufficiently complicated in their wiring.) This does
not mean, however, that we have reason now to conclude that computers of

the future cannot, or at least will not, be sufficiently like human brains in relevant respects to support such a belief.

Although a few computer experts have claimed that today's computers, armed with certain complicated programs, actually are conscious, even they seem to be backing off as they realize how incredibly complicated the human brain really is and how far they are from being able to construct computers that can, for example, translate ordinary talk from one language into another. This is true, in particular, with respect to the related question of whether these computers, in addition to being conscious, *understand* what they are doing. The point of John R. Searle's much-discussed "Chinese box" example (see pages 222–226) is that today's computing machines deal with language merely the way a thermometer shows temperature or a typewriter prints letters, thus not responding to the *meanings* of words or sentences. This leads Searle to conclude that they do not understand what they are doing any more than a thermostat understands that the temperature is rising when it turns down the heat. And surely, even given what little we know today about what causes consciousness and understanding, we ought to agree with Searle on this matter.

Note, however, that Searle does not say he has shown that *in principle* computers cannot ever be constructed so as to have true understanding. On the contrary, he sees "no reason in principle why we couldn't give a machine the capacity to understand English or Chinese, since in an important sense, our bodies with our brains are precisely such machines." His negative conclusion is directed, rather, just against the consciousness and understanding of computers like those we have today. Note also that Searle does not insist that only flesh and blood machines can be conscious, stating instead that whether this is so or not is an "empirical question."

My own belief is that the consciousness and understanding issues are indeed partly empirical questions of fact, as Searle believes, but also are a question of our responses as human beings to those facts. This is true because, as remarked before, we can't directly experience any minds other than our own. If computers ever do have streams of consciousness, we will never be able to prove it by direct observation. So these issues hinge in part on how we respond to whatever the observable facts about computers as compared to brains turn out to be. (Note that the matter is not one of pure *decision.* Just as no normal person can simply decide to become a true solipsist, so also we cannot just decide how a particular analogy between computers and brain will strike us, although we can have justified expectations on the matter.)

In addition to these partly philosophical questions about whether computers are or can be conscious, or have true understanding, there are more pressing issues about computer "intelligence." How many tasks now requiring human intelligence will computers be able to perform and what levels of skill will they be able to achieve?

Perhaps the best known pessimists on these questions are the Dreyfus brothers, Hubert and Stuart, who have made careers out of nay-saying the talents, potential or otherwise, of digital computers. Their view seems to be directed against the possibility that any sort of "artificial intelligence" ever will approach the human level, at least with respect to certain kinds of intelligence. Typical are these remarks with which Hubert Dreyfus begins the introduction to his 1970s book* on the subject:

> Even the most tough-minded men and women have a sense that, although they are made out of matter, they are not machines; yet lately they are . . . being told, as if it were obvious, that 'each human being is a superbly constructed . . . computer' [the quote is from astronomer Carl Sagan—see page 217 of this volume] and that computers will eventually behave as intelligently as people do. . . . [But] it is high time to look again at our assurance that we are not computers and that claims that computers can be intelligent must be nonsense.

The gist of their support for this view seems to be this: Computers are 15 programmed to follow rules and to define contexts (the Dreyfus brothers call them *situations*) in terms of the specific *features* of which they are composed. Thus, a computer might be programmed to label a small group of "well-dressed babies and new toys being presented" as a birthday party. But such a gathering may, in fact, be some other sort of party or even a baby beauty contest. So in programming a computer, we would have to take into account possible exceptions to the rule about well-dressed babies, toys, and birthday parties. The trouble is that there are possible exceptions to the exceptions, exceptions to the exceptions to the exceptions, and so on. The Dreyfus brothers therefore contend that we can never take into account all possible exceptions—every rule will have to say "other things being equal"—and yet other things may not be equal and we can't specify a rule for every case. Therefore, a computer could never be programmed with a sufficiently rich belief system (library of facts) to correctly determine contexts by sizing up their specific features.

Human beings, on the other hand, say the Dreyfus brothers, work some- 16 what differently. They grasp a context (situation) prior to grasping its features (they call them *aspects*). A chess master surveying a particular position sees it as similar to previously encountered positions and thus can determine its specific features, say the overextended nature of an opponent's position, and attack even though the chess computer, perhaps merely counting "material balance," might counsel a defensive move.

The mistake of many computer experts, contend the Dreyfus brothers, is 17 their "metaphysical assumption" that the "background of practices" can be put into a list of rules which then can be programmed into a computer. Instead, we must add an "other things being equal" clause to every such rule. And this points to the way that we human beings employ our *general* sense of what is normal or typical, gained through experience, which by definition cannot be situation specific—cannot be specified via a list of its specific features (aspects). When "explaining our actions we must always sooner or later fall back on our everyday practices and simply say 'this is what we do' or 'that is what it is to be

*Portions of which are reprinted on pages 226–235.

a human being.' Thus, in the last analysis all intelligibility and all intelligent behavior must be traced back to our sense of what we *are*, which is something we can never explicitly *know.*"

The idea that most everyday situations are sufficiently like previous cases   18
so that computers can be programmed to handle them with a set of situation-specific rules fails, the Dreyfus brothers claim, first, because even if similar to a preanalyzed case, "we still have the problem of deciding which situation it is similar to . . . for example, whether a situation where there are well-dressed babies and new toys . . . has more in common with a birthday party or a beauty contest," and second, because context must be specified in terms of what is normally the case, which requires adding an "other things being equal" clause and "only our *general* sense of what is typical can decide here . . ."

Finally, to the claim that human beings *must* somehow have rule-based   19
knowledge to handle everyday situations, perhaps of an unconscious nature, the brothers reply that instead, we "appeal to *concrete* representations (images or memories) based on our own experiences without having to make explicit the strict rules and their spelled out *ceteris paribus* conditions required by *abstract* symbolic descriptions."

The first thing to notice in assessing all of this is that the Dreyfus brothers   20
have not come close to proving their contention that human beings are not machines—are not superbly constructed computers. Those who claim we *are* machines, including, it should be said, this writer, do not mean that we are composed of nuts and bolts as are most humanly constructed machines. We mean that human bodies are composed of physical elements that follow the laws of physics and chemistry, as do all other bodies in the universe so far as science has been able to determine, and that all of our mental states—streams of consciousness—and all of our actions are determined by the physical/chemical events that take place in our bodies. This view can be defended by pointing to the ever increasing scientific knowledge of specific cases, two of which were mentioned at the beginning of this paper, plus an inductive leap to the conclusion that the other as yet not understood processes will be found to follow the same pattern. (Notice that no scientific evidence has ever been discovered that discounts this inductive conclusion.)

Now suppose for a moment that the Dreyfus brothers are right about how   21
human intelligence functions. That would prove nothing whatever against the idea that we are complicated machines, that, for instance, the general sense they speak about has no mechanical underpinning. The Dreyfus brothers themselves have suggested in recent writings* that human brains may work somewhat along the lines of holograms, which, of course, are a kind of machine.

Well, then, what about the Dreyfus brothers' other major contention,   22
namely that "claims that computers can be intelligent must be nonsense." Note first that at best they would have proved this only with respect to computers like

---

*See, for instance, their article "Why Computers May Never Think Like People," *Technology Review*, January 1986.

the ones we have today, and not, say, devices built on the model of holograms. But have they proved even this much? It depends in part on how intelligence is defined. Computers already in existence can perform all sorts of computations that are far beyond the capabilities of even the best mathematicians. They routinely solve equations no merely human computers could begin to tackle. Computer graphics picture events for us, such as simulated flights to Alpha Centauri, that otherwise would be far beyond our human ability to comprehend. And so on! We generally refer to the ability to do these things as kinds of intelligence, but for the Dreyfus brothers, they apparently are merely computational, and thus fail to qualify. (The philosophical point is that you can often win an argument by defining yourself into victory.)

Now consider their claim that rule-based computers will never be able to 23 deal correctly with everyday cases because of the "other things being equal" problem. Note first that physics and chemistry are based on this model. Isaac Newton, for instance, did not say that objects move according to his gravitation law, but rather that other things being equal, that is, other forces not intruding, they will do so. Yet science seems to progress quite well, these *ceteris paribus* clauses notwithstanding. Why can't computers also thrive using this model?

Take the actual cases the Dreyfus brothers mention, such as the birthday 24 party example. How in fact would someone determine that a given event is a birthday party and not a beauty contest? Certainly not via a general conceptual grasp but rather by taking account of specific factors which are indicative of birthday parties but not beauty contests, for instance, the fact that each gift given to one of the babies is given in the name of one of the other babies, that the parents sing "Happy Birthday," or perhaps even that we have received a birthday party invitation. In other words, in many, perhaps most or even all everyday cases, context is determined by noticing factors that can be programmed into rule-based computers of the general type that we have today.

But perhaps the most important objection to the Dreyfus brothers' position 25 is simply to wonder how they have discovered what they claim to be true. How do they know, for instance, that human beings don't experience situations (contexts) in terms of the aspects (specific features) of which they are composed? Why can't the "background of practices" be put into a list of rules or facts which then can be programmed into a computer? (If there is no such set of facts, how do human minds figure these things out?) And how do they know that the list of exceptions and exceptions to the exceptions is endless and not just very long or, indeed, in many cases rather short? Just how does our everyday sense of what is typical allow us to deal with situations without our even unconsciously doing so in terms of situation specifics gleaned first? (Does the Dreyfus brothers' position on this amount to the absurdity that situations are not determined by their parts?)*

---

*It's interesting to note that at least one of the Dreyfus brothers' predictions already has turned out to be false. They have indicated in several places that, while computers may be able to play a pretty good game of chess, they will never be able to play at an expert level (in their sense of

Nevertheless, isn't there *something* to the Dreyfus brothers' contentions, at 26
least to their claim that it takes creativity to discover new similarities between
disparate cases that cannot be put into a set of rules or facts? Perhaps *we*, when
using Newton's laws, are merely rule governed in some sense, but what about
Newton himself when he noticed the similarity in the apparently different cases
of objects falling toward the earth, planets moving around the sun, rising and
falling tides, and so on? Well, here the Dreyfus brothers have at least a small
point. Computers are now being constructed that can learn from experience,
but they cannot do so in the way Newton must have when he discovered
(constructed?) his laws of motion. We know, roughly, how to program computers to translate relatively straightforward prose from one language to another,
say "The young girl is pretty" into "La jeune fille est jolie," and even to handle
relatively dead metaphors and stock expressions such as "hit the nail on the
head" and "cross that bridge when we come to it," but we are very far indeed
from knowing how to construct computers that can handle even ordinary cases
in which context is not built into the language itself, to say nothing of translat-
ing a poem from one language to another without losing its poetic sense. Isn't
it possible that these require a kind of creative intelligence that is not based on
rules and facts of the kind that can be programmed into digital computers?

Certainly this much is true. *Today's* digital computers are not even close 27
to being sufficiently complicated to be creative in this way. (The portion of the
human brain that deals with face recognition alone is millions of times more
complicated than the entirety of any of today's computers.) But this, again,
proves nothing about very much more complicated digital computers, or about
machines based on some other mechanical system, say on the model of holograms.* And, finally, there is again this nagging question: How do the Dreyfus
brothers know that more complicated rule and fact based computers can never
be appropriately creative? This is a basically factual question of immense proportions that will require tremendous effort by scientific researchers, going back
and forth between theory and what observation and experiment disclose, even
to approach an answer. Yet the Dreyfus brothers, sitting in their armchairs, tell
us confidently what they know cannot be the case. Does this remind one of the
ancient Greek philosophers sitting in *their* armchairs speculating that the universe is composed of earth, air, fire and water?

---

that term) because they cannot take account of general situations in the correct manner. But
computers have already defeated master players under tournament conditions and the best of
them have now reached the *grand* master level. They have also shown that several of
the human analyses of chess positions are incorrect, for instance, they have shown that certain
end game positions believed to be draws when both sides play correctly can in fact be won by correct play.

*But note that the rod and cone construction of the human eye suggests, rather, the TV set
model in which situations are broken down into tiny component parts out of which the whole
is constructed.

ARTIFICIAL INTELLIGENCE

QUESTIONS AND SUGGESTIONS FOR WRITING

1. Sagan urges us to overcome our resistance to the idea that machines can be "intelligent" and to accept the benefits that these machines offer. Do you feel intimidated by sophisticated computers or do you use them with ease? Explain your response to those "intelligent" machines.

2. According to Searle, it is a mistake to conclude that "if a computer can simulate having a certain mental state, then we have the same grounds for supposing it really has that mental state as we have for supposing that human beings have that state." Explain in your own words what this complex idea means and then evaluate it.

3. What does Dreyfus mean when he argues that computers can never be intelligent in the way that human beings are? Do you agree or disagree? Defend your answer.

4. Examine a computer program that uses artificial intelligence to teach a particular subject and evaluate its effectiveness. Could you learn the subject better on the computer or in the classroom? Explain your response.

5. Kahane agrees with Sagan and Searle that human beings are a kind of machine, indeed a computing machine. Do you agree or disagree? Defend your answer.

6. Write a paper in which you defend or attack one of the following theses:
   a. Human beings are a kind of computing machine.
   b. Computers will never be able to translate, say, the John Searle text reprinted in this volume, into Chinese.
   c. Kahane is unfair comparing the Dreyfus brothers' speculations concerning computer intelligence to the ancient Greek philosophers' speculations about the ultimate constituents of the universe.

The feminist movement has brought question regarding sex roles to the fore-front of political discussion in recent years. The roles of men and women have been changing (this is particularly true of women), and allegedly unfair discrim-ination against women has been challenged. At the same time, homosexuals have been "coming out of the closet" and challenging discriminatory practices against homosexuals (for instance, in the military and in "sensitive" occupa-tions). Even the language we use to talk about these things and other sex-related matters has been challenged and is changing. The readings in this section discuss these and related matters, taking various sides of the issues in question.

⧖ **NOEL PERRIN**

The Androgynous Man

British born Noel Perrin is a minister and teacher who has written extensively on religious matters. In this essay he describes his worries about being a "wimp" after failing a test of masculinity/femininity and how he overcame them.

The summer I was sixteen, I took a train from New York to Steamboat 1
Springs, Colo., where I was going to be assistant horse wrangler at a camp. The trip took three days, and since I was much too shy to talk to strangers, I had quite a lot of time for reading. I read all of *Gone with the Wind*. I read all the interesting articles in a couple of magazines I had, and then I went back and read all the dull stuff. I also took all the quizzes, a thing of which magazines were even fuller then than now.

The one that held my undivided attention was called "How Masculine/ 2
Feminine Are You?" It consisted of a large number of inkblots. The reader was supposed to decide which of four objects each blot most resembled. The choices might be a cloud, a steam engine, a caterpillar, and a sofa.

When I finished the test, I was shocked to find that I was barely masculine ³ at all. On a scale of 1 to 10, I was about 1.2. Me, the horse wrangler? (And not just wrangler, either. That summer, I had to skin a couple of horses that died—the camp owner wanted the hides.)

The results of that test were so terrifying to me that for the first time in my ⁴ life I did a piece of original analysis. Having unlimited time on the train, I looked at the "masculine" answers over and over, trying to find what it was that distinguished real men from people like me—and eventually I discovered two very simple patterns. It was "masculine" to think the blots looked like man-made objects, and "feminine" to think they looked like natural objects. It was masculine to think they looked like things capable of causing harm, and feminine to think of innocent things.

Even at 16, I had the sense to see that the compilers of the test were using ⁵ rather limited criteria—maleness and femaleness are both more complicated than *that*—and I breathed a huge sigh of relief. I wasn't necessarily a wimp, after all.

That the test did reveal something other than the superficiality of its makers ⁶ I realized only many years later. What it revealed was that there is a large class of men and women both, to which I belong, who are essentially androgynous. That doesn't mean we're gay, or low in the appropriate hormones, or uncomfortable performing the jobs traditionally assigned our sexes. (A few years after that summer, I was leading troops in combat and, unfashionable as it now is to admit this, having a very good time. War is exciting. What a pity the 20th century went and spoiled it with high-tech weapons.)

What it does mean to be spiritually androgynous is a kind of freedom. ⁷ Men who are all-male, or he-man, or 100 percent red-blooded Americans, have a little biological set that causes them to be attracted to physical power, and probably also to dominance. Maybe even to watching football. I don't say this to criticize them. Completely masculine men are quite often wonderful people: good husbands, good (though sometimes overwhelming) fathers, good members of society. Furthermore, they are often so unself-consciously at ease in the world that other men seek to imitate them. They just aren't as free as us androgynes. They pretty nearly have to be what they are; we have a range of choices open.

The sad part is that many of us never discover that. Men who are not 100 ⁸ percent red-blooded Americans—say, those who are only 75 percent red-blooded—often fail to notice their freedom. They are too busy trying to copy the he-men ever to realize that men, like women, come in a wide variety of acceptable types. Why this frantic imitation? My answer is mere speculation, but not casual. I have speculated on this for a long time.

Partly they're just envious of the he-man's unconscious ease. Mostly ⁹ they're terrified of finding that there may be something wrong with them deep down, some weakness at the heart. To avoid discovering that, they spend their lives acting out the role that the he-man naturally lives. Sad.

One thing that men owe to the women's movement is that this kind of 10 failure is less common that it used to be. In releasing themselves from the single ideal of the dependent woman, women have more or less incidentally released a lot of men from the single ideal of the dominant male. The one mistake the feminists have made, I think, is in supposing that *all* men need this release, or that the world would be a better place if all men achieved it. It wouldn't. It would just be duller.

So far I have been pretty vague about just what the freedom of the 11 androgynous man is. Obviously it varies with the case. In the case I know best, my own, I can be quite specific. It has freed me most as a parent. I am, among other things, a fairly good natural mother. I like the nurturing role. It makes me feel good to see a child eat—and it turns me to mush to see a 4-year-old holding a glass with both small hands, in order to drink. I even enjoyed sewing patches on the knees of my daughter Amy's Dr. Dentons when she was at the crawling stage. All that pleasure I would have lost if I had made myself stick to the notion of the paternal role that I started with.

Or take a smaller and rather ridiculous example. I feel free to kiss cats. 12 Until recently it never occurred to me that I would want to, though my daughters have been doing it all their lives. But my elder daughter is now 22, and in London. Of course, I get to look after her cat while she is gone. He's a big, handsome farm cat named Petrushka, very unsentimental, though used from kittenhood to being kissed on the top of the head by Elizabeth. I've gotten very fond of him (he's the adventurous kind of cat who likes to climb hills with you), and one night I simply felt like kissing him on the top of the head, and did. Why did no one tell me sooner how silky cat fur is?

Then there's my relation to cars. I am completely unembarrassed by my 13 inability to diagnose even minor problems in whatever object I happen to be driving, and don't have to make some insider's remark to mechanics to try to establish that I, too, am a "Man with His Machine."

The same ease extends to household maintenance. I do it, of course. 14 Service people are expensive. But for the last decade my house has functioned better than it used to because I've had the aid of a volume called *Home Repairs Any Woman Can Do*, which is pitched just right for people at my technical level. As a youth, I'd as soon have touched such a book as I would have become a transvestite. Even though common sense says there is really nothing sexual whatsoever about fixing sinks.

Or take public emotion. All my life I have easily been moved by certain 15 kinds of voices. The actress Siobhan McKenna's, to take a notable case. Give her an emotional scene in a play, and within 10 words my eyes are full of tears. In boyhood, my great dread was that someone might notice. I struggled manfully, you might say, to suppress this weakness. Now, of course, I don't see it as a weakness at all, but as a kind of fulfillment. I even suspect that the true he-men feel the same way, or one kind of them does, at least, and it's only the poor imitators who have to struggle to repress themselves.

Let me come back to the inkblots, with their assumption that masculine   16
equates with machinery and science, and feminine with art and nature. I have
no idea whether the right pronoun for God is He, She or It. But this I'm pretty
sure of. If God could somehow be induced to take that test, God would not
come out macho, and not feminismo, either, but right in the middle. Fellow
androgynes, it's a nice thought.

⊠ JOHN LEO

Homosexuality: Tolerance Versus Approval

John Leo, associate editor of Time *magazine, argues in the following essay that
"the best public policy toward homosexuals is no public policy at all." But he
believes that tolerance does not mean approval.*

Homosexuality is . . . (check one): (1) unnatural and perverse, (2) a simple   1
sexual preference, (3) a result of childhood trauma, (4) learned behavior, morally neutral, (5) a problem of genes or hormones, (6) a private matter that is
none of the public's business.

As answers to this question would prove, the nation has never been so   2
confused on the subject of homosexuality as now.

In general, there has been a marked growth of tolerance. In the 1960s,   3
when an aide to President Johnson was arrested for committing a homosexual
act, he was expected to resign in disgrace—and did. This year (1979) a Congressman who apologized for trying to buy sex from a teen-age boy won his
party's support, and re-election. Homosexual publishing is booming, and gays
now receive far more sympathetic coverage in the media. Gay bars and bath-
houses operate unmolested in large communities and small. Police who were
once notorious for harassing homosexuals are now likely to be found playing
good-will softball games with gays. Although sodomy laws are still on the books
in many states, there is clearly little will to enforce them. The recent attempt
to pass major punitive legislation against gays—California's Proposition 6—was
soundly defeated.

At the same time, there is a strong reaction against the homosexual rights   4
movement. Polls show resistance to homosexuals as schoolteachers and to laws
that seem to enshrine homosexuals as a specially protected minority. Still, now

that homosexuals, and their opponents, are pressing for various laws, many Americans are questioning their own gut feeling that homosexuality is wrong. Many are downright ashamed or guilty about this aversion. Is their feeling merely instinct and prejudice? Or are there valid, respectable reasons for distaste for homosexuality and its public claims?

The most basic opposition to homosexuality seems to arise from religion.   5 In the Judaeo-Christian tradition, homosexual acts are considered sinful. Leviticus calls homosexuality "an abomination," and St. Paul condemns the practice three times. Homosexuals and their allies in the churches argue that these proscriptions are culture-bound and no longer apply. One argument is that the ancient Hebrews associated homosexuality with the competing Cannaanite religion and with the vengeance of conquering armies, which routinely sodomized the vanquished as a gesture of contempt. Some Christians suggest that St. Paul was attacking loveless sexuality and a refusal by heterosexuals to procreate. Another argument, received with some incredulity by conservative church members, is that Jesus Christ would have endorsed homosexual mating if he had been culturally able to envision Christians incapable of being attracted to the opposite sex.

What about other cultures? The only worldwide survey of sexual behavior,   6 published in 1951 by psychologist Frank Beach and anthropologist Clellan Ford, found that 49 out of 76 societies approved some form of homosexuality. Yet this approval extended only to sharply limited expressions of homosexuality, such as ritual acts, puberty rites, and youthful premarital affairs. Beach and Ford found no society where predominant or exclusive homosexuality was affirmed.

Even cultures and people not religiously oriented can object to homosex-   7 uality on broadly moral grounds. True, Kinsey considered bisexuality natural. Most researchers think that homosexuality, like heterosexuality, is learned behavior, the product of subtle interaction between a child and the significant people around the child. This argument now carries such weight in the academic world that researchers seem reluctant to investigate the origins of homosexuality without also investigating the origins of heterosexuality.

The main problem with this position is that heterosexuality requires no   8 complicated explanation. Even though most heterosexuals acts do not lead to reproduction, sex between a man and woman has an obvious biological function. Homosexuality has no such function, and cannot ever have it. The push of evolution and the survival of human culture are geared to heterosexual mating.

Another reason for opposing homosexuality—and one long considered   9 very liberal—is that it represents a sickness, or at least some form of biological or emotional disorder. Evidence to date casts doubt on the theory that homosexuality is biologically based. Freud, who believed that homosexuality was the fruit of early psychic stress, considered it to be a developmental arrest rather than an illness. As he wrote to the mother of an American homosexual, "It is assuredly no advantage, but it is nothing to be ashamed of, no vice, no degradation; it cannot be classified as an illness." Freudians have spun off dozens of theories of homosexuality, many of them focusing on mother fixation in males and a fear of aggression from other males.

In the hands of his successors Freud's view hardened into the theory that 10 homosexuality was pathological. But the rise of the Gay Liberation movement and the decline of popular support for the theories of psychoanalysis have seriously eroded the hard-line Freudian view. Militant gays have been strikingly successful in portraying Freudianism as a kind of conservative priestcraft devoted to enforcing the heterosexual status quo. When the gay rights movement demanded that the American Psychiatric Association remove the "sick" label from homosexuals, the association was in no mood to disagree. First, the homosexual lobby had demonstrated, in the words of one Freudian, "that there is a large ambulatory population of homosexuals out there who do not need psychiatric help." And second, the lobbyists argued, with heavy effect, that the "sick" label is the linchpin of society's oppression of homosexuals.

In a highly political compromise, the A.P.A. adopted a statement declar- 11 ing that "homosexuality, *per se*, cannot be classified as a mental disorder." The operative term, *per se*, left homosexuals free to think that they had been declared "normal" and traditional psychiatrists free to think that homosexuality, though not a disorder itself, was, or could be, a symptom of underlying problems. To compound the confusion, the association felt that it had to list homosexuality somewhere, so it created a new diagnostic category, "sexual orientation disturbance," for homosexuals dissatisfied with their sexuality. This diagnosis can only be applied with the patient's consent. It is a bit like dermatologists voting to ordain that acne is indeed a skin blemish, but only if the acne sufferer thinks it is. Though the A.P.A. vote seems to have pushed a great many therapists toward a more benign view of homosexuality, a strong body of psychiatric opinion still insistently holds that homosexuality reflects psychic disturbance. Last year an informal poll of 2,500 psychiatrists showed that a majority believed that homosexuals are sick.

Personality tests comparing heterosexuals and homosexuals have not been 12 of much help in resolving the confusion. Seven recent studies of lesbians and straight-women, for instance, conclude, variously, that: lesbians are not more neurotic but prone to anxiety; more neurotic; more depressed; less depressed; not more neurotic; not necessarily more neurotic; and less neurotic. The recent Kinsey Institute study of homosexuals, published as the book *Homosexualities,* reported that a minority of gays are indeed deeply disturbed, but that the majority function about as well as heterosexuals.

In the welter of conflicting studies, researchers tend to agree on at least 13 one point: homosexuals report more problems with their parents—unloving attitudes by at least one parent and parental conflict—than comparable groups of heterosexuals. This finding has been consistent among researchers who find homosexuals sick and those who find them well. Psychologists Seymour Fisher and Roger P. Greenberg, in their book *The Scientific Credibility of Freud's Theories and Therapy,* debunk much of Freud, but conclude that he was right about the fathers of male homosexuals. "In study after study," they write, "this father emerges as unfriendly, threatening or difficult to associate with."

Another area of agreement in the studies: there seem to be many more   14
male than female homosexuals. Kinsey estimated that there are two to three times as many males, and, though the actual figures are obviously unknowable, later researchers have roughly agreed. This evidence points away from the theory that homosexuality is a random variation (which ought to be randomly distributed by sex) and toward the theory that it is heavily related to special problems of male development, which appears to be more complicated and disaster-prone than that of the female. In this view, homosexuality is one of many unconscious strategies chosen by some children under great pressure, primarily pressure created by parents. It is, in short, nothing to despise, nothing to celebrate.

Many people disapprove of homosexuality because of the assumption,   15
long popular among some historians, that it is a sign of decadence and because of the fear of "contagion." About this, the evidence is, at best, mixed. The first point depends on what one means by decadence. The open, even glaring display of homosexuality may be seen simply as another sign of generally relaxed rules, which apply to heterosexual behavior as well. As for the "seduction of the innocent," there is little evidence that homosexual teachers, for example, are any more a threat to young pupils than heterosexual teachers. In most children, sexual orientation—the "learned" behavior that the psychologists talk about—is fixed early in life, probably by age five. In the rare cases when that orientation is not set until school age, it is doubtful that a homosexual teacher will have much impact. In fact, children raised by homosexual parents almost always grow up heterosexual. On the other hand, commonsense observation shows that in many fields homosexuals do function as admired role models, and that growing social acceptance allows potential homosexuals to follow their bent rather than trying to suppress it.

In sum, there are plenty of "respectable," valid reasons, including reasons   16
of taste, for opposing homosexuality. That is very different from trying to justify the persecution or oppression of homosexuals, for which there is no case at all. The trouble, however, is that for most heterosexuals the issue is not tolerance but social approval—the difference between placards that read I'M PROUD OF MY GAY SON and I'M PROUD MY SON IS GAY. Every oppressed group seeks a positive image, and some gays argue that homosexuals will never be truly free until society produces a positive image of homosexuality. That is precisely what the majority of Americans are unwilling to grant, however much they regret the past oppressions of homosexuals.

Many people who do not consider homosexuality either sinful or sick are   17
still not prepared to say that it is merely a matter of preference, just as good as—if not better than—other forms of sexual behavior. This question of social approval lurks behind the debate over gay teachers. Many parents believe that if current laws dictate the hiring of gay teachers, future ones may require that homosexuality and heterosexuality be discussed in sex education classes as

equally desirable choices. Richard Emery, a civil liberties lawyer in Manhattan, suggests just that. Gay activist Bruce Voeller says he believes that parents who try to push their children toward heterosexuality are guilty of an unjustified use of "straight power." This is understandable minority-group politics. And it is just as understandable if parents reply that this argument is absurd, and that they want to spare their children the kind of shocks and pressures that seem to be involved in homosexuality.

The same kind of fear is operating in the debate over gay rights laws. 18 Though polls show increasing tolerance of homosexuality, opposition to laws that might be read as endorsements of homosexuality or special treatment for gays is clearly rising. As if to clinch the point that Americans are leaning in both directions at once, homosexual activists report that when rights laws are defeated, as they were in Miami, discrimination against homosexuals declines.

Homosexuals counter that increased tolerance is not enough, that the 19 nation owes them protective laws like those passed in favor of blacks and women. A good many liberals have bought this argument, partly out of feelings of guilt over past cruelties to homosexuals. But it is possible to doubt that homosexuals are a class of citizens entitled to such legislation. The government's function is not to guarantee jobs or apartments for every disaffected group in society but only to step in where systematic or massive discrimination requires it. That is clearly not the case with homosexuals, who, unlike blacks and women, are already well integrated into the economy. Homosexuals ("We are everywhere") claim that they represent 10% of every profession—police, fire fighters, teachers, surgeons, even the psychiatrists who voted on the mental health of homosexuals.

The homosexual complaint is a claim that homosexuals should not have 20 their private behavior judged when it enters the public arena. No group in America enjoys that protection under the law. "It's a life-style question," said one opponent of a gay rights law in Eugene, Ore. "We've never seen legislation passed to protect a life-style." Simple-minded prejudice is, of course, a standard feature of many hiring decisions. But, in a free society, employers and landlords are granted considerable latitude in taking into account all publicly known aspects of an applicant's character and behavior.

The problem is that laws passed for blacks and women are not currently 21 viewed as rare exceptions to the general rule that employers and landlords can hire or rent to whom they please. Instead, such laws have come to be regarded as a basis for extending the same legal guarantees to a wide array of other aggrieved groups. The handicapped, for instance, have been included as protected persons in much legislation. Alcoholics may be next. In fact, a professor has sued Brooklyn College on grounds that he was let go because of alcoholism. The Government has entered the suit on the professor's side, arguing that alcoholics should be considered handicapped persons under the 1973 Rehabilitation Act. If he wins the suit, it will be illegal for federally assisted colleges to prefer teetotaling teachers over alcoholics. Enough. The Government has better things to do than proliferate categories of unfireable citizens. Like Masons, millenarians and est graduates, homosexuals must take their chances in the marketplace, just as everyone else does.

It is true that America has a great deal to be ashamed of in its treatment of   22 homosexual citizens. It owes them fairness, but not the kinds of legislation sought by gay groups. In their franker moments, homosexual activists refer to gay rights laws as educational efforts and many heterosexuals have no wish to be part of such efforts. The best policy toward homosexuals is no public policy at all—no sodomy laws, no special interventions pro or con. On matters of consensual adult sex, the law is, or should be, blind.

✎ **SUZANNAH LESSARD**

The Issue Was Women

Suzannah Lessard has written for several publications, including The Washington Monthly, *which published her article on Ted Kennedy's womanizing that brought her a good deal of recognition. She is now a staff writer for* The New Yorker. *In the following essay, written for Newsweek, she argues that it was philandering after all, not bad judgment, that ruined Gary Hart's chances in the 1988 presidential campaign.*

The way that the Hart controversy exploded into prominence and then brought   1 down the Democratic front runner in no time flat suggests that there have been some extraordinary changes since Teddy Kennedy's candidacy in 1980 and even since Hart's candidacy only four years ago. While Hart had a reputation as a womanizer then, the press respected the age-old tradition of overlooking behavior in this department. This tradition arose out of several incompatible attitudes. The first attitude—the only one that stands up to scrutiny—was respect for the privacy of candidates. A second was that the subject was of interest only to tabloid readers; that it was beneath the dignity of serious people to consider. Another attitude was a mixture of male solidarity and a commendable desire to judge not lest ye yourself be judged.

With the Hart episode, all these inhibitions have given way. That they   2 should do so suggests to me that we are in a period of transition toward a society in which the full humanity of women is recognized. Such transitions are never clear cut. For example, at some point along our path toward integration, racist remarks in many quarters became unattractive, then unacceptable and finally were a sign that the person who made them might have an emotional problem.

The reaction to the Hart incident reveals a transition in its early stage, 3 where most of us are still confused. But it seems more or less clear that the question of a presidential candidate's philandering has a meaning that it didn't have before. And while the interpretations surely vary, they must include the growing equality of women. A feminist sensibility has seeped into the public consciousness sufficiently to make philandering appear to many at best unattractive, maybe unacceptable and possibly even alarming where the candidate's emotions and psychology are concerned. Viewed from this perspective, the real issue in the Hart controversy was not Hart's "judgment," as some have argued, but the question of womanizing. Nor is the cause "moralism" in the sense of old-fashioned rectitude. Rather it is awareness of the dignity and equality of women.

As long as women were regarded as less than full-fledged human beings, a 4 man's behavior toward them was not a good gauge of his attitude toward human beings. It was not descriptive of his moral texture, not a sounding of his emotional depth. As long as women were assumed to be creatures of a generally lesser caliber than men, it made little sense to draw conclusions about a man's character from his relationships with them—any more than you could from his relationships with his pets. Unless of course, he was doing something extreme like beating or starving them. A pet was there to please and fulfill its owner, whose life was viewed as infinitely more significant. So it was with wives of politicians. The wives' pain wasn't significant, wasn't even real. And as for the women a politician dallied with, they were truly insignificant. What they felt or how they were affected by these liaisons was of no account. This began to change in the '70s. Mary Jo Kopechne's death at Chappaquidick and Joan Kennedy's devastation made an impression—though not enough of one to dissolve that magical protective circle around Kennedy, whose political life continued.

Worldly wise: Even then the ground was beginning to shift. During the 5 1980 campaign, when I did a piece on his womanizing as a political issue, a number of feminists were concerned about Kennedy's behavior. It meant to them that Kennedy did not respect women and would not put them in high posts and would respond to feminist causes only as an expedient. But they were not willing to be quoted by name because (and this was a reasonable assumption on their part) to come out against philandering was likely to jeopardize their standing as serious, worldly-wise political people. The same strange shield protected Hart in '84, but sometime between then and now the shield dissolved without anyone knowing it. Hart was so sure of its continued existence that he actually challenged reporters to follow him around. "I'm serious," he said. "If anybody wants to put a tail on me, go ahead. They'd be very bored."

It was almost as if he believed that he was invisible in this respect, or as if 6 his activities with women existed in a zone of reality entirely apart from the world of reporters and campaigns. A friend of Hart's was quoted as saying, "He never seemed to understand that it was his behavior that was the problem," and indeed, that was the impression he gave. "As I struggle to retain my integrity and my honor—and believe me I will—I hope you will also struggle to save our political system from its worst instincts," he said after the controversy broke. There is in this a capacity for a kind of extreme denial of reality—as if his life with women just wasn't real, as if he couldn't believe anyone else would think it meant anything. One might call this insane except that this split version of reality is a common trait in chauvinistic men. Certainly this split reality creates an insane atmosphere for women, both those who are lied to and those who are dallied with, although they accept it as normal—in fact, the whole society has.

There is an element of risk common to the Chappaquiddick tragedy and 7 the Hart episode that raises another concern about this kind of behavior. In Kennedy's case an actual death made this danger visible. In Hart's, it was the demise of his campaign. Neither of these costs could have been predicted, but neither are they beyond the bounds of what was imaginable, given the situations. And yet the risks were taken. There is a specter here of compulsion, self-deception and a delusory indifference to danger. The behavior surrounding Chappaquiddick was never resoundingly declared unacceptable. It could be that the force of the reaction against Hart drew upon pent-up feelings about the earlier incident.

When reporters accepted Hart's challenge to follow him we found out that 8 we had changed. We found out that many people now believe that if a man abuses his wife by womanizing there could be something abusive in his nature; that if a man deceives his wife and lies to the public about his relationship with other women he may well be generally untrustworthy. And that if he seems to seek out transitory relationships with women far younger than himself, there may be an immature, maybe even compulsive side to his nature. We found out that many of us now believe a man's life with women does reveal character and that we are not apologetic for thinking this way anymore.

Lovers and leaders: All that being said, we were wrenched from a deeply 9 rooted tradition in less than a week. Everybody, I think, would have preferred the process to be more evolutionary. To have Hart's campaign terminated over the issue seemed disproportionate. I, for one, agree with those who feel that a candidate's behavior in this respect is something that one weighs along with many other factors, that it is significant but not the kind of issue that by itself ought to decide one for or against a candidate. But it *is* something to take into account. It seems to me a blind form of free-thinking to say that only a fanatical or prejudiced or extremely religious person would take such a matter into account. I also share the almost universal recoil from probing into the private lives of candidates and feel very strongly that the matter is of significance only where presidential candidates are concerned—presidential candidates, and the men we choose as friends, husbands, lovers. It applies to presidential candidates and intimates, and no one in between. Perhaps this attitude merely reflects a particularly awkward stage in our transition to a more feminist world. Maybe it says something about how intimate a figure the president is for us. He is not a remote, godlike figure but a brother—and maybe someday a sister—who carries a power of life and death that no human being is qualified to bear. We need to be close to him. We need to know him heart and soul.

⊠ **ROBIN LAKOFF**

Making a Lady of Her

Robin Lakoff is a linguistics teacher and writer whose work on linguistic stereo-types and on language associated with sex roles has been very influential. In this essay taken from the July 1974 issue of Ms. *magazine, she discusses the uses of euphemisms and other locutions related chiefly to sexual topics and, in particu-lar, concentrates on uses of the terms* woman *and* lady.

When a word acquires a bad connotation by association with something unpleasant or embarrassing, people may search for substitutes that do not have the uncomfortable effect—that is, euphemisms. Since attitudes toward the orig-inal referent are not altered by a change of name, the new name itself takes on the adverse connotations, and a new euphemism must be found. It is no doubt possible to pick out areas of particular psychological strain or discomfort—areas where problems exist in a culture—by pinpointing items around which a great many euphemisms are clustered. An obvious example concerns the various words for that household convenience into which human wastes are eliminated: toilet, bathroom, rest room, comfort station, lavatory, water closet, loo, and all the others.

In the case of women, it may be encouraging to find no richness of euphemism; but it is discouraging to note that at least one euphemism for "woman" does exist and is very much alive. The word, of course, is "lady," which seems to be replacing "woman" in a great many contexts. Where both exist, they have different connotations; where only one exists, there is usually a reason, to be found in the context in which the word is uttered.

Related to the existence of euphemistic terms for "woman" is the existence of euphemistic terms for woman's principal role, that of "housewife." Most occupational terms do not have coexisting euphemisms: these seem to come into being only when the occupation is considered embarrassing or demeaning. Thus there is no euphemism for "professor," "doctor," "bank president"; but we do find "mortician" and "funeral director" for "undertaker"; "custodian" and "sanitary engineer" for "janitor"; "domestic" for "cleaning woman"; and so forth. Similarly one keeps running into hopeful suggestions, principally in the pages of women's magazines, that the lot of the housewife would be immeasurably improved if she though of herself as "homemaker," "household executive," "household engineer," or any of several others. I am not sure what to make of the fact that none of these (unlike the bona fide occupational euphemisms) have taken hold: is it because the "housewife" doesn't consider her status demeaning? Then why the search for euphemisms? Or does she feel that there is no escape through a change in nomenclature, or lack pride in her job to such an extent that she doesn't feel up to making the effort? This is a question for the sociologist.

It may be objected that *lady* has a masculine counterpart, namely *gentle-* 4 *man*, occasionally shortened to *gent*. But I don't think this is a fair comparison. *Lady* is much more common than *gent(leman)*. and, since *gent* exists, the reason is not ease of pronunciation. *Lady* is really a euphemism for *woman*, but *gentleman* is not nearly frequent enough to classify as a euphemism for *man*. Just as we do not call whites "Caucasian-Americans," there is no felt need to refer to men commonly as "gentlemen." And just as there is a need for such terms as "Afro-Americans," there is similarly a felt need for "lady." One might even say that when a derogatory epithet exists, a parallel euphemism is deemed necessary. (The term WASP, white Anglo-Saxon Protestant, may occur to the reader as a possible derogatory term which has no parallel euphemism. But in fact, WASP is not parallel in usage to *nigger, polack,* or *yid*. One can refer to himself as a WASP, as one cannot refer to himself as a *nigger* without either a total lack of self-pride or bitter sarcasm. Thus one can say: "Sure I'm a WASP, and proud of it!" but probably not: "Sure I'm a nigger, and proud of it!" without special sarcastic inflection in the voice suggesting that it is an imitation of the addressee.) To avoid having to resort to terms like "Afro-American," we need only get rid of all expressions like "nigger"; to banish "lady" in its euphemistic sense from the vocabulary of English, we need only first get rid of "broad" and its relations. But of course, as already pointed out, we cannot achieve this commendable simplification of the lexicon unless we somehow remove from our minds the idea that blacks *are* niggers and that women *are* broads. The presence of the words is a signal that something is wrong, rather than (as too often interpreted by well-meaning reformers) the problem itself. The point here is that, unless we start feeling more respect for women and, at the same time, less uncomfortable about them and their roles in society in relation to men, we cannot avoid *ladies* any more than we can avoid *broads*.

In the past, some ethnic groups that today are relatively respectable were 5 apparently considered less so. And in looking at reports of the terms used to describe those groups at the earlier time, we find two interesting facts: first, there is a much greater incidence of derogatory epithets for that group (as might be expected); and second (which one might not be led to expect automatically), there exist euphemistic terms for that group that are no longer in general use.

One can only conclude that euphemisms vanish as they are no longer needed. The example I have in mind is that of the words used to describe Jews. Aside from the uncomplimentary epithets which still exist today, though not encountered very often, one finds, in reading novels written and set more than half a century ago, a number of euphemisms that are not found any more, such as "hebrew gentleman" and "Israelite." The disappearance of the euphemisms concurrently with the derogatory terms suggests that women will be *ladies* until some more dignified status can be found for them.

It might also be claimed that *lady* is no euphemism because it has exactly 6 the same connotations as *woman*, is usable under the same semantic and contextual conditions. But a cursory inspection will show that this is not always the case. The decision to use one term rather than the other may considerably alter the sense of a sentence. The following are examples:

> (*a*) A (woman) that I know makes amazing things out of
>   (lady)
> shoelaces and old boxes.
> (*b*) A (woman) I know works at Woolworth's.
>   (lady)
> (*c*) A (woman) I know is a dean at Berkeley.
>   (lady)

(These facts are true for some speakers of English. For others, *lady* has taken over the functions of *woman* to such an extent that *lady* can be used in all these sentences.)

In my speech, the use of *lady* in (*c*) imparts a frivolous or nonserious tone 7 to the sentence: the matter under discussion is one of not too great moment. In this dialect, then, *lady* seems to be the more colloquial word: it is less apt to be used in writing, or in discussing serious matters. Similarly in (*a*), using *lady* would suggest that the speaker considered the "amazing things" not to be serious art, but merely a hobby or an aberration. If *woman* is used, she might be a serious (pop art) sculptor.

Related to this is the use of *lady* in job terminology. For at least some 8 speakers, the more demeaning the job, the more the person holding it (if female, of course) is likely to be described as a *lady*. Thus *cleaning lady* is at least as common as *cleaning woman*, *saleslady* as *saleswoman*. But one says, normally, *woman doctor*. To say *lady doctor* is to be very condescending: it constitutes an insult. For men, there is no such dichotomy. *Garbageman* or *salesman* is the only possibility, never **garbage gentleman*. And of course, since in the professions the male is unmarked, we never have **man (male) doctor*.[1]

Numerous other examples can be given, all tending to prove the same 9 point: that if, in a particular sentence, both *woman* and *lady* might be used, the use of the latter tends to trivialize the subject matter under discussion, often subtly ridiculing the woman involved. Thus, for example, a mention in the

---

[1]Like many other linguists, Lakoff sometimes uses asterisks in front of words to indicate that they are being used in an unusual way that falls outside normal or expected usage.

San Francisco Chronicle of January 31, 1972, of Madalyn Murray O'Hair as the "lady atheist" reduces her position to that of scatterbrained eccentric, or at any rate, one who need not be taken seriously. Even *woman atheist* is scarcely defensible: first, because her sex is irrelevant to her philosophical position, and second, because her name makes it clear in any event. But *lady* makes matters still worse. Similarly a reference to a *woman sculptor* is only mildly annoying (since there is no term **male sculptor*, the discrepancy suggests that such activity is normal for a man, but not for a woman), but still it could be used with reference to a serious artist. *Lady sculptor*, on the other hand, strikes me as a slur against the artist, deliberate or not, implying that the woman's art is frivolous, something she does to fend off the boredom of suburban housewifery, or at any rate, nothing of moment in the art world. Serious artists have shows, not dilettantes. So we hear of *one-woman shows*, but never *one-lady shows*.

Another realm of usage in which *lady* contrasts with *woman* is in titles of 10 organizations. It seems that organizations of women who have a serious purpose (not merely that of spending time with one another) cannot use the word *lady* in their titles, but less serious ones may. Compare the *Ladies' Auxiliary* of a men's group, or the *Thursday Evening Ladies Browning and Garden Society*, with **Ladies' Lib* or **Ladies Strike for Peace*.

What is curious about this split is that *lady* is, as noted, in origin a 11 euphemism for *woman*. What kind of euphemism is it that subtly denigrates the people to whom it refers, suggests that they are not to be taken seriously, are laughing stocks? A euphemism, after all, is supposed to put a better face on something people find uncomfortable. But this is not really contradictory. What a euphemism is supposed to do, actually, is to remove from thought *that part* of the connotations of a word that creates the discomfort. So each of the euphemisms for toilet, starting with *toilet*, seems to be trying to get further from the notion of excrement, by employing successively more elegant terminology that seems designed to suggest that the piece of furniture in question has really other primary uses, for performing one's toilette, for washing, for comfort, for resting, but never for those other things. Perhaps the notion of the nonseriousness of women is not the thing that makes men—the devisers of euphemism— as well as women, uncomfortable. Perhaps it is some other aspect of the man-woman relationship. How can we determine whether this is in fact the case?

One way of identifying the precise source of discomfort is, perhaps, by 12 looking at the derogatory terms for something. Many of the terms for blacks refer to their physical characteristics. And the latest euphemism for blacks, *Afro-Americans*, seems to be a specific attempt to get away from color names. (The term *black* is not a euphemism, but rather an attempt to confront the issue squarely and make color into a source of pride.) And as has often been noted, derogatory terms for women are very often overtly sexual: the reader will have no difficulty recalling what I allude to here.

The distinction between *lady* and *woman*, in those dialects of American 13 English in which it is found, may be traceable to other causes than the sexual connotations present in *woman*. Most people who are asked why they have chosen to use *lady* where *woman* would be as appropriate will reply that *lady* seemed more polite. The concept of politeness thus invoked is the politeness used in dignifying or ennobling a concept that normally is not thought of as having dignity or nobility. It is this notion of politeness that explains why we have *cleaning lady*, but not, normally, *lady doctor*. A doctor does not need to be exalted by conventional expressions: she has dignity enough from her professional status. But a cleaning woman is in a very different situation, in which her occupational category requires ennobling. Then perhaps we can say that the very notion of womanhood, as opposed to manhood, requires ennobling since it lacks inherent dignity of its own: hence the word *woman* requires the existence of a euphemism like *lady*. Besides or possibly because of being explicitly devoid of sexual connotation, *lady* carries with it overtones recalling the age of chivalry: the exalted stature of the person so referred to, her existence above the common sphere. This makes the term seem polite at first, but we must also remember that these implications are perilous: they suggest that a "lady" is helpless, and cannot do things for herself. In this respect the use of a word like *lady* is parallel to the act of opening doors for women—or ladies. At first blush it is flattering: the object of the flattery feels honored, cherished, and so forth; but by the same token, she is also considered helpless and not in control of her own destiny. Women who protest that they *like* receiving these little courtesies, and object to being liberated from them, should reflect a bit on their deeper meaning and see how much they like *that*.

⬚ **PHYLLIS SCHLAFLY**

The Power of the Positive Woman

Phyllis Schlafly is best known as an outspoken opponent of women's liberation. In her book, The Power of the Positive Woman, *from which this essay is taken, she argues that women liberationists are imprisoned by their own negative image of themselves.*

The first requirement for the acquisition of power by the Positive Woman is to   1 understand the differences between men and women. Your outlook on life, your faith, your behavior, your potential for fulfillment, all are determined by the parameters of your original premise. The Positive Woman starts with the assumption that the world is her oyster. She rejoices in the creative capability

within her body and the power potential of her mind and spirit. She understands that men and women are different, and that those very differences provide
the key to her success as a person and fulfillment as a woman.

The women's liberationist, on the other hand, is imprisoned by her own   2
negative view of herself and of her place in the world around her. This view of
women was most succinctly expressed in an advertisement designed by the
principal women's liberationist organization, the National Organization for
Women (NOW), and run in many magazines and newspapers and as spot
announcements on many television stations. The advertisement showed a darling curlyheaded girl with the caption: "This healthy, normal baby has a handicap. She was born female."

This is the self-articulated dog-in-the-manger, chip-on-the-shoulder, fun-   3
damental dogma of the women's liberation movement. Someone—it is not
clear who, perhaps God, perhaps the "Establishment," perhaps a conspiracy of
male chauvinist pigs—dealt women a foul blow by making them female. It
becomes necessary, therefore, for women to agitate and demonstrate and hurl
demands on society in order to wrest from an oppressive male-dominated social
structure the status that has been wrongfully denied to women through the
centuries.

By its very nature, therefore, the women's liberation movement precipitates   4
a series of conflict situations—in the legislatures, in the courts, in the schools,
in industry—with man targeted as the enemy. Confrontation replaces cooperation as the watchword of all relationships. Women and men become adversaries
instead of partners.

The second dogma of the women's liberationists is that, of all the injustices   5
perpetrated upon women through the centuries, the most oppressive is the cruel
fact that women have babies and men do not. Within the confines of the
women's liberationist ideology, therefore, the abolition of this overriding inequality of women becomes the primary goal. This goal must be achieved at
any and all costs—to the woman herself, to the baby, to the family, and to
society. Women must be made equal to men in their ability *not* to become
pregnant and *not* to be expected to care for babies they may bring into the
world.

This is why women's liberationists are compulsively involved in the drive   6
to make abortion and child-care centers for all women, regardless of religion or
income, both socially acceptable and government-financed. Former Congress-
woman Bella Abzug has defined the goal: "to enforce the constitutional right
of females to terminate pregnancies that they do not wish to continue."

If man is targeted as the enemy, and the ultimate goal of women's libera-   7
tion is independence from men and the avoidance of pregnancy and its consequences, then lesbianism is logically the highest form in the ritual of women's
liberation. Many, such as Kate Millett, come to this conclusion, although
many others do not.

The Positive Woman will never travel that dead-end road. It is self-evident   8
to the Positive Woman that the female body with its baby-producing organs was

not designed by a conspiracy of men but by the Divine Architect of the human race. Those who think it is unfair that women have babies, whereas men cannot, will have to take up their complaint with God because no other power is capable of changing that fundamental fact. On some college campuses, I have been assured that other methods of reproduction will be developed. But most of us must deal with the real world rather than with the imagination of dreamers.

Another feature of the woman's natural role is the obvious fact that women 9 can breast-feed babies and men cannot. This functional role was not imposed by conspiratorial males seeking to burden women with confining chores, but must be recognized as part of the plan of the Divine Architect for the survival of the human race through the centuries and in the countries that know no pasteurization of milk or sterilization of bottles.

The Positive Woman looks upon her femaleness and her fertility as part of 10 her purpose, her potential, and her power. She rejoices that she has a capability for creativity that men can never have.

The third basic dogma of the women's liberation movement is that there 11 is no difference between male and female except the sex organs, and that all those physical, cognitive, and emotional differences you *think* are there, are merely the result of centuries of restraints imposed by a male-dominated society and sex-stereotyped schooling. The role imposed on women is, by definition, inferior, according to the women's liberationists.

The Positive Woman knows that, while there are some physical competi- 12 tions in which women are better (and can command more money) than men, including those that put a premium on grace and beauty, such as figure skating, the superior physical strength of males over females in competitions of strength, speed, and short-term endurance is beyond rational dispute. . . .

The Positive Woman remembers the essential validity of the old prayer: 13 "Lord, give me the strength to change what I can change, the serenity to accept what I cannot change, and the wisdom to discern the difference." The women's liberationists are expending their time and energies erecting a make-believe world in which they hypothesize that *if* schooling were gender-free, and *if* the same money were spent on male and female sports programs, and *if* women were permitted to compete on equal terms, *then* they would prove themselves to be physically equal. Meanwhile, the Positive Woman has put the ineradicable physical differences into her mental computer, programmed her plan of action, and is already on the way to personal achievement. . . .

Despite the claims of the women's liberation movement, there are count- 14 less physical differences between men and women. The female body is 50 to 60 percent water, the male 60 to 70 percent water, which explains why males can dilute alcohol better than women and delay its effect. The average woman is about 25 percent fatty tissue, while the male is 15 percent, making women more buoyant in water and able to swim with less effort. Males have a tendency to color blindness. Only 5 percent of persons who get gout are female. Boys are born bigger. Women live longer in most countries of the world, not only in the

United States where we have a hard-driving competitive pace. Women excel in manual dexterity, verbal skills, and memory recall. . . .

Does the physical advantage of men doom women to a life of servility and 15 subservience? The Positive Woman knows that she has a complementary advantage which is at least as great—and, in the hands of a skillful woman, far greater. The Divine Architect who gave men a superior strength to lift weights also gave women a different kind of superior strength.

The women's liberationists and their dupes who try to tell each other that the sexual drive of men and women is really the same, and that it is only societal restraints that inhibit women from an equal desire, an equal enjoyment, and an equal freedom from the consequences, are doomed to frustration forever. It just isn't so, and pretending cannot make it so. The differences are not a woman's weakness but her strength. . . .

The new generation can brag all it wants about the new liberation of the 16 new morality, but it is still the woman who is hurt the most. The new morality isn't just a "fad"—it is a cheat and a thief. It robs the woman of her virtue, her youth, her beauty, and her love—for nothing, just nothing. It has produced a generation of young women searching for their identity, bored with sexual freedom, and despondent from the loneliness of living a life without commitment. They have abandoned the old commandments, but they can't find any new rules that work.

The Positive Woman recognizes the fact that, when it comes to sex, 17 women are simply not the equal of men. The sexual drive of men is much stronger than that of women. That is how the human race was designed in order that it might perpetuate itself. The other side of the coin is that it is easier for women to control their sexual appetites. A Positive Woman cannot defeat a man in a wrestling or boxing match, but she can motivate him, inspire him, encourage him, teach him, restrain him, reward him, and have power over him that he can never achieve over her with all his muscle. How or whether a Positive Woman uses her power is determined solely by the way she alone defines her goals and develops her skills.

The differences between men and women are also emotional and psycho- 18 logical. Without woman's innate maternal instinct, the human race would have died out centuries ago. There is nothing so helpless in all earthly life as the newborn infant. It will die within hours if not cared for. Even in the most primitive, uneducated societies, women have always cared for their newborn babies. They didn't need any schooling to teach them how. They didn't need any welfare workers to tell them it is their social obligation. Even in societies to whom such concepts as "ought," "social responsibility," and "compassion for the helpless" were unknown, mothers cared for their new babies.

Why? Because caring for a baby serves the natural maternal need of a 19 woman. Although not nearly so total as the baby's need, the woman's need is nonetheless real.

The overriding psychological need of a woman is to love something alive. 20 A baby fulfills this need in the lives of most women. If a baby is not available to fill that need, women search for a baby-substitute. This is the reason why women have traditionally gone into teaching and nursing careers. They are doing what comes naturally to the female psyche. The schoolchild or the patient of any age provides an outlet for a woman to express her natural maternal need.

This maternal need in women is the reason why mothers whose children 21
have grown up and flown from the nest are sometimes cut loose from their psychological moorings. The maternal need in women can show itself in love for grandchildren, nieces, nephews, or even neighbors' children. The maternal need in some women has even manifested itself in an extraordinary affection lavished on a dog, a cat, or a parakeet.

This is not to say that every woman must have a baby in order to be 22
fulfilled. But it is to say that fulfillment for most women involves expressing their natural maternal urge by loving and caring for someone.

The women's liberation movement complains that traditional stereotyped 23
roles assume that women are "passive" and that men are "aggressive." The anomaly is that a woman's most fundamental emotional need is not passive at all, but active. A woman naturally seeks to love affirmatively and to show that love in an active way by caring for the object of her affections.

The Positive Woman finds somebody on whom she can lavish her mater- 24
nal love so that it doesn't well up inside her and cause psychological frustrations. Surely no woman is so isolated by geography or insulated by spirit that she cannot find someone worthy of her maternal love. All persons, men and women, gain by sharing something of themselves with their fellow humans, but women profit most of all because it is part of their very nature.

One of the strangest quirks of women's liberationists is their complaint 25
that societal restraints prevent men from crying in public or showing their emotions, but permit women to do so, and that therefore we should "liberate" men to enable them, too, to cry in public. The public display of fear, sorrow, anger, and irritation reveals a lack of self-discipline that should be avoided by the Positive Woman just as much as by the Positive Man. Maternal love, however, is not a weakness but a manifestation of strength and service, and it should be nurtured by the Positive Woman.

Most women's organizations, recognizing the preference of most women 26
to avoid hard driving competition, handle the matter of succession of officers by the device of a nominating committee. This eliminates the unpleasantness and the tension of a competitive confrontation every year or two. Many women's organizations customarily use a prayer attributed to Mary, Queen of Scots, which is an excellent analysis by a woman of women's faults:

> Keep us, O God, from pettiness; let us be large in thought, in word, in deed. Let us be done with fault-finding and leave off self-seeking. . . . Grant that we may realize it is the little things that create differences, that in the big things of life we are at one.

Another silliness of the women's liberationists is their frenetic desire to 27
force all women to accept the title *Ms* in place of *Miss* or *Mrs*. If Gloria

Steinem and Betty Friedan want to call themselves *Ms* in order to conceal their marital status, their wishes should be respected.

But that doesn't satisfy the women's liberationists. They want all women   28
to be compelled to use *Ms* whether they like it or not. The woman's liberation movement has been waging a persistent campaign to browbeat the media into using *Ms* as the standard title for all women. The women's liberationists have already succeeded in getting the Department of Health, Education and Welfare to forbid schools and colleges from identifying women students as *Miss* or *Mrs*. . . .

Finally, women are different from men in dealing with the fundamentals   29
of life itself. Men are philosophers, women are practical, and 'twas ever thus. Men may philosophize about how life began and where we are heading; women are concerned about feeding the kids today. No woman would ever, as Karl Marx did, spend years reading political philosophy in the British Museum while her child starved to death. Women don't take naturally to a search for the intangible and the abstract. The Positive Woman knows who she is and where she is going, and she will reach her goal because the longest journey starts with a very practical first step. . . .

An effort to eliminate the differences [between men and women] by social   30
engineering or legislative or constitutional tinkering cannot succeed, which is fortunate, but social relationships and spiritual values can be ruptured in the attempt. Thus the role reversals being forced upon high school students, under which guidance counselors urge reluctant girls to take "shop" and boys to take "home economics," further confuse a generation already unsure about its identity. They are as wrong as efforts to make a left-handed child right-handed.

DOROTHY L. SAYERS

Women and Work

In this excerpt from her book, Are Women Human?, *Dorothy L. Sayers argues against the idea that "it is the women who are always trying to ape the man," now even taking away some of the male's jobs, by showing how over the years men have been taking away jobs that women used to do in the home.*

. . . When we hear that women have once more laid hands upon something   1
which was previously a man's sole privilege, I think we have to ask ourselves:
. . . Is it something useful, convenient, and suitable to a human being as such?
Or is it merely something unnecessary to us, ugly, and adopted merely for the

sake of collaring the other fellow's property? These jobs and professions, now. It is ridiculous to take on a man's job just in order to be able to say that "a woman has done it—yah!" The only decent reason for tackling any job is that it is *your* job, and *you* want to do it.

At this point, somebody is likely to say: "Yes, that is all very well. But it *is*   2 the woman who is always trying to ape the man. She *is* the inferior being. You don't as a rule find the men trying to take the women's jobs away from them. They don't force their way into the household and turn women out of their rightful occupations."

Of course they do not. They have done it already.   3

Let us accept the idea that women should stick to their own jobs—the jobs   4 they did so well in the good old days before they started talking about votes and women's rights. Let us return to the Middle Ages and ask what we should get then in return for certain political and educational privileges which we should have to abandon.

It is a formidable list of jobs: the whole of the spinning industry, the whole   5 of the dyeing industry, the whole of the weaving industry. The whole catering industry and . . . the whole of the nation's brewing and distilling. All the preserving, pickling, and bottling industry, all the bacon-curing. And (since in those days a man was often absent from home for months together on war or business) a very large share in the management of landed estates. Here are the women's jobs—and what has become of them? They are all being handled by men. It is all very well to say that woman's place is the home—but modern civilization has taken all these pleasant and profitable activities out of the home, where the women looked after them, and handed them over to big industry, to be directed and organized by men at the head of large factories. Even the dairy-maid in her simple bonnet has gone, to be replaced by a male mechanic in charge of a mechanical milking plant.

Now, it is very likely that men in big industries do these jobs better than   6 the women did them at home. The fact remains that the home contains much less of interesting activity than it used to contain. What is more, the home has so shrunk to the size of a small flat that—even if we restrict woman's job to the bearing and rearing of families—there is no room for her to do even that. It is useless to urge the modern woman to have twelve children, like her grand-mother. Where is she to put them when she has got them? And what modern man wants to be bothered with them? It is perfectly idiotic to take away women's traditional occupations and then complain because she looks for new ones. Every woman is a human being—one cannot repeat that too often—and a human being *must* have occupation, if he or she is not to become a nuisance to the world.

I am not complaining that the brewing and baking were taken over by the   7 men. If they can brew and bake as well as women or better, then by all means let them do it. But they cannot have it both ways. If they are going to adopt the very sound principle that the job should be done by the person who does it best, then that rule must be applied universally. If the women make better office-workers than men, they must have the office work. If any individual woman is able to make a first-class lawyer, doctor, architect, or engineer, then she must be allowed to try her hand at it. Once lay down the rule that the job comes first and you throw that job open to every individual, man or woman, fat or thin, tall or short, ugly or beautiful, who is able to do that job better than the rest of the world.

Now, it is frequently asserted that, with women, the job does not come 8 first. What (people cry) are women doing with this liberty of theirs? What woman really prefers a job to a home and family? Very few, I admit. It is unfortunate that they should so often have to make the choice. A man does not, as a rule, have to choose. He gets both. In fact, if he wants the home and family, he usually has to take the job as well, if he can get it. Nevertheless, there have been women, such as Queen Elizabeth and Florence Nightingale, who had the choice, and chose the job and made a success of it. And there have been and are many men who have sacrificed their careers for women— sometimes, like Antony or Parnell, very disastrously. When it comes to a *choice*, then every man or woman has to choose as an individual human being, and, like a human being, take the consequences.

As human beings! I am always entertained—and also irritated—by the 9 newsmongers who inform us, with a bright air of discovery, that they have questioned a number of female workers and been told by one and all that they are "sick of the office and would love to get out of it." In the name of God, what human being is *not*, from time to time, heartily sick of the office and would *not* love to get out of it? The time of female office-workers is daily wasted in sympathizing with disgruntled male colleagues who yearn to get out of the office. No human being likes work—not day in and day out. Work is noto- riously a curse—and if women *liked* everlasting work they would not be human beings at all. *Being* human beings, they like work just as much and just as little as anybody else. They dislike perpetual washing and cooking just as much as perpetual typing and standing behind shop counters. Some of them prefer typing to scrubbing—but that does not mean that they are not, as human beings, entitled to damn and blast the typewriter when they feel that way. The number of men who daily damn and blast typewriters is incalculable; but that does not mean that they would be happier doing a little plain sewing. Nor would the women.

I have admitted that there are very few women who would put their job 10 before every earthly consideration. I will go further and assert that there are very few men who would do it either. In fact, there is perhaps only one human being in a thousand who is passionately interested in his job for the job's sake. The difference is that if that one person in a thousand is a man, we say, sim- ply, that he is passionately keen on his job; if she is a woman, we say she is a freak. . . .

Which brings us back to this question of what jobs, if any, are women's 11 jobs. Few people would go so far as to say that all women are well fitted for all men's jobs. When people do say this, it is particularly exasperating. It is stupid to insist that there are as many female musicians and mathematicians as male— the facts are otherwise, and the most we can ask is that if a Dame Ethel Smyth or a Mary Somerville turns up, she shall be allowed to do her work without having aspersions cast either on her sex or her ability. What we ask is to be human individuals, however peculiar and unexpected. It is no good saying: "You are a little girl and therefore you ought to like dolls"; if the answer is, "But I don't," there is no more to be said. Few women happen to be natural born mechanics; but if there is one, it is useless to try and argue her into being something different. What we must *not* do is to argue that the occasional appearance of a female mechanical genius proves that all women would be mechanical geniuses if they were educated. They would not.

⊠ USA TODAY

Court Ruling Opens Doors for Women

This editorial from USA Today *(May 12, 1987) argues in favor of the recent U.S. Supreme Court rulings opening to women the doors of private clubs where business is commonly transacted.*

Ten years ago, the men-only Rotary club in tiny Duarte, Calif., was languish- 1
ing. Women had begun to occupy the community leadership slots that Rotary had traditionally turned to for members-to-be. So Duarte's Rotarians did the gentlemanly thing: They opened the door for the ladies.

And a very ungentlemanly squabble ensued.   2

Rotary International banished the club. Both sides went to court. The 3
fisticuffs ended last week when the Supreme Court ruled 7-0 for the Duarte Rotarians.

Echoing an earlier ruling that ended the men-only status of the Jaycees, 4
the court said states have the right to forbid sex discrimintion by local Rotary clubs.

Why? Because, while truly private clubs have a constitutional right of free 5
association, the Jaycees and the Rotary clubs aren't "private," the court said: They are too big, too business-related, too community service-oriented.

Does this spell the end to men-only clubs? The court said decisions must 6
be made case by case. But across the USA, die-hard men's clubs are manning the barricades:

• In Salt Lake City, when a judge warned he would yank the beer license 7
  if the Alta Club didn't stop discriminating, the club quit selling beer—
  rather than admit women.

- In Bethesda, Md., the men-only Burning Tree Club forfeited $186,000 in tax breaks—rather than admit women. 8

- In New York City, the Century Association is so afraid that its income from non-members will jeopardize its private status that it is considering selling its art collection to substitute for that revenue—rather than admit women. 9

How *ungentlemanly.* 10

Professional and business people use private clubs to make contacts and clinch deals. Women should have the same opportunities. Today, 44 percent of the work force is female. There are 130,000 women bankers, 104,000 women lawyers. It is unfair that they must stand outside while their male clients and competitors dine in the clubroom. 11

Now that the Supreme Court has sent the message that Rotary and the Jaycees must accept women, other men-only service groups should follow suit. 12

And what of the smaller, more exclusive private clubs where the socially prominent eat and play? 13

The court's message was less clear. But there's no mistaking the moral message: Closing the doors of opportunity to women is just plain wrong. 14

Clubs that have evolved into meeting places where members transact business must admit members without regard to race, religion, or sex. 15

The gentlemen of Duarte found that welcoming women helped their club. So did the men of Philadelphia's Union League Club, Washington's University Club, Pittsburgh's Duquesne Club, and others that have recently stopped discriminating. Old members say that since the ladies joined, the change has been negligible. 16

But for women, the change can be dramatic and positive. When opportunity knocks, they're there to answer. 17

It's time to open the door for the ladies. 18

⊠ **DOUG BANDOW**

Court Ruling Threatens the Rights of Women

In this essay that appeared in USA Today *on the same day and page as the above editorial, Doug Bando takes the other side of the issue and argues that the Supreme Court's decision threatens everyone's right to free association guaranteed by the Constitution's First Amendment.*

The latest feminist victory against discrimination—the Supreme Court's ruling 1
that the state of California can force the Rotary club to admit women—is a
major blow against everyone's freedom.

The government may still allow small, independent clubs to set their own 2
admission standards if, in the court's words, the group involves "the kind of
intimate or private relation that warrants constitutional protection." But organizations like the Lions, Kiwanis, and Elks apparently have lost control over
their memberships.

While forcibly opening up such clubs obviously benefits women, it vastly 3
increases state interference with the most minute and personal of social and
business relationships.

Indeed, in the name of nondiscrimination, governments have banned 4
discounts for women during "ladies' nights" at bars and restaurants. A children's
hair salon in Los Angeles was sued for charging girls, who tend to have longer
hair, more than boys. Price breaks for women at a car wash have been ruled
discriminatory and illegal. One male patron even sued a night club that barred
men, but not women, from wearing shorts.

In none of these cases was the discrimination invidious. Irritating, per- 5
haps. But nothing like the old Jim Crow rules that treated blacks as sub-
humans.

And while there's no logical reason for organizations like Rotary to exclude 6
women, human relationships are not logical. Which is why freedom of association—a right protected by the First Amendment—is so important.

Indeed, there are women's-only organizations, like the Cosmopolitan and 7
Colony clubs in New York and the Spa Lady chain of fitness centers. They,
along with establishments that cater to homosexuals, are threatened by rules
that ban all discrimination.

In a free society like ours, the government should stay out of interpersonal 8
relations whenever possible. Social change may take longer as a result, but it
will still occur.

In fact, the Rotary case arose after the local club in Duarte, Calif., decided 9
to induct women to help counteract a declining membership. Three dozen
Kiwanis clubs have also defied their international organization by admitting
women. And many women's colleges have gone coed because of economic
pressure.

This sort of voluntary movement toward non-discrimination is preferable 10
to heavy-handed government regulation. Where innocuous discrimination persists, whether it be men's business clubs or ladies' discount nights, it should be
accepted as inevitable in a pluralistic society.

A free people must tolerate intolerance, for the cost to liberty of trying to 11
expunge every last vestige of discrimination from society is too high.

SEX AND SEXUAL POLITICS

QUESTIONS AND SUGGESTIONS FOR WRITING

1. Perrin gives many personal examples to support his argument that spiritual androgyny offers a kind of personal freedom. In what ways have you experienced freedom by allowing yourself to do the work traditionally assigned to a man (if you are a woman) or to a woman (if you are a man)?

2. Leo claims that "the best policy towards homosexuals is no public policy at all—no sodomy laws, no special interventions pro or con." Explain why he takes this position, and evaluate his reasoning.

3. In discussing the demise of Gary Hart's campaign, Lessard suggests that many people now believe "that if a man abuses his wife by womanizing, there could be something abusive in his nature; that if a man deceives his wife and lies to the public about his relationship with other women, he may well be generally untrustworthy." Do you agree or disagree with this assessment? Why?

4. Look up the word *lady* in the unabridged *Oxford English Dictionary* and explain how the definition has changed over the years. How would you account for the current use of the word as defined by Lakoff?

5. Schlafly, an outspoken opponent of the women's liberation movement, asserts that "women are different [from men] in dealing with the fundamentals of life. . . . Men are philosophers, women are practical. . . . Women don't take naturally to a search for the intangible and abstract." In your personal experience, have you found this to be a relevant difference between men and women? Explain, using examples of people you know or have read about to support your position.

6. Sayers counters the argument that women should stick to their own jobs by asserting that the jobs they did so well for centuries have been usurped by men. Among others, she lists the spinning, dyeing, and weaving industries; the catering, brewing, and distilling industries; and the preserving, pickling, and bottling industries. Is Sayer's contention that men have taken over women's work relevant to the issues facing women today?

7. Both Lakoff and Schlafly are concerned with terms used to describe women. What fundamental difference in world view is evident in Lakoff's concern over our current misuse of *lady* and Schlafly's criticism of women's liberationists for insisting that the media use *Ms.* as the standard title for all women?

8. Both men and women have been victims of sexual stereotyping. Argue against the stereotyping of men or of women, drawing from your own experience for support.

PORNOGRAPHY

One recently published dictionary defines *pornography* as "written, graphic, or other forms of communication intended to excite lascivious feelings," and *lascivious* as "of or characterized by lust." The widespread dissemination of pornography has generated a good deal of controversy. Should we prohibit communications intended to excite lustful feelings? Is there something wrong in itself with this kind of communication? Or should it be forbidden because of its harmful effects? Do feminists oppose the arousal of lustful feelings, or is their target pornography that degrades women? Does, or doesn't, the First Amendment to the Constitution guarantee freedom of speech, including the kind that arouses lustful feelings? And, in any case, is the dictionary definition of pornography cited above narrow or inaccurate?

⊗ IRVING KRISTOL

Pornography, Obscenity, and the Case for Censorship

Irving Kristol is a well-known neoconservative teacher and writer. In the following essay he argues in favor of the censorship of pornography on the grounds that "if you care for the quality of life in our American democracy, then you have to be for censorship" of pornography.

Being frustrated is disagreeable, but the real disasters in life begin when you get 1
what you want. For almost a century now, a great many intelligent, well-meaning, and articulate people—of a kind generally called liberal or intellectual, or both—have argued eloquently against any kind of censorship of art

273

and/or entertainment. And within the past ten years, the courts and the legislatures of most Western nations have found these arguments persuasive—so persuasive that hardly a man is now alive who clearly remembers what the answers to these arguments were. Today, in the United States and other democracies, censorship has to all intents and purposes ceased to exist.

Is there a sense of triumphant exhilaration in the land? Hardly. There is, 2 on the contrary, a rapidly growing unease and disquiet. Somehow, things have not worked out as they were supposed to, and many notable civil libertarians have gone on record as saying this was not what they meant at all. They wanted a world in which *Desire under the Elms* could be produced, or *Ulysses* published, without interference by philistine busybodies holding public office. They have got that, of course; but they have also got a world in which homosexual rape takes place on the stage, in which the public flocks during lunch hours to witness varieties of professional fornication, in which Times Square has become little more than a hideous market for the sale and distribution of printed filth that panders to all known (and some fanciful) sexual perversions.

But disagreeable as this may be, does it really matter? Might not our 3 unease and disquiet be merely a cultural hangover—a "hang-up," as they say? What reason is there to think that anyone was ever corrupted by a book?

This last question, oddly enough, is asked by the very same people who 4 seem convinced that advertisements in magazines or displays of violence on television do indeed have the power to corrupt. It is also asked, incredibly enough and in all sincerity, by people—for example, university professors and schoolteachers—whose very lives provide all the answers one could want. After all, if you believe that no one was ever corrupted by a book, you have also to believe that no one was ever improved by a book (or a play or a movie). You have to believe, in other words, that all art is morally trivial and that, consequently, all education is morally irrelevant. No one, not even a university professor, really believes that.

To be sure, it is extremely difficult, as social scientists tell us, to trace the 5 effects of any single book (or play or movie) on an individual reader or any class of readers. But we all know, and social scientists know it too, that the ways in which we use our minds and imaginations do shape our characters and help define us as persons. That those who certainly know this are nevertheless moved to deny it merely indicates how a dogmatic resistance to the idea of censorship can—like most dogmatism—result in a mindless insistence on the absurd.

I have used these harsh terms—"dogmatism" and "mindless—advisedly. I 6 might also have added "hypocritical." For the plain fact is that none of us is a complete civil libertarian. We all believe that there is some point at which the public authorities ought to step in to limit the "self-expression" of an individual or a group, even where this might be seriously intended as a form of artistic expression, and even where the artistic transaction is between consenting adults. A playwright or theatrical director might, in this crazy world of ours, find someone willing to commit suicide on the stage, as called for by the script. We would not allow that—any more than we would permit scenes of real physical torture on the stage, even if the victim were a willing masochist. And I know of no one, no matter how free in spirit, who argues that we ought to permit gladiatorial contests in Yankee Stadium, similar to those once performed in the Colosseum at Rome—even if only consenting adults were involved.

The basic point that emerges is one that Walter Berns has powerfully   7
argued: No society can be utterly indifferent to the ways its citizens publicly entertain themselves. Bearbaiting and cockfighting are prohibited only in part out of compassion for the suffering animals; the main reason they were abolished was because it was felt that they debased and brutalized the citizenry who flocked to witness such spectacles. And the question we face with regard to pornography and obscenity is whether, now that they have such strong legal protection from the Supreme Court, they can or will brutalize and debase our citizenry. We are, after all, not dealing with one passing incident—one book, or one play, or one movie. We are dealing with a general tendency that is suffusing our entire culture.

I say pornography *and* obscenity because, though they have different dic-   8
tionary definitions and are frequently distinguishable as "artistic" genres, they are nevertheless in the end identical in effect. Pornography is not objectionable simply because it arouses sexual desire or lust or prurience in the mind of the reader or spectator; this is a silly Victorian notion. A great many nonpornographic works—including some parts of the Bible—excite sexual desire very successfully. What is distinctive about pornography is that, in the words of D. H. Lawrence, it attempts "to do dirt on [sex] . . . [It is an] insult to a vital human relationship."

In other words, pornography differs from erotic art in that its whole purpose   9
is to treat human beings obscenely, to deprive human beings of their specifically human dimension. That is what obscenity is all about. It is light years removed from any kind of carefree sensuality—there is no continuum between Fielding's *Tom Jones* and the Marquis de Sade's *Justine.* These works have quite opposite intentions. To quote Susan Sontag: "What pornographic literature does is precisely to drive a wedge between one's existence as a full human being and one's existence as a sexual being—while in ordinary life a healthy person is one who prevents such a gap from opening up." This definition occurs in an essay *defending* pornography—Miss Sontag is a candid as well as gifted critic—so the definition, which I accept, is neither tendentious nor censorious.

Along these same lines, one can point out—as C. S. Lewis pointed out   10
some years back—that it is no accident that in the history of all literatures obscene words, the so-called four-letter words, have always been the vocabulary of farce or vituperation. The reason is clear; they reduce men and women to some of their mere bodily functions—they reduce man to his animal component, and such a reduction is an essential purpose of farce or vituperation.

Similarly, Lewis also suggested that it is not an accident that we have no   11
offhand, colloquial, neutral terms—not in any Western European language at

any rate—for our most private parts. The words we do use are either (1) nursery terms, (2) archaisms, (3) scientific terms, or (4) a term from the gutter (i.e., a demeaning term). Here I think the genius of language is telling us something important about man. It is telling us that man is an animal with a difference: He has a unique sense of privacy, and a unique capacity for shame when this privacy is violated. Our "private parts" are indeed private, and not merely because convention prescribes it. This particular convention is indigenous to the human race. In practically all primitive tribes, men and women cover their private parts; and in practically all primitive tribes, men and women do not copulate in public.

It may well be that Western society, in the latter half of the twentieth 12 century, is experiencing a drastic change in sexual mores and sexual relationships. We have had many such "sexual revolutions" in the past—the bourgeois family and bourgeois ideas of sexual propriety were themselves established in the course of a revolution against eighteenth-century "licentiousness"—and we shall doubtless have others in the future. It is, however, highly improbable (to put it mildly) that what we are witnessing is the Final Revolution which will make sexual relations utterly unproblematic, permit us to dispense with any kind of ordered relationships between the sexes, and allow us freely to redefine the human condition. And so long as humanity has not reached that utopia, obscenity will remain a problem.

One of the reasons it will remain a problem is tht obscenity is not merely 13 about sex, any more than science fiction is about science. Science fiction, as every student of the genre knows, is a peculiar vision of power: What it is really about is politics. And obscenity is a peculiar vision of humanity: What it is really about is ethics and metaphysics.

Imagine a man—a well-known man, much in the public eye—in a hos- 14 pital ward, dying an agonizing death. He is not in control of his bodily functions, so that his bladder and his bowels empty themselves of their own accord. His consciousness is overwhelmed and extinguished by pain, so that he cannot communicate with us, nor we with him. Now, it would be, technically, the easiest thing in the world to put a television camera in his hospital room and let the whole world witness this spectacle. We do not do it—at least we do not do it as yet—because we regard this as an *obscene* invasion of privacy. And what would make the spectacle obscene is that we would be witnessing the extinguishing of humanity in a human animal.

Incidentally, in the past our humanitarian crusaders against capital punish- 15 ment understood this point very well. The abolitionist literature goes into great physical detail about what happens to a man when he is hanged or electrocuted or gassed. And their argument was—and is—that what happens is shockingly obscene, and that no civilized society should be responsible for perpetrating such obscenities, particularly since in the nature of the case there must be spectators to ascertain that this horror was indeed being perpetrated in fulfillment of the law.

Sex—like death—is an activity that is both animal and human. There are 16 human sentiments and human ideals involved in this animal activity. But when sex is public, the viewer does not see—cannot see—the sentiments and the ideals. He can only see the animal coupling. And that is why, when men and women make love, as we say, they prefer to be alone—because it is only when you are alone that you can make love, as distinct from merely copulating in an animal and casual way. And that, too, is why those who are voyeurs, if they are not irredeemably sick, also feel ashamed at what they are witnessing. When sex is a public spectacle, a human relationship has been debased into a mere animal connection. . . .

. . . What is at stake is civilization and humanity, nothing less. The idea 17 that "everything is permitted," as Nietzsche put it, rests on the premise of nihilism and has nihilistic implications. I will not pretend that the case against nihilism and for civilization is an easy one to make. We are here confronting the most fundamental of philosophical questions, on the deepest levels. In short, the matter of pornography and obscenity is not a trivial one, and only superficial minds can take a bland and untroubled view of it. . . .

I am already touching upon a political aspect of pornography when I 18 suggest that it is inherently and purposefully subversive of civilization and its institutions. But there is another and more specifically political aspect, which has to do with the relationship of pornography and/or obscenity to democracy, and especially to the quality of public life on which democratic government ultimately rests. . . .

. . . This idea starts from the proposition that democracy is a form of self- 19 government, and that if you want it to be a meritorious polity, you have to care about what kind of people govern it. Indeed, it puts the matter more strongly and declares that if you want self-government, you are only entitled to it if the "self" is worthy of governing. There is no inherent right to self-government if it means that such government is vicious, mean, squalid, and debased. Only a dogmatist and a fanatic, an idolater of democratic machinery, could approve of self-government under such conditions.

And because the desirability of self-government depends on the character 20 of the people who govern, the older idea of democracy was very solicitous of the condition of this character. It was solicitous of the individual self, and felt an obligation to educate it into what used to be called "republican virtue." And it was solicitous of that collective self which we call public opinion and which, in a democracy, governs us collectively. Perhaps in some respects it was nervously oversolicitous—that would not be surprising. But the main thing is that it cared, cared not merely about the machinery of democracy but about the quality of life that this machinery might generate.

And because it cared, this older idea of democracy had no problem in 21 principle with pornography and/or obscenity. It censored them—and it did so with a perfect clarity of mind and a perfectly clear conscience. It was not about to permit people capriciously to corrupt themselves. Or, to put it more precisely:

In this version of democracy, the people took some care not to let themselves be governed by the more infantile and irrational parts of themselves.

I have, it may be noticed, uttered that dreadful word censorship. And I   22
am not about to back away from it. If you think pornography and/or obscenity is a serious problem, you have to be for censorship. I will go even further and say that if you want to prevent pornography and/or obscenity from becoming a problem, you have to be for censorship. And lest there be any misunderstanding as to what I am saying, I will put it as bluntly as possible: If you care for the quality of life in our American democracy, then you have to be for censorship.

But can a liberal be for censorship? Unless one assumes that being a liberal   23
must mean being indifferent to the quality of American life, then the answer has to be yes, a liberal can be for censorship—but he ought to favor a liberal form of censorship.

Is that a contradiction in terms? I do not think so. We have no problem in   24
contrasting *repressive* laws governing alcohol and drugs and tobacco with laws *regulating* (i.e., discouraging the sale of) alcohol and drugs and tobacco. Laws encouraging temperance are not the same thing as laws that have as their goal prohibition or abolition. We have not made the smoking of cigarettes a criminal offense. We have, however, and with good liberal conscience, prohibited cigarette advertising on television, and may yet, again with good liberal conscience, prohibit it in newspapers and magazines. The idea of restricting individual freedom, in a liberal way, is not at all unfamiliar to us.

I therefore see no reason why we should not be able to distinguish repres-   25
sive censorship from liberal censorship of the written and spoken word. In Britain, until a few years ago, you could perform almost any play you wished, but certain plays, judged to be obscene, had to be performed in private theatrical clubs, which were deemed to have a "serious" interest in theater. In the United States, all of us who grew up using public libraries are familiar with the circumstances under which certain books could be circulated only to adults, while still other books had to be read in the library reading room, under the librarian's skeptical eye. In both cases, a small minority that was willing to make a serious effort to see an obscene play or read an obscene book could do so. But the impact of obscenity was circumscribed and the quality of public life was only marginally affected.*

I am not saying it is easy in practice to sustain a distinction between liberal   26
and repressive censorship, especially in the public realm of a democracy, where popular opinion is so vulnerable to demagoguery. Moreover, an acceptable system of liberal censorship is likely to be exceedingly difficult to devise in the United States today, because our educated classes, upon whose judgment a

---

*It is fairly predictable that someone is going to object that this point of view is "elitist"—that, under a system of liberal censorship, the rich will have privileged access to pornography and obscenity. Yes, of course, they will—just as, at present, the rich have privileged access to heroin if they want it. But one would have to be an egalitarian maniac to object to this state of affairs on the grounds of equality.

liberal censorship must rest, are so convinced that there is no such thing as a problem of obscenity, or even that there is no such thing as obscenity at all. But, to counterbalance this, there is the further, fortunate truth that the tolerable margin for error is quite large, and single mistakes or single injustices are not all that important.

This possibility of error, of course, occasions much distress among artists   27 and academics. It is a fact, one that cannot and should not be denied, that any system of censorship is bound, upon occasion, to treat unjustly a particular work of art—to find pornography where there is only gentle eroticism, to find obscenity where none really exists, or to find both where its existence ought to be tolerated because it serves a larger moral purpose. Though most works of art are not obscene, and though most obscenity has nothing to do with art, there are some few works of art that are, at least in part, pornographic and/or obscene. There are also some few works of art that are in the special category of the comic-ironic "bawdy" (Boccaccio, Rabelais). It is such works of art that are likely to suffer at the hands of the censor. That is the price one has to be prepared to pay for censorship—even liberal censorship.

But just how high is this price? If you believe, as so many artists seem to   28 believe today, that art is the only sacrosanct activity in our profane and vulgar world—that any man who designates himself an artist thereby acquires a sacred office—then obviously censorship is an intolerable form of sacrilege. But for those of us who do not subscribe to this religion of art, the costs of censorship do not seem so high at all.

If you look at the history of American or English literature, there is pre-   29 cious little damage you can point to as a consequence of the censorship that prevailed throughout most of that history. Very few works of literature—of real literary merit, I mean—ever were suppressed; and those that were, were not suppressed for long. Nor have I noticed, now that censorship of the written word has to all intents and purposes ceased in this country, that hitherto suppressed or repressed masterpieces are flooding the market. Yes, we can now read *Fanny Hill* and the Marquis de Sade. Or, to be more exact, we can now openly purchase them, since many people were able to read them even though they were publicly banned, which is as it should be under a liberal censorship. So how much have literature and the arts gained from the fact that we can all now buy them over the counter, that indeed, we are all now encouraged to buy them over the counter? They have not gained much that I can see.

And one might also ask a question that is almost never raised: How much   30 has literature lost from the fact that everything is now permitted? It has lost quite a bit, I should say. In a free market, Gresham's Law can work for books or theater as efficiently as it does for coinage— driving out the good, establishing the debased. The cultural market in the United States today is being preempted by dirty books, dirty movies, dirty theater. A pornographic novel has a far better chance of being published today than a nonpornographic one, and quite a few pretty good novels are not being published at all simply because they are not pornographic, and are therefore less likely to sell. Our cultural condition has not improved as a result of the new freedom. American cultural life was not much to brag about twenty years ago; today one feels ashamed for it.

Just one last point, which I dare not leave untouched. If we start censoring 31 pornography or obscenity, shall we not inevitably end up censoring political opinion? A lot of people seem to think this would be the case—which only shows the power of doctrinaire thinking over reality. We had censorship of pornography and obscenity for 150 years, until almost yesterday, and I am not aware that freedom of opinion in this country was in any way diminished as a consequence of this fact. Fortunately for those of us who are liberal, freedom is not indivisible. If it were, the case for liberalism would be indistinguishable from the case for anarchy; and they are two very different things.

But I must repeat and emphasize: What kinds of laws we pass governing 32 pornography and obscenity, what kind of censorship—or, since we are still a federal nation, what kinds of censorship—we institute in our various localities may indeed be difficult matters to cope with; nevertheless the real issue is one of principle. I myself subscribe to a liberal view of the enforcement problem: I think that pornography should be illegal *and* available to anyone who wants it so badly as to make a pretty strenuous effort to get it. We have lived with under-the-counter pornography for centuries now, in a fairly comfortable way. But the issue of principle, of whether it should be over or under the counter, has to be settled before we can reflect on the advantages and disadvantages of alternative modes of censorship. I think the settlement we are living under now, in which obscenity and democracy are regarded as equals, is wrong; I believe it is inherently unstable; I think it will, in the long run, be incompatible with any authentic concern for the quality of life in our democracy.

SUSAN BROWNMILLER

Pornography Hurts Women

Susan Brownmiller, feminist writer, is the author of the well-known Against Our Will: Men, Women, and Rape *(1975), from which the following essay is taken. She argues that "pornography, like rape, is a male invention, designed to dehumanize women" and to assure "his rule by force over her."*

Pornography has been so thickly glossed over with the patina of chic these 1
days in the name of verbal freedom and sophistication that important distinctions between freedom of political expression (a democratic necessity), honest
sex education for children (a societal good) and ugly smut (the deliberate deval-
uation of the role of women through obscene, distorted depictions) have been
hopelessly confused. Part of the problem is that those who traditionally have
been the most vigorous opponents of porn are often those same people who
shudder at the explicit mention of any sexual subject. Under their watchful,
vigilante eyes, frank and free dissemination of educational materials relating
to abortion, contraception, the act of birth, and female biology in general is
also dangerous, subversive and dirty. (I am not unmindful that a frank and
free discussion of rape, "the unspeakable crime," might well give these
righteous vigilantes further cause to shudder.) Because the battle lines were
falsely drawn a long time ago, before there was a vocal women's movement, the
anti-pornography forces appear to be, for the most part, religious, Southern,
conservative and right-wing, while the pro-porn forces are identified as Eastern,
atheistic and liberal.

But a woman's perspective demands a totally new alignment, or at least a 2
fresh appraisal. The majority report of the President's Commission on Obscenity and Pornography (1970), a report that argued strongly for the removal of all
legal restrictions on pornography, soft and hard, made plain that 90 percent of
all pornographic material is geared to the male heterosexual market (the other
10 percent is geared to the male homosexual taste), that buyers of porn are
"predominantly white, middle-class, middle-aged married males" and that the
graphic depictions, the meat and potatoes of porn, are of the naked female
body and of the multiplicity of acts done to that body.

Discussing the content of stag films, "a familiar and firmly established part 3
of the American scene," the commission report dutifully, if foggily, explained,
"Because pornography historically has been thought to be primarily a masculine interest, the emphasis in stag films seems to represent the preferences of
the middle-class American male. Thus male homosexuality and bestiality are
relatively rare, while lesbianism is rather common."

The commissioners in this instance had merely verified what purveyors of 4
porn have always known: hard-core pornography is not a celebration of sexual
freedom; it is a cynical exploitation of female sexual activity through the device
of making all such activity, and consequently all females, "dirty." Heterosexual
male consumers of pornography are frankly turned on by watching lesbians in
action (although never in the final scenes, but always as a curtain raiser); they
are turned off with the sudden swiftness of a water faucet by watching naked
men act upon each other. One study quoted in the commission report came to
the unastounding conclusion that "seeing a stag film in the presence of male
peers bolsters masculine esteem." Indeed. The men in groups who watch the
films, it is important to note, are *not* naked.

When male response to pornography is compared to female response, a 5
pronounced difference in attitude emerges. According to the commission,

"Males report being more highly aroused by depictions of nude females, and show more interest in depictions of nude females than [do] females." Quoting the figures of Alfred Kinsey, the commission noted that a majority of males (77 percent) were "aroused" by visual depictions of explicit sex while a majority of females (68 percent) were not aroused. Further, "females more often than males reported 'disgust' and 'offense.' "

From whence comes this female disgust and offense? Are females sexually 6 backward or more conservative by nature? The gut distaste that a majority of women feel when we look at pornography, a distaste that, incredibly, it is no longer fashionable to admit, comes, I think, from the gut knowledge that we and our bodies are being stripped, exposed and contorted for the purpose of ridicule to bolster that "masculine esteem" which gets its kick and sense of power from viewing females as anonymous, panting playthings, adult toys, dehumanized objects to be used, abused, broken and discarded.

This, of course, is also the philosophy of rape. It is no accident (for what 7 else could be its purpose?) that females in the pornographic genre are depicted in two cleanly delineated roles: as virgins who are caught and "banged" or as nymphomaniacs who are never sated. The most popular and prevalent pornographic fantasy combines the two: an innocent, untutored female is raped and "subjected to unnatural practices" that turn her into a raving, slobbering nymphomaniac, a dependent sexual slave who can never get enough of the big, male cock.

There can be no "equality" in porn, no female equivalent, no turning of 8 the tables in the name of bawdy fun. Pornography, like rape, is a male invention, designed to dehumanize women, to reduce the female to an object of sexual access, not to free sensuality from moralistic or parental inhibition. The staple of porn will always be the naked female body, breasts and genitals exposed, because as man devised it, her naked body is the female's "shame," her private parts the private property of man, while his are the ancient, holy, universal, patriarchal instrument of his power, his rule by force over *her.*

Pornography is the undiluted essence of anti-female propaganda. Yet the 9 very same liberals who were so quick to understand the method and purpose behind the mighty propaganda machine of Hitler's Third Reich, the consciously spewed-out anti-Semitic caricatures and obscenities that gave an ideological base to the Holocaust and the Final Solution, the very same liberals who, enlightened by blacks, searched their own conscience and came to understand that their tolerance of "nigger" jokes and portrayals of shuffling, rolling-eyed servants in movies perpetuated the degrading myths of black inferiority and gave an ideological base to the continuation of black oppression—these very same liberals now fervidly maintain that the hatred and contempt for women that find expression in four-letter words used as expletives and in what are quaintly called "adult" or "erotic" books and movies are a valid extension of freedom of speech that must be preserved as a Constitutional right.

To defend the right of a lone, crazed American Nazi to grind out propa- 10 ganda calling for the extermination of all Jews, as the ACLU has done in the

name of free speech, is, after all, a self-righteous and not particularly coura-
geous stand, for American Jewry is not currently threatened by storm troopers,
concentration camps and imminent extermination, but I wonder if the ACLU's
position might change if, come tomorrow morning, the bookstores and movie
theaters lining Forty-second Street in New York City were devoted not to the
humiliation of women by rape and torture, as they currently are, but to a
systematized, commercially successful propaganda machine depicting the sa-
distic pleasures of gassing Jews or lynching blacks?

Is this analogy extreme? Not if you are a woman who is conscious of the   11
ever-present threat of rape and the proliferation of a cultural ideology that makes
it sound like "liberated" fun. The majority report of the President's Commission
on Obscenity and Pornography tried to pooh-pooh the opinion of law enforcement agencies around the country that claimed their own concrete experience
with offenders who were caught with the stuff led them to conclude that pornographic material is a causative factor in crimes of sexual violence. The
commission maintained that it was not possible at this time to scientifically
prove or disprove such a connection.

But does one need scientific methodology in order to conclude that the   12
anti-female propaganda that permeates our nation's cultural output promotes a
climate in which acts of sexual hostility directed against women are not only
tolerated but ideologically encouraged? A similar debate has raged for many
years over whether or not the extensive glorification of violence (the gangster as
hero; the loving treatment accorded bloody shoot-'em-ups in movies, books and
on TV) has a causal effect, a direct relationship to the rising rate of crime,
particularly among youth. Interestingly enough, in this area—nonsexual and
not specifically related to abuses against women—public opinion seems to be
swinging to the position that explicit violence in the entertainment media does
have a deleterious effect; it makes violence commonplace, numbingly routine
and no longer morally shocking.

More to the point, those who call for a curtailment of scenes of violence   13
in movies and on television in the name of sensitivity, good taste and what's
best for our children are not accused of being pro-censorship or against freedom
of speech. Similarly, minority group organizations, black, Hispanic, Japanese,
Italian, Jewish, or American Indian, that campaign against ethnic slurs and
demeaning portrayals in movies, on television shows and in commercials are
perceived as waging a just political fight, for if a minority group claims to be
offended by a specific portrayal, be it Little Black Sambo or the Frito Bandido,
and relates it to a history of ridicule and oppression, few liberals would dare to
trot out a Constitutional argument in theoretical opposition, not if they wish to
maintain their liberal credentials. Yet when it comes to the treatment of
women, the liberal consciousness remains fiercely obdurate, refusing to be
budged, for the sin of appearing square or prissy in the age of the so-called
sexual revolution has become the worst offense of all.

✄ G. L. SIMONS

Is Pornography Beneficial?

In the following excerpt from his book Pornography Without Prejudice, *G. L. Simons, an English writer on human sexuality, argues against censorship of pornography on grounds that it has not been shown to be excessively harmful and, indeed, is beneficial in several different ways, for example, as an aid to normal sexual development and a release from sexual frustration.*

It is not sufficient, for the objectors' case, that they demonstrate that some harm   1
has flowed from pornography. It would be extremely difficult to show that pornography had *never* had unfortunate consequences, but we should not make too much of this. Harm has flowed from religion, patriotism, alcohol and cigarettes without this fact impelling people to demand abolition. The harm, if established, has to be weighed against a variety of considerations before a decision can be reached as to the propriety of certain laws. Of the British Obscenity Laws the Arts Council Report comments[1] that "the harm would need to be both indisputable and very dire indeed before it could be judged to outweigh the evils and anomalies inherent in the Acts we have been asked to examine."

The onus therefore is upon the anti-pornographers to demonstrate not   2
only that harm is caused by certain types of sexual material but that the harm is considerable: if the first is difficult the second is necessarily more so, and the attempts to date have not been impressive. It is even possible to argue that easily available pornography has a number of benefits. Many people will be familiar with the *catharsis* argument whereby pornography is said to cut down on delinquency by providing would-be criminals with substitute satisfactions. This is considered later but we mention it here to indicate that access to pornography may be socially beneficial in certain instances, and that where this is possible the requirement for anti-pornographers to *justify* their objections must be stressed.

The general conclusion[2] of the U.S. Commission was that no adequate   3
proof had been provided that pornography was harmful to individual or society—"if a case is to be made out against 'pornography' [in 1970] it will have to be made on grounds other than demonstrated effects of a damaging personal or social nature." . . .

The heresy (to some ears) that pornography is harmless is compounded by   4
the even greater impiety that it may be beneficial. Some of us are managing to adjust to the notion that pornography is unlikely to bring down the world in

[1]In *The Obscenity Laws* (London: André Deutsch, 1969), p. 33.
[2]The *Report of the Commission on Obscenity and Pornography*, Part Three, (New York: Bantam Books, 1970), p. 169.

moral ruin, but the idea that it may actually do good is altogether another thing. When we read of Professor Emeritus E. T. Rasmussen, a pioneer of psychological studies in Denmark, and a government adviser, saying that there is a possibility "that pornography can be beneficial", many of us are likely to have *mixed* reactions, to say the least. In fact this thesis can be argued in a number of ways.

The simplest approach is to remark that people enjoy it. This can be seen 5 to be true whether we rely on personal testimony or the most respectable index of all in capitalist society—"preparedness to pay." The appeal that pornography has for many people is hardly in dispute, and in a more sober social climate that would be justification enough. Today we are not quite puritan enough to deny that *pleasure* has a worthwhile place in human life: not many of us object to our food being tasty or our clothes being attractive. It was not always like this. In sterner times it was *de rigueur* to prepare food without spices and to wear the plainest clothes. The cult of puritanism reached its apotheosis in the most fanatical asceticism, where it was fashionable for holy men to wander off into a convenient desert and neglect the body to the point of cultivating its lice as "pearls of God." In such a bizarre philosophy pleasure was not only condemned in its sexual manifestations but in all areas where the body could conceivably take satisfaction. These days we are able to countenance pleasure in most fields but in many instances still the case for *sexual* pleasure has to be argued.

Pleasure is not of course its own justification. If it clearly leads to serious 6 malaise, early death, or the *dis*pleasure of others, then there is something to be said against it. But the serious consequences have to be demonstrated: it is not enough to condemn certain forms of pleasurable experience on the grounds of *possible* ill effect. With such an approach any human activity could be censured and freedom would have no place. In short, if something is pleasurable and its bad effects are small or nonexistent then it is to be encouraged: opposition to such a creed should be recognized as an unwholesome antipathy to human potential. Pleasure is a good except where it is harmful (and where the harmfulness is *significant*). . . .

That pornography is enjoyable to many people is the first of the arguments 7 in its favour. In any other field this would be argument enough. It is certainly sufficient to justify many activities that have—unlike a taste for pornography—demonstrably harmful consequences. Only in a sexually neurotic society could a tool for heightening sexual enjoyment be regarded as reprehensible and such as to warrant suppression by law. The position is well summarized[3] in the *first* of the Art Council's twelve reasons for advocating the repeal of the Obscenity Publications Acts:

> It is not for the State to prohibit private citizens from choosing what they may or may not enjoy in literature or art unless there were incontrovertible evidence that the result would be injurious to society. There is no such evidence.

[3]*The Obscenity Laws*, p. 35.

A further point is that availability of pornography may *aid*, rather than frustrate normal sexual development. Thus in 1966, for example, the New Jersey Committee for the Right to Read presented the findings of a survey conducted among nearly a thousand psychiatrists and psychologists of that state. Amongst the various personal statements included was the view that "sexually stimulating materials" might help particular people develop a normal sex drive.[4] In similar spirit, Dr. John Money writes[5] that pornography "may encourage normal sexual development and broadmindedness," a view that may not sound well to the anti-pornographers. And even in circumstances where possible dangers of pornography are pointed out conceivable good effects are sometimes acknowledged. In a paper issued[6] by The Danish Forensic Medicine Council it is pointed out that neurotic and sexually shy people may, by reading pornographic descriptions of normal sexual activity, be freed from some of their apprehension regarding sex and may thereby attain a freer and less frustrated attitude to the sexual side of life. . . .

One argument in favour of pornography is that it can serve as a substitute   8 for actual sexual activity involving another person or other people. This argument has two parts, relating as it does to (1) people who fantasize over *socially acceptable* modes of sexual involvement, and (2) people who fantasize over types of sexual activity that would be regarded as illegal or at least immoral. The first type relates to lonely and deprived people who for one reason or another have been unable to form "normal" sexual contacts with other people; the second type are instances of the much quoted *catharsis* argument.

One writer notes[7] that pornography can serve as a substitute for both the   9 knowledge of which some people have been deprived and the pleasure in sexual experience which they have not enjoyed. One can well imagine men or women too inhibited to secure sexual satisfaction with other adults and where explicit sexual material can alleviate some of their misery. It is facile to remark that such people should seek psychiatric assistance or even "make an effort": the factors that prevent the forming of effective sexual liaisons are just as likely to inhibit any efforts to seek medical or other assistance. Pornography provides sex *by proxy*, and in such usage it can have a clear justification.

It is also possible to imagine circumstances in which men or women—for   10 reasons of illness, travel or bereavement—are unable to seek sexual satisfaction with spouse or other loved one. Pornography can help here too. Again it is easy to suggest that a person abstain from sexual experience, or, if having *permanently* lost a spouse, seek out another partner. Needless to say such advice is often quite impractical—and the alternative to pornography may be prostitution

[4]Quoted by Isadore Rubin, "What Should Parents Do About Pornography?" *Sex in the Adolescent Years* (London: Fontana, 1969), p. 202.
[5]John Money, contribution to "Is Pornography Harmful to Young Children?" in Isadore Rubin and Lester Kirkendall, eds., *Sex in the Childhood Years* (London: Fontana, 1971), p. 181–185.
[6]Paper from the Danish Forensic Medicine Council to the Danish Penal Code Council, published in *The Penal Code Council Report on Penalty for Pornography*, Report No. 435, Copenhagen, 1966, pp. 78–80, and as appendix to *The Obscenity Laws*, pp. 120–124.
[7]Ashley Montagu, "Is Pornography Harmful to Young Children?" in *Sex in the Childhood Years*, p. 182.

or adultery. Montagu notes that pornography can serve the same purpose as "dirty jokes", allowing a person to discharge harmlessly repressed and unsatisfied sexual desires.

In this spirit, Mercier (1970) is quoted by the U.S. Commission: 11

> . . . it is in periods of sexual deprivation—to which the young and the old are far more subject than those in their prime—that males, at any rate, are likely to reap psychological benefit from pornography.

And also Kenneth Tynan (1970):

> For men on long journeys, geographically cut off from wives and mistresses, pornography can act as a portable memory, a welcome shortcut to remembered bliss, relieving tension without involving disloyalty.

It is difficult to see how anyone could object to the use of pornography in such circumstances, other than on the grounds of a morbid anti-sexuality.

The *catharsis argument* has long been put forward to suggest that avail-   12
ability of pornography will neutralize "aberrant" sexual tendencies and so reduce the incidence of sex crime or clearly immoral behaviour in related fields. (. . . it is worth remarking that it should not be necessary to demonstrate a *reduction* in sex crime to justify repeal of the Obscenity Laws. It should be quite sufficient to show that an *increase* in crime will not ensue following repeal. We may even argue that a small increase may be tolerable if other benefits from easy access to pornography could be shown: but it is no part of the present argument to put this latter contention.) . . .

. . . The popularity of all forms of sexual literature—from the superficial,   13
sexless, sentimentality of the popular women's magazine to the clearest "hardcore" porn—has demonstrated over the ages the perennial appetite that people have for fantasy. To an extent, a great extent with many single people and frustrated married ones, the fantasy constitutes an important part of the sex-life. The experience may be vicarious and sterile but it self-evidently fills a need for many individuals. If literature, as a *symbol* of reality, can so involve human sensitivities it is highly likely that when the sensitivities are *distorted* for one reason or another the same sublimatory function can occur: the "perverted" or potentially criminal mentality can gain satisfaction, as does the lonely unfortunate, in sex *by proxy*. If we wanted to force the potential sex criminal on to the streets in search of a human victim perhaps we would do well to deny him his sublimatory substitutes: deny him fantasy and he will be forced to go after the real thing. . . .

The importance of this possibility should be fully faced. If a causal con-   14
nection *does* exist between availability of pornographic material and a *reduction* in the amount of sex crime—and the evidence is wholly consistent with this possibility rather than its converse—then people who deliberately restrict pornography by supporting repressive legislation are prime architects of sexual offences against the individual. The anti-pornographers would do well to note that their anxieties may be driving them into a position the exact opposite of

the one they explicitly maintain—their commitment to reduce the amount of sexual delinquency in society.

The most that the anti-pornographers can argue is that at present the   15 evidence is inconclusive—a point that would be taken by Kutschinsky et al. But if the inconclusive character of the data is once admitted then the case for repressive legislation falls at once. For in a *free* society, or one supposedly aiming after freedom, social phenomena are, like individuals, innocent until proven guilty—and an activity will be permitted unless there is clear evidence of its harmful consequences. . . . Any other view is *totalitarian*.

If human enjoyment *per se* is not to be condemned then it is not too rash   16 to say that we *know* pornography does good. We can easily produce our witnesses to testify to experiencing pleasure. If in the face of this—and no other favourable argument—we are unable to demonstrate a countervailing harm, then the case for easy availability of pornography is unassailable. If, in such circumstances, we find some people unconvinced it is futile to seek out further empirical data. Once we commit ourselves to the notion that the evil nature of something is axiomatic we tacitly concede that evidence is largely irrelevant to our position. If pornography never fails to fill us with predictable loathing then statistics on crime, or measured statements by careful specialists, will not be useful: our reactions will stay the same. But in this event we would do well to reflect on what our emotions tell us of our own mentality. . . .

⧗ JOHN STUART MILL

On Liberty

John Stuart Mill (1806–1873), the nineteenth century English philosopher of the empiricist school, economist, and writer on social and political issues, is perhaps best known as a champion of utilitarianism, the theory that, roughly, the best course of action in any situation is the one most likely to yield the most benefit for all concerned. His best known works are A System of Logic *(1843),* Utilitarianism *(1863),* On the Subjection of Women *(1869), and* On Liberty *(1859). In the following passage from* On Liberty, *Mill argues against social interference with private behavior that does no harm to others on the utilitarian grounds that we're all better off tolerating behavior that does no harm to others than by "compelling each to live as seems good to the rest."*

The object of this Essay is to assert one very simple principle, as entitled to   1 govern absolutely the dealings of society with the individual in the way of compulsion and control, whether the means used be physical force in the form of legal penalties, or the moral coercion of public opinion. That principle is, that the sole end for which mankind are warranted, individually or collectively, in interfering with the liberty of action of any of their number, is self-protection. That the only purpose for which power can be rightfully exercised over any member of a civilized community, against his will, is to prevent harm to others. His own good, either physical or moral, is not a sufficient warrant. He cannot rightfully be compelled to do or forbear because it will be better for him to do so, because it will make him happier, because, in the opinions of others, to do so would be wise, or even right. These are good reasons for remonstrating with him, or reasoning with him, or persuading him, or entreating him, but not for compelling him, or visiting him with any evil in case he do otherwise. To justify that, the conduct from which it is desired to deter him, must be calculated to produce evil to some one else. The only part of the conduct of any one, for which he is amenable to society, is that which concerns others. In the part which merely concerns himself, his independence is, of right, absolute. Over himself, over his own body and mind, the individual is sovereign.

It is, perhaps, hardly necessary to say that this doctrine is meant to apply 2 only to human beings in the maturity of their faculties. We are not speaking of children, or of young persons below the age which the law may fix as that of manhood and womanhood. Those who are still in a state to require being taken care of by others, must be protected against their own actions as well as against external injury. . . .

There is a sphere of action in which society, as distinguished from the 3 individual, has, if any, only an indirect interest; comprehending all that portion of a person's life and conduct which affects only himself, or if it also affects others, only with their free, voluntary, and undeceived consent and participation. When I say only himself, I mean directly, and in the first instance: for whatever affects himself, may affect others through himself; and the objection which may be grounded on this contingency, will receive consideration in the sequel. This, then, is the appropriate region of human liberty. It comprises, first, the inward domain of consciousness; demanding liberty of conscience, in the most comprehensive sense; liberty of thought and feeling; absolute feedom of opinion and sentiment on all subjects, practical or speculative, scientific, moral, or theological. The liberty of expressing and publishing opinions may seem to fall under a different principle, since it belongs to that part of the conduct of an individual which concerns other people; but, being almost of as much importance as the liberty of thought itself, and resting in great part on the same reasons, is practically inseparable from it. Secondly, the principle requires liberty of tastes and pursuits; of framing the plan of our life to suit our own character; of doing as we like, subject to such consequences as may follow; without impediment from our fellow-creatures, so long as what we do does not harm them, even though they should think our conduct foolish, perverse, or wrong. Thirdly, from this liberty of each individual, follows the liberty, within the same limits, of combination among individuals; freedom to unite, for any purpose not involving harm to others: the persons combining being supposed to be of full age, and not forced or deceived.

No society in which these liberties are not, on the whole, respected, is 4 free, whatever may be its form of government; and none is completely free in which they do not exist absolute and unqualified. The only freedom which deserves the name is that of pursuing our own good in our own way, so long as we do not attempt to deprive others of theirs, or impede their efforts to obtain it. Each is the proper guardian of his own health, whether bodily, or mental and spiritual. Mankind are greater gainers by suffering each other to live as seems goods to themselves, than by compelling each to live as seems good to the rest. . . .

Again, there are many acts which, being directly injurious only to the 5 agents themselves, ought not to be legally interdicted, but which, if done publicly, are a violation of good manners, and coming thus within the category of offences against others, may rightfully be prohibited. Of this kind are offences against decency; on which it is unnecessary to dwell, the rather as they are only connected indirectly with our subject, the objection to publicity being equally strong in the case of many actions not in themselves condemnable, nor supposed to be so. . .

PORNOGRAPHY

QUESTIONS AND SUGGESTIONS FOR WRITING

1. Kristol believes that we can censor pornography without inevitably ending up censoring political opinion, citing as evidence his claim that it has not done so in the past. Do you agree or disagree? Why?

2. Brownmiller argues that "pornography, like rape, is a male invention designed to dehumanize women." In essence it is "antifemale propaganda." If you find this argument convincing, explain the adverse social or psychological consequences pornography might have on men and women in our society.

3. Simons claims that there is no evidence that pornography is seriously harmful while Kristol and Brownmiller argue the other way. Which side does the evidence favor in this disagreement. Indicate what evidence convinces you.

4. Do you agree with the libertarian position taken by Mill in his *On Liberty*? Does his view imply that censorship of pornography is wrong, given the facts as you see them about the nature and consequences of pornography?

5. Argue for or against censoring pornography. When appropriate, draw supporting evidence from the articles in this section and outside sources, taking care to cite all sources and to explain the world view underlying your position on the issue.

The quality of life depends on all sorts of things, from the amount of pollution to the amount of wealth available to the quality of entertainment to the treatment of the sexes. This section contains essays on all of these topics as well as several others, for instance, the nature of class distinctions in America and the problem of endangered species. Modern life is so radically different from anything that has gone before that it is difficult to know how to deal with most of the problems that industry and science have created.

※ **PAUL FUSSELL**

The Middle Class

Paul Fussell is best known for The Great War and Modern Memory, *his book about the horrors of World War I. The following is excerpted from his 1983 book,* Class: A Guide Through the American Status System, *and explains Fussell's negative views on mass culture and the middle class.*

The middle class is distinguishable more by its earnestness and psychic inse-   1
curity than by its middle income. I have known some very rich people who remain stubbornly middle class, which is to say they remain terrified at what others think of them, and to avoid criticism are obsessed with doing everything right. The middle class is the place where table manners assume an awful importance and where net curtains flourish to conceal activities like hiding the salam' (a phrase no middle-class person would indulge in, surely; the fatuous

making love is the middle-class equivalent). The middle class, always anxious about offending, is the main market for "mouthwashes," and if it disappeared the whole "deodorant" business would fall to the ground. If physicians tend to be upper-middle-class, dentists are gloomily aware that they're middle, and are said to experience frightful status anxieties when introduced socially to "physicians"—as dentists like to call them. (Physicians call themselves *doctors*, and enjoy doing this in front of dentists, as well as college professors, chiropractors, and divines.)

"Status panic": that's the affliction of the middle class, according to   2 C. Wright Mills, author of *White Collar* (1951) and *The Power Elite* (1956). Hence the middles' need to accumulate credit cards and take in *The New Yorker*, which it imagines registers upper-middle taste. Its devotion to that magazine, or its ads, is a good example of Mills's description of the middle class as the one that tends "to borrow status from higher elements." *New Yorker* advertisers have always known this about their audience, and some of their pseudo-upper-middle gestures in front of the middles are hilarious, like one recently flogging expensive stationery, here, a printed invitation card. The pretentious Anglophile spelling of the second word strikes the right opening note:

> In honour of
> Dr and Mrs Leonard Adam Westman,
> Dr and Mrs Jeffrey Logan Brandon
> request the pleasure of your company for

[at this point the higher classes might say *cocktails*, or, if thoroughly secure, *drinks*. But here, "Dr." and Mrs. Brandon are inviting you to consume specifically—]

> Champagne and Caviar
> on Friday, etc., etc.
> Valley Hunt Club
> Stamford, Conn., etc.

The only thing missing is the brand names of the refreshments.

If the audience for that sort of thing used to seem the most deeply rooted   3 in time and place, today it seems the class that's the most rootless. Members of the middle class are not only the sort of people who buy their own heirlooms, silver, etc. They're also the people who do most of the moving long-distance (generally to very unstylish places), commanded every few years to pull up stakes by the corporations they're in bondage to. They are the geologist employed by the oil company, the computer programmer, the aeronautical engineer, the salesman assigned a new territory, and the "marketing" (formerly *sales*) manager deputed to keep an eye on him. These people and their families occupy the suburbs and developments. Their "Army and Navy," as William H. Whyte, Jr., says, is their corporate employer. IBM and DuPont hire these people from second-rate colleges and teach them that they are nothing if not members of the team. Virtually no latitude is permitted to individuality or the milder forms of eccentricity, and these employees soon learn to avoid all ideological statements, notably, as we'll see, in the furnishing of their living rooms. Terrified of losing their jobs, these people grow passive, their humanity diminished as they perceive themselves mere parts of an infinitely larger structure. And interchangeable parts, too. "The training makes our men interchangeable," an IBM executive was once heard to say.

It's little wonder that, treated like slaves most of the time, the middle class 4 lusts for the illusion of weight and consequence. One sign is their quest for heraldic validation ("This beautiful embossed certificate will show your family tree"). Another is their custom of issuing annual family newsletters announcing the most recent triumphs in the race to become "professional":

> John, who is now 22, is in his first year at the Dental School of Wayne State University.
>
> Caroline has a fine position as an executive secretary for a prestigious firm in Boise, Idaho.

Sometimes these letters really wring the heart, with their proud lists of new "affiliations" achieved during the past year: "This year Bob became a member of the Junior Chamber of Commerce, the Beer Can Collectors League of North America, the Alumni Council of the University of Evansville, and the Young Republicans of Vanderburgh County." (Cf. Veblen: "Since conservatism is a characteristic of the wealthier and therefore more reputable portion of the community, it has acquired a certain honorific or decorative value.") Nervous lest she be considered nobody, the middle-class wife is careful to dress way up when she goes shopping. She knows by instinct what one middle-class woman told an inquiring sociologist: "You know there's class when you're in a department store and a well-dressed lady gets treated better."

"One who makes birth or wealth the sole criterion of worth": that's a 5 conventional dictionary definition of a *snob*, and the place to look for the snob is in the middle class. Worried a lot about their own taste and about whether it's working for or against them, members of the middle class try to arrest their natural tendency to sink downward by associating themselves, if ever so tenuously, with the imagined possessors of money, power, and taste. "Correctness" and doing the right thing become obsessions, prompting middle-class people to write thank-you notes after the most ordinary dinner parties, give excessively expensive or correct presents, and never allude to any place—Fort Smith, Arkansas, for example—that lacks known class. It will not surprise readers who have traveled extensively to hear that Neil Mackwood, a British authority on snobbery, finds the greatest snobs worldwide emanating from Belgium, which can also be considered world headquarters of the middle class.

The desire to belong, and to belong by some mechanical act like purchas- 6 ing something, is another sign of the middle class. Words like *club* and *guild* (as in Book-of-the-Month Club and Literary Guild) extend a powerful invitation. The middle class is thus the natural target for developers' ads like this:

You Belong
  in Park Forest!
The moment you come to our town you know:
  You're Welcome.
  You're part of a big group. . . .

Oddity, introversion, and the love of privacy are the big enemies, a total reversal of the values of the secure upper orders. Among the middles there's a convention that erecting a fence or even a tall hedge is an affront. And there's also a convention that you may drop in on neighbors or friends without a telephone inquiry first. Being naturally innocent and well disposed and aboveboard, a member of the middle class finds it hard to believe that all are not. Being timid and conventional, no member of the middle class would expect that anyone is copulating in the afternoon instead of the evening, clearly, for busy and well-behaved corporate personnel, the correct time for it. When William H. Whyte, Jr., was poking around one suburb studying the residents, he was told by one quintessentially middle-class woman: "The street behind us is nowhere near as friendly. They knock on doors over there."

If the women treasure "friendliness," the men treasure having a genteel   7 occupation (usually more important than money), with emphasis on the word (if seldom the thing) *executive*. (As a matter of fact, an important class divide falls between those who feel veneration before the term *executive* and those who feel they want to throw up.) Having a telephone-answering machine at home is an easy way of simulating (at relatively low cost) high professional desirability, but here you wouldn't think of a facetious or eccentric text (delivered in French, for example, or in the voice of Donald Duck or Richard Nixon) asking the caller to speak his bit after the beeping sound. For the middle-class man is scared. As C. Wright Mills notes, "He is always somebody's man, the corporation's, the government's, the army's. . . ." One can't be too careful. One "management adviser" told Studs Terkel: "Your wife, your children have to behave properly. You've got to fit in the mold. You've got to be on guard." In *Coming Up for Air* (1939) George Orwell, speaking for his middle-class hero, gets it right:

> There's a lot of rot talked about the sufferings of the working class. I'm not so sorry for the proles myself. . . . The prole suffers physically, but he's a free man when he isn't working. But in every one of those little stucco boxes there's some poor bastard who's *never* free except when he's fast asleep.

Because he is essentially a salesman, the middle-class man develops a   8 salesman's style. Hence his optimism and his belief in the likelihood of self-improvement if you'll just hurl yourself into it. One reason musicals like *Annie* and *Man of La Mancha* make so much money is that they offer him and his wife songs, like "Tomorrow" and "The Impossible Dream," that seem to promise that all sorts of good things are on the way. A final stigma of the middle class, an emanation of its social insecurity, is its habit of laughing at its own jests. Not entirely certain what social effect he's transmitting, and yet obliged, by his role as "salesman," to promote goodwill and optimism, your middle-class man serves as his own enraptured audience. Sometimes, after uttering some would-be clever formulation in public, he will look all around to gauge the response of the audience. Favorable, he desperately hopes.

The young men of the middle class are chips off the old block. If you want 9 to know who reads John T. Molloy's books, hoping to break into the upper-middle class by formulas and mechanisms, they are your answer. You can see them on airplanes especially, being forwarded from one corporate training program to another. Their shirts are implausibly white, their suits are excessively dark, their neckties resemble those worn by undertakers, and their hair is cut in the style of the 1950s. Their talk is of *the bottom line,* and for *no* they are likely to say *no way.* Often their necks don't seem long enough, and their eyes tend to be too much in motion, flicking back and forth rather than up and down. They will enter adult life as corporate trainees and, after forty-five faithful years, leave it as corporate personnel, wondering whether this is all.

PEREGRINE WORSTHORNE

The New Inequality

Peregrine Worsthorne is a well-known British writer recently employed by a London newspaper. In the essay that follows, she argues against what she takes to be the new inequality based on merit rather than on birth, rank, or class. She says that if "equality of opportunity, as at present practiced, is assumed to be the basis for a just society, then this cannot fail to legitimize inequality in ways that we are only now beginning to discover."

To most of us it now seems very strange, almost incomprehensible, that for 1 centuries gross hereditary inequalities of wealth, status and power were universally accepted as a divinely ordained fact of life. The lord in his castle, like the peasant at his gate, both believed that this was where God wished them to remain. If anybody had then suggested that such an arrangement was manifestly unfair he would have been dismissed as a little crazed, not to say blasphemous.

Modern man, as I say, finds this awfully difficult to understand. To him it 2 seems absolutely axiomatic that each individual ought to be allowed to make his grade according to merit, regardless of the accident of birth. All positions of power, wealth and status should be open to talent. To the extent that this ideal is achieved a society is deemed to be just.

If our feudal forebears thought it perfectly fair that the lord should be in his castle and the peasant at his gate, their liberal successors—which means most of us—have tended to believe it to be fair enough that the man of merit should be on top and the man without merit should be underneath. Anybody who challenged this assumption was thought a little crazed.

Much of the current political and social malaise springs, in my view, from the increasing evidence that this assumption should be challenged. The ideal of a meritocracy no longer commands such universal assent.

It used to be considered manifestly unjust that a child should be given an enormous head-start in life simply because he was the son of an earl, or a member of the landed gentry. But what about a child today born of affluent, educated parents whose family life gets him off to a head-start in the educational ladder? Is he not the beneficiary of a form of hereditary privilege no less unjust than that enjoyed by the aristocracy?

It used to be assumed that a system of universal public education would eventually overcome this difficulty. But all the recent evidence suggests that this is an illusion. Family life is more important than school life in determining brain power, and children from poor, uneducated homes will do worse than children from affluent, educated homes, even if they are sent to better schools, let alone comparable schools.

So much is beginning to become inescapably obvious. Educational qualifications are today what armorial quarterings were in feudal times. Yet access to them is almost as unfairly determined by accidents of birth as was access to the nobility. Clearly this makes a nonsense of any genuine faith in equality of opportunity.

It is the realization of this that accounts for the current populist clamor to do away with educational distinctions such as exams and diplomas, since they are seen as the latest form of privilege which, in a sense, they are.

It is perfectly true, of course, that in theory socialism has always been critical of the ideal of equality of opportunity. But hitherto, at least in the free world, it has preferred to concentrate its energies on the old injustices which stemmed from the feudal past and the capitalist present rather than to address itself to the injustices of the future.

For these purposes the ideal of equality of opportunity has been exploited as at least a way of moving in the right, that is to say the Left direction. But today, for the first time, a new school of radical thinkers is becoming acutely aware that equality of opportunity may be a dead end instead of the thin end of the egalitarian wedge—more a buttress behind which a new form of privilege has taken shelter than a slippery slope down which hereditary privilege is moving to its doom.

And up to a point they are right in this conclusion. If equality of opportunity, as at present practiced, is assumed to be the basis for a just society, then this cannot fail to legitimize inequality in ways that we are only now beginning to discover.

But there is a problem here for the Right quite as much as for the Left. It   12
seems to me that there will be a growing awareness in the coming decades of
the unfairness of existing society, of the new forms of arbitrary allocation of
power, status and privilege. Resentment will build up against the new meritocracy just as it built up against the old aristocracy and plutocracy.

The task of the Right must be to devise new ways of disarming this resent-   13
ment, without so curbing the high-fliers, so penalizing excellence, or so imposing uniformity as to destroy the spirit of a free and dynamic society.

What will be required of the new meritocracy is a formidably revived and   14
re-animated spirit of *noblesse oblige*, rooted in the recognition that they *are*
immensely privileged and must, as a class, behave accordingly, being prepared
to pay a far higher social price, in terms of taxation, in terms of service, for the
privilege of exercising their talents.

This is not an easy idea for a meritocracy to accept. They like to think that   15
they deserve their privileges, having won them by their own efforts. But this is
an illusion, or at any rate a half truth. The other half of the truth is that they
are terribly lucky and if their luck is not to run out they must be prepared to
pay much more for their good fortune than they had hoped or even feared.

⊠ EUGENE H. METHVIN

TV Violence: The Shocking New Evidence

Eugene H. Methvin is a senior editor on the staff of the Reader's Digest. *In the
following* Reader's Digest *article (January 1983), he argues that watching violence on the tube increases violent behavior in everyday life and urges parents to
"curtail the total time children watch television."*

- SAN DIEGO: A high-school honor student watches a lurid ABC-TV fic-   1
  tionalization of the 1890s Lizzie Borden ax murder case; then chops his
  own parents and sister to death and leaves his brother a quadriplegic.

- DENVER: *The Deer Hunter* is telecast and a seventeen-year-old kills him-   2
  self with a revolver, acting out the movie's climactic game of Russian
  roulette. He is the twenty-fifth viewer in two years to kill himself that
  way after watching the drama on TV.

- DECATUR, ILL.: A twelve-year-old overdoses on sleeping pills after her   3
mother forbids her to date a sixteen-year-old boy. "What gave you the
idea of suicide?" an investigating psychiatrist asks. The answer: A little
girl tried it on a TV show, was quickly revived and welcomed back by
her parents with open arms.

Ten years ago, after studying massive research on the subject, the U.S.   4
Surgeon General, Jesse L. Steinfeld, declared, "The casual relationship between televised violence and antisocial behavior is sufficient to warrant immediate remedial action." Called before Congress, the presidents of the three
networks solemnly agreed.

Yet the University of Pennsylvania's Annenberg School of Communi-   5
cations, which for fourteen years has charted mayhem in network programming, reports that violent acts continue at about six per prime-time hour and
in four out of every five programs. The weekend children's programs are even
worse.

Last May the National Institute of Mental Health (NIMH) issued a report   6
summarizing over 2500 studies done in the last decade on television's influence
on behavior. Evidence from the studies—with more than 100,000 subjects in
dozens of nations—is so "overwhelming," the NIMH found, that there is a
consensus in the research community "that violence on television does lead to
aggressive behavior."

Television ranks behind only sleep and work as a consumer of our time.   7
In fact, according to the 1982 Nielsen Report on Television, the average American family keeps its set on for forty-nine and one-half hours each week. The
typical youngster graduating from high school will have spent almost twice as
much time in front of the tube as he has in the classroom—the staggering
equivalent of ten years of forty-hour weeks. He will have witnessed some
150,000 violent episodes, including an estimated 25,000 deaths.

Despite the mayhem, the viewer sees little pain or suffering, a false picture   8
that influences young and old. At a Capitol Hill hearing on TV violence, a
dismayed Rep. Billy Tauzin complained to network executives that his three-
year-old son had poked his fist through a glass door—in imitation of a TV
cartoon character—and almost bled to death. In New Rochelle, N.Y., a killer
who re-enacted a TV bludgeon murder told police of his surprise when his
victim did not die with the first crunch of his baseball bat, as on the tube, but
instead threw up a hand in defense and groaned and cried piteously.

The effect of all this? Research points toward these conclusions: 9

1. *TV violence produces lasting and serious harm.* University of Illinois   10
psychology professor Leonard Eron and colleagues compared the television
diets and level of aggressive behavior of 184 boys at age eight and again at
eighteen. His report: "The more violent the programs watched in childhood,
the more combative the young adults became. We found their behavior studded
with antisocial acts, from theft and vandalism to assault with a deadly weapon.
The children appeared to learn aggressive habits that persisted for at least ten
years."

2. *Those "action" cartoons on children's programs are decidedly damaging.* 11
Stanford University psychologist Albert Bandura found cartoon violence as
potent as real-life models in increasing violence among youngsters. A University of Kansas researcher reported that Saturday-morning cartoons markedly
decreased imaginative play and hiked aggression among sixty-six preschoolers.
In a year-long study of two hundred preschoolers, Yale University Drs. Jerome
L. and Dorothy Singer found that playground depredations like fighting and
kicking were far greater among steady action-cartoon viewers.

Indeed, the Saturday-morning "kid vid" ghetto is the most violent time in 12
TV. It bathes the prime audience of youngsters from three to thirteen years old
with twenty-five violent acts per hour, much of it in a poisonous brew of violent
programs and aggressive commercials designed to sell such products as breakfast
cereals and action toys. According to one study, these commercials have a rate
of violence about three times that of the programs themselves.

3. *TV erodes inhibitions.* With a $290,000 grant from CBS, British psy- 13
chologist William A. Belson studied the television diets and subsequent behavior of 1,565 London boys ages twelve to seventeen. He found cartoon, slapstick,
or science-fiction violence less harmful at this age; but realistic fictional violence, violence in close personal relationships, and violence "in a good cause"
were deadly poison. Heavy viewers were 47 percent more likely to commit acts
such as knifing during a school fight, burning another with a cigarette, slashing
car tires, burglary and attempted rape. To Belson's surprise, the TV exposure
did not seem to change the boys' opinions toward violence but rather seemed
to crumble whatever constraints family, church, or school had built up. "It is
almost as if the boys then tend to let go whatever violent tendencies are in
them. It just seems to explode in spontaneous ways."

4. *The sheer quantity of TV watching by youngsters increases hurtful be-* 14
havior and poor academic performance. "When the TV set is on, it freezes
everybody," says Cornell University psychologist Urie Bronfenbrenner. "Everything that used to go on between people—the games, the arguments, the
emotional scenes out of which personality and ability develop—is stopped.
When you turn on the TV, you turn off the process of making human beings
human."

Studies in the United States, Canada, Israel, Australia, and Europe show 15
that the amount of TV watched, regardless of program content, is a critical
variable that contributes heavily to children's later aggressive attitudes and behavior. Dozens of other studies indicate that TV impairs the children's verbal
skills and creativeness.

WHAT PARENTS CAN DO

First of all, they can help by realizing that their own TV viewing affects the 16
quality of family life. Until recently most adults worried that violent programming might be harmful to children, but assumed they could gorge themselves
with impunity on whatever programs caught their fancy. Not so.

In one study, U.C.L.A. researchers Roderic Gorney and David Loye divided 183 husbands, ages twenty to seventy, into five comparable groups. The groups were assigned twenty-one hours of varied TV fare at home during a single week, and each man kept a diary of his "moods." Wives, without knowing which TV diet the husbands watched, recorded "hurtful" and "helpful" behaviors. The result: husbands who watched violent programming recorded a significantly higher level of aggressive moods. Furthermore, their wives noted about 35 percent more daily incidents of hurtful behavior than did wives whose husbands watched "prosocial" programming.   17

"The important lesson of our experiment is that adults, by their own programming choices, may actually *reduce* aggressive moods and hurtful behavior," says Gorney. "In a home the climate generated by parental moods and conduct is surely as crucial as what children see on TV in determining the family's mental health."   18

Further, parents can curtail the total time children watch television. Investigators find that parents are consistently unaware of how long their children are watching, and underestimate how much violence they see and how much it disturbs them. Experts agree that three hours a day should be an absolute maximum for subteen children and far less than that of action drama, cartoons, and other violence-packed programming. Advises syndicated columnist Ann Landers: "Be firm. You wouldn't allow your child to eat garbage, would you? Why, then, let him put it in his head?"   19

Parents can avoid using TV as a baby-sitter, and they can watch with their children—making sure that incidents of violence or sex never go without comment. Parents can encourage children to identify and watch programs of educational and social value. They should not hesitate to change channels or turn off the set. As an aid, Yale University's Family Television Research and Consultation Center has produced a carefully tested program for parents and teachers of children ranging from nursery to junior high: *Getting the Most Out of TV.*   20

WHAT EVERYONE CAN DO

In legal theory, "the airwaves belong to the people," and the nation's 1,067 television stations enjoy their federally awarded monopoly only in return for programming "in the public interest." In general, the government cannot deny any corporation the right to advertise on any program it chooses. But the viewer has a right to declare that he is not going to help pay for those programs by buying the advertised products.   21

Both the American Medical Association and the National PTA have urged their members to bring public pressure against advertisers on high-violence programs. The National Coalition on Television Violence (NCTV), formed by psychiatrists, pediatricians and educators, carefully grades network prime-time and weekend children's programs. Each quarter it publishes lists of the compa-   22 nies and products that sponsor the most mayhem, and also companies that allot the largest portion of their television budgets to violent programming. It promotes legislative action and urges school, church and parent groups to publish its lists and to complain to advertisers.

Some companies need little prompting. Kodak has always shunned violent 23 programming and consistently ranks low in NCTV monitoring lists. Kraft, Inc., also has a long-standing policy against programming that depicts excessive violence. Other companies that rate well with NCTV include Hallmark Cards, Schering-Plough and Campbell Soup.

Too much TV watching—and violent programming in general—can indeed be harmful to viewers' health. Says NCTV's chairman, Dr. Thomas Radecki, a psychiatry professor at Southern Illinois University, "Each of us bears a responsibility in stopping this ubiquitous teacher of rage and hate. Each of us must live in the world it is destroying."

ERIC JULBER

Let's Open Up Our Wilderness Areas

Eric Julber is a lawyer who wrote the following essay out of the conviction that a large part of America's natural beauty is wasted, unlike Switzerland's, for instance. He recommends several ways in which this waste might be remedied.

The prevailing philosophy with regard to the use of some 40 million acres of 1 America's magnificent wilderness has become what I term "purist-conservationist." The purist is, generally speaking, against everything. He is against roads, campgrounds, ski lifts and restaurants. He has very strong ideas about who deserves to enjoy natural beauty and, ideally, would reserve beauty for those who are willing and able to hike, climb, crawl or cliffhang to achieve it. The purist believes that those who do not agree with him desire to "rape the landscape."

The purist standards were embodied in the Wilderness Act of 1964, which 2 provides that in such areas there shall be "no permanent road . . no temporary road . . . no mechanical transport and no structure or installation." The practical effect of this philosophy, thus frozen into federal law, has been to make many of the most beautiful areas of the United States "off limits" to anyone who is not willing and able to backpack into them. Statistics show that this means 99 *percent* of Americans.

In 1965, there were 1,475,000 visitors to the Wilderness areas. In 1970, 3 the number of visitors had increased only to 1,543,000. This represents use by less than 1 percent of our population. Moreover, a survey on behalf of the President's Outdoor Recreation Resources Review Commission (ORRRC) showed, by statistical analysis, that the users are the intellectual and financial elite of our nation.

Reports the ORRRC: "In the sample of Wilderness users interviewed, 4 more than 75 percent had at least a college degree, and a high proportion have done post-graduate work or hold advance degrees. . . . Wilderness users are disproportionately drawn from the higher income levels. Professional and semi-professional people, and those in white-collar occupations, account for approximately three quarters of those interviewed."

And what of ordinary Americans, those whose favorite recreations are 5 driving, sightseeing, easy walking, and camping? What of the too-old, the too-young, the timid, the inexperienced, the frail, the hurried, the out-of-shape or the just-plain-lazy, all of whose taxes acquired and maintain the Wilderness areas?

For this group—99 percent of the American population—federal agencies 6 provide 73,700 acres of campgrounds and 39,100 acres of picnic sites: a total of 112,800 acres. And I believe that the areas provided to the common American are not the prime scenic areas; they are the fringes, the leftovers, the secondary scenic areas.

I feel I can speak with some authority as to purist philosophy, because I 7 was once a purist myself. I have carried many a fifty-pound pack; I've hiked to the top of Mt. Whitney, there to think beautiful thoughts; I've hiked the two-hundred-mile length of California's John Muir Trail, running from Yosemite to Sequoia. And even in later years, when the press of law practice kept me physically away from the wilderness, in spirit I remained a purist. Keep those roads and crowds out, I said!

But no more. Recently I paid a visit to Switzerland. What I saw there 8 made a non-purist out of me. Switzerland has, within the boundaries of a country half as large as South Carolina, one of the most astonishing concentrations of natural beauty on the face of the earth. Not only was I overwhelmed by Switzerland's beauty, but I was amazed to find that virtually every part of it was accessible and thoroughly used by people of all shapes and ages. It was, in fact, exploited to the ultimate—crisscrossed with roads, its mountain valleys heavily grazed and farmed, hotels and restaurants everywhere. Where the automobile cannot go, railroads take you; and where the going gets too steep for cogwheel trains, you catch an aerial tramway.

The most remarkable viewpoints in the country have been deliberately 9 made accessible by some kind of comfortable transportation. People from all over Europe sit on Switzerland's restaurant patios, 10,000 feet high, admiring the magnificent views—views that in America would be excluded from 99 percent of our population without days of the most arduous struggle.

The Swiss philosophy says: Invite people in; the more the better. The 10 purist says: Keep people out. The Swiss say: Let the strong climb if they choose (and many of them do), but let the children, the aged, the hurried, or just-plain-lazy ride.

I, who have now done it both ways, say: My thoughts were just as beautiful 11 on top of Switzerland's Schilthorn—9,757 feet up; restaurant lunch of fondue, wine, strawberry pastry, and coffee; reached by thirty-minute tram ride—as they were on top of Mt. Lyell in America's Yosemite—13,095 feet up; lunch of peanut butter sandwich; reached by two-day hike. I conclude that the purist philosophy which keeps Americans out of their own land is an unwise misuse of our wilderness resources.

Let me propose an alternative philosophy. For want of a better term, call 12 it an "access" philosophy. Consider as an example Muir Trail in California, with its magnificent Wilderness scenery—peaks, meadows, hundreds of lakes, streams, even glaciers. Its southern end is 212 miles from Los Angeles, its northern end 215 miles from San Francisco. Under present purist conditions, the Muir Trail is inaccessible to all except the hardiest, for only two roads touch it between its two ends. To reach its most beautiful parts you have to hike over mountain passes averaging 10,000 feet in height, packing supplies on your back.

Under the "access" philosophy, I would install aerial tramways at three or 13 four locations within easy driving distance of Los Angeles. These tramways would have large gondola cars suspended from cables between towers that can be up to a mile apart; the cars would move silently high above the landscape. At the terminal of each tramway—after, say, an hour's ride—there would be restaurant facilities, picnic areas, observation points. A family could stay for a few hours or camp for weeks. General access would be year-round, as compared to the present ninety-day, snow-free period.

Why not also put a tramway in Grand Canyon?   14

The visitor now cannot get from the South Rim to the North Rim (a 15 distance of from 8 to 18 miles) without driving 217 miles around, and he cannot get to the bottom of the canyon (the most interesting part), except on foot or muleback. I would install an aerial tramway in an inconspicuous fold of the canyon, so that visitors could ride from the South Rim to the bottom, and from the bottom to the North Rim, thus getting a feel for its immense depths.

That brings up the ultimate argument that purists always fall back on: that 16 the Swiss can do such things with taste, judgment and reverence for the land-scape; that we Americans would botch it up. This is neither altogether true nor altogether false. We are capable of abominations, but we are just as capable of tasteful building as Europeans. Witness the beautiful aerial tramway at Palm Springs, Calif., which carries visitors to the slopes of Mt. San Jacinto. Built in 1963, after fifteen years of battle with purists, this tramway has taken 2.5 million people to a lovely area which before was a full day's arduous climb away.

Surprisingly, the litter problem is often least great in precisely those areas 17 where access is provided to beautiful spots. The Palm Springs aerial tramway, for instance, and Glacier Point in Yosemite are remarkably free of litter despite heavy visitation. This, I think, is because people will not litter when they feel others are watching; and also because purchasing a ticket on a tramway gives one a proprietary interest in keeping the premises clean.

It is my firm belief that if Americans were permitted access to Wilderness   18
areas in the manner I have suggested, we would soon create a generation of avid nature lovers. Americans would cease to be "alienated" from their landscape, and would mend their littering tendencies. If you question any purist or wilderness buff, you will find that what initially "turned him on," in almost every case, was an experience in which he was provided access to natural beauty—be it Glacier Park, Yellowstone, Grand Canyon, or Yosemite (as in my own case)—by roads, bus, or other similar non-purist means. Yet, if purists had had the influence 100 years ago that they have today, there would be no roads or other facilities in Yosemite Valley, and the strong possibility is that neither I nor millions of other Americans would ever have seen its beauties, except on postcards.

I believe that the purist philosophy is unfair and undemocratic, and that   19
an alternate philosophy, one of enlightened, carefully controlled "access," is more desirable and also ecologically sound. If the Swiss can do it, why can't we?

⧄ **LANDON LOCKETT**

Whales Off the Faeroe Islands

Landon Lockett has taught linguistics in South and Central America. In this essay that appeared in Newsweek *(November 23, 1987) he argues that conservationists have missed the point. He says that ". . . those who would save whales, and wildlife, have a lesson to learn: what counts is not the individual animal but the species and its habitat—save the habitat and you will probably save the species."*

I recently received an appeal, the second this year, from an organization called   1
the International Wildlife Coalition. Having failed to raise my consciousness with tales of carnage in the North Atlantic, they were trying again.

The letter, accompanied by color photographs of the Faeroese—who live   2
north of Scotland but are under the control of Denmark—up to their knees in bloodstained surf as they hack away at pilot whales, does its utmost to exploit the squeamishness of animal lovers. Readers who, unlike their forebears, have never gutted a squirrel or helped butcher a hog, or in fact faced anything

bloodier than a supermarket lamb chop, are urged, in language dripping with self-righteousness, to send their dollars to stop "this monstrous, mass-scale savagery against nature." The letter also mentions the "modern homes and new cars" of the islanders, implying that were they Third Worlders instead of Europeans their barbarism could be excused.

I get this kind of mail because I am a lifelong conservationist. I belong to 3 several organizations that are active in the fight to save the world's natural environment and its endangered species. I support the National Audubon Society, the Sierra Club, and the Nature Conservancy, and over the years my name has migrated from one mailing list to another.

But as a conservationist, I am bothered more by the International Wildlife 4 Coalition/Whale Rescue Project's solicitations than I am by the whaling practices of the Faeroese. The coalition's plea seems aimed at arousing reader sensibilities and strikes me as an appeal in behalf of individual animals rather than one for real conservation needs.

I believe that those who would save whales, and wildlife, have a lesson to 5 learn: what counts is not the individual animal but the species and its habitat— save the habitat and you will probably save the species, even if individual members of it die. They must also learn more about the differences among the creatures they champion. Some species of larger whales like the humpback and blue are genuinely threatened with extinction. These urgently need protection. Can the same be said of the smaller pilot whales?

Although the coalition's letter speaks of protection being "desperately 6 needed," and accuses the Faeroese of killing 3,000 pilot whales a year, a recent "Audubon Wildlife Report" says nothing about the species being endangered. Nor does it appear on the official list of endangered species published by the U.S. Fish and Wildlife Service.

Because it's not easy to kill a large animal quickly, I have no doubt that 7 the whales suffer, as some animals always suffer so that others, including man, may eat. What the coalition seems to be trying to sell us, however, is the illusion that all such suffering can be stopped. Or that at the least we can keep our own hands clean if we have the wealth to distance ourselves from life's messier realities, or if we can bully people like the Faeroese into sharing our humane sentiments.

We are all involved in spilling blood—even those who give to the Inter- 8 national Wildlife Coalition. When we buy meat or any animal product, including leather shoes, we in effect pay others to do our bloodletting. The killing that takes place in the slaughterhouses is no more respectable than what happens to pilot whales. Just contemplate the dismal lot of cows, calves, and lambs that we breed and fatten only to herd to their deaths.

Vegetarians do not escape responsibility, either. To raise the crops they eat, 9 we have to clear land. The clearing of land destroys various species' habitats. Deprived of a source of food, wild animals crowd out other animals, or suffer slow death by starvation. Then to harvest the vegetarians' foods, we poison, trap, shoot, or drive off creatures (such as the raccoon that last night raided my fig tree) that also need to feed on them.

Anyone who loves nature beyond the level of "Bambi" must recognize and   10
accept its brutality along with its beauty. But we do not promote such understanding—essential to saving our environment and its wildlife—by pretending
that violent death is not part of nature, or that we human beings, in order to
survive, do not play a part in that violence.

The point is that saving animals from suffering is not the same thing as   11
saving wildlife. In preserving the natural environment, we also preserve the
suffering that goes with it. Species prey upon species in the wild world. And in
the civilized world, too. It's the only way the human species can survive.

I don't think that sending dollars to the coalition will wash away the stain   12
of blood. Yet great harm can be done, however appealing pilot whales may be.
Money spent on a species that is not really endangered is money not spent on
those actually threatened and that, for a lack of resources, we may lose. Like
the sperm whale or the Florida panther.

Emotional campaigns can only undermine the environmental movement   13
and encourage the tendency to dismiss conservationists as hand-wringing sen-
timentalists. Concern for the suffering of animals is legitimate but, whatever
the members of the coalition may imagine, the Faeroese do not kill whales just
to watch them suffer. Whale meat is still a dietary staple; it accounts for 25
percent of the meat Faeroese consume. And whale drives are organized on a
communal and noncommercial basis—the Faeroese do not sell their catch.

The letters I received informed me that even Faeroese children are in-   14
volved in the whale slaughter, yet I think these children will probably grow up
with a deeper understanding of man's relation to and dependence on nature
than those for whom all meat comes wrapped in a plastic package and all wild
animals are images on TV. Indeed, herding whales from small boats seems not
the easiest way to gather one's supper and is an experience that should leave the
participant with a sense of just what is involved in reducing a living creature
to food.

⬙ **WOODY ALLEN**

Don't Colorize Old Black and White Films

*Here are excerpts from comedian and movie director Woody Allen's testimony
before the U.S. Senate Judiciary Subcommittee on Technology and the Law
(May 12, 1987). The issue was whether to legally ban the colorization of old
black-and-white movies, a process that computer technology had just made
possible. Woody argues that the director's wishes should be adhered to.*

. . . You might get the impression . . . that I am against colorization of black 1
and white films, but . . . you'd be wrong. If a movie director wishes his film to
be colorized, then I say by all means, let him color it. If he prefers it to remain
in black and white then it is sinful to force him to change it. If the director is
not alive and his work has been historically established in black and white it
should remain true to its origin. . . .

The colorizers will tell you that it's proven no one wants black and white 2
but this is not true. . . . [A]nd even if it were [true that people prefer coloriza-
tion]—if audiences who have grown up on mindless television were so desen-
sitized that a movie like *It Happened One Night*, which has been delighting
people in black and white for generations, now had to be viewed in color to be
appreciated—then the task would be to cultivate the audience back to some
level of maturity rather than to doctor the film artificially to keep up with
lowered tastes. . . .

A large number of American movies are classics both at home and all over 3
the world. Thinking they were making popular entertainment, American film
makers have produced numerous motion pictures that are considered genuine
works of art comparable to fine literature, painting, and music. . . .

The colorizers also tell us that a viewer can simply turn off the color and 4
see the film [*The Maltese Falcon*] in black and white. The fact that the man
who made the film wants no one at all to see it in color [because it would make
this "hard-boiled Bogart film silly-looking"] means nothing to them. . . .

If members of the public had the right to demand alterations to suit their 5
taste the world would have no real art. Nothing would be safe. Picasso would
have been changed years ago, and James Joyce and Stravinsky and the list goes
on. . . .

. . . [T]he different effect between color and black and white is often so 6
wide it alters the meaning of scenes. If I had portrayed New York City in color
rather than black and white in my movie, *Manhattan*, all the nostalgic
connotations would have vanished. All the evocation of the city from old
photographs and films would have been impossible to achieve in glorious tech-
nicolor. . . .

If a producer insists on color and if a helpless director is forced to film it 7
the studio's way, despite his own feelings that it should be black and white—
well a deal's a deal. But once a film exists in black and white and has been
thrilling audiences for years, then to suddenly color it seems too great an insult. . . .

Only in America are films so degraded. In other countries the artist is 8
often protected by the government. No one can change a French film director's
film without his consent. They have too much respect for people who contribute to the society by doing creative work to allow anyone to subvert their
creations at random.

My personal belief is of course that no one should ever be able to tamper 9
with any artist's work in any medium against the artist's will. . . .

◁▷ U.S. COMMITTEE FOR ENERGY AWARENESS

This is one of several ads by the U.S. Committee for Energy Awareness. Compare its contents with the remarks by Benjamin Spock in the essay that follows.

NUCLEAR ENERGY
Is America being left behind?

"In Europe, it's still full speed ahead for nuclear power"
New York Times, December 4, 1983
"Japan pursuing aggressive nuclear energy program"
Business Week, September 19, 1983
"Britain, China sign agreement for Chinese nuclear power plant"
Wall Street Journal, December 8, 1983

News stories like these raise questions about what, if anything, America stands to lose if we fall behind in nuclear energy development.
Eighty-four nuclear power plants are now licensed to operate across the U.S., and fifty more are being built. But since 1978, no future nuclear plants have been planned in this country. During the same period, at least 40 such plants have been ordered in other parts of the world.

Nuclear electricity is growing worldwide
There are now close to 300 nuclear power plants producing electricity in 25 countries throughout the world. Japan, France, the Soviet Union, and China are among the many nations committed to nuclear electricity as an economic, safe alternative to oil-fired and coal-fired power—despite reduced rates of growth in energy consumption.
In Japan, eight new nuclear plants are due to start producing electricity over the next three years. Japanese companies are designing their own advanced reactors and making it

possible to gain the edge in nuclear energy technology.
Soon, over 50 percent of France's electricity will be nuclear-generated. It takes only six years or so to get a nuclear plant built there, which is half the average time needed to build one in the U.S.

A secure America needs a balanced mix of energy sources
Our country has a lot more oil, natural

NUCLEAR SHARE OF ELECTRICITY GENERATED BY COUNTRY, 1982

Country	Share
Finland	40%
France	39%
Sweden	39%
Belgium	30%
Switzerland	28%
Japan	20%
W. Germany	17%
England	16%
U.S.A.	13%

Source: Organization for Economic Cooperation and Development

In many countries throughout the world, nuclear power is now supplying a substantial share of the electricity that people consume.

gas, and coal than either France or Japan. But oil supplies are uncertain. Natural gas is more valuable for other uses than for burning in power plants. And coal, though essential, can't be expected to do the job alone.
What is best for the practical generation of large amounts of electricity? The National Academy of Sciences has stated that "Coal and nuclear power are the only economic alternatives for large-scale application in the remainder of this century."

The cost of not pushing ahead
Through the growing use of nuclear electricity, countries all over the world are reducing their dependence on oil and strengthening their position in increasingly competitive world markets. They realize that a healthy national economy needs a healthy supply of energy.
Will we have to play a costly game of catch-up in the competition ahead? America runs the risk of doing just that—if we ignore the growing international reliance on nuclear energy, and the reasons behind that growth.

Free booklet tells more
For a free booklet that covers nuclear electricity in more detail, write to the U.S. Committee for Energy Awareness, P.O. Box 37012 (   ), Washington, D.C. 20013.

Information about energy
America can count on today
U.S. COMMITTEE FOR ENERGY AWARENESS

◿ BENJAMIN SPOCK

A Statement on Nuclear Energy

Benjamin Spock is the author of The Common Sense Book of Baby and Child Care *(first edition, 1946), the best-known book on the topic and one of the best-selling books of any kind in history (over 28 million sold so far). He was a prominent opponent of the Vietnam War and has remained politically active since then. In this essay, written in the late 1970s, he argues against the production of nuclear power on the grounds that it is unsafe and unnecessary.*

By coincidence I had this article on the dangers of nuclear power, especially 1 to children, almost finished when the frightening accident occurred at the Three Mile Island nuclear power plant near Harrisburg, Pennsylvania, a few months ago.

In 1962 I joined the National Committee for a Sane Nuclear Policy 2 because I was convinced then that if the United States and the Soviet Union did not negotiate a nuclear weapons test ban treaty, more and more children around the world would die of cancer and leukemia or be born with mental and physical defects as a result of radiation from fallout. (This conviction has been borne out by a veritable epidemic of cancer in Utah as a result of the bomb tests made in Nevada between 1951 and 1962.) As a pediatrician I saw this as a pediatrics issue, since children—born and unborn—are particularly susceptible to radiation. It was this and the horrible danger of nuclear war that led me to become an advocate of world disarmament, and later an opponent of the disastrous war in Vietnam.

Earlier, after the end of World War II, when our government and people 3 were feeling anxious and guilty about having invented and used the atom bomb, the suggestion of "atoms for peace" was received with enthusiasm. The chairman of the Atomic Energy Commission promised that nuclear power would be limitless, safe, clean, and "so cheap that it would not need to be metered."

As the years have passed all these promises have proved false. And many 4 of us have come to realize that nuclear power—on a smaller scale for peacetime use—is just as dangerous as nuclear weapons. Furthermore, the rising cost of nuclear power is mind-boggling.

As the supply of vital uranium is dwindling its cost is skyrocketing. The 5 frequency of breakdowns and of dangerous accidents in nuclear power plants has compelled more and more elaborate safeguards, and the price of a plant has gone up 1,000 percent in fifteen years. All this has caused a rapid escalation of the price of nuclear power, which is now almost as expensive as power made from oil or coal when the cost of the plant is taken into account.

There are five distinct dangers in nuclear power; the most horrible would   6
be a complete "meltdown" caused by a failure of the cooling system. Highly
lethal radioactive materials would melt through the containing walls and be
dispersed into the ground and into the atmosphere. This might promptly kill
50,000 people downwind from the plant from radiation sickness, and many
more in the succeeding thirty years from leukemia and cancer, especially in
children. And the irradiation of the germ cells in the ovaries and testicles of
exposed adults, children and unborn babies would produce mental and physical
defects for endless generations. For when mutations are produced in the germ
cells, they are passed on forever.

Most commentators spoke as if the Three Mile Island nuclear accident   7
was the first serious such accident, but it wasn't. The worst near disasters were
at Brown's Ferry, Alabama, in 1975 and at the Fermi Plant, near Detroit, in
1966. But every year there have been dozens of lesser accidents and malfunc-
tions that were threatening. Many plants have been shut down for long periods
for decontamination after accidents, for repairs and for improvements in the
safety systems. Yet our nuclear-utilities and government officials have kept
reassuring us that the plants are safe, pointing to the multiple safeguards. The
revelations of the poor functioning of the staff of Three Mile Island and of the
Nuclear Regulatory Commission showed how ill prepared and helpless are the
people who are supposed to know what to do when a nuclear plant gets out of
control.

There have been serious accidents in Canadian and European plants too.   8
And in the Soviet Union in 1958 there was a truly major disaster at Kyshtym
that devastated a large area; it is now so radioactive that it will have to be barred
to occupancy for thousands of years. It presumably killed hundreds of people,
though the Soviet Government never acknowledged the accident.

A second danger from nuclear power plants is the regular leakage of low-   9
level radiation into the atmosphere and into the water in the ground. It is now
known that low levels of radiation are harmful to at least small percentages of
the exposed population, depending on the intensity of the exposure. Thousands
of cases of leukemia and cancer are calculated to have been caused in the past
by diagnostic x-rays and by atomic weapons tests. Whether the radiation leaking
from power plants has already caused an increase in leukemia and cancer in
downwind areas is still a matter of controversy among scientists.

A third danger is from the transportation of uranium to nuclear plants—   10
and of wastes from power plants to burial sites—by railway, by highway and
through city streets. The wastes contain many radioactive substances, but the
worst by far is plutonium. An invisibly small amount of plutonium is enough
to kill a person. One pound dispersed evenly into the lungs of the world's
people would kill them all. Its poisonous effects will last for hundreds of thousands of years. The government assures us that all necessary precautions are
being taken. But the fact is that there have already been serious accidents
involving radioactive materials on the highways.

A fourth danger—and a great one—is in the permanent disposal of lethal 11
nuclear wastes. (Now they are in temporary storage at the power plants where
they were created, or in other temporary depositories.) Even the authorities,
with all their optimism, admit that they have no solution. These corrosive
mixtures in a relatively few-score years will eat through steel or concrete. If they
are buried in deep caves or mines, they will work their way into the water
supply. If they are dumped in steel drums into the ocean, which has already
happened, they will, when they begin to leak, be ingested and progressively
concentrated, as smaller fish are consumed by larger and larger fish, and eventually they will be eaten by human beings. To try to shoot the wastes into space
would be prohibitively expensive. What moral right do we have to jeopardize
the lives of our children, grandchildren and further descendants by creating a
menace against which there is no known protection?

A fifth danger looms: the theft of nuclear materials, including plutonium, 12
by terrorists. The experts agree that it would not be too difficult to steal the
materials or to make a crude bomb.

Defenders of nuclear power answer their critics by saying, "But we need 13
the power!"

My first answer is that we can surely find ways to get along without a type 14
of power that threatens to kill us, to kill our children with leukemia and cancer
and to produce deformities in our descendants till the end of time.

My second reply is that all the energy experts whose opinions I've read 15
agree that America *wastes* half the energy it now consumes. One of the largest
causes of waste is the insufficiency or absence of insulation in the walls of
houses, especially in the houses of those who can't afford the cost of insulation.

Unnecessarily hot buildings in winter, unnecessarily cold buildings in 16
summer, unnecessarily powerful cars, are other examples of energy waste.

Why is there such a strong bias in favor of nuclear power in certain 17
industries and in the federal government despite the grave dangers it entails?
The great oil companies now control the mining and processing of uranium,
the source of nuclear power, and expect to profit from it long after the oil is
gone. General Electric, Westinghouse, and two other companies make practically all the nuclear power plant equipment, and hope to make a good thing of
it. Many utility companies have planned to make an ever-increasing portion of
their profits from nuclear power. The utilities in turn are largely owned and
controlled by the most powerful banks in the country. So there is strong industrial and financial pressure for nuclear power. And since our presidents, governors, and legislators depend mainly on industry for their campaign funds, they
are obligated to listed to industry's wishes.

Most of the staff of the Nuclear Regulatory Commission, who now make 18
the decisions about safety, would no longer have their jobs if they finally concluded that nuclear power was too dangerous to be worth the risk. This being
the case, most of them, naturally, are inclined to believe that the problems can
be licked with a little more ingenuity and time. But a few who have become

convinced that the dangers are too great to justify nuclear power expansion, at least for now, have resigned or have been forced out. Three nuclear engineers at General Electric resigned in 1976 for that reason.

James Schlesinger, the secretary of the Energy Department, who always　19 pushes nuclear energy as against "renewable" energy sources, was formerly head of the Atomic Energy Commission, the precursor of the Nuclear Regulatory Commission. Both commissions have been accused many times by scientists of cover-ups, silencing critical employees and distortions of the truth.

Our Energy Department spends huge sums subsidizing nuclear power.　20 Instead it should be spending generously to encourage further research and more rapid development of power from the sun, from the winds, from the tides, from small dams, from "biomass" (manure, sewage, garbage, trash, crop residues, weeds, wood) that can be burned directly or converted to fuels such as methane gas or alcohol. These are renewable sources of energy, in contrast to oil and coal. (Coal involves serious environmental problems.)

Actually our government is spending only piddling sums to develop renew-　21 able energies. The main reasons are that the sun and winds and the tides don't promise big profits to big industries and they don't make contributions to political parties.

So it is up to ordinary citizens to tackle the job of stopping the construction　22 of more nuclear power plants and later dismantling those already built. This will take a long time and persistent effort.

You can—and should, if you agree—write letters to . . . your senators and　23 representatives, not once but every time you are reminded of the dangers. Some people don't write because they worry about how to express a letter or how to address it. Don't worry; the official may not even read your letter, but someone will count it and report on its contents. Just show how you feel. Address letters to the White House or the Energy Department or to the Senate or House of Representatives—or, better still, to all four—Washington, D.C.

Vote in coming elections for candidates who promise to work against　24 nuclear power. Join an antinuclear group and contribute to it.

Participate in demonstrations if you can overcome your shyness. This is a　25 particularly effective way to spread the word and to show the depth of your convictions, as was shown by the spiraling numbers of participators at four successive demonstrations at Seabrook, New Hampshire, over a two-year period—18 at the first demonstration, 180 at the second, 2,400 at the third and 20,000 at the fourth, and as was shown by the participation of an estimated 100,000 people in an anti-nuclear-energy demonstration in Washington, D.C., shortly after the dangerous accident at Three Mile Island plant.

PETER FREUNDLICH

Gazing into Bergdorf's Window

Peter Freundlich is a writer who has reflected on several topics for Harper's *magazine. This essay appeared in the December 1987 issue and concerns what he takes to be the fact that we are, "thanks to the yuppie, mad with connoisseurship, nuts with our own discriminations."*

A while back I saw a piece on the evening news, a cutesy-poo feature about a   1
summer camp in Palm Beach. Wholesome, innocent, happy-seeming eight-
and ten- and twelve-year olds, boys and girls both, were at this camp to sit at
the knees of professional deal-makers, to learn the ins and out of the buck-
turning arts and sciences: stocks, bonds, corporate mergers, leveraged buy-outs,
portfolio management, you know.

The kids, blonde and blue-eyed mostly, were enthusiastic and clearly   2
much interested in the claptrap being expounded. Their whole bodies shook,
the way the tail wags the happy dog, when they raised their hands to signal
their desire to ask a question. And they asked *deep* questions, I am sorry to say,
about debentures and junk bonds and accounting methods and the Japanese
challenge.

Sic transit Huck Finn.   3

We were ordinary folk once, our dreams simple: a few chickens, a tar-   4
paper shack to call our own, an extra pair of overalls into which to change on
Sundays, a crystal radio. But now something new has been loosed among us,
loosed as the H-bomb was loosed, and we are red hot in mid-mutation. Instead
of being satisfied with a ham sandwich, we want for a snack goat-cheese pizza
with sun-dried morels; instead of all-cotton, we wear for our tennis athletic
socks of lapin fur; instead of refrigerator ice, we plop hearts of glacier ice cubes
into our Cartesian well water.

How did we get from there to here? What fantastic dream dreamed by the   5
world's merchants—by haberdashers and restaurateurs and real-estate developers and automobile salesmen lost in transports of nocturnal greed—revealed
to the multitude the wonder of the higher shopping? By what pure act of will
did the dream become flesh? How did the divine word turn first into a fat
wallet, clay-soft so that it could tease and stretch itself into a Giacometti-like
human being? When the dream was done, there stood the yuppie: the smooth-
faced monster of consumerism, teeth like pearls, eyes like coals, slouching
toward Bloomingdale's to be born.

The yuppie is the dream buyer, the dream buyer in both senses of that   6
phrase: the buyer dreamed of by sellers everywhere, the buyer with money to
burn; and the one who, just like that, buys what the rest of us only dream
about, the one who buys dreams, easily, without huddling to consider, or

agonizing, or feeling his parents' guilt and trepidation over laying out what took so long to amass. Because it *didn't* take long, you see. Easy come, easy go. Nice car. I'll take it. Nice house. I'll take it. Nice dog. I'll take two.

And now the world. I mean the *made* world, the world as fashioned by 7 manufacturers and offered for sale, is being fashioned for *him*.

Look you everywhere, and see! The search now is for the very best, the 8 most rare, the empyrean, the nonpareil. We need not ask anymore who or what it is that has inherited the earth: we *know*. It is the walking wallet with the coal-black eyes, in search of underwear handwoven by Tibetan virgins, in search of silk foulard toilet paper, badger-bristle johnny-mops, microchip-controlled shoelaces of braided platinum wire that make a fine little beep when they come untied, fish-tank gravel of pulverized moonrock, coffee beans certified to have ripened in the very first shaft of morning light at the tippy top of a sacred mountain in Kenya, ham from the hock of a pig that has drunk only spring water and which has been read Japanese love poetry at bedtime from piglet-hood on.

We are, thanks to the yuppie, mad with connoisseurship, nuts with our 9 own discriminations.

Maybe we inhabit a dream, a fiction, a continentwide mirage that may 10 dissipate at any moment. But in the meantime, we *will* have hand-sewn mattresses stuffed with angora fleeces, bedframes laminated of twigs gathered atop Mount Sinai, briefcases of tooled llama-leather, bespoke shoes of water-buffalo hide cured with the spittle of Saint Bernard puppies.

I tell you we are discriminating ourselves out of existence. If our hanker- 11 ings become any more refined, we shall die of hunger and go naked and unhoused. We are incapable of settling anymore, incapable of compromising. If the jam was not compounded of berries from the sunny side of the bush, we will not have it. If the grain of the bread was not milled between stones quarried in Jerusalem, we will not eat it. If the time is not told by a movement that turns on diamonds and is housed in a case carved of a single hollowed ingot of gold, we will not know it. We turn away from the base and the common. We are like Geiger counters calibrated for preciousness, our hearts clicking harder, faster in the presence of the rare.

We do not blanch anymore at the hundred-dollar snack, the several- 12 hundred-dollar shirt, the hundred-thousand-dollar car, the forty-million-dollar painting. Van Gogh was mad? Piffle. Look at us.

Lunch now is a horrifying business. There is the speaking menu, for one 13 thing: the tanned waiter with the slicked-back hair who recites the miracles the chef has this day performed. Are the tomatoes from Provence? Are they vine ripened? Was baroque music piped into the field in which they grew, and was that music from an analogue or a digital source? Are those who picked the tomatoes graduates of an *école normale* or *supérieure*? What, other than tomatoes, are their larger interests in life? Philosophy, music, painting, dance? For lunch to have its fullest efflorescence, we need to know something about those who gathered the ingredients of which it was made.

And what of the chef? What has been the main influence on his style, St. 14
Thomas Aquinas or the Veda, or is he a Kantian or a pantheist or what? Tell,
man, tell.

And speak, I pray you, the long list of arcane fruits and vegetables from 15
which, with a flutter of my eyes, I may choose. Say the names, man; say them.
Be, for this little time, like Adam or Eve on Naming Day: chicory, radicchio,
endive, chard, roquette, purslane, sorrel, pepper grass, frankincense, myrrh.

And recite, as once the oracles recited their portending dreams, with eyes 16
rolled back, the dishes available and their manners of preparation: say the shark
has been a fortnight steeped in a caper-laced brine of Aegean water and old
retsina, and then wrapped in parchment and baked underground in clay. Say
it. Say that there is rose-hip sorbet for dessert, surmounted with sheep's milk
whipped-cream and individually glazed elderberries. Go on, man: don't make
me drag it out of you. Tell me you have loin-of-pork salad at room temperature,
made monastery-style and served with a chain-mail doublet of pasta links.

We need now to know the provenance of everything, of our snacks and 17
our trinkets and our bits of garb, so as to be assured that, having paid ransoms
for the stuff, we have indeed gotten the goods. All our purchases must have
attached to them certificates of pedigree and booklets telling the little-known
stories of their evolution in out-of-the-way places among generations of kindly,
nature-loving, magic-touched peoples whose wisdom is far too simple for us to
understand. Indeed, it is the certificates and the storybooks we buy, really, not
the things from which they hang these pretty tags.

Step into the clothing department, please. Here at the *schmatterer* it is as 18
it is at the bistro too. We have dangled before us first the crème de la crème
and then the crème de la crème de la crème: Sea Island cotton, pima cotton,
Egyptian cotton, Swiss cotton, tweeds from the Outer Hebrides. The winding-
sheet of the Inca himself could not have been of finer stuff.

The designers are all celebrities, artists really, *soi*-(and by all the rest of us) 19
disant and, as such, they sign their works in conspicuous places. We would not
have it otherwise. So we walk around in scrawled-upon silk caftans, and suit
jackets the shoulders of which fall down over our own shoulders, like dogs'
ears, and in trousers three sizes too big at the waist so that they need to be
gathered like the neck of a highwayman's loot bag. Only we do the gathering
with a lizard belt ($550, Jacques B. Nimble; shoes of hand-stitched marmoset
pelts, $2,540, O Sole Mio; pumpkin-colored burlap-weave linen tie, $105,
Buck Neckèd; puce fisherman's cardigan of hand-shorn, -carded, -loomed, and
-knitted Nepalese mountain-goat wool, $38,950, Bon Dieu, by appointment
only).

Thus attired, we taxi home. Home ain't what it used to be either. 20

On nearly every corner now in Manhattan, condominium apartments sell 21
for many hundreds of thousands of dollars or, when they rent, for many thousands of dollars a month. A quick calculation shows that, in order for a person
to live in a $3,000-a-month apartment (which comes to $36,000-a-year), that
person needs to be making much more than twice that amount; after taxes,

making only seventy-two Gs, he'd be meeting the rent only, and would be squatting hungry and naked on his parquet floor.

The buildings are ersatz grand, sold in their prospectuses as throwbacks to   22 the rambling baronial palazzi built in the Twenties on Park and West End and Riverside. In all but a few, though (and those few cost millions, not hundreds of thousands), the baronial touches are tiny ones: fancy faucets, video intercoms, built-in kitchen gee-gaws. The rooms themselves are otherwise the same nasty dual-purpose boxes found in most postwar buildings: living/dining, bed/study, bath/dressing, entrance/foyer. The slash is the builder's best friend these days; I expect soon to see floorplans boasting bath/guest room, closet/library, hall/stables, pantry/swimming pool.

From our vantage point in the doorway/wine cellar, let us scan panorami-   23 cally one such set of digs. Immediately we see the BMW Effect. In the hopes of making whatever they produce as much the wanted thing as the BMW is among cars, manufacturers have streamlined and attempted to imbue with engineering mystique every article of dreck they turn out. Thus we have racing blenders and racing toasters and racing coffee-makers. We have racing desk lamps that have clearly been tested in wind tunnels and that have lower coefficients of drag than jet fighters.

Perhaps it was the Sexual Revolution that brought us here. For a decade   24 or so, we were our own toys. With religious, with almost childlike intensity, we played with ourselves and with each other. But see where all that got us. We have loosed a horde of dreadful new diseases upon ourselves, spawned oceanic schools of invisible love-borne piranhas that eat their ways into us and then eat their ways back out again, leaving us riven, as dry and drilled as dead coral.

So we have turned to things, which we can feel but which cannot feel us.   25
Not that we *really* feel.   26

It would be easy to dismiss the yuppie as the bellwether of materialism.   27 But the truth is sadder than that. For the yuppie is not a materialist, and those of us exhausted by the yuppie's example are not materialists either. Would that we were, really were, materialists, genuinely in love with the stuff of which the world is made. But we are not. Yuppies are, and we have by them been forced to become, symbolists. The yuppie covets not the thing itself but the thing as symbol. The Rolex on the yuppie's wrist is a statement only of his ability to spend on a watch what most cannot scratch together for a used car. He is blind to the material itself, mindless of the coming of gold by sweat and hatred and death out of the ground.

The yuppie is, he thinks, the point toward which the striving restless riches   28 of the world tend. Thus, the glittering fish lashing itself along past the atolls off Key West is *meant* for him, means itself for him, knows its destiny to be a bath of snail butter on a gold-rimmed plate in a sconce-lighted and palm-fronded room on Columbus Avenue. Enormities before which we should quail, we tame by buying.

The tall teak felled in some wild green forest by men in breechclouts and   29 then elephant-dragged out of the tangle down to a brown river to be lashed onto a raft with other trees to be floated from village to village to town to city to great port, there to be put aboard some rusting many-funneled freighter, and to end at last in the plank-making spray of the buzz saw at a dockside mill and under the shaping hands of a few craftsmen—that tree from the heart of darkness squats in our living rooms, holding up our coffee-table books and a piece or two of well-chosen art glass. We can put our hands upon the wood and feel nothing: not the beating heart of the mahout, not the slapping of the river, not the pulse of the ship's engines, not the wind of the saw, not the creak in the knee of the craftsman as he crouches to look at eye-level at the joint he has made.

We are dead to the things we covet, understanding them only as show-   30
pieces, show-off pieces, albeit we show them off, in the main, properly, understatedly. Not long ago, William Carlos Williams urged that we have "no ideas but in things." Ah, but wouldn't he be surprised now to find that what was only a plank in his aesthetic platform we have taken up literally as an all-purpose creed. We have now no ideas but in things.

What we have here is a New Romanticism, except now we adore the   31
manufactured instead of the natural world. Where once Tennysonians swooned, literally swooned, on the banks of peaceful rivers, soul-struck by the perfection of a world not dependent in the least on man, now we swoon over artificial beauties. We would have "Ode to a Mercedes-Benz" now or "Upon First Looking into Bergdorf's Window."

✂ **SIDNEY HOOK**

In Defense of Voluntary Euthanasia

Sidney Hook is a very well known pragmatist philosopher who in addition to technical philosophical tracts has written many essays on social/political issues, including this essay that draws on bitter personal experience to argue in favor of voluntary euthanasia.

A few short years ago, I lay at the point of death. A congestive heart failure was   1
treated for diagnostic purposes by an angiogram that triggered a stroke. Violent and painful hiccups, uninterrupted for several days and nights, prevented the ingestion of food. My left side and one of my vocal cords became paralyzed.

Some form of pleurisy set in, and I felt I was drowning in a sea of slime. At one point, my heart stopped beating; just as I lost consciousness, it was thumped back into action again. In one of my lucid intervals during those days of agony, I asked my physician to discontinue all life-supporting services or show me how to do it. He refused and predicted that someday I would appreciate the unwisdom of my request.

A month later, I was discharged from the hospital. In six months, I re-   2 gained the use of my limbs, and although my voice still lacks its old resonance and carrying power I no longer croak like a frog. There remain some minor disabilities and I am restricted to a rigorous, low sodium diet. I have resumed my writing and research.

My experience can be and has been cited as an argument against honoring   3 requests of stricken patients to be gently eased out of their pain and life. I cannot agree. There are two main reasons. As an octogenarian, there is a reasonable likelihood that I may suffer another "cardiovascular accident" or worse. I may not even be in a position to ask for the surcease of pain. It seems to me that I have already paid my dues to death—indeed, although time has softened my memories they are vivid enough to justify my saying that I suffered enough to warrant dying several times over. Why run the risk of more?

Secondly, I dread imposing on my family and friends another grim round   4 of misery similar to the one my first attack occasioned.

My wife and children endured enough for one lifetime. I know that for   5 them the long days and nights of waiting, the disruption of their professional duties and their own familial responsibilities counted for nothing in their anxiety for me. In their joy at my recovery they have been forgotten. Nonetheless, to visit another prolonged spell of helpless suffering on them as my life ebbs away, or even worse, if I linger on into a comatose senility, seems altogether gratuitous.

But what, it may be asked, of the joy and satisfaction of living, of basking   6 in the sunlight, listening to music, watching one's grandchildren growing into adolescence, following the news about the fate of freedom in a troubled world, playing with ideas, writing one's testament of wisdom and folly for posterity? Is not all that one endured, together with the risk of its recurrence, an acceptable price for the multiple satisfactions that are still open even to a person of advanced years?

Apparently those who cling to life, no matter what, think so. I do not.   7

The zest and intensity of these experiences are no longer what they used   8 to be. I am not vain enough to delude myself that I can in the few remaining years make an important discovery useful for mankind or can lead a social movement or do anything that will be historically eventful, no less event-making. My autobiography, which describes a record of intellectual and political experiences of some historical value, already much too long, could be posthumously published. I have had my fill of joys and sorrows and am not greedy for more life. I have always thought that a test of whether one had found happiness in one's life is whether one would be willing to relive it—whether, if it were possible, one would accept the opportunity to be born again.

Having lived a full and relatively happy life, I would cheerfully accept the 9 chance to be reborn, but certainly not to be reborn again as an infirm octogenarian. To some extent, my views reflect what I have seen happen to the aged and stricken who have been so unfortunate as to survive crippling paralysis. They suffer, and impose suffering on others, unable even to make a request that their torment be ended.

I am mindful too of the burdens placed upon the community, with its 10 rapidly diminishing resources, to provide the adequate and costly services necessary to sustain the lives of those whose days and nights are spent on mattress graves of pain. A better use could be made of these resources to increase the opportunities and qualities of life for the young. I am not denying the moral obligation the community has to look after its disabled and aged. There are times, however, when an individual may find it pointless to insist on the fulfillment of a legal and moral right.

What is required is no great revolution in morals but an enlargement of 11 imagination and an intelligent evaluation of alternative uses of community resources.

Long ago, Seneca observed that "the wise man will live as long as he 12 ought, not as long as he can." One can envisage hypothetical circumstances in which one has a duty to prolong one's life despite its costs for the sake of others, but such circumstances are far removed from the ordinary prospects we are considering. If wisdom is rooted in knowledge of the alternatives of choice, it must be reliably informed of the state one is in and its likely outcome. Scientific medicine is not infallible, but it is the best we have. Should a rational person be willing to endure acute suffering merely on the chance that a miraculous cure might presently be at hand? Each one should be permitted to make his own choice—especially when no one else is harmed by it.

The responsibility for the decision, whether deemed wise or foolish, must 13 be with the chooser.

THE QUALITY OF MODERN LIFE

QUESTIONS AND SUGGESTIONS FOR WRITING

1. Fussell claims "the middle class is distinguishable more by its earnestness and psychic insecurity than by its middle income." It is "obsessed with doing everything right"; it is afflicted with "status panic." What is the tone of his essay? Does it help persuade you to his point of view? Explain.

2. How does Worsthorne define the new "meritocracy"? What do you think of the idea that members of this group are "immensely privileged and must, as a class, behave accordingly . . . by paying a far higher social price, in terms of taxation, in terms of service, for the privilege of exercising their talents"?

3. Methvin provides evidence to support the theory that violence on television leads to aggressive behavior. Evaluate his evidence carefully to determine whether it is convincing. Further, supposing that it is convincing, would this be sufficient reason to campaign for a reduction in TV violence, given the obvious fact that masses of people enjoy and even prefer violent programs?

4. Do you agree with Julber that America's wilderness areas should be made more accessible to the public? Or do you think that access to these areas should remain restricted? Why?

5. Although Lockett has been a lifelong conservationist, he is opposed to the International Wildlife Coalition's whale rescue project. What reasons does he give in support of his position? Do you find his reasoning convincing? Why or why not?

6. Spock sees the dangers of nuclear power as a definite threat to the quality of modern life. Do some research on the five dangers he discusses and try to determine how serious the threat of nuclear power really is.

7. Why does Freundlich title his essay "Gazing into Bergdorf's Window"? What does the title have to do with his notion that we are celebrating a New Romanticism, "except now we adore the manufactured world instead of the natural world"? What do you think of his use of exaggeration to make his point? Explain his position and provide evidence from your own experience to support or refute this idea.

8. Write a short essay arguing for or against voluntary euthenasia.

9. Do some research on the life of people in another century. Choose members of a particular class and contrast them to members of the same class in America today. Then discuss whether the quality of life is better today or in another century.

POLITICAL RHETORIC

Although most of the readings in this section contain genuinely argumentative parts, they differ from the readings in the other sections of the text in the proportion of rational and emotional appeals they contain, and in general they are less likely to be cogent. But they all are excellent examples of *persuasive* rhetoric; indeed, one or two of them have probably had a serious effect on the course of history (for instance, Winston Churchill's World War II speech that helped to buck up the spirits and resolve of the English people to fight to the end against Hitler and the Nazis).

✄ WILLIAM SHAKESPEARE

Mark Antony: Oration on the Dead Body of Julius Caesar

While the following oration was written by Shakespeare, it is based on historical accounts of Mark Antony's (83 – 30 B.C.) actual address. The circumstances were that Julius Caesar had just been murdered by Brutus ("Et tu Brute?") and others disgruntled by Caesar's leadership.

ANTONY.   Friends, Romans, countrymen, lend me your ears;   1
I come to bury Caesar, not to praise him.
The evil that men do lives after them;
The good is oft interred with their bones;
So let it be with Caesar. The noble Brutus
Hath told you Caesar was ambitious:
If it were so, it was a grievous fault,
And grievously hath Caesar answer'd it.
Here, under leave of Brutus and the rest,—
For Brutus is an honourable man;   2
So are they all, all honourable men;

Come I to speak in Caesar's funeral.
He was my friend, faithful and just to me:
But Brutus says he was ambitious;
And Brutus is an honourable man.
He hath brought many captives home to Rome,
Whose ransoms did the general coffers fill:
Did this in Caesar seem ambitious?
When that the poor have cried, Caesar hath wept:
Ambition should be made of sterner stuff: 3
Yet Brutus says he was ambitious;
And Brutus is an honourable man.
You all did see that on the Lupercal
I thrice presented him a kingly crown,
Which he did thrice refuse: was this ambition?
Yet Brutus says he was ambitious;
And, sure, he is an honourable man.
I speak not to disprove what Brutus spoke,
But here I am to speak what I do know.
You all did love him once, not without cause: 4
What cause withholds you then to mourn for him?
O judgment; thou are fled to brutish beasts,
And men have lost their reason. Bear with me;
My heart is in the coffin there with Caesar,
And I must pause till it come back to me.
FIRST CITIZEN.   Methinks there is much reason in his sayings.
SECOND CITIZEN.   If you consider rightly of the matter, Caesar has had great
    wrong.
THIRD CITIZEN.   Has he, masters?
I fear there will a worse come in his place.   5
FOURTH CITIZEN.   Mark'd ye his words? He would not take the crown;
Therefore 'tis certain he was not ambitious.
FIRST CITIZEN.   If it be found so, some will dear abide it.
SECOND CITIZEN.   Poor soul! his eyes are red as fire with weeping.
THIRD CITIZEN.   There's not a nobler man in Rome than Antony.
FOURTH CITIZEN.   Now mark him, he begins again to speak.
ANTONY.   But yesterday the word of Caesar might
Have stood against the world: now lies he there,
And none so poor to do him reverence.
O masters, if I were disposed to stir   6
Your hearts and minds to mutiny and rage,
I should do Brutus wrong and Cassius wrong
Who, you all know, are honourable men.
I will not do them wrong; I rather choose
To wrong the dead, to wrong myself and you,
Than I will wrong such honourable men.

But here's a parchment with the seal of Caesar;
I found it in his closet; 'tis his will:
Let but the commons hear this testament—   7
Which pardon me, I do not mean to read—
And they would go and kiss dead Caesar's wounds
And dip their napkins in his sacred blood,
Yea, beg a hair of him for memory,
And, dying, mention it within their wills,
Bequeathing it as a rich legacy
Unto their issue.
FOURTH CITIZEN.   We'll hear the will; read it, Mark Antony.
ALL.   The will, the will! we will hear Caesar's will.
ANTONY.   Have patience, gentle friends, I must not read it;
It is not meet you know how Caesar loved you.   8
You are not wood, you are not stones, but men;
And, being men, hearing the will of Caesar,
It will inflame you, it will make you mad:
'Tis good you know not that you are his heirs;
For if you should, O, what would come of it.
FOURTH CITIZEN.   Read the will; we'll hear it, Antony;
You shall read the will, Caesar's will.
ANTONY.   Will you be patient? will you stay awhile?
I have o'ershot myself to tell you of it:
I fear I wrong the honourable men   9
Whose daggers have stabb'd Caesar; I do fear it.
FOURTH CITIZEN.   They were traitors: honourable men!
ALL.   The will! the testament!
SECOND CITIZEN.   They were villains, murderers: the will! read the will.
ANTONY.   You will compel me then to read the will?
Then make a ring about the corpse of Caesar,
And let me show you him that made the will.
Shall I descend? and will you give me leave?
ALL.   Come down.
SECOND CITIZEN.   Descend.   [*He comes down from the pulpit.*]   10
THIRD CITIZEN.   You shall have leave.
FOURTH CITIZEN.   A ring; stand round.
FIRST CITIZEN.   Stand from the hearse, stand from the body.
SECOND CITIZEN.   Room for Antony, most noble Antony.
ANTONY.   Nay, press not so upon me; stand far off.
ALL.   Stand back. Room. Bear back.
ANTONY.   If you have tears, prepare to shed them now.
You all do know this mantle: I remember
The first time ever Caesar put it on;
'Twas on a summer's evening, in his tent,   11
That day he overcame the Nervii:

Look, in this place ran Cassius' dagger through:
See what a rent the envious Casca made:
Through this the well-belov'd Brutus stabb'd;
And as he pluck'd his cursed steel away,
Mark how the blood of Caesar follow'd it,
As rushing out of doors, to be resolved
If Brutus so unkindly knock'd, or no:
For Brutus, as you know, was Caesar's angel:
Judge, O you gods, how dearly Caesar loved him.   12
This was the most unkindest cut of all;
For when the noble Caesar saw him stab,
Ingratitude, more strong than traitors' arms,
Quite vanquish'd him: then burst his mighty heart;
And, in his mantle muffling up his face,
Even at the base of Pompey's statue,
Which all the while ran blood, great Caesar fell.
O, what a fall was there, my countrymen!
Then I, and you, and all of us fell down,
Whilst bloody treason flourish'd over us.
O, now you weep, and I perceive you feel   13
The dint of pity: these are gracious drops.
Kind souls, what weep you when you but behold
Our Caesar's vesture wounded? Look you here,
Here is himself, marr'd, as you see, with traitors.
FIRST CITIZEN.   O piteous spectacle!
SECOND CITIZEN.   O noble Caesar!
THIRD CITIZEN.   O woful day!
FOURTH CITIZEN.   O traitors, villains!
FIRST CITIZEN.   O most bloody sight!   14
SECOND CITIZEN.   We will be revenged.
ALL.   Revenge! About! Seek! Burn! Fire!
Kill! Slay! Let not a traitor live!
ANTONY.   Stay, countrymen.
FIRST CITIZEN.   Peace there! hear the noble Antony.
SECOND CITIZEN.   We'll hear him, we'll follow him, we'll die with him.
ANTONY.   Good friends, sweet friends, let me not stir you up
To such a sudden flood of mutiny.
They that have done this deed are honourable;   15
What private griefs they have, alas, I know not,
That made them do it; they are wise and honourable,
And will, no doubt, with reasons answer you.
I come not, friends, to steal away your hearts: I am no orator, as Brutus is;
But, as you know me all, a plain blunt man,
That love my friend; and that they know full well

That gave me public leave to speak of him:
For I have neither wit, nor words, nor worth,   16
Action, nor utterance, nor the power of speech,
To stir men's blood: I only speak right on;
I tell you that which you yourselves do know;
Show you sweet Caesar's wounds, poor poor dumb mouths,
And bid them speak for me: but were I Brutus,
And Brutus Antony, there were an Antony
Would ruffle up your spirits, and put a tongue
In every wound of Caesar, that should move
The stones of Rome to rise and mutiny.
ALL.   We'll mutiny.
FIRST CITIZEN.   We'll burn the house of Brutus.   17
THIRD CITIZEN.   Away, then! come, seek the conspirators.
ANTONY.   Yet hear me, countrymen; yet hear me speak.
ALL.   Peace, ho! Hear Antony. Most noble Antony!
ANTONY.   Why, friends, you go to do you know not what: wherein hath Caesar
    thus deserved your loves?
Alas, you know not; I must tell you then:
You have forgot the will I told you of.
ALL.   Most true: the will! Let's stay and hear the will.
ANTONY.   Here is the will, and under Caesar's seal.
To every Roman citizen he gives,   18
To every several man, seventy-five drachmas.
SECOND CITIZEN.   Most noble Caesar! we'll revenge his death.
THIRD CITIZEN.   O royal Caesar!
ANTONY.   Hear me with patience.
ALL.   Peace, ho!
ANTONY.   Moreover, he hath left you all his walks,
His private arbours and new-planted orchards,
On this side Tiber; he hath left them you,
And to your heirs for ever; common pleasures,
To walk abroad and recreate yourselves.
Here was a Caesar! when comes such another?   19
FIRST CITIZEN.   Never, never. Come, away, away!
We'll burn his body in the holy place,
And with the brands fire the traitors' houses.
Take up the body.
SECOND CITIZEN.   Go fetch fire.
THIRD CITIZEN.   Pluck down benches.
FOURTH CITIZEN.   Pluck down forms, windows, anything.
                            [*Exeunt Citizens with the body.*]
ANTONY.   Now let it work. Mischief, thou art afoot, take thou what course
thou wilt.

⊠ **PATRICK HENRY**

Give Me Liberty, or Give Me Death

Patrick Henry (1736–1799), Virginia patriot, who may or may not have said "If this be treason, make the most of it," when his challenges to the authority of the British crown were charged with treason, delivered this oration at a crucial moment just before the birth of a new nation—the United States of America. His intent, obviously, was to stir the colonies into rebellion.

MR. PRESIDENT: No man thinks more highly than I do of the patriotism, as 1 well as abilities of the very worthy gentlemen who have just addressed the House. But different men often see the same subject in different lights; and, therefore, I hope that it will not be thought disrespectful to those gentlemen, if, entertaining as I do, opinions of a character very opposite to theirs, I shall speak forth my sentiments freely and without reserve. This is no time for ceremony. The question before the House is one of awful moment to this country. For my own part I consider it as nothing less than a question of freedom or slavery; and in proportion to the magnitude of the subject ought to be the freedom of the debate. It is only in this way that we can hope to arrive at truth, and fulfill the great responsibility which we hold to God and our country. Should I keep back my opinions at such a time, through fear of giving offence, I should consider myself as guilty of treason towards my country, and of an act of disloyalty towards the majesty of heaven, which I revere above all earthly kings.

Mr. President, it is natural to man to indulge in the illusions of hope. We 2 are apt to shut our eyes against a painful truth, and listen to the song of that siren, till she transforms us into beasts. Is this the part of wise men, engaged in a great and arduous struggle for liberty? Are we disposed to be of the number of those who, having eyes, see not, and having ears, hear not, the things which so nearly concern their temporal salvation? For my part, whatever anguish of spirit it may cost, I am willing to know the whole truth; to know the worst and to provide for it.

I have but one lamp by which my feet are guided; and that is the lamp of 3 experience. I know of no way of judging of the future but by the past. And judging by the past, I wish to know what there has been in the conduct of the British ministry for the last ten years, to justify those hopes with which gentlemen have been pleased to solace themselves and the House? Is it that insidious smile with which our petition has been lately received? Trust it not, sir; it will prove a snare to your feet. Suffer not yourselves to be betrayed with a kiss. Ask yourselves how this gracious reception of our petition comports with these warlike preparations which cover our waters and darken our land. Are fleets and armies necessary to a work of love and reconciliation? Have we shown ourselves so unwilling to be reconciled, that force must be called in to win back our love? Let us not deceive ourselves, sir. These are the implements of war and subjugation; the last arguments to which kings resort.

I ask gentlemen, sir, what means this martial array, if its purpose be not to   4 force us to submission? Can gentlemen assign any other possible motives for it? Has Great Britain any enemy, in this quarter of the world, to call for all this accumulation of navies and armies? No, sir, she has none. They are meant for us; they can be meant for no other. They are sent over to bind and rivet upon us those chains which the British ministry have been so long forging. And what have we to oppose to them? Shall we try argument? Sir, we have been trying that for the last ten years. Have we anything new to offer on the subject? Nothing. We have held the subject up in every light of which it is capable; but it has been all in vain. Shall we resort to entreaty and humble supplication? What terms shall we find which have not been already exhausted? Let us not, I beseech you, sir, deceive ourselves longer. Sir, we have done everything that could be done, to avert the storm which is now coming on. We have petitioned; we have remonstrated; we have supplicated; we have prostrated ourselves before the throne, and have implored its interposition to arrest the tyrannical hands of the ministry and Parliament. Our petitions have been slighted; our remonstrances have produced additional violence and insult; our supplications have been disregarded; and we have been spurned, with contempt, from the foot of the throne. In vain, after these things, may we indulge the fond hope of peace and reconciliation. There is no longer any room for hope. If we wish to be free—if we mean to preserve inviolate those inestimable privileges for which we have been so long contending—if we mean not basely to abandon the noble struggle in which we have been so long engaged, and which we have pledged ourselves never to abandon until the glorious object of our contest shall be obtained, we must fight! I repeat it, sir, we must fight! An appeal to arms and to the God of Hosts is all that is left us!

They tell us, sir, that we are weak; unable to cope with so formidable an   5 adversary. But when shall we be stronger? Will it be the next week, or the next year? Will it be when we are totally disarmed, and when a British guard shall be stationed in every house? Shall we gather strength by irresolution and inaction? Shall we acquire the means of effectual resistance, by lying supinely on our backs, and hugging the delusive phantom of hope, until our enemies shall have bound us hand and foot? Sir, we are not weak, if we make proper use of the means which the God of nature hath placed in our power. Three millions of people, armed in the holy cause of liberty, and in such a country as that which we possess, are invincible by any force which our enemy can send against us. Besides, sir, we shall not fight our battles alone. There is a just God who presides over the destinies of nations; and who will raise up friends to fight our battles for us. The battle, sir, is not to the strong alone; it is to the vigilant, the active, the brave. Besides, sir, we have no election. If we were base enough to desire it, it is now too late to retire from the contest. There is no retreat, but in submission and slavery! Our chains are forged! Their clanking may be heard on the plains of Boston! The war is inevitable—and let it come! I repeat it, sir, let it come!

It is in vain, sir, to extenuate the matter. Gentlemen may cry peace, 6 peace—but there is no peace. The war is actually begun! The next gale that sweeps from the north will bring to our ears the clash of resounding arms! Our brethren are already in the field! Why stand we here idle? What is it that gentlemen wish? What would they have? Is life so dear, or peace so sweet, as to be purchased at the price of chains and slavery? Forbid it, Almighty God! I know not what course others may take; but as for me, give me liberty, or give me death!

⊠ **ABRAHAM LINCOLN**

Address at Gettysburg

Abraham Lincoln (1809–1865), the sixteenth and some would say the greatest American president, delivered this succinct gem at the site of what was perhaps the decisive battle of the Civil War. It illustrates the power of a few well-chosen ordinary words to provide an inspirational justification for that war.

Fourscore and seven years ago our fathers brought forth on this continent a new nation, conceived in liberty and dedicated to the proposition that all men are created equal. Now we are engaged in a great civil war, testing whether that nation, or any nation so conceived and so dedicated, can long endure. We are met on a great battlefield of that war. We have come to dedicate a portion of that field as a final resting place for those who here gave their lives that that nation might live. It is altogether fitting and proper that we should do this. But, in a larger sense, we cannot dedicate—we cannot consecrate—we cannot hallow—this ground. The brave men, living and dead, who struggled here have consecrated it far above our poor power to add or to detract. The world will little note nor long remember what we say here, but it can never forget what they did here. It is for us, the living, rather to be dedicated here to the unfinished work which they who fought here have thus far so nobly advanced. It is rather for us to be here dedicated to the great task remaining before us—that from these honored dead we take increased devotion to that cause for which they gave the last full measure of devotion; that we here highly resolve that these dead shall not have died in vain; that this nation, under God, shall have a new birth of freedom; and that government of the people, by the people, for the people, shall not perish from the earth.

☒ FRANKLIN D. ROOSEVELT

The Only Thing We Have to Fear Is Fear Itself

Franklin D. Roosevelt (1882–1945) is the only U.S. president to serve more than two terms in office. He was also the first president to make effective use of the radio in communicating with the American people. The following excerpts are taken from his 1933 inaugural address, delivered at the height of the Great Depression when American spirits were low. Millions of people heard and were cheered by his immortal statement that "the only thing we have to fear is fear itself." (The statement was a lie, of course, but a great one nevertheless—exactly what a dispirited people needed to hear.)

I am certain that my fellow Americans expect that on my induction into the   1
Presidency I will address them with a candor and a decision which the present situation of our Nation impels. This is preeminently the time to speak the truth, the whole truth, frankly and boldly. Nor need we shrink from honestly facing conditions in our country today. This great Nation will endure as it has endured, will revive and will prosper. So, first of all, let me assert my firm belief that the only thing we have to fear is *fear itself*—nameless, unreasoning, unjustified terror which paralyzes needed efforts to convert retreat into advance. In every dark hour of our national life a leadership of frankness and vigor has met with that understanding and support of the people themselves which is essential to victory. I am convinced that you will again give that support to leadership in these critical days.

In such a spirit on my part and on yours we face our common difficulties.   2
They concern, thank God, only material things. Values have shrunken to fantastic levels; taxes have risen; our ability to pay has fallen; government of all kinds is faced by serious curtailment of income; the means of exchange are frozen in the currents of trade; the withered leaves of industrial enterprise lie on every side; farmers find no markets for their produce; the savings of many years in thousands of families are gone.

More important, a host of unemployed citizens face the grim problem of ₃ existence, and an equally great number toil with little return. Only a foolish optimist can deny the dark realities of the moment. . . .

Our greatest primary task is to put people to work. This is no unsolvable ₄ problem if we face it wisely and courageously. It can be accomplished in part by direct recruiting by the Government itself, treating the task as we would treat the emergency of a war, but at the same time, through this employment, accomplishing greatly needed projects to stimulate and reorganize the use of our natural resources.

Hand in hand with this we must frankly recognize the overbalance of ₅ population in our industrial centers and, by engaging on a national scale in a redistribution, endeavor to provide a better use of the land for those best fitted for the land. The task can be helped by definite efforts to raise the values of agricultural products and, with this, the power to purchase the output of our cities. It can be helped by preventing realistically the tragedy of the growing loss through foreclosure of our small homes and our farms. It can be helped by insistence that the federal, state, and local governments act forthwith on the demand that their cost be drastically reduced. It can be helped by the unifying of relief activities which today are often scattered, uneconomical, and unequal. It can be helped by national planning for and supervision of all forms of transportation and of communications and other utilities which have a definitely public character. There are many ways in which it can be helped, but it can never be helped merely by talking about it. We must act and act quickly.

Finally, in our progress toward a resumption of work we require two safe- ₆ guards against a return of the evils of the old order: there must be a strict supervision of all banking and credits and investments, so that there will be an end to speculation with other people's money; and there must be provisions for an adequate but sound currency.

These are the lines of attack. I shall presently urge upon a new Congress, ₇ in special session, detailed measures for their fulfillment, and I shall seek the immediate assistance of the several States.

Through this program of action we address ourselves to putting our own ₈ national house in order. . . . Our Constitution is so simple and practical that it is possible always to meet extraordinary needs by changes in emphasis and arrangements without loss of essential form. That is why our constitutional system has proved itself the most superbly enduring political mechanism the modern world has produced. It has met every stress of vast expansion of territory, of foreign wars, of bitter internal strife, of world relations.

It is to be hoped that the normal balance of Executive and legislative ₉ authority may be wholly adequate to meet the unprecedented task before us. But it may be that an unprecedented demand and need for undelayed action may call for temporary departure from that normal balance of public procedure.

I am prepared under my constitutional duty to recommend the measures ₁₀ that a stricken Nation in the midst of a stricken world may require. These measures, or such other measures as the Congress may build out of its experience and wisdom, I shall seek, within my constitutional authority, to bring to speedy adoption.

But in the event that the Congress shall fail to take one of these two 11 courses, and in the event that the national emergency is still critical, I shall not evade the clear course of duty that will then confront me. I shall ask the Congress for the one remaining instrument to meet the crisis—broad Executive power to wage a war against the emergency, as great as the power that would be given to me if we were in fact invaded by a foreign foe.

For the trust reposed in me I will return the courage and the devotion that 12 befit the time. I can do no less.

We face the arduous days that lie before us in the warm courage of national 13 unity; with the clear consciousness of seeking old and precious moral values; with the clear satisfaction that comes from the stern performance of duty by old and young alike. We aim at the assurance of a rounded and permanent national life.

We do not distrust the future of essential democracy. The people of the 14 United States have not failed. In their need they have registered a mandate that they want direct, vigorous action. They have asked for discipline and direction under leadership. They have made me the present instrument of their wishes. In the spirit of the gift I take it.

In this dedication of a Nation we humbly ask the blessing of God. May 15 He protect each and every one of us. May He guide me in the days to come.

⚜ WINSTON CHURCHILL

We Shall Never Surrender

Winston Churchill (1874–1965) became prime minister at one of the darkest moments in British history. The German panzer divisions had swept through Luxembourg and the Ardennes forest to the French coast, trapping the entire Belgian and British armies and, as Churchill knew but did not say in his speech, effectively defeating the French army. The British Expeditionary Force (BEF) in France retreated to the French coast where, following a German military error, the British managed almost miraculously to transport almost their whole army back to Britain, surely one reason that Hitler did not invade England, where with hindsight we know he almost certainly would have been victorious.

. . . When a week ago today I asked the House [of Parliament] to fix this 1
afternoon for the occasion of a statement, I feared it would be my hard lot to
announce from this box the greatest military disaster of our long history.

I thought, and there were good judges who agreed with me, that perhaps 2
20,000 or 30,000 men might be re-embarked, but it certainly seemed that the
whole French First Army and the whole B.E.F. north of the Amiens-Abbeville
gap would be broken up in open field or else have to capitulate for lack of food
and ammunition.

These were the hard and heavy tidings I called on the House and nation 3
to prepare themselves for.

The whole root and core and brain of the British Army, around which and 4
upon which we were building and were able to build the great British armies of
later years, seemed due to perish upon the field. That was the prospect a week
ago, but another blow which might have proved final was still to fall upon us.

The King of the Belgians called upon us to come to his aid. Had not this 5
ruler and his government severed themselves from the Allies who rescued their
country from extinction in the late war, and had they not sought refuge in what
has proved to be fatal neutrality, then the French and British armies at the
outset might well have saved not only Belgium but perhaps even Holland.

At the last moment, when Belgium was already invaded, King Leopold 6
called upon us to come to his aid, and even at the last moment we came. He
and his brave and efficient army of nearly half a million strong guarded our
eastern flank; this kept open our only retreat to the sea.

Suddenly, without any prior consultation and with the least possible no- 7
tice, without the advice of his ministers and on his own personal act, he sent a
plenipotentiary to the German Command surrendering his army and exposing
our flank and the means of retreat.

I asked the House a week ago to suspend its judgment because the facts 8
were not clear. I do not think there is now any reason why we should not form
our own opinions upon this pitiful episode. The surrender of the Belgian Army
compelled the British Army at the shortest notice to cover a flank to the sea of
more than thirty miles' length which otherwise would have been cut off.

In doing this and closing this flank, contact was lost inevitably between 9
the British and two of three corps forming the First French Army who were
then further from the coast than we were. It seemed impossible that large
numbers of Allied troops could reach the coast. The enemy attacked on all
sides in great strength and fierceness, and their main power, air force, was
thrown into the battle.

The enemy began to fire cannon along the beaches by which alone ship- 10
ping could approach or depart. They sowed magnetic mines in the channels
and seas and sent repeated waves of hostile aircraft, sometimes more than 100
strong, to cast bombs on a single pier that remained and on the sand dunes.

Their U-boats, one of which was sunk, and motor launches took their toll 11
of the vast traffic which now began. For four or five days the intense struggle

raged. All armored divisions, or what was left of them, together with great masses of German infantry and artillery, hurled themselves on the ever narrowing and contracting appendix within which the British and French armies fought.

Meanwhile the Royal Navy, with the willing help of countless merchant 12 seamen and a host of volunteers, strained every nerve and every effort and every craft to embark the British and Allied troops.

Over 220 light warships and more than 650 other vessels were engaged. 13 They had to approach this difficult coast, often in adverse weather, under an almost ceaseless hail of bombs and increasing concentration of artillery fire. Nor were the seas themselves free from mines and torpedoes.

It was in conditions such as these that our men carried on with little or no 14 rest for days and nights, moving troops across dangerous waters and bringing with them always the men whom they had rescued. The numbers they brought back are the measure of their devotion and their courage.

Hospital ships, which were plainly marked, were the special target for Nazi 15 bombs, but the men and women aboard them never faltered in their duty.

Meanwhile the R.A.F., who already had been intervening in the battle so 16 far as its range would allow it to go from home bases, now used a part of its main metropolitan fighter strength to strike at German bombers.

The struggle was protracted and fierce. Suddenly the scene has cleared. 17 The crash and thunder has momentarily, but only for the moment, died away. The miracle of deliverance achieved by the valor and perseverance, perfect discipline, faultless service, skill and unconquerable vitality is a manifesto to us all.

The enemy was hurled back by the British and French troops. He was so 18 roughly handled that he dare not molest their departure seriously. The air force decisively defeated the main strength of the German Air Force and inflicted on them a loss of at least four to one.

The navy, using nearly 1,000 ships of all kinds, carried over 335,000 men, 19 French and British, from the jaws of death back to their native land and to the tasks which lie immediately before them.

We must be very careful not to assign to this deliverance attributes of a 20 victory. Wars are not won by evacuations, but there was a victory inside this deliverance which must be noted. . . .

May it not be that the cause of civilization itself will be defended by the 21 skill and devotion of a few thousand airmen? There never has been, I suppose, in all the history of the world such opportunity for youth.

The Knights of the Round Table and the Crusaders have fallen back into 22 distant days, not only distant but prosaic; but these young men are going forth every morning, going forth holding in their hands an instrument of colossal shattering power, of whom it may be said that every morn brought forth a noble chance and every chance brought forth a noble deed. These young men deserve our gratitude, as all brave men who in so many ways and so many occasions are ready and will continue to be ready to give their life and their all to their native land. . . .

. . . our thankfulness at the escape of our army with so many men, and 23
the thankfulness of their loved ones, who passed through an agonizing week, must not blind us to the fact that what happened in France and Belgium is a colossal military disaster.

The French Army has been weakened, the Belgian Army has been lost 24
and a large part of those fortified lines upon which so much faith was reposed has gone, and many valuable mining districts and factories have passed into the enemy's possession. . . .

We were told that Hitler has plans for invading the British Isles. This has 25
often been thought of before. When Napoleon lay at Boulogne for a year with his flat-bottomed boats and his Grand Army, someone told him there were bitter weeds in England. There certainly were and a good many more of them have since been returned. . . .

Turning once again to the question of invasion, there has, I will observe, 26
never been a period in all those long centuries of which we boast when an absolute guarantee against invasion, still less against serious raids, could have been given to our people. In the days of Napoleon the same wind which might have carried his transports across the Channel might have driven away a block-ading fleet. There is always the chance, and it is that chance which has excited and befooled the imaginations of many continental tyrants.

We are assured that novel methods will be adopted, and when we see the 27
originality, malice, and ingenuity of aggression which our enemy displays we may certainly prepare ourselves for every kind of novel stratagem and every kind of brutal and treacherous manoeuvre. I think no idea is so outlandish that it should not be considered and viewed with a watchful, but at the same time steady, eye.

We must never forget the solid assurances of sea power and those which 28
belong to air power if they can be locally exercised. I have myself full confi-dence that if all do their duty and if the best arrangements are made, as they are being made, we shall prove ourselves once again able to defend our island home, ride out the storms of war and outlive the menace of tyranny, if neces-sary, for years, if necessary, alone.

At any rate, that is what we are going to try to do. That is the resolve 29
of His Majesty's Government, every man of them. That is the will of Parlia-ment and the nation. The British Empire and the French Republic, linked together in their cause and their need, will defend to the death their native soils, aiding each other like good comrades to the utmost of their strength, even though a large tract of Europe and many old and famous States have fallen or may fall into the grip of the Gestapo and all the odious apparatus of Nazi rule.

We shall not flag nor fail. We shall go on to the end. We shall fight in 30
France and on the seas and oceans; we shall fight with growing confidence and growing strength in the air.

We shall defend our island whatever the cost may be; we shall fight on 31 beaches, landing grounds, in fields, in streets and on the hills. We shall never surrender and even if, which I do not for the moment believe, this island or a large part of it were subjugated and starving, then our empire beyond the seas, armed and guarded by the British Fleet, will carry on the struggle until in God's good time the New World, with all its power and might, sets forth to the liberation and rescue of the Old.

⌖ RICHARD M. NIXON

Checkers Speech

Richard M. Nixon, the only U.S. president forced to resign from office, delivered the following television speech during the 1952 presidential campaign, when he was Eisenhower's vice presidential running mate. Nixon was accused of diverting $18,000 in campaign contributions for personal use, and the question was whether he should be removed from the Republican ticket. The speech was favorably received, and Eisenhower decided to keep Nixon as his running mate—a decision of some consequence for future events.

My fellow Americans: I come before you tonight as a candidate for the vice 1 presidency and as a man whose honesty and integrity has been questioned.

Now, the usual political thing to do when charges are made against you is 2 to either ignore them or to deny them without giving details. I believe we have had enough of that in the United States, particularly with the present Administration in Washington, D.C.

To me the office of the vice presidency of the United States is a great 3 office, and I feel that the people have got to have confidence in the integrity of the men who run for that office and who might attain them.

I have a theory, too, that the best and only answer to a smear or to an 4 honest misunderstanding of the facts is to tell the truth. And that is why I am here tonight. I want to tell you my side of the case.

I am sure that you have read the charge, and you have heard it, that I, 5 Senator Nixon, took $18,000 from a group of my supporters.

Now, . . . let me say this: 6

Not one cent of the $18,000 or any other money of that type ever went to   7
me for my personal use. Every penny of it was used to pay for political expenses
that I did not think should be charged to the taxpayers of the United States.

It was not a secret fund. As a matter of fact, when I was on *Meet the Press*,   8
some of you may have seen it last Sunday—Peter Edson came up to me after
the program and he said, "Dick, what about this fund we hear about?" And I
said, Well, there's no secret about it. Go out and see Dana Smith, who was the
administrator of the fund. And I gave him his address, and I said that you will
find that the purpose of the fund simply was to defray political expenses that I
did not feel should be charged to the government.

And third, let me point out, and I want to make this particularly clear,   9
that no contributor to this fund, no contributor to any of my campaign, has
ever received any consideration that he would not have received as an ordinary
constituent. . . .

But then some of you will say and rightly, "Well, what did you use the   10
fund for, Senator? Why did you have to have it?"

Let me tell you in just a word how a Senate office operates. First of all, a   11
senator gets $15,000 a year in salary. He gets enough money to pay for one trip
a year, a round trip that is, for himself and his family between his home and
Washington, D.C.

And then he gets an allowance to handle the people that work in his office,   12
to handle his mail. And the allowance for my state of California is enough to
hire thirteen people.

And let me say, incidentally, that that allowance is not paid to the sena-   13
tor—it's paid directly to the individuals that the senator puts on his payroll, that
all of these people and all of these allowances are for strictly official business.
Business, for example, when a constituent writes in and wants you to go down
to the Veterans Administration and get some information about his GI policy.
Items of that type, for example.

But there are other expenses which are not covered by the government.   14
And I think I can best discuss those expenses by asking you some questions. Do
you think that when I or any other senator makes a political speech, has it
printed, [he] should charge the printing of that speech and the mailing of that
speech to the taxpayers?

Do you think, for example, when I or any other senator makes a trip to his   15
home state to make a purely political speech that the cost of that trip should be
charged to the taxpayers?

Do you think when a senator makes political broadcasts or political tele-   16
vision broadcasts, radio or television, that the expense of those broadcasts
should be charged to the taxpayer?

Well, I know what your answer is. The same answer that audiences give   17
me whenever I discuss this particular problem. The answer is, No. The taxpayers shouldn't be required to finance items which are not official business but
which are primarily political business.

But then the question arises, you say, "Well, how do you pay for these and   18
how can you do it legally?"

And there are several ways that it can be done, incidentally, and that it is   19
done legally in the United States Senate and in the Congress.

The first way is to be a rich man. I don't happen to be a rich man so I   20
couldn't use that.

Another way that is used is to put your wife on the payroll. Let me say,   21
incidentally, my opponent, my opposite number for the vice presidency on the
Democratic ticket, does have his wife on the payroll. And has had her on his
payroll for the ten years—the past ten years.

Now just let me say this. That's his business and I'm not critical of him   22
for doing that. You will have to pass judgment on that particular point. But I
have never done that for this reason. I have found that there are so many
deserving stenographers and secretaries in Washington that needed the work
that I just didn't feel it was right to put my wife on the payroll.

My wife's sitting over here. She's a wonderful stenographer. She used to   23
teach stenography and she used to teach shorthand in high school. That was
when I met her. And I can tell you folks that she's worked many hours at night
and many hours on Saturdays and Sundays in my office and she's done a fine
job. And I'm proud to say tonight that in the six years I've been in the House
and the Senate of the United States, Pat Nixon has never been on the government payroll.

There are other ways that these finances can be taken care of. Some who   24
are lawyers, and I happen to be a lawyer, continue to practice law. But I haven't
been able to do that. I'm so far away from California and I've been so busy with
my senatorial work that I have not engaged in any legal practice.

And also as far as law practice is concerned, it seemed to me that the   25
relationship between an attorney and the client was so personal that you
couldn't possibly represent a man as an attorney and then have an unbiased
view when he presented his case to you in the event that he had one before the
government.

And so I felt that the best way to handle these necessary political expenses   26
of getting my message to the American people and the speeches I made, the
speeches that I had printed, for the most part, concerned this one message—
that exposing this administration, the communism in it, the corruption in it—
the only way that I could do that was to accept the aid which people in my
home state of California who contributed to my campaign and who continued
to make these contributions after I was elected were glad to make.

And let me say I am proud of the fact that not one of them has ever asked   27
me for a special favor. I'm proud of the fact that not one of them has ever asked
me to vote on a bill other than as my own conscience would dictate. And I am
proud of the fact that the taxpayers by subterfuge or otherwise have never paid
one dime for expenses which I thought were political and shouldn't be charged
to the taxpayers.

Let me say, incidentally, that some of you may say, "Well, that's all right,   28
Senator; that's your explanation, but have you got any proof?"

And I'd like to tell you this evening that just about an hour ago we received   29
an independent audit of this entire fund. . . .

It's an audit made by the Price, Waterhouse & Co. firm, and the legal   30
opinion by Gibson, Dunn & Crutcher, lawyers in Los Angeles, the biggest law
firm and incidentally one of the best ones in Los Angeles. . . .

> It is our conclusion that Senator Nixon did not obtain any financial gain from
> the collection and disbursement of the fund by Dana Smith; that Senator Nixon
> did not violate any federal or state law by reason of the operation of the fund,
> and that neither the portion of the fund paid by Dana Smith directly to third
> persons nor the portion paid to Senator Nixon to reimburse him for designated
> office expenses constituted income to the Senator which was either reportable
> or taxable as income under applicable tax laws. (Signed) Gibson, Dunn &
> Crutcher by Alma H. Conway.

Now that, my friends, is not Nixon speaking, but that's an independent   31
audit which was requested because I want the American people to know all the
facts and I'm not afraid of having independent people go in and check the facts,
and that is exactly what they did.

But then I realize that there are still some who may say, and rightly so,   32
and let me say that I recognize that some will continue to smear regardless of
what the truth may be, but that there has been understandably some honest
misunderstanding on this matter, and there's some that will say:

"Well, maybe you were able, Senator, to fake this thing. How can we   33
believe what you say? After all, is there a possibility that you may have feathered
your own nest?"

And so now what I am going to do—and incidentally this is unprecedented   34
in the history of American politics—I am going at this time to give to this
television and radio audience a complete financial history; everything I've
earned; everything I've spent; everything I owe. And I want you to know the
facts. I'll have to start early.

I was born in 1913. Our family was one of modest circumstances and   35
most of my early life was spent in a store out in East Whittier. It was a grocery
store—one of those family enterprises. The only reason we were able to make
it go was because my mother and dad had five boys and we all worked in the
store.

I worked my way through college and to a great extent through law school.   36
And then, in 1940, probably the best thing that ever happened to me happened,
I married Pat—sitting over here. We had a rather difficult time after we were
married, like so many of the young couples who may be listening to us. I
practiced law; she continued to teach school. I went into the service.

Let me say that my service record was not a particularly unusual one. I   37
went to the South Pacific. I guess I'm entitled to a couple of battle stars. I got
a couple of letters of commendation but I was just there when the bombs were
falling and then I returned. I returned to the United States and in 1946 I ran
for the Congress.

When we came out of the war, Pat and I—Pat during the war had worked   38
as a stenographer and in a bank and as an economist for a governmental
agency—and when we came out the total of our savings from both my law

practice, her teaching, and all the time that I was in the war—the total for that entire period was just a little less than $10,000. Every cent of that, incidentally, was in government bonds.

Well, that's where we start when I go into politics. Now what have I earned   39 since I went into politics? Well, here it is—I jotted it down, let me read the notes. First of all I've had my salary as a congressman and as a senator. Second, I have received a total in this past six years of $1,600 from estates which were in my law firm at the time that I severed my connection with it.

And, incidentally, as I said before, I have not engaged in any legal practice   40 and have not accepted any fees from business that came into the firm after I went into politics. I have made an average of approximately $1,500 a year from nonpolitical speaking engagements and lectures. And then, fortunately, we've inherited a little money. Pat sold her interest in her father's estate for $3,000 and I inherited $1,500 from my grandfather.

We live rather modestly. For four years we lived in an apartment in Park   41 Fairfax, in Alexandria, Va. The rent was $80 a month. And we saved for the time that we could buy a house.

Now, that was what we took in. What did we do with this money? What   42 do we have today to show for it? This will surprise you, because it is so little, I suppose, as standards generally go, of people in public life. First of all, we've got a house in Washington which cost $41,000 and on which we owe $20,000.

We have a house in Whittier, California, which cost $13,000 and on   43 which we owe $10,000. My folks are living there at the present time.

I have just $4,000 in life insurance, plus my GI policy which I've never   44 been able to convert and which will run out in two years. I have no life insurance whatever on Pat. I have no life insurance on our two youngsters, Patricia and Julie. I own a 1950 Oldsmobile car. We have our furniture. We have no stocks and bonds of any type. We have no interest of any kind, direct or indirect, in any business.

Now, that's what we have. What do we owe? Well, in addition to the   45 mortgage, the $20,000 mortgage on the house in Washington, the $10,000 one on the house in Whittier, I owe $4,500 to the Riggs Bank in Washington, D.C. with interest 4½ percent.

I owe $3,500 to my parents and the interest on that loan which I pay   46 regularly, because it's the part of the savings they made through the years they were working so hard, I pay regularly 4 percent interest. And then I have a $500 loan which I have on my life insurance.

Well, that's about it. That's what we have and that's what we owe. It isn't   47 very much but Pat and I have the satisfaction that every dime that we've got is honestly ours. I should say this—that Pat doesn't have a mink coat. But she does have a respectable *Republican* cloth coat. And I always tell her that she'd look good in anything. [At this point, the TV cameras that had been focused on Nixon switched to a smiling Pat Nixon.]

One other thing I probably should tell you because if I don't they'll prob-   48 ably be saying this about me too, we did get something—a gift—after the election. A man down in Texas heard Pat on the radio mention the fact that our two youngsters would like to have a dog. And, believe it or not, the day before we left on this campaign trip we got a message from Union Station in Baltimore saying they had a package for us. We went down to get it. You know what it was?

It was a little cocker spaniel dog, in a crate that he had sent all the way 49 from Texas, black and white, spotted, and our little girl, Tricia, the six-year-old, named it Checkers.

And, you know, the kids, like all kids, loved the dog, and I just want to 50 say this, right now, that regardless of what they say about it, we are going to keep it.

It isn't easy to come before a nation-wide audience and bare your life, as I 51 have done. But I want to say some things before I conclude, that I think most of you will agree on.

Mr. Mitchell, the chairman of the Democratic National Committee, 52 made the statement that if a man couldn't afford to be in the United States Senate, he shouldn't run for the Senate. And I just want to make my position clear.

I don't agree with Mr. Mitchell when he says that only a rich man should 53 serve his government, in the United States Senate or in the Congress. I don't believe that represents the thinking of the Democratic party, and I know it doesn't represent the thinking of the Republican party.

I believe that it's fine that a man like Governor Stevenson, who inherited 54 a fortune from his father, can run for president. But I also feel that it is essential in this country of ours that a man of modest means can also run for president, because, you know—remember Abraham Lincoln—you remember what he said—"God must have loved the common people, he made so many of them."

And now I'm going to suggest some courses of conduct. 55

First of all, you have read in the papers about other funds, now. Mr. 56 Stevenson apparently had a couple. One of them in which a group of business people paid and helped to supplement the salaries of state employees. Here is where the money went directly into their pockets, and I think that what Mr. Stevenson should do should be to come before the American people, as I have, give the names of the people that contributed to that fund, give the names of the people who put this money into their pockets, at the same time that they were receiving money from their state government and see what favors, if any, they gave out for that.

I don't condemn Mr. Stevenson for what he did, but until the facts are in 57 there is a doubt that would be raised. And as far as Mr. Sparkman is concerned, I would suggest the same thing. He's had his wife on the payroll. I don't condemn him for that, but I think that he should come before the American people and indicate what outside sources of income he has had. I would suggest that under the circumstances both Mr. Sparkman and Mr. Stevenson should come before the American people, as I have, and make a complete financial statement as to their financial history, and if they don't it will be an admission that they have something to hide.

And I think you will agree with me—because, folks, remember, a man 58
that's to be president of the United States, a man that is to be vice president of
the United States, must have the confidence of all the people. And that's why
I'm doing what I'm doing, and that is why I suggest that Mr. Stevenson and
Mr. Sparkman, if they are under attack, that should be what they are doing.

Now, let me say this: I know that this is not the last of the smears. In spite 59
of my explanation tonight, other smears will be made. Others have been made
in the past. And the purpose of the smears, I know, is this, to silence me, to
make me let up.

Well, they just don't know who they are dealing with. I'm going to tell 60
you this: I remember, in the dark days of the [Alger] Hiss trial, some of the
same columnists, some of the same radio commentators who are attacking me
now and misrepresenting my position, were violently opposing me at the time
I was after Alger Hiss. But I continued to fight, because I knew I was right, and
I can say to this great television and radio audience that I have no apologies to
the American people for my part in putting Alger Hiss where he is today. And
as far as this is concerned, I intend to continue to fight.

Why do I feel so deeply? Why do I feel that in spite of the smears, the 61
misunderstanding, the necessity for a man to come up here and bare his soul,
as I have—why is it necessary for me to continue this fight? And I want to tell
you why.

Because, you see, I love my country. And I think my country is in danger. 62
And I think the only man that can save America at this time is the man that's
running for president, on my ticket, Dwight Eisenhower. . . .

☒ **JOHN F. KENNEDY**

Inaugural Address

*John F. Kennedy (1917–1963), the charismatic thirty-fifth president of the
United States, delivered the now immortal lines ". . . ask not what your country
can do for you—ask what you can do for your country" as part of his inaugural
address to the nation in January 1961.*

. . . Let every nation know, whether it wishes us well or ill, that we shall pay 1
any price, bear any burden, meet any hardship, support any friend, oppose any
foe to assure the survival and the success of liberty.

This much we pledge—and more. . . .   2

To that world assembly of sovereign states, the United Nations, our last   3
best hope in an age where the instruments of war have far outpaced the instruments of peace, we renew our pledge of support—to prevent it from becoming
merely a forum for invective—to strengthen its shield of the new and the weak
and to enlarge the area in which its writ may run.

Finally, to those nations who would make themselves our adversary, we   4
offer not a pledge but a request: that both sides begin anew the quest for peace,
before the dark powers of destruction unleashed by science engulf all humanity
in planned or accidental self-destruction.

We dare not tempt them with weakness. For only when our arms are   5
sufficient beyond doubt can we be certain beyond doubt that they will never be
employed. . . .

So let us begin anew—remembering on both sides that civility is not a   6
sign of weakness, and sincerity is always subject to proof. Let us never negotiate
out of fear. But let us never fear to negotiate.

Let both sides explore what problems unite us instead of laboring those   7
problems which divide us. . . .

And if a beachhead of cooperation may push back the jungle of suspicion,   8
let both sides join in creating a new endeavor—not a new balance of power,
but a new world of law, where the strong are just and the weak secure and the
peace preserved. . . .

In the long history of the world, only a few generations have been granted   9
the role of defending freedom in its hour of maximum danger. I do not shrink
from this responsibility—I welcome it. I do not believe that any of us would
exchange places with any other people or any other generation. The energy, the
faith, the devotion which we bring to this endeavor will light our country and
all who serve it—and the glow from that fire can truly light the world.

And so, my fellow Americans: ask not what your country can do for you—   10
ask what you can do for your country.

My fellow citizens of the world: ask not what Americans will do for you,   11
but what together we can do for the freedom of man.

§ ADLAI STEVENSON

The Cat Bill Veto

Adlai Stevenson (1900–1965), who ran unsuccessfully for president twice against Eisenhower and later served as ambassador to the United Nations, wrote this veto while he was governor of Illinois. He was known for his dry wit, including his remark when accused of being an intellectual egghead: "Eggheads of the world, unite. All we have to lose is our yolks." The "Cat Bill Veto," though little more than a footnote in the annals of political rhetoric, has unusual charm and persuasive appeal.

To the Honorable, the Members of the Senate of the Sixty-sixth
General Assembly:

I herewith return, without my approval, Senate Bill No. 93 entitled "An Act to   1
Provide Protection to Insectivorous Birds by Restraining Cats." This is the so-
called "Cat Bill." I veto and withhold my approval from this bill for the following reasons:

   It would impose fines on owners or keepers who permitted their cats to   2
run at large off their premises. It would permit any person to capture, or call
upon the police to pick up and imprison, cats at large. It would permit the use
of traps. The bill would have statewide application—on farms, in villages, and
in metropolitan centers.

   This legislation has been introduced in the past several sessions of the   3
Legislature, and it has, over the years, been the source of much comment—
not all of which has been in a serious vein. It may be that the General Assembly
has now seen fit to refer it to one who can view it with a fresh outlook. Whatever
the reasons for passage at this session, I cannot believe there is a widespread
public demand for this law or that it could, as a practical matter, be enforced.

   Furthermore, I cannot agree that it should be the declared public policy   4
of Illinois that a cats visiting a neighbor's yard or crossing the highway is a
public nuisance. It is in the nature of cats to do a certain amount of unescorted
roaming. Many live with their owners in apartments or other restricted premises, and I doubt if we want to make their every brief foray an opportunity for a
small game hunt by zealous citizens—with traps or otherwise. I am afraid this
bill could only create discord, recrimination and enmity. Also consider the
owner's dilemma: To escort a cat abroad on a leash is against the nature of the
cat, and to permit it to venture forth for exercise unattended into a night of new
dangers is against the nature of the owner. Moreover, cats perform useful service, particularly in rural areas, in combatting rodents—work they necessarily
perform alone and without regard for property lines.

We are all interested in protecting certain varieties of birds. That cats ⁵ destroy some birds, I well know, but I believe this legislation would further but little the worthy cause to which its proponents give such unselfish effort. The problem of the cat versus the bird is as old as time. If we attempt to resolve it by legislation who knows but what we may be called upon to take sides as well in the age-old problems of dog versus cat, bird versus bird, or even bird versus worm. In my opinion, the state of Illinois and its local governing bodies already have enough to do without trying to control feline delinquency.

For these reasons, and not because I love birds the less or cats the more, I ⁶ veto and withhold my approval from Senate Bill No. 93.

POLITICAL RHETORIC

QUESTIONS AND SUGGESTIONS FOR WRITING

1. What rhetorical devices and tricks of reasoning does Marc Antony use to turn the citizens of Rome against Brutus?

2. Patrick Henry's speech is charged with emotive fervor. Describe the tone of the speech and explain how the language works to persuade the American colonists to wage war against the British.

3. In his eloquent address at Gettysburg, Abraham Lincoln turns a eulogy for soldiers killed in battle into an inspirational justification for the Civil War. How does he manage to persuade so well in so few words? (Difficult question.)

4. Franklin Roosevelt took office during the worst of the Depression. His speech is intended to address that crisis realistically yet to provide hope for the future. Does he succeed in his purpose? Explain your answer.

5. Winston Churchill's speech was given to Parliament just after the "miracle" of Dunkirk during World War II. It was quoted from often during the war and is still considered among the most stirring speeches of the century. How do you explain the persuasive power of this speech?

6. What is the appeal of John F. Kennedy's much quoted line: ". . . ask not what your country can do for you—ask what you can do for your country"? Why shouldn't you ask what your country can do for you as well as what you can do for your country?

7. Explain how the use of language, tone, and irony contribute to the appeal of Stevenson's "Cat Bill Veto."

8. Do some research on the historic background of one of the speeches in this section and explain how that speech is particularly suited to its time and purpose.

This section contains readings that don't quite fit into any of the above categories but are, we believe, interesting in their own right, argue well for their theses, and should be of some value in inspiring creative and cogent argumentative essay writing.

⊠ **ALDOUS HUXLEY**

Propaganda Under a Dictatorship

Aldous Huxley (1894–1963), grandson of Thomas Huxley, was a well-known English novelist and essayist. His most famous work, Brave New World, *all too accurately pictured the direction a good deal of modern life was about to take. In the following essay, taken from his 1958 work,* Brave New World Revisited, *he gives us an account of propaganda during the Nazi period in Germany and raises the question of how in "an age of accelerating over-population, of accelerating over-organization and ever more efficient means of mass communication, . . . [we can] preserve the integrity and reassert the value of the human individual."*

At his trial after the Second World War, Hitler's Minister for Armaments, Albert 1
Speer, delivered a long speech in which, with remarkable acuteness, he described the Nazi tyranny and analyzed its methods. "Hitler's dictatorship," he said, "differed in one fundamental point from all its predecessors in history. It was the first dictatorship in the present period of modern technical development, a dictatorship which made complete use of all technical means for the domination of its own country. Through technical devices like the radio and the loud-speaker, eighty million people were deprived of independent thought. It was thereby possible to subject them to the will of one man. . . . Earlier dictators needed highly qualified assistants even at the lowest level—men who could think and act independently. The totalitarian system in the period of

modern technical development can dispense with such men; thanks to modern methods of communication, it is possible to mechanize the lower leadership. As a result of this there has arisen the new type of the uncritical recipient of orders."

In the Brave New World of my prophetic fable technology had advanced 2 far beyond the point it had reached in Hitler's day; consequently the recipients of orders were far less critical than their Nazi counterparts, far more obedient to the order-giving elite. Moreover, they had been genetically standardized and postnatally conditioned to perform their subordinate functions, and could therefore be depended upon to behave almost as predictably as machines. . . . this conditioning of the "lower leadership" is already going on under the Communist dictatorships. The Chinese and the Russians are not relying merely on the indirect effects of advancing technology; they are working directly on the psychophysical organisms of their lower leaders, subjecting minds and bodies to a system of ruthless and, from all accounts, highly effective conditioning. "Many a man," said Speer, "has been haunted by the nightmare that one day nations might be dominated by technical means. That nightmare was almost realized in Hitler's totalitarian system." Almost, but not quite. The Nazis did not have time—and perhaps did not have the intelligence and the necessary knowledge—to brainwash and condition their lower leadership. This, it may be, is one of the reasons why they failed.

Since Hitler's day the armory of technical devices at the disposal of the 3 would-be dictator has been considerably enlarged. As well as the radio, the loud-speaker, the moving picture camera and the rotary press, the contemporary propagandist can make use of television to broadcast the image as well as the voice of his client, and can record both image and voice on spools of magnetic tape. Thanks to technological progress, Big Brother can now be almost as omnipresent as God. Nor is it only on the technical front that the hand of the would-be dictator has been strengthened. Since Hitler's day a great deal of work has been carried out in those fields of applied psychology and neurology which are the special province of the propagandist, the indoctrinator and the brainwasher. In the past these specialists in the art of changing people's minds were empiricists. By a method of trial and error they had worked out a number of techniques and procedures, which they used very effectively without, however, knowing precisely why they were effective. Today the art of mind-control is in process of becoming a science. The practitioners of this science know what they are doing and why. They are guided in their work by theories and hypotheses solidly established on a massive foundation of experimental evidence. Thanks to the new insights and the new techniques made possible by these insights, the nightmare that was "all but realized in Hitler's totalitarian system" may soon be completely realizable.

But before we discuss these new insights and techniques let us take a look 4 at the nightmare that so nearly came true in Nazi Germany. What were the methods used by Hitler and Goebbels for "depriving eighty million people of independent thought and subjecting them to the will of one man"? And what was the theory of human nature upon which those terrifyingly successful methods were based? These questions can be answered, for the most part, in Hitler's own words. And what remarkably clear and astute words they are! When he writes about such vast abstractions as Race and History and Providence, Hitler is strictly unreadable. But when he writes about the German masses and the methods he used for dominating and directing them, his style changes. Nonsense gives place to sense, bombast to a hard-boiled and cynical lucidity. In his philosophical lucubrations Hitler was either cloudily daydreaming or reproducing other people's half-baked notions. In his comments on crowds and propaganda he was writing of things he knew by firsthand experience. In the words of his ablest biographer, Mr. Alan Bullock, "Hitler was the greatest demagogue in history." Those who add, "only a demagogue," fail to appreciate the nature of political power in an age of mass politics. As he himself said, "To be a leader means to be able to move the masses." Hitler's aim was first to move the masses and then, having pried them loose from their traditional loyalties and moralities, to impose upon them (with the hypnotized consent of the majority) a new authoritarian order of his own devising. "Hitler," wrote Hermann Rauschning in 1939, "has a deep respect for the Catholic church and the Jesuit order; not because of their Christian doctrine, but because of the 'machinery' they have elaborated and controlled, their hierarchical system, their extremely clever tactics, their knowledge of human nature and their wise use of human weaknesses in ruling over believers." Ecclesiasticism without Christianity, the discipline of a monastic rule, not for God's sake or in order to achieve personal salvation, but for the sake of the State and for the greater glory and power of the demagogue turned Leader—this was the goal toward which the systematic moving of the masses was to lead.

Let us see what Hitler thought of the masses he moved and how he did 5 the moving. The first principle from which he started was a value judgment: the masses are utterly contemptible. They are incapable of abstract thinking and uninterested in any fact outside the circle of their immediate experience. Their behavior is determined, not by knowledge and reason, but by feelings and unconscious drives. It is in these drives and feelings that "the roots of their positive as well as their negative attitudes are implanted." To be successful a propagandist must learn how to manipulate these instincts and emotions. "The driving force which has brought about the most tremendous revolutions on this earth has never been a body of scientific teaching which has gained power over the masses, but always a devotion which has inspired them, and often a kind of hysteria which has urged them into action. Whoever wishes to win over the masses must know the key that will open the door of their hearts." . . . In post-Freudian jargon, of their unconscious.

Hitler made his strongest appeal to those members of the lower middle 6 classes who had been ruined by the inflation of 1923, and then ruined all over again by the depression of 1929 and the following years. "The masses" of whom he speaks were these bewildered, frustrated, and chronically anxious millions. To make them more mass-like, more homogeneously subhuman, he assembled them, by the thousands and the tens of thousands, in vast halls and arenas, where individuals could lose their personal identity, even their elementary humanity, and be merged with the crowd. A man or woman makes direct contact with society in two ways: as a member of some familial, professional or religious group, or as a member of a crowd. Groups are capable of being as moral and intelligent as the individuals who form them; a crowd is chaotic, has no purpose of its own and is capable of anything except intelligent action and realistic thinking. Assembled in a crowd, people lose their powers of reasoning and their capacity for moral choice. Their suggestibility is increased to the point where they cease to have any judgment or will of their own. They become very excitable, they lose all sense of individual or collective responsibility, they are subject to sudden accesses of rage, enthusiasm and panic. In a word, a man in a crowd behaves as though he had swallowed a large dose of some powerful intoxicant. He is a victim of what I have called "herd-poisoning." Like alcohol, herd-poison is an active, extraverted drug. The crowd-intoxicated individual escapes from responsibility, intelligence and morality into a kind of frantic, animal mindlessness.

During his long career as an agitator, Hitler had studied the effects of herd-poison and had learned how to exploit them for his own purposes. He had discovered that the orator can appeal to those "hidden forces" which motivate men's actions, much more effectively than can the writer. Reading is a private, not a collective activity. The writer speaks only to individuals, sitting by themselves in a state of normal sobriety. The orator speaks to masses of individuals, already well primed with herd-poison. They are at his mercy and, if he knows his business, he can do what he likes with them. As an orator, Hitler knew his business supremely well. He was able, in his own words, "to follow the lead of the great mass in such a way that from the living emotion of his hearers the apt word which he needed would be suggested to him and in its turn this would go straight to the heart of his hearers." Otto Strasser called him a "loud-speaker, proclaiming the most secret desires, the least admissible instincts, the sufferings and personal revolts of a whole nation." Twenty years before Madison Avenue embarked upon "Motivational Research," Hitler was systematically exploring and exploiting the secret fears and hopes, the cravings, anxieties and frustrations of the German masses. It is by manipulating "hidden forces" that the advertising experts induce us to buy their wares—a toothpaste, a brand of cigarettes, a political candidate. And it is by appealing to the same hidden forces—and to others too dangerous for Madison Avenue to meddle with—that Hitler induced the German masses to buy themselves a Fuehrer, an insane philosophy and The Second World War.

Unlike the masses, intellectuals have a taste for rationality and an interest in facts. Their critical habit of mind makes them resistant to the kind of propaganda that works so well on the majority. Among the masses "instinct is supreme, and from instinct comes faith. . . . While the healthy common folk instinctively close their ranks to form a community of the people" (under a Leader, it goes without saying) "intellectuals run this way and that, like hens in a poultry yard. With them one cannot make history; they cannot be used as elements composing a community." Intellectuals are the kind of people who demand evidence and are shocked by logical inconsistencies and fallacies. They regard over-simplification as the original sin of the mind and have no use for the slogans, the unqualified assertions and sweeping generalizations which are the propagandist's stock in trade. "All effective propaganda," Hitler wrote, "must be confined to a few bare necessities and then must be expressed in a few stereotyped formulas." These stereotyped formulas must be constantly repeated, for "only constant repetition will finally succeed in imprinting an idea upon the memory of a crowd." Philosophy teaches us to feel uncertain about the things that seem to us self-evident. Propaganda, on the other hand, teaches us to accept as self-evident matters about which it would be reasonable to suspend our judgment or to feel doubt. The aim of the demagogue is to create social coherence under his own leadership. But, as Bertrand Russell has pointed out, "systems of dogma without empirical foundations, such as scholasticism, Marxism and fascism, have the advantage of producing a great deal of social coherence among their disciples." The demagogic propagandist must therefore be consistently dogmatic. All his statements are made without qualification. There are no grays in his picture of the world; everything is either diabolically black or celestially white. In Hitler's words, the propagandist should adopt "a systematically one-sided attitude towards every problem that has to be dealt with." He must never admit that he might be wrong or that people with a different point of view might be even partially right. Opponents should not be argued with; they should be attacked, shouted down, or, if they become too much of a nuisance, liquidated. The morally squeamish intellectual may be shocked by this kind of thing. But the masses are always convinced that "right is on the side of the active aggressor."

Such, then, was Hitler's opinion of humanity in the mass. It was a very 9 low opinion. Was it also an incorrect opinion? The tree is known by its fruits, and a theory of human nature which inspired the kind of techniques that proved so horribly effective must contain at least an element of truth. Virtue and intelligence belong to human beings as individuals freely associating with other individuals in small groups. So do sin and stupidity. But the subhuman mindlessness to which the demagogue makes his appeal, the moral imbecility on which he relies when he goads his victims into action, are characteristic not of men and women as individuals, but of men and women in masses. Mindlessness and moral idiocy are not characteristically human attributes; they are symptoms of herd-poisoning. In all the world's higher religions, salvation and enlightenment are for individuals. The kingdom of heaven is within the mind of a person, not within the collective mindlessness of a crowd. Christ promised to be present where two or three are gathered together. He did not say anything about being present where thousands are intoxicating one another with herd-poison. Under the Nazis enormous numbers of people were compelled to spend an enormous amount of time marching in serried ranks from point A to point B and back again to point A. "This keeping of the whole population on the march seemed to be a senseless waste of time and energy. Only much later," adds Hermann Rauschning, "was there revealed in it a subtle intention based on a well-judged adjustment of ends and means. Marching diverts men's thoughts. Marching kills thought. Marching makes an end of individuality. Marching is the indispensable magic stroke performed in order to accustom the people to a mechanical, quasi-ritualistic activity until it becomes second nature."

From his point of view and at the level where he had chosen to do his 10 dreadful work, Hitler was perfectly correct in his estimate of human nature. To those of us who look at men and women as individuals rather than as members of crowds, or of regimented collectives, he seems hideously wrong. In an age of accelerating over-population, of accelerating over-organization and ever more efficient means of mass communication, how can we preserve the integrity and reassert the value of the human individual? This is a question that can still be asked and perhaps effectively answered. A generation from now it may be too late to find an answer and perhaps impossible, in the stifling collective climate of that future time, even to ask the question.

◿ **GORDON ALLPORT**

The Nature of Prejudice

Gordon Allport (1897–1967) was a psychology professor. In this essay, he argues against prejudice by defining it so as to reveal its odiousness.

Before I attempt to define prejudice, let us have in mind four instances that I 1 think we all would agree are prejudice.

The first is the case of the Cambridge University student, who said, "I 2 despise all Americans. But," he added, a bit puzzled, "I've never met one that I didn't like."

The second is the case of another Englishman, who said to an American, 3 "I think you're awfully unfair in your treatment of Negroes. How *do* Americans feel about Negroes?" The American replied, "Well, I suppose some Americans feel about Negroes just the way you feel about the Irish." The Englishmen said, "Oh, come now. The Negroes are human beings."

Then there's the incident that occasionally takes place in various parts of 4 the world (the West Indies, for example, I'm told). When an American walks down the street the natives conspicuously hold their noses till the American goes by. The case of odor is always interesting. Odor gets mixed up with prejudice because the odor has great associative power. We know that some Chinese deplore the odor of Americans. Some white people think Negroes have a distinctive smell and vice versa. An intrepid psychologist recently did an experiment; it went as follows. He brought to a gymnasium an equal number of white and colored students and had them take shower baths. When they were nice and clean he had them exercise vigorously for fifteen minutes. Then he brought his judges in, each went to the sheeted figures and sniffed. They were to say "white" or "black," guessing at the identity of the subject. The experiment seemed to prove that when we are sweaty we all smell the same way. It's good to have experimental demonstration of the fact.

The fourth example I'd like to bring before you is a piece of writing that I 5 quote. Please ask yourselves who, in your judgment, wrote it. It's a passage about the Jews.

> The synagogue is worse than a brothel. It's a den of scoundrels. It's a criminal assembly of Jews, a place of meeting for the assassins of Christ, a den of thieves, a house of ill fame, a dwelling of iniquity. Whatever name more horrible to be found, it could never be worse than the synagogue deserves.
>
> I would say the same things about their souls. Debauchery and drunkenness have brought them to the level of lusty goat and pig. They know only one thing: to satisfy their stomachs and get drunk, kill, and beat each other up. Why should we salute them? We should have not even the slightest converse with them. They are lustful, rapacious, greedy, perfidious robbers.

Now who wrote that? Perhaps you say Hitler, or Goebbels, or one of our 6 local anti-Semites? No, it was written by Saint John Chrysostom, in the fourth century A.D. Saint John Chrysostom, as you know, gave us the first liturgy in the Christian church still used in the Orthodox churches today. From it all services of the Holy Communion derive. Episcopalians will recognize him also as the author of that exalted prayer that closes the offices of both matin and evensong in the *Book of Common Prayer*. I include this incident to show how complex the problem is. Religious people are by no means necessarily free from prejudice. In this regard be patient even with our saints.

What do these four instances have in common? You notice that all of 7 them indicate that somebody is "down" on somebody else—a feeling of rejection, or hostility. But also, in all these four instances, there is indication that the person is not "up" on his subject—not really informed about Americans, Irish, Jews, or bodily odors.

So I would offer, first a slang definition of prejudice: *Prejudice is being* 8 *down on somebody you're not up on.* If you dislike slang, let me offer the same thought in the style of St. Thomas Aquinas. Thomists have defined prejudice as *thinking ill of others without sufficient warrant.*

You notice that both definitions, as well as the examples I gave, specify 9 two ingredients of prejudice. First there is some sort of faulty generalization in thinking about a group. I'll call this the process of *categorization*. Then there is the negative, rejective, or hostile ingredient, a *feeling* tone. "Being down on something" is the hostile ingredient; "that you're not up on" is the categorization ingredient; "thinking ill of others" is the hostile ingredient; "without sufficient warrant" is the faulty categorization.

Parenthetically I should say that of course there is such a thing as *positive* 10 prejudice. We can be just as prejudiced *in favor of* as we are *against*. We can be biased in favor of our children, our neighborhood, or our college. Spinoza makes the distinction neatly. He says that *love prejudice* is "thinking well of others, through love, more than is right." *Hate prejudice,* he says, is "thinking ill of others, through hate, more than is right."

⌧ LEWIS H. LAPHAM

Spoils of War

Lewis H. Lapham is the long-time editor of Harper's *magazine. He writes an essay for each issue of* Harper's *and this one appeared in the December 1987 issue. In it he argues that the cold war between the United States and the U.S.S.R. is foolish in the extreme, and that there is nothing to be gained by either side in a war between the two.*

> But what good came of it at last?
> Quoth little Peterkin.
> Why, that I cannot tell, said he,
> But 'twas a famous victory.
> —Robert Southey,
> "The Battle of Blenheim"

For the better part of forty years I have been listening to people talk about the 1 chance of war with the Soviet Union, but I have yet to hear anybody say anything about what might be gained from such a war. What would be its objectives, and what spoils would belong to the victor?

The ancient Romans at least had it in mind to loot the tents of their 2 enemies. Their legions marched east and south in the hope of stealing somebody else's grain or elephants or gold. The British empire in the eighteenth century employed its armies to protect its trade in molasses or slaves or tea.

Napoleon sacked Europe in the early years of the nineteenth century to pay off the debts of the French Revolution.

But what profit could the United States or the Soviet Union discover in ³ the other's defeat? Suppose that both nations avoided the stupidity of nuclear self-annihilation. Suppose further that one of the two nations managed to win World War III—either by means of conventional arms (Soviet tanks rolling unhindered across the plain of northern Europe or American troops marching triumphantly north from the Black Sea) or because one of the two nations simply got tired of paying the bills for next year's collection of new weapons. On the American side, the second eventuality assumes that during one of Senator Jesse Helms's brief absences from Washington a consortium of frightened liberal politicians surrendered the United States without firing as much as a single naval salute.

Say, for whatever reason, that the war ends in a flutter of parades and that ⁴ a chorus of new voices, slightly accented, begins telling the story of the evening news. What then? Who distributes the prize money, and how does the conquering host preserve the innocence of its ideological faith?

Consider first the consequences of a Soviet triumph. Imagine a Soviet ⁵ fleet at anchor in New York harbor and the White House occupied by the proconsuls of the Soviet empire. Among the official classes of Washington the transition probably could be accomplished in a matter of days. Certainly the federal bureaucracy would welcome the expansion of its powers and dominions. Because so much of the nation's nominally private industry feeds—even now, at the zenith of the conservative ascendancy—on the milk of government charity, none of the city's accomplished lobbyists would have any trouble grasping the principles of socialist enterprise.

The directives handed down by the Politburo presumably would do little ⁶ more than magnify the frown of paranoid suspicion already implicit in the Reagan administration's insistence on loyalty oaths, electronic surveillance, urine testing, and censorship. In return for the trifling gestures that accompany any change of political venue—replacing the portraits on the walls, learning a few words of a new flattery—the government ministries would receive the gifts of suzerainty over the whole disorderly mess of American democracy. After so many years of writing so many querulous memoranda and bearing the insults of so many ungrateful journalists, the government would be free at last—free to meddle in everybody's business, free to indulge its passion for rules and its habit of sloth, free to tap all the telephones in all the discotheques in west Los Angeles.

The intellectual classes would go even more quietly into the totalitarian ⁷ night. The American intelligentsia never has been notable for its courage or the tenacity of its convictions. If the Soviets took the trouble to shoot three or four television anchormen, the rest of the class would quickly learn the difference between a right and a wrong answer. The big media inevitably applaud the wisdom in office (whether announced by Gerald Ford or Jimmy Carter) and the universities teach the great American lesson of going along to get along.

Many of the most vehement apostles of the Reagan revolution (among them Norman Podhoretz and Michael Novak) once professed themselves loyal to the liberal, even radical, left. Given their talent for conversion I expect that they wouldn't have much trouble working out the dialectics of a safe return to the winning side. Literary bureaucrats—in the United States as in the Soviet Union and whether construed as priests or commissars or English professors—prefer the kind of world in which words take precedence over things and statements of theory overrule the insolence of facts.

Nor would the monied classes offer much of an objection to a Soviet 8 victory. The financial magnates who weren't traveling in Europe at the time and who even bothered to notice that the war had come and gone almost certainly would make some sort of deal with the new owners of the American franchise. Over the last seven years Americans have sold off (to the Japanese, the French, the British, the Saudis) one trillion dollars in assets (land, bank debt, manufacturing capacity, real estate, office buildings), and we have gotten into the habit of deferring to the whims of a foreign buyer.

Again, as with the unoffending anchormen, the Soviets might make a 9 halfhearted show of ideological seriousness. The Communist state certainly would confiscate a fair number of yachts and racing stables, and it might subject a few conspicuous slumlords and investment bankers to the formalities of a trial for crimes against the working poor. But too zealous a schedule of punishments would violate the spirit of *glasnost*, and I expect that most of the native oligarchy would be allowed to keep as much of its property as it could decently hide.

People might have to reduce their standards of extravagance and forgo the 10 comfort of the fourth Mercedes or the convenience of a choice between forty-seven Italian white wines, but within a matter of weeks the opulent magazines would reflect the craze for wood carvings, caftans, and oriental colors. The fashionable people in New York and Los Angeles soon would discover a remarkable similarity between the Marxist aesthetic ("so simple, so pure") and the Puritan charm of seventeenth century New England. Henry Kissinger could be relied upon to teach the television audience about the greatness of Peter the Great.

So far, so good, but not quite good enough. Among the privileged classes 11 in the larger cities the Soviets might discover a crowd of new and eager friends, but in the *terra incognita* beyond the lights of New York, Washington, and Beverly Hills, I'm afraid that they wouldn't have such an easy time of it. The county is too big, and too many citizens like to carry guns. The Russians have trouble enough with the illiterate and poorly armed Afghans. What would they do with the subscribers to *Soldier of Fortune* magazine, with hundreds of thousands of restless adolescents looking for a reason (any reason) to dynamite a train, with bands of guerrillas trained at M.I.T. and capable of reading the instruction manuals for automatic weapons, with the regiments of elderly duck-hunters in Florida and Texas who have been waiting patiently ever since 1945 for the chance to blast the Communist birds of prey? Lacking the sophistication of the New York police, how could the Soviets contain a crowd at a Bruce

Springsteen concert, or suppress the computer networking in the San Fernando Valley? Where would the Politburo recruit the army of censors necessary to silence all the CB radios, raid all the pornographic newsstands, shut down all the telephone lines, and foreclose all the means of free and seditious expression?

Even with the enthusiastic help of Pat Robertson and William Bennett, 12 the secretary of education, it is unlikely that the Soviet Union could accomplish so herculean a labor of purification. But unless the Russians operated the United States as a labor camp, how could they preserve the belief in the Marxist fairy tale? Let too many Russians loose in the streets of Orlando or Kansas City and they might succumb to the heresy of supermarkets or fall into the temptation of department stores. Within a generation Communism would be as dead as the last czar.

Nor would the Americans fare much better if we were unlucky enough to 13 win the war. We are a people who lack both the talent and stomach for empire. Shooting partisans on sight doesn't sit well with what remains of the American conscience, and we complain bitterly (Mr. Reagan's Orange County friends foremost among the complainants) about the cost of keeping a military garrison in a terrain as comfortable as Western Europe. Where would we find the troops to stand guard on the marches of Uzbekistan? How could we administer the 8,649,000 square miles of the Union of Soviet Socialist Republics? We can't provide enough of our own citizens with decent housing, fair employment, or a fifth-grade education. What empty political promises could George Bush or Michael Dukakis offer 283,520,000 people speaking 130 languages who expect to be fed and clothed by the state? Do we imagine that we can staff Siberia with graduates of the Harvard Business School, that we can teach the hard lessons of independence to a people used to the comforts of depotism?

If we cannot do for the vast expanse of the Soviet Union what we cannot 14 do for downtown Detroit, then either we operate the country as a penal institution or, as with Germany and Japan in the aftermath of World War II, we lend money, provide technical assistance, and instruct our wards in the perfections of capitalism. By choosing the first option we transform the American republic into a police state. The second option probably dooms America to economic ruin. To our sorrow we have seen what wonders can be worked by people released from the sterile task of making the toys of war. Within a generation we would be importing Russian cars, wearing Russian silk, borrowing Russian currency to finance the miraculous debt incurred by our military triumph.

No, I'm afraid that World War III lacks the motive of enlightened self- 15 interest. No matter whose troops march through which capital city, the conquerors become the conquered, their systems of political and economic thought changed into their dreaded opposites.

The certain defeat implicit in anybody's victory seems to me worth bearing 16 firmly in mind. Yet, in all the official gabbling about missiles and tanks and the fierce portrait of "American credibility" in the Persian Gulf, I never hear anybody asking the questions "Why?" and "What for?" Maybe this is because the answers would sound like nightclub jokes.

⚶ ANDREW MARVELL

To His Coy Mistress

Andrew Marvell (1621–1678), was a poet and British statesman. The poem that follows, published posthumously, is his most famous work. In it he tries to persuade a coy mistress into action now, while alive, and before "your quaint honor turn to dust. And into ashes all my lust."

Had we but world enough, and time,   1
This coyness, Lady, were no crime.
We would sit down and think which way
To walk and pass our long love's day.
Thou by the Indian Ganges' side
Shouldst rubies find; I by the tide
Of Humber would complain. I would
Love you ten years before the Flood,
And you should, if you please, refuse
Till the conversion of the Jews.
My vegetable love would grow
Vaster than empires and more slow;
An hundred years would go to praise
Thine eyes and on thy forehead gaze;
Two hundred to adore each breast,
But thirty thousand to the rest;
An age at least to every part,
And the last age should show your heart.
For, Lady, you deserve this state,
Nor would I love at lower rate.

But at my back I always hear   2
Time's wingèd chariot hurrying near;
And yonder all before us lie
Deserts of vast eternity.
Thy beauty shall no more be found,
Nor, in thy marble vault, shall sound
My echoing song; then worms shall try
That long preserved virginity,
And your quaint honor turn to dust,
And into ashes all my lust:
The grave's a fine and private place,
But none, I think, do there embrace.

Now therefore, while the youthful hue   3
Sits on thy skin like morning dew,

And while thy willing soul transpires
At every pore with instant fires,
Now let us sport us while we may,
And now, like amorous birds of prey,
Rather at once our time devour
Than languish in his slow-chapped power.
Let us roll all our strength and all
Our sweetness up into one ball,
And tear our pleasures with rough strife
Through the iron gate of life:
Thus, though we cannot make our sun
Stand still, yet we will make him run.

⊠ PLATO

What Is Justice?

The ancient Greek philosopher Plato is generally considered one of the greatest philosophers in the history of Western philosophy. In this excerpt from his book, The Republic, *he has Socrates argue against the Sophist Thrasymachus' cynical definition of justice as whatever is in the interests of the stronger party and present his own ideas on the nature of justice.*

I proclaim that justice is nothing else than the interest of the stronger [said 1 Thrasymachus]. And now why do you not praise me? . . .

[Socrates:] we are both agreed that justice is interest of some sort, but you go on to say "of the stronger"; about this addition I am not so sure. Tell me, Do you not likewise admit that it is just for subjects to obey their rulers? . . . Are the rulers of the various states infallible, or are they sometimes liable to err?

To be sure, he replied, they are liable to err.   2

Then in making their laws they may sometimes make them rightly, and 3 sometimes not?

When they make them rightly, they make them agreeably to their interest; 4 when they are mistaken, contrary to their interest; you admit that?

And whatever laws they make must be obeyed by their subjects,—and that 5 is what you call justice?

Doubtless.   6

Then justice, according to your argument, is not only observance of the 7 interest of the stronger but the reverse?

What is that you are saying? he asked.   8

I am only repeating what you are saying, I believe. But let us consider: 9
Have we not agreed that the rulers, in commanding some actions, may be
mistaken about their own interest but that it is just for the subjects to do
whatever their rulers command?

I think so.   10

Then think that you have acknowledged that it is just to do actions which 11
are contrary to the interest of the government or the stronger, when the governors unintentionally command things to be done which are to their own injury,
assuming with you that the obedience which the subject renders to their commands, is just.

[Now] . . . let me ask [said Socrates], in what sense do you speak of a ruler 12
or stronger whose interest, as you were saying, he being the superior, it is just
that the inferior should execute—is he a ruler in the popular or in the strict
sense of the term?

In the strictest of all senses, he said. . . .   13

[Then] tell me: Is the physician, taken in that strict sense of which you are 14
speaking, a healer of the sick or a maker of money? And remember that I am
now speaking of the true physician.

A healer of the sick, he replied.   15

Now, I said, has not each of these craftsmen an interest? . . .   16

For which the art has to consider and provide, that being its origin and 17
purpose? . . .

And the interest of any art consists in its being, as far as possible, perfect— 18
this and nothing else?

What do you mean?   19

I mean what I may illustrate negatively by the example of the body. Sup- 20
pose you were to ask me whether the body is self-sufficing or wants assistance,
I should reply: Certainly it does so; that is why the science, which we call
medicine, was invented, because the body is unsound and cannot survive by
itself. The art has been established in order to provide it with things which are
beneficial to it.

But is the art of medicine or any other art faulty or deficient in any quality 21
in the same way that the eye may be deficient in sight or the ear fail of hearing,
and therefore require another art to provide for the interests of seeing and
hearing? Or is each of them able to look after its own interest? Or have they no
need either of themselves or of another to provide the remedy for their own
unsoundness—for there is no such thing as a fault or unsoundness in any art,
and the only benefit which an art need consider is that of its subject? For every
art remains pure and faultless while remaining true—that is to say, while perfect
and unimpaired. Take the words in your precise sense, and tell me whether I
am not right.

Yes, clearly.   22

Then medicine does not consider the interest of medicine, but the interest 23
of the body?

True, he said.   24

But surely, Thrasymachus, the arts are the superiors and rulers of their 25 own subjects?

To this he assented with a good deal of reluctance. 26

Then, I said, no science or art considers or enjoins the interest of the 27 stronger [or superior], but only the interest of the subject and weaker?

He made an attempt to contest this proposition also, but finally 28 acquiesced.

Then, I continued, no physician, in so far as he is a physician, considers 29 his own good in what he prescribes, but the good of his patient; for the true physician is also a ruler having the human body as a subject, and is not a mere money-maker; that has been admitted?

Yes. . . . 30

And such a . . . ruler will provide and prescribe for the interest of the 31 sailor who is under him, and not for his own interest?

He gave a reluctant "Yes." 32

Then, I said, Thrasymachus, there is no one in any rule who, in so far as 33 he is a ruler, considers or enjoins what is for his own interest. On the contrary, a ruler attends to the subject which he has undertaken to direct; to that he looks, and in everything which he says and does, considers what is suitable or advantageous to it.

When we had got to this point in the argument, and everyone saw that the 34 definition of justice had been completely turned round, Thrasymachus, instead of replying to me, said: Tell me, Socrates, have you got a nurse?

Why do you ask such a question, I said. . . . 35

Because she leaves you to snivel, and never wipes your nose: she has not 36 even taught you to know the shepherd from the sheep.

What makes you say that? I replied. 37

Because you fancy that the shepherd or neatherd fattens and tends the 38 sheep or oxen with a view to something other than the good of himself or his master; and you further imagine that the rulers of states, if they are true rulers, never think of their subjects as sheep, and that they are not studying their own advantage day and night. Oh, no; and so entirely astray are you in your ideas about the just and the unjust as not even to know that justice and the just are in reality another's good, that is to say, the interest of the ruler and stronger, and the loss of the subject and servant; and injustice, the opposite, for the unjust is lord over the truly simple and just: he is the stronger, and his subjects do what is for his interest, and minister to his happiness, which is very far from being their own. . . . Mankind censure injustice, fearing that they may be the victims of it and not because they shrink from committing it. And thus, as I have shown, Socrates, injustice, when on a sufficient scale, has more strength and freedom and mastery than justice; and, as I said at first, justice is in fact the interest of the stronger, whereas injustice is a man's own profit and interest. . . .

I must remark, Thrasymachus, if you will recall what was previously said 39 [replied Socrates], that although you began by defining the true physician in an exact sense, you did not observe a like exactness when speaking of the shepherd;

you thought that the shepherd as a shepherd tends the sheep not with a view to their own good, but like a mere diner or banqueter with a view to the pleasures of the table; or, again, as a trader, for sale in the market, and not as a shepherd. Yet surely the art of the shepherd is concerned only with the good of his subjects; he has only to provide the best for them, since the perfection of the art itself is already ensured whenever the shepherd's work is perfectly performed. And that was what I was saying just now about the ruler. I conceived that the art of the ruler, considered as ruler, whether in a state or in private life, could only have regard to the maximum good of those ruled. Do you think that rulers and office holders—true rulers—willingly hold office and rule?

Think! Nay, I am sure of it.   40

Then why in the case of lesser offices do men never take them willingly   41 without payment, unless because they assume that their rule is to be advantageous not to themselves but to the governed? Let me ask you a question: Are not the several arts different, by reason of their each having a separate function? . . .

And each art gives us a particular good and not merely a general one—   42 medicine, for example, gives us health; navigation, safety at sea; and so on?

Yes, he said.   43

And the art of earning has the special function of giving pay: but we do   44 not confuse this with other arts, any more than the art of the pilot is to be confused with the art of medicine, because the health of the pilot may be improved by a sea voyage. . . .

And we have admitted, I said, that the good of each art is specially con-   45 fined to the art? . . .

Then, if there be any good which all craftsmen have in common, that is   46 to be attributed to something of which they all make common use? . . .

Moreover, we say that if the craftsman is benefited by receiving pay, that   47 comes from his use of the art of earning in addition to his own?

He gave a reluctant assent to this.   48

Then the benefit, or receipt of pay, is not derived by the several craftsmen   49 from their respective crafts. But it is more accurate to say that while the art of medicine gives health, and the art of the builder builds a house, another art attends them which is the art of earning. The various arts may be doing their own business and benefiting that over which they preside, but would the craftsman receive any benefit from his art unless he were paid as well?

I suppose not.   50

But does he therefore confer no benefit when he works for nothing?   51

Then now, Thrasymachus, there is not longer any doubt that neither arts   52 nor governments provide for their own interests; but, as we were before saying, they rule and provide for the interest of their subjects who are the weaker and not the stronger—to their good they attend and not to the good of the superior. And this is the reason, my dear Thrasymachus, why, as I was just now saying, no one is willing to govern; because no one likes to take in hand the reformation of evils which are not his concern without remuneration. For in the execution of his work, and in giving his orders to another, the true artist does not regard his own interest, but always that of his subjects; and therefore in order that rulers may be willing to rule, they must be paid in one of three modes of payment—money, or honour, or a penalty for refusing. . . .

⊠ I. F. STONE

Plato's Ideal Bedlam

I. F. Stone wrote and published his own periodical, I. F. Stone's Weekly *(later a bi-weekly), for many years before retiring to study the classics he had not had time for before. This essay reflects his disappointment at discovering that Plato favored an authoritarian society in which there is no freedom.*

The oldest and hoariest idea of political philosophy is that ordinary people 1
cannot be trusted to govern themselves. It is also the most persistent. For if one looks closely enough, one will find that it is still the hidden first premise of all bureaucracies, however diverse they may otherwise be, whether in the capitalist democracies, the Communist dictatorships, or the makeshift military despotisms into which most of the Third World has been liberated.

The most glamorous packaging of this ancient and disdainful notion was 2
provided more than two millennia ago by Plato. No other thinker has ever gotten away with so much egregious nonsense as this fastidious Athenian aristocrat, so seductive are his artistry and charm. The foremost example, and the best known, is his proposal for government by "philosopher kings."

This, the most famous of Plato's utterances about politics, appears midway 3
in the *Republic*. There, as almost everyone knows, Plato has Socrates say that until philosophers become kings or kings become philosophers, there is no prospect of happiness for the human race.

Plato waged a lifelong vendetta against democracy, although that vendetta 4
was only made possible by the free speech and free inquiry the democratic institutions of his native Athens allowed him. It was democracy that enabled him to pursue his teaching unmolested and to found an Academy that lasted for nearly a thousand years. It was closed down by two forces that shared his own belief that absolute government was best: the Roman Empire and the Roman Catholic Church. It is ironic but fitting that the Academy should have fallen victim to the very doctrine its founder propounded.

Plato's preference in government assumes different forms in different dia- 5
logues, but the underlying theme is the same. In the *Politicus*, or *Statesman*,
Plato taught that the "right form of government must be sought in some small
number, or one person" with absolute power, *unrestricted even by law*, to the
point where the ruler or rulers may "purge the city for its good by killing or
banning some of its citizens." This practice is no stranger to our turbulent
times.

In Plato's *Laws*, the government is a gloomy theocracy, buttressed by an 6
inquisition that is embodied in a Nocturnal Synod empowered to execute those
whose heretical or dissident views it cannot "correct." The best-known form of
the Platonic ideal is sketched in his *Republic*, which was not a republic at all
in the modern meaning of the term, but what we would call an absolute and
authoritarian regime, presided over by one or more philosopher kings. . . .

Neither Plato nor the Platonists, dazzled by the genius of their master, 7
recognize the fundamental difficulty that at once strikes the fresh and irreverent
reader of the *Republic*. Philosophers spend their lives disagreeing with one
another, and they disagree about everything. How could a government of philosopher kings be kept from breaking down into a disputatious bedlam? How
would they ever come to agreement and decision? Even those who call themselves the followers of the selfsame teacher manage to disagree, often violently,
about just what it was that their master actually taught them. The warring sects
of Christianity provide the most notorious example. The followers of Socrates
were busily disagreeing and founding rival schools of Socratic philosophy even
while he was still alive. . . .

Plato took a firm though somewhat startling step for dealing with philo- 8
sophic feuding. He decided, in effect—and quite conveniently—to outlaw all
but one school of philosophy from his utopia. He never says so explicitly in the
Republic, but in his Seventh Letter we find it clearly stated that it is not just
philosophers who must come to power but the "right kind" of philosophers.
This means, of course, those who agree with Plato. Even the philosophers,
indeed the philosophers especially, have to toe the party line in his utopia. In
short, the concept of the philosopher king is a cloak for the dictatorship of one
school of philosophy, Plato's own. . . .

Once in his life, Plato was given his chance to reform a government and 9
create a utopia. Plutarch tells the story, and it illustrates how differently Plato's
mind worked from that of such latter-day followers as Bosanquet. The opportunity came in Sicily, where a new tyrant, Dionysius II, summoned Plato to
his court in Syracuse and asked him to reform the government. Such an
invitation had long been Plato's dream. One way to achieve his utopia, as Plato
tells us in his *Republic*, would be to find a tyrant willing to place his dictatorial
power at the disposal of a philosopher. This is what Dionysius seemed ready
to do.

Plato did not proceed by mobilizing experts in trade, economics, law, and 10
government for their "best and deepest ideas." From Plutarch's account, he
seems to have sought the reformation of society by teaching the rulers higher
mathematics.

Plato was deeply influenced by the Pythagoreans, for whom the secrets of 11 existence were to be found in mathematics, particularly geometry. Plato's first step was to set the tyrant and his associates to work on geometry lessons. Geometry in those days was learned and taught by drawing diagrams in the sand. Plutarch tells us the tyrant's palace was soon strewn with sand "owing to the multitude of geometricians there." Every courtier was eager to curry favor by conforming to this strange new fashion. . . .

[Plato's reforms were soon overturned. But the] point here is that Plato's 12 procedure as a reformer bore no resemblance to what we think of as government by "experts." Plato was not concerned with the here and now, but with the eternal. His idea of a perfect government was a hierarchical society governed by mathematical mystics free to devote their lives to the contemplation of ineffable metaphysical mysteries while a special policing caste kept the lower, but producing, classes in awed submission.

The strangest aspect of Plato's utopia is that it put the reins of government 13 in the hands of those who care least about human concerns. Plato makes Socrates say outright that "the man whose mind is truly fixed on eternal realities has no leisure to turn his eyes downward upon the petty affairs of men." Instead, "he fixes his gaze upon the things of the eternal unchanging order." This may qualify him to be the abbot of a monastery, where men retire to meditate. But is such a man the kind to run a government?

If novels—and utopias—can be read psychoanalytically as daydreams, the 14 vicarious fulfillment of subconscious fantasies, then the *Republic* may be read as a schoolmaster's daydream, the vision of society as an enlarged schoolroom, peopled by dutiful, submissive, and adoring pupils and ruled over by a professor who brooks no disagreement.

The most paradoxical feature of Plato's republic is that although it was to 15 be ruled by philosophers, in it no further philosophizing was to be allowed. To maintain the one "correct" philosophy, the Platonic party line, there was to be no freedom of speech or of teaching or of inquiry.

Plato's philosopher kings were to establish a monopoly of education, 16 screen out potential dissenters from higher schooling, control the content and means of communication, censor the poets and especially the theater, establish a state religion, and formulate a theology to which all must conform. . . .

. . . Since the visible universe was constantly changing, he rejected it as 17 unreal. He sought refuge in a world of invisible "forms" or "ideas" in which he saw the only unchanging, and therefore true, reality. This perfect world existed somewhere in the celestial stratosphere, beyond even the stars, and was perceptible only to the mystical vision of the initiated. . . .

Plato's bold aim in the *Republic* is nothing less than to fashion a New 18 Man. He has Socrates explain the process of this creation, or re-creation, in the most beguiling and spiritual terms. First the philosopher refashions himself and then he refashions mankind.

Socrates begins by saying that the "true" philosopher "contemplates a world 19 of unchanging and harmonious order, where reason governs and nothing can do or suffer wrong." The true philosopher, "like one who imitates an admired companion," tries to fit his own self to this celestial vision, so that he himself will, "so far as man may, become godlike."

If summoned to take the reins of power, our godlike philosopher will show 20 that he does not lack "the skill to produce such counterparts of temperance, justice, and all the virtues as can exist in the ordinary man." Like an artist, he will remake man and state "after the divine pattern."

Sounds lovely, doesn't it? Then Socrates is asked how this "artist" will set 21 to work. And here the shivers begin, for Socrates replies:

> He will take society and human character as his canvas and begin by scraping it clean. That is no easy matter; but as you know, unlike other reformers [i.e., the moderates and gradualists] he will not consent to take in hand either an individ-ual or a state or to draft laws, until he is given a clean surface to work on or has cleansed it himself.

In other words, the philosopher will not take over rule unless given total and absolute power. Socrates uses the metaphor of the painter, and this is charm-ing—until one begins to see what it really entails. . . .

The nightmarish climax of this wacky mystic vision comes in a too-little- 22 noticed passage at the end of Book VII of the *Republic*. There, finally, Socrates says he will show the "speediest and easiest way" a perfect city and perfect people "could be established and prosper." He says the philosopher kings could simply expel all inhabitants over the age of ten, "take over the children, remove them from the manners and habits of their parents," and bring them up in accord with the new customs and laws imposed by the philosopher kings. This would indeed be a "clean slate."

The Platonic commentators skip over this frightful suggestion with embar- 23 rassment. None of the questions that would arise in a real discussion of such a proposal is raised. We are not told how these self-proclaimed practitioners of the highest virtue would justify the condemnation of every adult inhabitant to the loss of his city, his home, and his children. Plato's suggestion seems the archetypal model for the utopias we have seen in this century. In every one of them some sort of genocide has lain across the threshold to the earthly paradise they promised.

In the construction of Plato's utopia, fundamental problems of morality 24 and power are glossed over or ignored. The underside and scaffolding have to be kept in the dark; they would otherwise make the process of erecting Plato's ideal society too repulsive. The gruesome details are made easy to hide by the absence of normal thrust and rejoinder in the dialogue, which needs only be compared with the agonizing debates in Thucydides to see how far the highly touted Socratic dialectic falls short of the genuine article. In these fixed boxing matches, the opposition always takes the count, and Socrates always walks off with the verdict while smugly advertising his humility.

But when it comes to maintaining power in the new ideal state, the 25 mechanism is clear to all whose eyes are not too clouded by Platonic piety. The fundamental step is to disarm the citizenry and to allow weapons only to a professional police-soldier caste.

Plato calls them *phylakes*, which basically means watchmen or guards, 26 but which is usually translated into English with a word of gentler connotation, *Guardians*. According to Socrates, the Guardians are to serve as "watchers against foemen without and friends within, so that the latter *shall not wish* [my italics] and the former shall not be able to work harm to the City." Of course, nobody asks Socrates how these Guardians are to make sure that the disarmed citizenry will not even "wish" to throw a monkey wrench into the works. Apparently the citizenry was not only to be spied upon but to be brainwashed against any desire to dissent.

Aristotle once observed that politics was the struggle between the rich and 27 the poor. One way of easing the struggle was to achieve internal peace by widening the rights of citizenship to the poorest class, as in the participatory democracy of Athens, thus creating a sense of community. The other was to hold down the lower classes by denying them fundamental rights and treating them as a race apart, as was done in Sparta and Crete. That was also Plato's solution.

Plato was an absolutist in every aspect of his thought, and his politics ran 28 true to form. As Aristotle, his first and most famous critic, pointed out, "There will inevitably be [in Plato's republic] two states in one, and these antagonistic to one another": on one side the Guardians, "a sort of garrison" or occupying army; on the other "the Farmers, Artisans, and other classes." Aristotle saw a parallel between Plato's divided state and Crete, where the ruling class forbade the workers gymnastic exercises and the right to bear arms, thereby ensuring their inferiority in physique and in weaponry.

But these lower classes in Crete were slaves, and their lack of strength kept 29 them so. Were the common people in Plato's republic to be slaves, or citizens? It is difficult to answer the question. Certainly both commoner and slave would be accorded fewer rights than they had in Athens. In Plato's republic the common man, like the slave, would be taught to know and observe his place. But the *Republic* sometimes blurs the distinction between them by equating the status of a free commoner with that of a slave. . . .

Paul Shorey's masterly translation [of key phrases] provides the most exact 30 rendering of the Greek text when he has it say that the ordinary citizen of the republic "ought to be the slave of that best man who has within himself the divine governing principle." The word in Greek is *doulos*, which unambiguously means slave, although in this passage it has rarely been translated that bluntly.

Plato explains that this subordination is of course for the common man's 31 own good, and not for his exploitation. . . .

Plato knew that submission could not be won by force alone. How did he 32 propose to make this new bondage acceptable? His answer was that a sense of irremediable inferiority had to be inculcated in the minds and souls of the lower classes. This bit of mental engineering was to be the achievement of what Plato called the Noble Lie.

To understand the Noble Lie one must understand that in Plato's utopia 33 the truth is demanded of the governed but mendacity is to be a creative tool in the hands of the philosopher kings. Socrates is quite specific about this:

> For if we were right in what we were just saying and falsehood is in very deed useless to gods, but to men useful as remedy or form of medicine, it is obvious that such a thing [i.e., lying] must be assigned to physicians, and laymen should have nothing to do with it.
>
> Obviously, he [Socrates' interlocutor] replied.
>
> The rulers then of the city may . . . fitly lie on account of enemies or citizens for the benefit of the state; . . . .

This kind of sophistry is still the rationalization for what the CIA calls its "disinformation" activities. Socrates goes on to make sure that mendacity and perjury* remain a monopoly of the state:

> No others may have anything to do with it [i.e., lying], but for a layman to lie to rulers . . . we shall affirm to be as great a sin, nay a greater, than it is for a patient not to tell his physician or an athlete his trainer the truth about his bodily condition, or for a man to deceive the pilot about the ship.

The questions inevitably following from this—for instance, what happens 34 when a citizen contradicts an official lie, will he be punished for telling the truth?—are not aired in the *Republic*. What Socrates is leading up to there is the propagation of the one whopping falsehood upon which the whole structure depends: those in the ideal city were to be taught that, although all citizens are brothers, the god of creation used an admixture of gold in fashioning those fitted to rule, silver in making the Guardians, and, for the lowest class, composed of the farmers and craftsmen, iron and brass.

The common folk were to be taught that the rulers and soldiers had 35 precious metal in their makeup and were intrinsically superior to the lower class. Thus, the myth would stamp a sense of inferiority on the lower class so indelibly that it would be forever submissive to its "betters." This would be a caste system, like India's, not merely a division into classes; in short, social status would be inherited, although provision would be made for ruthlessly upgrading or downgrading occasional "sports" in the breeding process. . . .

. . . the human landscape for most of the two-and-a-half millennia since 36 Plato wrote has resembled his ideal city. Until the comparatively recent Ameri-

---

*Victor S. Navasky's new book, *Naming Names*, on the witch-hunt of the Fifties, gives on pages 14 and 15 the sworn testimony of an FBI man in which he says, in quite Platonic fashion, that where the interests of the government were at stake he was ready to lie even "under oath in a court of law," something he would do "a thousand times." Similarly, in 1975, Richard Helms admitted that as head of the CIA he had lied under oath to the Senate Foreign Relations Committee, to hide the CIA's covert efforts to overthrow the Allende government in Chile. He escaped with a suspended sentence in a plea bargain with the Justice Department that allowed him to plead no contest to a mere misdemeanor. Platonism still has its triumphs.

can and French revolutions, the common man almost everywhere was regarded, and conditioned to regard himself, as of a nature inferior to his betters.

Most of the Platonists, and the classical scholars over the intervening 37 centuries, have reflected—as Plato did—the ethos of the landed aristocracy, of the gentlemen born to no pursuit other than that of governing, policing, and indoctrinating the lower classes, whether in the officer corps of the armed forces, in the various churches and universities, or in the government itself.

The English gentleman, like the Prussian Junker and the landed nobility 38 of Europe well into the nineteenth century—and some even to this day—shared the lofty condescensions of the Attic gentry, which Plato embodied in its utmost perfection. And most of mankind until recently provided the mire in the human garden where these exquisite creatures bloomed for their day.

Plato remains the darling of the hierarchs, whatever their guise, a sacred 39 cow to both the Left and Right. To dare an irreverent look at him and his doctrines is to unite even the otherwise irreconcilables of Right and Left in his defense. His philosopher kings are still with us, though in new guise, in wide stretches of the earth.

⊠ **JONATHAN SWIFT**

A Modest Proposal

Jonathan Swift (1667–1745), author of Gulliver's Travels, *wrote this ironic gem in protest against the terrible famine Ireland was experiencing under British rule. He used irony (saying one thing while clearly meaning another) to force British readers to face the horrors of the mass starvation for which they were partly responsible.*

It is a melancholy object to those who walk through this great town or travel in 1 the country, when they see the streets, the roads, and cabin doors, crowded with beggars of the female sex, followed by three, four, or six children, all in rags and importuning every passenger for an alms. These mothers, instead of being able to work for their honest livelihood, are forced to employ all their time strolling to beg sustenance for their helpless infants, who, as they grow up, either turn thieves for want of work, or leave their dear native country to fight for the Pretender in Spain, or sell themselves to the Barbados.

I think it is agreed by all parties that this prodigious number of children in 2 the arms, or on the backs, or at the heels of their mothers, and frequently of their fathers, is in the present deplorable state of the kingdom a very great additional grievance; and therefore whoever could find out a fair, cheap, and easy method of making these children sound, useful members of the commonwealth would deserve so well of the public as to have his statue set up for a preserver of the nation.

But my intention is very far from being confined to provide only for the 3 children of professed beggars; it is of a much greater extent, and shall take in the whole number of infants at a certain age who are born of parents in effect as little able to support them as those who demand our charity in the streets.

As to my own part, having turned my thoughts for many years upon this 4 important subject, and maturely weighed the several schemes of other projectors, I have always found them grossly mistaken in their computation. It is true, a child just dropped from its dam may be supported by her milk for a solar year, with little other nourishment; at most not above the value of two shillings, which the mother may certainly get, or the value in scraps, by her lawful occupation of begging; and it is exactly at one year that I propose to provide for them in such a manner as instead of being a charge upon their parents or the parish, or wanting food and raiment for the rest of their lives, they shall on the contrary contribute to the feeding, and partly to the clothing, of many thousands.

There is likewise another great advantage in my scheme, that it will prevent 5 those voluntary abortions, and that horrid practice of women murdering their bastard children, alas, too frequent among us, sacrificing the poor innocent babes, I doubt, more to avoid the expense than the shame, which would move tears and pity in the most savage and inhuman breast.

The number of souls in this kingdom being usually reckoned one million 6 and a half, of these I calculate there may be about two hundred thousand couples whose wives are breeders; from which number I subtract thirty thousand couples who are able to maintain their own children, although I apprehend there cannot be so many under the present distress of the kingdom; but this being granted, there will remain an hundred and seventy thousand breeders. I again subtract fifty thousand for those women who miscarry, or whose children die by accident or disease within the year. There only remain an hundred and twenty thousand children of poor parents annually born. The question therefore is, how this number shall be reared and provided for, which, as I have already said, under the present situation of affairs, is utterly impossible by all the methods hitherto proposed. For we can neither employ them in handicraft or agriculture; we neither build houses (I mean in the country) nor cultivate land. They can very seldom pick up a livelihood by stealing till they arrive at six years old, except where they are of towardly parts; although I confess they learn the rudiments much earlier, during which time they can however be looked upon only as probationers, as I have been informed by a principal gentleman in the country of Cavan, who protested to me that he never knew above one or two instances under the age of six, even in a part of the kingdom so renowned for the quickest proficiency in that art.

I am assured by our merchants that a boy or a girl before twelve years old 7 is no salable commodity; and even when they come to this age they will not yield above three pounds, or three pounds and half a crown at most on the Exchange; which cannot turn to account either to the parents or the kingdom, the charge of nutriment and rags having been at least four times that value.

I shall now therefore humbly propose my own thoughts, which I hope 8 will not be liable to the least objection.

I have assured by a very knowing American of my acquaintance in Lon- 9 don, that a young healthy child well nursed is at a year old a most delicious, nourishing, and wholesome food, whether stewed, roasted, baked, or boiled; and I make no doubt that it will equally serve in a fricassee or a ragout.

I do therefore humbly offer it to public consideration that of the hundred 10 and twenty thousand children, already computed, twenty thousand may be reserved for breed, whereof only one-fourth part to be males, which is more than we allow to sheep, black cattle, or swine; and my reason is that these children are seldom the fruits of marriage, a circumstance not much regarded by our savages, therefore one male will be sufficient to serve four females. That the remaining hundred thousand may at a year old be offered in sale to the persons of quality and fortune through the kingdom, always advising the mother to let them suck plentifully in the last month, so as to render them plump and fat for a good table. A child will make two dishes at an entertainment for friends; and when the family dines alone, the fore or hind quarter will make a reason- able dish and seasoned with a little pepper or salt will be very good boiled on the fourth day, especially in winter.

I have reckoned upon a medium that a child just born will weigh twelve 11 pounds, and in a solar year if tolerably nursed increaseth to twenty-eight pounds.

I grant this food will be somewhat dear, and therefore very proper for 12 landlords, who, as they have already devoured most of the parents, seem to have the best title to the children.

Infant's flesh will be in season throughout the year, but more plentiful in 13 March, and a little before and after. For we are told by a grave author, an eminent French physician, that fish being a prolific diet, there are more chil- dren born in Roman Catholic countries about nine months after Lent than at any other season; therefore, reckoning a year after Lent, the markets will be more glutted than usual, because the number of popish infants is at least three to one in this kingdom; and therefore it will have other collateral advantage, by lessening the number of Papists among us.

I have already computed the charge of nursing a beggar's child (in which 14 list I reckon all cottagers, laborers, and four-fifths of the farmers) to be about two shillings per annum, rags included; and I believe no gentleman would repine to give ten shillings for the carcass of a good fat child, which, as I have said, will make four dishes of excellent nutritive meat, when he hath only some particular friend or his own family to dine with him. Thus the squire will learn to be a good landlord, and grow popular among the tenants; the mother will have eight shillings net profit, and be fit for work until she produces another child.

Those who are more thrifty (as I must confess the times require) may flay   15
the carcass; the skin of which artificially dressed will make admirable gloves for ladies, and summer boots for fine gentlemen.

As to our city of Dublin, shambles may be appointed for this purpose in   16
the most convenient parts of it, and butchers we may be assured will not be wanting; although I rather recommend buying the children alive, and dressing them hot from the knife as we do roasting pigs.

A very worthy person, a true lover of his country, and whose virtues I   17
highly esteem, was lately pleased in discoursing on this matter to offer a refinement upon my scheme. He said that many gentlemen of his kingdom, having of late destroyed their deer, he conceived that the want of venison might be well supplied by the bodies of young lads and maidens, not exceeding fourteen years of age nor under twelve, so great a number of both sexes in every county being now ready to starve for want of work and service; and these to be disposed of by their parents, if alive, or otherwise by their nearest relations. But with due deference to so excellent a friend and so deserving a patriot, I cannot be altogether in his sentiments; for as to the males, my American acquaintance assured me from frequent experience that their flesh was generally tough and lean, like that of our schoolboys, by continual exercise, and their taste disagreeable; and to fatten them would not answer the charge. Then as to the females, it would, I think with humble submission, be a loss to the public, because they soon would become breeders themselves; and besides, it is not improbable that some scrupulous people might be apt to censure such a practice (although indeed very unjustly) as a little bordering upon cruelty; which, I confess, hath always been with me the strongest objection against any project, how well soever intended.

But in order to justify my friend, he confessed that this expedient was put   18
into his head by the famous Psalmanazar, a native of the island Formosa, who came from thence to London above twenty years ago, and in conversation told my friend that in his country when any young person happened to be put to death, the executioner sold the carcass to persons of quality as a prime dainty; and that in his time the body of a plump girl of fifteen, who was crucified for attempt to poison the emperor, was sold to his Imperial Majesty's prime minister of state, and other great mandarins of the court, in joints from the gibbet, at four hundred crowns. Neither indeed can I deny that if the same use were made of several plump young girls in this town, who without one single groat to their fortunes cannot stir abroad without a chair, and appear at the playhouse and assemblies in foreign fineries which they never will pay for, the kingdom would not be the worse.

Some persons of a desponding spirit are in great concern about that vast   19
number of poor people who are aged, diseased, or maimed, and I have been desired to employ my thoughts what course may be taken to ease the nation of

so grievous an encumbrance. But I am not in the least pain upon that matter, because it is very well known that they are every day dying and rotting by cold and famine, and filth and vermin, as fast as can be reasonably expected. And as to the younger laborers, they are now in almost as hopeful a condition. They cannot get work, and consequently pine away for want of nourishment to a degree that if any time they are accidentally hired to common labor, they have not strength to perform it; and thus the country and themselves are happily delivered from the evils to come.

I have too long digressed, and therefore shall return to my subject. I think 20 the advantages by the proposal which I have made are obvious and many, as well as of the highest importance.

For first, as I have already observed, it would greatly lessen the number of 21 Papists, with whom we are yearly overrun, being the principal breeders of the nation as well as our most dangerous enemies; and who stay at home on purpose to deliver the kingdom to the Pretender, hoping to take their advantage by the absence of so many good Protestants, who have chosen rather to leave their country than to stay at home and pay tithes against their conscience to an Episcopal curate.

Secondly, the poorer tenants will have something valuable of their own, 22 which by law may be made liable to distress, and help to pay their landlord's rent, their corn and cattle being already seized and money a thing unknown.

Thirdly, whereas the maintenance of an hundred thousand children, from 23 two years old and upwards, cannot be computed at less than ten shillings a piece per annum, the nation's stock will be thereby increased fifty thousand pounds per annum, besides the profit of a new dish introduced to the tables of all gentlemen of fortune in the kingdom who have any refinement in taste. And the money will circulate among ourselves, the goods being entirely of our own growth and manufacture.

Fourthly, the constant breeders, besides the gain of eight shillings sterling 24 per annum by the sale of their children, will be rid of the charge of maintaining them after the first year.

Fifthly, this food would likewise bring great custom to taverns, where the 25 vintners will certainly be so prudent as to procure the best receipts for dressing it to perfection, and consequently have their houses frequented by all the fine gentlemen, who justly value themselves upon their knowledge in good eating; and a skillful cook, who understands how to oblige his guests, will contrive to make it as expensive as they please.

Sixthly, this would be a great inducement to marriage, which all wise 26 nations have either encouraged by rewards or enforced by laws and penalties. It would increase the care and tenderness of mothers toward their children, when they were sure of a settlement for life to the poor babes, provided in some sort by the public, to their annual profit instead of expense. We should see an honest emulation among the married women, which of them could bring the fattest child to the market. Men would become as fond of their wives during the time of their pregnancy as they are now of their mares in foal, their cows in calf, or sows when they are ready to farrow; nor offer to beat or kick them (as is too frequent a practice) for fear of a miscarriage.

Many other advantages might be enumerated. For instance, the addition 27 of some thousand carcasses in our exportation of barreled beef, the propagation of swine's flesh, and improvements in the art of making good bacon, so much wanted among us by the great destruction of pigs, too frequent at our tables, which are no way comparable in taste or magnificence to a well-grown, fat, yearling child, which roasted whole will make a considerable figure at a lord mayor's feast or any other public entertainment. But this and many others I omit, being studious of brevity.

Supposing that one thousand families in this city would be constant cus- 28 tomers for infants' flesh, besides other who might have it at merry meetings, particularly weddings and christenings, I compute that Dublin would take off annually about twenty thousand carcasses, and the rest of the kingdom (where probably they will be sold somewhat cheaper) the remaining eighty thousand.

I can think of no one objection that will possibly be raised against this 29 proposal, unless it should be urged that the number of people will be thereby much lessened in the kingdom. This I freely own, and it was indeed one principal design in offering it to the world. I desire the reader will observe, that I calculate my remedy for this one individual kingdom of Ireland and for no other that ever was, is, or I think ever can be upon earth. Therefore let no man talk to me of other expedients: of taxing our absentees at five shillings a pound: of using neither clothes nor household furniture except what is of our own growth and manufacture: of utterly rejecting the materials and instruments that promote foreign luxury: of curing the expensiveness of pride, vanity, idleness, and gaming in our women: of introducing a vein of parsimony, prudence, and temperance: of learning to love our country, in the want of which we differ even from Laplanders and the inhabitants of Topinamboo: of quitting our animosities and factions, nor acting any longer like the Jews, who were murdering one another at the very moment their city was taken: of being a little cautious not to sell our country and conscience for nothing: of teaching landlords to have at least one degree of mercy toward their tenants: lastly, of putting a spirit of honesty, industry, and skill into our shopkeepers; who, if a resolution could now be taken to buy only our native goods, would immediately unite to cheat and exact upon us in the price, the measure, and the goodness, nor could ever yet be brought to make one fair proposal of just dealing, though often and earnestly invited to it.

Therefore I repeat, let no man talk to me of these and the like expedients, 30 till he hath at least some glimpse of hope that there will ever be some hearty and sincere attempt to put them in practice.

But as to myself, having been wearied out for many years with offering 31 vain, idle, visionary thoughts, and at length utterly despairing of success, I fortunately fell upon this proposal, which, as it is wholly new, so it hath something solid and real, of no expense and little trouble, full in our own power, and whereby we can incur no danger in disobliging England. For this kind of commodity will not bear exportation, the flesh being of too tender a consistence to admit a long continuance in salt, although perhaps I could name a country which would be glad to eat up our whole nation without it.

After all, I am not so violently bent upon my own opinion as to reject any 32 offer proposed by wise men, which shall be found equally innocent, cheap, easy, and effectual, But before something of that kind shall be advanced in contradiction to my scheme, and offering a better, I desire the author or authors will be pleased maturely to consider two points. First, as things now stand, how they will be able to find food and raiment for an hundred thousand useless mouths and backs. And secondly, there being a round million of creatures in human figure throughout this kingdom, whose sole subsistence put into a common stock would leave them in debt two millions of pounds sterling, adding those who are beggars by profession to the bulk of farmers, cottagers, and laborers, with their wives and children who are beggars in effect; I desire those politicians who dislike my overture, and may perhaps be so bold to attempt an answer, that they will first ask the parents of these mortals whether they would not at this day think it a great happiness to have been sold for food at a year old in this manner I prescribe, and thereby have avoided such a perpetual scene of misfortunes as they have since gone through by the oppression of landlords, the impossibility of paying rent without money or trade, the want of common sustenance, with neither house nor clothes to cover them from the inclemencies of the weather, and the most inevitable prospect of entailing the like or greater miseries upon their breed forever.

I profess, in the sincerity of my heart, that I have not the least personal 33 interest in endeavoring to promote this necessary work, having no other motive than the public good of my country, by advancing our trade, providing for infants, relieving the poor, and giving some pleasure to the rich. I have no children by which I can propose to get a single penny; the youngest being nine years old, and my wife past childbearing.

Author/Title Index

378   *Author/Title Index*

Index of Useful Terms*

*Initial and/or important occurrences.

Acknowledgments

Gordon Allport, "The Nature of Prejudice," is from the Seventeenth Claremont Reading Conference Yearbook, 1952, Claremont College, Claremont, California. Reprinted with permission.

Doug Bandow, "This Ruling Threatens the Rights of Women," is from *USA TODAY*, May 12, 1987. Copyright © 1987 USA TODAY. Reprinted with permission of the author.

Walter Berns, "For Capital Punishment," is from Walter Berns, *For Capital Punishment: Crime and Morality of the Death Penalty* (Basic Books, 1979). Reprinted with permission of the author.

Alan Bloom, "The Student and the University," is from *The Closing of the American Mind*. Copyright © 1987 by Alan Bloom. Reprinted by permission of Simon & Schuster, Inc.

Susan Brownmiller, "Pornography Hurts Women," is from *Against Our Will*. Copyright © 1975 by Susan Brownmiller. Reprinted by permission of Simon & Schuster, Inc.

Patrick J. Buchanan, "Never Strike a King," is from the *San Francisco Chronicle*, July 20, 1987. Reprinted by permission: Tribune Media Services.

William F. Buckley, Jr., "Identify All the Carriers," is from *The New York Times*, March 8, 1986. Copyright © 1986 by The New York Times Company. Reprinted by permission.

Clarence Darrow, "The Futility of the Death Penalty," is from *Verdicts Out of Court* (Quadrangle Books, 1963). Reprinted with permission of Arthur Weinberg.

Hubert Dreyfus, 'Why Computers Can't Be Intelligent," is from *What Computers Can't Do*. Copyright © 1972, 1979 by Hubert L. Dreyfus. Reprinted by permission of Harper & Row, Publishers, Inc.

James K. Fitzpatrick, "AIDS: It Is Not Just Another Disease," is from *The Wanderer*, August 15, 1985. Reprinted by permission.

Sigmund Freud, "Consciousness and What Is Unconscious," is reprinted from *The Ego and the Id* by Sigmund Freud, translated by Joan Riviere, revised and newly edited by James Strachey, by permission of W. W. Norton & Company,

Benjamin Spock, "A Statement on Nuclear Energy," is from *Redbook*, November 1979. Reprinted by permission of the author.

I. F. Stone, "Plato's Ideal Bedlam," is from Harper's Magazine. Copyright © 1980 by Harper's magazine. All rights reserved. Reprinted from the January 1981 issue by special permission.

USA Today, "Court Ruling Opens Doors for Women," appeared in the May 12, 1987 edition of *USA TODAY*. Copyright 1987, USA TODAY. Reprinted with permission.

U.S. Committee for Energy Awareness, "Nuclear Energy: Is America Being Left Behind?" is reprinted by permission of the U.S. Committee for Energy Awareness.

Gore Vidal, "Drugs," is from *The Case for Legalizing Marijuana*. Reprinted by permission of William Morris Agency, Inc. on behalf of the author. Copyright © 1970 by Gore Vidal.

Marie Winn, "Television and Reading," is from *The Plug in Drug*. Copyright © 1977, 1978 by Marie Winn Miller. Reprinted by permission of Viking Penguin, Inc.

Peregrine Worsthorne, "The New Inequality," is from *The Sunday Telegraph*, December 3, 1972 (London). Reprinted by permission of The Sunday Telegraph.